How Russia
Became a
Market
Economy

ANDERS ÅSLUND

How Russia Became a Market Economy

THE BROOKINGS INSTITUTION
Washington, D.C.

Library of Congress Cataloging-in-Publication data:

Åslund, Anders, 1952–
    How Russia became a market economy / Anders Åslund.
        p.   cm.
    Includes bibliographical references.
    ISBN 0-8157-0426-7 (cl. : alk. paper).—ISBN 0-8157-0425-9 (pbk.
: alk. paper)
        1. Russia (Federation)—Economic conditions—1991–   2. Russia
(Federation)—Economic policy—1991–   3. Soviet Union—Economic
conditions—1986–1991.   4. Soviet Union—Economic
policy—1986–1991.   I. Title.
    HC340.12.A84   1995
    338.947—dc20   95-786
                                                                            CIP

9 8 7 6 5 4 3 2 1

The paper used in this publication meets the minimum requirements of the American
National Standard for Information Sciences—Permanence of Paper for Printed Library
Materials, ANSI Z39.48-1984.

Typeset in Times Roman

Composition by Harlowe Typography, Inc.
Cottage City, Maryland

Printed by R.R. Donnelley and Sons Co.
Harrisonburg, Virginia

To my parents

Foreword

THE TRANSFORMATION of the Russian economy into a market economy has been marred by controversy in both Russia and the West. While taking a clear line in favor of a radical approach, this book tries to investigate a multitude of problems involved and underlines the extent of the collapse of the Soviet economy and system. It provides an account of how the economic reform program was developed, highlighting the acrimony of the internal Russian debate.

In his analysis of the Russian economic transformation, Anders Åslund gives many examples of how halfway measures caused problems, but he notes that new radical measures eventually resolved many of the difficulties. Specifically, Åslund argues that inflation could only be controlled after the ruble zone had been broken up. He acknowledges that liberalization was not far-reaching enough. It brought well-placed people large rents. Moreover, macroeconomic stabilization was fought by state enterprise managers who did not want to adjust to a market economy and who wanted to make as much as possible from state subsidies during the transition. Privatization appears to have been surprisingly successful, however, because of clever policies proposed by the reformers. On the whole, Åslund believes that Russia has really become a market economy, however imperfect.

The Brookings Institution gratefully acknowledges the financial support provided for this project by The Carnegie Corporation of New York and The John D. and Catherine T. MacArthur Foundation.

The views expressed in this study are those of the author alone and should not be ascribed to any of the persons or organizations mentioned above, or to the trustees, officers, or other staff members of the Brookings Institution.

Bruce K. MacLaury
President

April 1995
Washington, D.C.

Acknowledgments

I WROTE this book from March to August 1994 as a guest scholar in the Foreign Policy Studies program at the Brookings Institution, during a sabbatical leave from the Stockholm Institute of East European Economics at the Stockholm School of Economics. I am grateful to John Steinbruner, who invited me to Brookings, and to my research assistant, Natasha Hritzuk, who provided excellent support of my efforts.

This volume is based on my work as an economic advisor to the Russian government from November 1991 to January 1994. By its very nature, such a job necessitates having extensive conversations with many people and reading countless unpublished memoranda from various sources. I am grateful to every person whom I contacted.

I want to express my great admiration and appreciation of Yegor Gaidar, Anatoly Chubais, and Boris Fedorov, the men behind the great Russian transformation to a market economy. In the Russian government, I also appreciated working with Aleksandr Shokhin, Sergei Vasil'ev, Yevgeny Yasin, Andrei Illarionov, Petr Fillipov, Vladimir Kosmarsky, Andrei Kazmin, Sergei Aleksashenko, Petr Aven, Aleksei Ulyukaev, Vladimir Mau, Maxim Boycko, Konstantin Kagalovsky, Leonid Grigor'ev, Alexei Mozhin, and Anna Tyagunenko, and I have met and learned from a great many other Russian officials.

Among the Western advisors to the Russian government, I am particularly indebted to Jeffrey D. Sachs, who has been our undisputed intellectual leader. In any situation, he can conceptualize the problems, structure them, and immediately propose viable, concrete solutions. I also learned much from my colleagues David Lipton, Marek Dabrowski, Jacek Rostowski, Richard Layard, Andrei Shleifer, and Charles Wyplosz. Other valuable interlocutors include Stanley Fischer, Lawrence Summers, and Peter Oppenheimer. Primarily at the Macroeconomic and Finance Unit (MFU) at the Russian Ministry of Finance, which Jeffrey Sachs and I codirected, we had a large number of Western and Russian associates employed in Moscow. They tracked down facts, analyzed them, and formulated policy proposals. Out of many people, I would particularly like to express my gratitude to Mstislav Afanasiev, John Anderson, Martin Andersson, Andrew Berg, Lars Bergström, Peter Boone, Vladimir Capelik, Jacques Delpla, Bouzidar Djelic, Aleksandr Dynkin, Michael Ellam, Douglas Galbi, Alla Gantman, Brigitte Granville, Jonathan Hay, Torun Hedbäck, Georg Kjällgren, Andrei Lushin, Rory MacFarquhar, Mark Nagel, Aleksandr Naumenkov, Aleksandr Nichiporuk, Peter Orszag, Andrea Richter, Mikhail Sarafanov, Judith Shapiro, Christopher Smart, Pavel Teplukhin, Andrew Warner, Oliver Weeks, Jochen Wermuth, and Anastasiya Zoteeva. Our work was financed by the Swedish government and the Ford Foundation, whose generous support is gratefully acknowledged.

In addition, I have benefitted from my contacts with many perceptive Russian interlocutors. I would especially like to thank Mikhail Berger, Tatyana Dolgopiatova, Aleksei Kudrin, Mikhail Leont'ev, Nina Oding, Vasily Selyunin, Lilya Shevtsova, Nikolai Shmelev, Galina Starovoitova, Dmitry Travin, Valentina Vedeneeva, Maria Vishnevskaya, Arkady Volsky, Ina Voennaya, Ruben Yevstigneev, and Gennady Zoteev. Among my Western interlocutors in Moscow, I am particularly grateful to Örjan Berner, Charles Blitzer, Pilar Bonet, Leyla Boulton, Andrew Cowley, Steven Erlanger, Christopher Granville, Akio Kawato, John Lloyd, Pierre Morell, Geoffrey Murrel, and John Parker.

At the Stockholm Institute of East European Economics, Gun Malmquist and Eva Johansson have provided me with administrative help, and Ardo Hansson, Sten Luthman, Örjan Sjöberg, and Eva Sundquist with intellectual exchange. Göran Ennerfelt and Michael Sohlman have been my mainstays in many ways, and Carl Bildt and Margaretha af Ugglas have given me moral support and public recognition.

While in Washington, I have given seminars and benefitted from discussion of my book with colleagues at various institutions. These venues have included the American Enterprise Institute, the Brookings Institution, the Carnegie Endowment for International Peace, the Cato Institute, the Center for Strategic and International Studies, the Council for Foreign Relations, the George Washington University, the Federal Reserve Board, Georgetown University, the Institute of International Economics, the Kennan Institute for Advanced Russian Studies, the National Committee on American Foreign Policy, the *New York Times*, the University of Pennsylvania, and Princeton University.

Fred Pryor and John Hardt meticulously read the whole manuscript and offered many helpful comments. I also benefitted from suggestions from John Steinbruner, Andrei Shleifer, Mancur Olson, John Anderson, Douglas Galbi, and two anonymous reviewers, who read all or parts of my draft manuscript. Steph Selice edited the manuscript; Melanie Allen, Diane Chido, and Andrew Solomon verified it; and Stacey Seaman answered my computer questions and prepared the manuscript for publication. My current employer, the Carnegie Endowment for International Peace, has allowed me the necessary time for revisions, and Melissa Meeker has assisted me ably here.

I am grateful to all who helped me with this book. As it stands, the published result represents my own views, and I alone am responsible for any mistake that may remain.

Anders Åslund

Contents

1. Introduction   1
   Purpose of This Book   *1*
   What Becoming a Market Economy Means   *3*
   What Should Be Done?   *5*
   Why Soviet and Chinese Reforms Had to Differ   *13*
   The Author's Personal Involvement as an Economic
       Advisor   *16*
   Sources and Statistics   *21*
   Structure of This Book   *25*

2. Preconditions of Economic Reform   26
   Gorbachev's Legacy: Institutional Breakdown   *27*
   The Transformation of Economic Thinking   *36*
   The Depth of the Economic Crisis in 1991   *41*
   Conclusions: The End of the Soviet System   *50*

3. Formation of a Reform Program   53
   Stages of the Economic Reform   *53*
   A New Political Setting Takes Form   *57*
   A Program of Radical Economic Reform   *63*
   Formation of the Economic Reform Team   *70*
   An Acrimonious Critique   *73*
   Political and Institutional Impediments   *86*
   The Political Undoing of Radical Reform   *93*
   Conclusions   *100*

4. Relations With Other Former Soviet Republics   102
   From the USSR to the CIS   *103*
   Dilemmas Posed by the Collapse of the Soviet Union   *106*
   Alternative Currency and Payments Arrangements   *109*
   Alternative Strategies of Other Former Soviet Republics   *115*

Decay of the Ruble Zone   *119*
A Ruble Zone of a New Type   *131*
Conclusions: A Costly Failure   *134*

5. Liberalization   137
Domestic Liberalization   *139*
Liberalization of Foreign Trade   *145*
Antimonopoly Policy   *152*
Problems With the Deregulation of the Energy Sector   *156*
Agriculture: Intertwined Rent-Seeking Monopolies   *161*
Economic Crime as a Threat to Liberalization   *167*
Conclusion: Accomplishing Liberalization, However
   Slowly   *171*

6. Macroeconomic Stabilization   174
Why Macroeconomic Stabilization Is So Important   *174*
Is Russia Unique?   *177*
How to Fight Inflation in Russia   *181*
Radical Reform: January–May 1992   *187*
Backsliding: June–December 1992   *191*
Stalemate: January–September 1993   *193*
The Second Reform Wave: September–December 1993   *198*
A Policy of Passivity: January–October 1994   *200*
How to Deal With Interenterprise Arrears   *207*
The Role of the West   *214*
Conclusions: Money Is Money in Russia, Too   *220*

7. Privatization   223
Private Enterprise at the End of the USSR   *223*
Early Russian Ideas on Privatization   *226*
The Russian Reformers' Ideas on Privatization   *228*
The Great Privatization Debate   *232*
A Radical Privatization Program   *241*
Skillful Administration   *244*
Ordinary Small-Scale Privatization   *248*
Large-Scale Mass Privatization   *252*
Undramatic Housing Privatization   *257*
Stalled Land Reform   *259*
Development of New Private Enterprises   *263*
Tardy Bankruptcy   *264*
Conclusions: A Successful Privatization   *265*

8. Conclusions   272
    Economic Results *272*
    How Was the Window of Opportunity Used? *291*
    Why Did the Military-Industrial Complex Fail as a
      Lobby? *298*
    Lessons From the Russian Transformation *311*

    Abbreviations   317

    Chronology   319

    Cast of Characters   321

    Endnotes   327

    Index   369

Tables

2-1. Average Annual Growth of the Soviet Economy, 1961–85,
      Net Material Product   43
2-2. Structure of Production: Distribution of GDP, 1991   44
2-3. Production Per Capita of Selected Products, 1989   45
2-4. Russian Trade With Countries Outside the Former Soviet
      Union, 1990–92   46
2-5. Consolidated State Budget Deficit of the USSR, 1985–90 47
2-6. Soviet Wage Increases, 1986–90   48
2-7. Soviet Foreign Debt and Debt Service Obligations in
      Convertible Currencies, 1986–91   49
4-1. Introduction of New Currencies   118
4-2. Annual Inflation in the Former Soviet Republics,
      1992 and 1993   119
4-3. Trade Between Russia and Other Former Soviet Republics
      1992 and 1993   122
4-4. Russia's Trade Surplus With Other Former Soviet Republics,
      1992 and 1993   123
4-5. Financing of Other States by the Central Bank of Russia
      (CBR), 1992   123
4-6. Financing From Russia to Other Former Soviet Republics,
      1992 and 1993   126
5-1. Size Distribution of Soviet Industrial Enterprises as of
      January 1, 1988   152
6-1. Monthly Inflation and the Expansion of the Money Supply,
      1992–94   184
6-2. Wages, 1985–93   185

6-3.   Interest Rates and Inflation, 1992–94   195
6-4.   Consolidated State Budget, 1992 and 1993 (Outcomes)   197
6-5.   Party Factions in the State Duma, June 1994   201
7-1.   Russian Employment by Ownership, 1991   224
7-2.   Number of Enterprises Privatized, March 1992–August 1994   250
7-3.   Results of Voucher Auctions, December 1992–June 1994   256
7-4.   Privatization of Apartments, 1989–94   259
7-5.   Expansion of Private Farms, 1990–93   262
7-6.   Employment by Ownership, 1990–93   266
8-1.   Macroeconomic Stabilization, 1991–94   275
8-2.   Production, 1991–94   278
8-3.   Consumption and Accumulation, 1990–94: Structure of
       Utilization of GDP   279
8-4.   Conversion of Enterprises in the Military-Industrial Complex,
       1991–94   280
8-5.   Foreign Trade, 1991–94   281
8-6.   Russia Foreign Debt as of January 1, 1994   283
8-7.   Demographic Indicators, 1991–94   288

Figure

8-1.   Decline of the Ruble: Ruble/Dollar Exchange Rates, 1991–94   277

The market economy exists in Russia.
. . . Any aberration can only be
short term.
Boris Fedorov, January 22, 1994[1]

But you cannot avoid noticing the obvious:
the market economy already exists
in Russia.
Viktor Chernomyrdin, March 4, 1994[2]

CHAPTER ONE

Introduction

THE ABORTIVE coup of August 1991 in Moscow had many of the trappings of an operetta. One hundred thousand people gathered around the heroic White House. The first democratically elected Russian president, Boris Yeltsin, mounted a tank whose soldiers had deserted the communist dictators for the Russian people. High above this memorable scene the Russian tricolor swayed. In the end, only three people were killed.

This was one of the great moments in history. The crushing of the coup symbolized the collapse of the totalitarian communist ideology, the Soviet economic and political system, and the country known as the Soviet Union. A window of opportunity—a chance to build a new society—had opened. This book investigates how the Russians took the opportunity to build a new economic system.

Purpose of This Book

My purpose in writing this book is empirical: to clarify what actually happened when Russia attempted a radical transformation to a market economy based on private ownership and the rule of law. As a natural consequence, this discussion leads me to draw conclusions on which theories and methods are applicable and which are not. My intention is not to give policy advice but rather to analyze events and their causes.

1

As an economic advisor to the Russian government from November 1991 until January 1994, I was closely involved in the reform process. My intention is to take what I saw as a basis for examining problems, actual aims of the reform government, plausible options, choices made, and outcomes. Far too often, criticism is directed against ideas that were never presented and events that never happened, and impossible solutions are then suggested. For those who did not witness these events, it is difficult to imagine the real range of options. Usually it was more limited than many realize, but sometimes the futility of piecemeal approaches made radical options necessary.

Since I have spent most of my adult life studying Eastern Europe, the Soviet Union, and their economies and politics, this is an academic study and not a memoir. It is a sequel to my book *Gorbachev's Struggle for Economic Reform*, which dealt with the degeneration of the Soviet economic system under perestroika from 1985 until 1991.[3] It is written for the lay public, specifically those readers with a general interest in the transformation of Russia. The issues I discuss are fundamental. No special knowledge of the Soviet Union, the communist system, Russia, or economics is necessary, though some technical economic language is occasionally called for, primarily in the discussion of macroeconomic stabilization.

The period covered starts with the appointment of the Russian economic reform team in November 1991 and continues to the present (early 1995). The end of 1991 heralded a series of profound changes in Russia, including the fall of a political and economic system, an ideology, and a country. December 1993 marked the end of fundamental reforms. A large number of reformist measures had previously been introduced. On December 12, 1993, a new constitution with a normal division of powers was adopted through a referendum. The simultaneous parliamentary elections created a new democratically elected parliament structured through political parties. Both radical liberalism and communist insurrection had come to an end. Russia entered a stage of normal politics—that is, one in which interests take precedence over ideas. Since December 1993, the changes previously made have been maintained and their effects more widely felt, but few new reforms have been introduced. An analysis of the last three years should be sufficient to allow us to pass judgment on the qualitative achievements and failures of the Russian transition, though more time would be needed to assess the quantitative performance of this change appropriately.

What Becoming a Market Economy Means

A central thesis of this book is that the main goal of the Russian economic transition has been accomplished: Russia has become a market economy. The essential feature of such an economy is that the market is the main instrument of allocation. A multitude of markets must exist, including product, labor, capital, and property markets.[4] For the purposes of this discussion, the implications of a market are best understood by delineating the typical features of the socialist or communist system. (The terms socialist and communist will be used interchangeably in this book.) An excellent hierarchy of key characteristics has been outlined by János Kornai.[5]

First, Kornai states, "[the] key to explaining the classical socialist system is an understanding of the political structure. The starting point is the undivided political power of the ruling party, the interpenetration of the party and the state, and the suppression of all forces that depart from or oppose the party's policy." Moreover, both the party and the state were dominated by the Marxist-Leninist ideology.[6] After the August 1991 coup, the hegemony of the Communist party of the Soviet Union was gone. The economy had been emancipated from politics.

A second characteristic of the classic socialist system was the dominant position of state and quasi-state ownership. As early as the spring of 1994, the massive privatization program had shifted more than half the jobs in the Russian labor force to the private sector. Ownership had been depoliticized.

A third feature of the socialist economy was the preponderance of bureaucratic coordination. This could be defined as a planned, command, or bargaining economy, an administrative allocation, or centralized rationing. In any case, its essence was a vertical state-party control over enterprises and their production and flows of resources. Centralized state allocation, with vertical commands to enterprises regarding production targets and deliveries, ended with the liberalization of 1992. Even if a large number of state orders lingered on into 1993, they were not commands in the old sense. By 1994 these bureaucratic directives were gone (with rare exceptions), and allocation had been depoliticized.

To Kornai's criteria, a fourth requirement of a market economy should be added. If a market is not monetized, that market is ineffective and transaction costs are excessive. Since liberalization, the Russian ruble has become a real, reasonably convertible currency, with a floating, unified exchange rate that is market determined. It is true that the volume of U.S. dollars in circulation in Russia and in Russian bank accounts exceeds the volume of Russian rubles in Russia, but the dollar is also money. The problem is no longer a lack of monetization but the stabilization of the ruble.

A fifth characteristic of a socialist economy was the last major hurdle Russia had to overcome on the road to becoming a market economy: the lack of hard budget constraints for enterprises. Introducing such constraints implies that money should be scarce. That is, enterprises should be barred from negotiating further means from the state, through subsidies, subsidized credits, price controls, tax exemption, or customs exemption. The last important source of soft budget constraints was subsidized credits, which were prohibited by Council of Ministers decree on September 25, 1993. Credit and pricing have thus been essentially (although not completely) depoliticized.

A great deal follows from these five basic transformations. The vertical command structure between enterprises and the state has been replaced by horizontal links and free bargaining between both domestic and foreign enterprises. There are no quantitative production targets left. Monopoly and concentration are lingering structural problems, but much has been achieved through domestic deregulation and the liberalization of foreign trade. Fixed arbitrary prices as well as administrative wage controls have disappeared altogether. With few exceptions (notably energy prices), prices have been liberalized. Wages have been free from regulations since the beginning of 1992. The foreign trade monopoly, with its extraordinary protectionism, separation of domestic and foreign prices, and nonconvertible currency, belongs to history. Foreign trading rights have been liberalized. Export restrictions persist only on a dozen important items. After an initial and complete deregulation of imports, tariffs have gradually been raised; but they conform to the market, and Russia has no quantitative import barriers. Money became active instantly after the decontrol of prices in January 1992, as is obvious from the high rate of inflation. Even so, and regardless of earlier Russian inclinations to barter, the economy has become thoroughly monetized. Although cash and noncash money have not been unified by law, they are unified on the market, as is reflected in cross-exchange rates.

The characteristics of a socialist economy have been replaced by those of a market economy. Chronic shortages, including labor scarcity, are gone. The market has taken hold, but requires further penetration. The predominance of producers over consumers has weakened; but the seller's market prevails, though monopolies have gradually been undermined. All kinds of markets have emerged. Interenterprise markets exist for goods and services as well as markets for money, foreign exchange, capital, credit, shares, and property. Even state enterprises no longer take orders from Moscow and barely maintain contacts with the capital. They are on their own and work for profit.

At this point in the discussion, three objections may be raised. The first is that the Russian legal system remains extremely poor; however, that is an issue of lowering transaction costs and improving efficiency and does not disqualify Russia as a market economy. The second objection is that private ownership is not firmly established on a large scale in Russia. But the fundamental issues are the mutual independence of enterprises from one another (as well as from the state) and their profit orientation. Under such conditions, owners will forcefully try to ascertain their property rights. A third concern is that inflation remains far too high. But after all, inflation is a market economic concept, and it is not disqualifying as long as it does not rise to hyperinflation. Hyperinflation is usually defined as a rate of more than 50 percent inflation during one month. Such a rate of inflation endangers monetization of the economy and entices strict regulations.

However messy and imperfect, Russia is a market economy, and has been at least since the end of 1993. The task now is to explain how this market economy was created.

What Should Be Done?

The choice of economic system is profoundly ideological. Therefore, if this book is to provide the reader with a comprehensive analytical framework, the book's very structure cannot but reflect basic values. Otherwise, there is little ground for judging what is an achievement or a failure. I have elaborated on my views of how the transformation should be undertaken in detail in another book, and I have gone on record regarding what I had hoped to achieve in Russia in June 1991.[7] In this introduction I only intend to clarify the tenets of my reasoning.

It has often been said that there was no theory of transition from communism to capitalism. Although this is true, there are many partial theories and historical parallels that are applicable. The real issue is to choose those that are relevant for the actual situation in Russia and for the aims of building a democracy and a market economy based on private ownership and the rule of law. When choosing theories and parallels, the choices made implicitly suggest how the economic transition should be undertaken.

The defining characteristic of Russia in 1991 was the depth of the collapse of the state, which had occurred in at least four ways. First, and most obviously, the Soviet Union broke up in December 1991. Second, the communist political system fell apart in the fall of 1991. Third, the command economy system foundered in 1990 and 1991. Fourth, state finances faltered as well, as a massive budget deficit of perhaps 30 percent of GDP mounted up in 1991. Production fell precipitously because of all-pervasive shortages; yet a huge monetary overhang (that is, excess of money over available goods and services at controlled prices) and the fiscal imbalance made hyperinflation almost inevitable. It is important to observe how fundamental the collapse was (which will be discussed further in chapter 2). The old Soviet system was no longer functioning, and Russia was close to chaos. Perestroika destroyed the old system but did not construct anything new to take its place. The much-sought "third way" was not found.[8]

Another Russian peculiarity was the extraordinary strength of the old elite, the *nomenklatura*, while civil society was weak and rule of law all but absent. The numerous civil servants worked for themselves rather than for any common interest, and the old elite exploited the state to its own advantage. Thus the collapsing Soviet state was extraordinarily corrupt by nature, and few forces could counteract it apart from the top politicians.

A society cannot exist in chaos. Pillars of a new, tenable order needed to be raised as quickly as possible after the collapse of the old communist state. The capacity for forming policy was limited, but so was the resistance against radical change immediately after the democratic breakthrough. A brief spell of technocratic policymaking emerged, which could be used to construct a new system.

Essentially, three major tasks needed to be resolved quickly. The first was to build both a state and a democracy. Therefore, an ordinary democratic constitution with a division and balance of powers needed to be adopted and democratic elections to a parliament with political parties held, as well as elections of regional democratic bodies. The second assignment was to build a market economy. On the one hand, markets—that is, prices, trade, production, and enterprise—must be given free rein. On the other hand, when prices are liberalized in the presence of a huge monetary overhang of unsatisfied demand at regulated prices, they rise. Therefore, it was necessary to impose financial and monetary stabilization simultaneously to prevent the instant price rises from turning into inflation. The third fundamental task involved large-scale privatization, which called for quick implementation, wide distribution, and the introduction of real individual property rights.

A fourth vital task was to build a legal system. Unfortunately, this could not be resolved in the short term, because it required not only the adoption of many laws and the establishment of numerous courts, but also the training of thousands of lawyers and the evolution of a business ethic. The introduction of an adequate economic system should lead to structural changes, raising economic efficiency.

On the basis of these brief premises, the relevant theories and empirical parallels are already evident. The first task is to build a democratic state. An ample and highly applicable literature on transition from authoritarian rule has evolved. The general conclusion in this literature is that it is important to quickly consolidate democratic achievements immediately after a democratic breakthrough, with frequent democratic elections and the early adoption of a constitution.[9]

The social forces of the postcommunist state can be well understood through Mancur Olson's analysis of the logic of collective action. Acknowledging the weakness of the civil society and the strength of the old nomenklatura, it follows from Olson's theory that the main threat to common public interest comes from the few—the old elite—who can exploit the state institutions for rent-seeking if their actions go unchecked.[10] The strongest instrument to keep the *nomenklatura* in check is the authority of a democratically elected leadership.

However, the state is so weak that democratization cannot strengthen it enough in the short term. Corruption is an overwhelming concern. The whole economic strategy must thus be based on recognition of the state's limited capacity. A judicious application of new institutional economics and economic history is required. (Douglass C. North provides the general framework.[11]) One relevant historical parallel is Western Europe and the United States in the nineteenth century before capitalist institutions had evolved and when the rule of law was comparatively rudimentary. The Western response to the weak legal system at the time was *laissez-faire* until the legal system had gained strength. Although it took a long time for capitalism to evolve as a comprehensive system, many elements of the capitalist system were introduced quickly, notably the complete economic liberalization in Britain in 1846.

Another appropriate historical parallel is Latin America in recent decades. In various Latin American nations, the state has degenerated because of overextension, and the eventual successful solution appears to be far-reaching liberalization and firm macroeconomic stabilization—a back-to-basics approach. A large body of both theoretical and empirical research has been done on macroeconomic stabilization under conditions of high inflation, rendering this the best-investigated part of the transition.[12] The experiences of Japan and Germany after World War II appear far less applicable; both countries were occupied, which limited the problems of the weakness of the state, and the systemic changes were far less radical. They had possessed vast human skills, and most of the human capital remained intact.

For an understanding of what is likely to happen at the enterprise level, Oliver E. Williamson's study of transaction costs is helpful.[13] Interestingly, Yegor Gaidar's doctoral dissertation on economic reforms and hierarchies applied Mancur Olson and Oliver Williamson's ideas to the situation in the USSR. Gaidar's general conclusion is that "a hierarchical organization can function efficiently only in the presence of social forces and mechanisms which allow effective control over its activity."[14] With poor management and little trust within enterprises, markets most likely provide lower transaction costs than hierarchies.

Economic history shows how market economies evolve. They always start from trade. When supply is limited and demand great, entrepreneurs skim the market and concentrate on the sales of goods with high markups—luxury goods, such as perfumes, consumer electronics, and liquor—and focus on selling in big, rich cities. Only when the market has been reasonably saturated do sellers provide cheaper goods; entrepreneurship then begins to permeate the market, and production starts to adjust. The adjustment process moves upstream from small-scale, consumer-oriented production and services toward heavier production.

Moreover, a market with its multiple communication channels requires far more infrastructure than a command economy. The more quickly the market is saturated, the more swiftly output will be restructured.

The breakup of the Soviet Union was hardly unique. Many empires have broken up before. The most appropriate parallel appears to be the Hapsburg Empire, which was composed of several neighboring countries that were relatively highly developed. The lessons of the Hapsburg collapse were well analyzed and widely studied at the time, and they have been kept alive.[15] A general conclusion was that it was vital to break up the monetary area at the same time as the state was dissolving. This would prohibit various central banks from issuing the same currency, which would thus prevent extreme inflation.

Finally, when Russia launched its transformation, the experiences of Eastern Europe were already well known. Both the Gaidar team and their foreign advisors were primarily inspired by the Polish transformation; a substantial early literature on postcommunist transition remains highly relevant.[16] Mass privatization of large enterprises was certainly a novelty, but Czechoslovakia had already developed a good technique. Presumably nowhere else had such great need for restructuring arisen; but thanks to the East European experience, the size of plausible structural change could be anticipated. It had been huge in Eastern Europe, but because of a longer period of communism (and thus economic irrationality) in the USSR, the necessary structural destruction was likely to be even greater in Russia.[17]

There are many reasons to emphasize the need for speed in such a transformation.[18] Politically, it is easier to have a big package of radical measures accepted early on, when a deep sense of crisis prevails and various interest groups cannot yet fully evaluate what they may gain or lose. People are prepared to suffer quite a bit if it is to the benefit for their society, but not for long. Both politically and economically, a comprehensive and consistent package of reforms better serves the purpose. It is vital to break inflationary expectations and to turn state enterprise managers from the parasitical seeking of rents or subsidies from the state to profit-seeking endeavors. They must be convinced to shift their attention from supply to demand. They will only do so if they both face a demand barrier because of a strict budgetary and monetary policy and if they believe it will last. Any lingering regulation will lead to corruption and rent-seeking. Therefore, a sudden and far-reaching liberalization of domestic as well as foreign trade is necessary.

A normal market economy has millions of markets. The more radical the liberalization, the sooner the markets will be cleansed of distortions and corruption. A swift transition will also have positive social effects. On the income side, strict stabilization and far-reaching liberalization squeeze the excessive incomes of the rent-seeking elite (notably their access to underpriced export goods, import subsidies, and subsidized credits). On the expenditure side, a market that functions more effectively offers consumers better choice, service, products, and value. Production and investment will only recover after sufficient liberalization and stabilization have occurred.[19] In the fall of 1989, the term "shock therapy" was applied to this kind of policy in Poland. It is an expressive allusion to the need to break old stereotypes, thus forcing enterprises to adjust to the market rather than trying to extract resources from the state. However, such a term evokes varied emotions. A more general description of these policies is a "big bang." The essence, however, is radical, market-oriented economic reform.

A standard objection to radical economic reform has been that Russia is unique. However, the essential starting point of most inquiry in the social sciences is that regular processes are to be found in most societies assuming preconditions are the same. The question needs to be made more specific: what preconditions are peculiar to Russia, and what adjustments do they call for? The special features emphasized in the case of Russia are the collapse of the state and the strength of the old elite, both of which call for particularly speedy action.

Many Russian peculiarities have been inferred as objections to reform. One objection is the backwardness of Russian political, economic, or legal culture. With my strong belief in modern institutional economics, I treat culture as a residuum that can explain what cannot be explicated by other means. Far too often, it has been argued that people of one religious creed or culture cannot survive the shift to capitalism, but such statements have eventually been proven wrong. Another objection has been the structure of the Russian economy, notably its degree of monopolization. As shall be seen in chapter 5, there are uncommonly few production monopolies in the Russian economy, and its monopolization is essentially the result of a lack of liberalization of trade and prices. A third objection is that certain laws, institutions, privatization efforts, and even infrastructure should be developed before liberalization. However, all these measures are undertaken more easily and appropriately after liberalization; it is extremely difficult to carry them out in advance. Any observer needs to ask why such changes had not been undertaken already. He or she will find that these changes contradict the interests of the old establishment, which will rule until its powers are reduced through liberalization.

Under the circumstances prevailing in Russia in late 1991, it would have been lethal to hesitate or move slowly. On the contrary, it was vital to act fast and decisively and to concentrate on the most important issues. Russia's weak state and strong rent-seeking elite called for a more robust and radical approach than that taken in east central Europe, where both the state and civil society were comparatively stronger. The main social endeavor had to be to rebuild basic state institutions and to abolish the mechanisms of rent-seeking that were exploited by the old elite. Thus, there were important Russian peculiarities, but they warranted more emphasis on speed than in other countries.

General objections to a swift solution are that democracy requires time and that speed and technocratic decisionmaking are by definition undemocratic. However, such thoughts reflect confusion regarding the essence of democracy. In the case of Russia, the issue was to build a democracy, not to govern an established democratic state. Democratic breakthroughs are usually momentary, and the survival of a democracy depends on a swift consolidation of democratic institutions. It is therefore vital to use time effectively. If civil society is weak and the old establishment strong, the real implication of compromise would be to surrender power to the old antidemocratic establishment.

Rather than being based on any alternative theory, ideas regarding a gradual transition to a market economy tend to be intuitive. If a theory or broader perspective is not adopted, it seems less risky to move forward in small steps. Moreover, many proponents of a gradual approach have disregarded Russia's extraordinary crisis, as is evident by suggestions that Russia should have followed the course of such orderly countries as Japan, Germany, and Sweden. One reason why the Russian reformers focused on Poland was that it was in a much deeper crisis than Hungary or Czechoslovakia but still pursued a comprehensive policy. Other proposed model countries included South Korea, Taiwan, Singapore, and Chile, each of which is characterized by very small public sectors, orderly state administrations, and limited democracy. But it is difficult to see any relevant similarity in the preconditions of these nations and those of Russia.

Characteristically, as the prime representative of the old elite, Arkady Volsky, chairman of the Russian Union of Industrialists and Entrepreneurs, has consistently proposed such models. He has argued against haste and early elections and in favor of compromise, consensus, and roundtable agreements.[20] A democrat should not compromise on the foundation of democracy; similarly, a supporter of a market economy should not compromise on the fundamentals of such an economy. After the foundations of a democracy and a market economy have been laid, the initial period of extraordinary politics has presumably come to an end.[21] What follows is the period of what might be called ordinary politics—that is, one in which interests dominate over ideals, and institutions have grown strong enough to balance the flamboyance of the old elite. Then compromises in a democratic sense are the order of the day.

I have written this book from such a perspective, and the Russian experience has reinforced my convictions. My general conclusion is that the essence of our ideas as economic advisers was correct, but that there was insufficient consistency in many regards. Yet I try to present a detailed account of the actual developments to allow the reader to draw his or her own conclusions. To my mind, the question "what should be done?" was answered correctly with regard to fundamentals in Poland and Czechoslovakia. A more interesting question is "why was the best possible solution not chosen in Russia?" To a considerable extent, therefore, my interest focuses on political economy. A suboptimal solution can be chosen for many reasons: lack of understanding, analysis, and conceptualization among decisionmakers; incorrect information; poor technical advice; weak legislative design; technical traps; inadequate implementation; lack of political will; political resistance. The respective significance of these factors varies from issue to issue.

In general, given Russia's much more difficult preconditions, the change of economic system should be expected to be more arduous in Russia and the former USSR than it has been in east central Europe. However, the differences between the former Soviet republics have been enormous. For example, many predicted that Ukraine would fare better than Russia because its initial economic and political conditions were considered superior to Russia's. However, the opposite happened. From 1991 to 1994, Ukraine experienced much higher inflation than Russia and also saw a greater drop in national income. This comparison reflects the fundamental importance of the political and economic strategy chosen by a country's political leadership.

Why Soviet and Chinese Reforms Had to Differ

A substantial literature argues that the Soviet Union (and later, Russia) should have followed the Chinese path of economic reform.[22] The arguments are so prevalent that they deserve a special section in this book. However, to a considerable extent, Mikhail Gorbachev did try to follow the path taken by Deng Xiaoping, but he failed. The primary reason for this failure appears to be that the Soviet preconditions were so different from China's.[23]

The Chinese and Soviet approaches to economic reform were initially more similar than is generally recognized. Reform was started by the top leadership in both China and the USSR (by Deng Xiaoping and Mikhail S. Gorbachev, respectively). Each wanted to reform socialism in order to reinforce it, the power of the Communist party, and his country. Each had a clear sense of direction, but not a clear goal. Both adopted an eclectic, gradual approach.[24]

However, the initial reforms became much more radical in China than in the USSR. The underlying reasons were both political and economic. The political starting points of the Chinese economic reforms in 1978 and the Soviet *perestroika* that began in 1985 were completely different. In the USSR, the Communist party, its *nomenklatura*, and the ideology of Marxism-Leninism were essentially intact. Even though Gorbachev had been elected on a mandate of revitalization, the prevailing mood was conservative. Nor was there any sense of economic crisis; the net material product in the USSR grew officially by an average of 3.2 percent a year during the first half of the 1980s.[25] The government's perceived concern was to arrest a slight downturn in the growth rate and return to a growth rate of 4 percent a year.

The situation in China was completely different. The cultural revolution had cost millions of Chinese their lives. It had devastated society as well as public confidence in the Communist party and Marxism-Leninism. Moreover, it had reduced and weakened the cadres of the Communist party and left the economy in tatters. The mood in China favored radical change in a pragmatic direction. Deng made his way by opposing the ideological excesses of Maoism, while Gorbachev rose as a seemingly obedient servant of Leonid Brezhnev. Deng had a mandate for pragmatic change, whereas Gorbachev had only a mandate for revitalizing the old communist system. A precondition for the Chinese path was the bloody massacres and devastation wrought by the cultural revolution, which had weakened the old communist system.

The Chinese economic reforms produced substantial positive economic results from the outset; the Soviet reforms, to the contrary, prompted a serious economic crisis. One group of causes was structural. The Chinese economic reform took off in agriculture and small-scale enterprises. No less than 71 percent of the labor force in China worked in agriculture in 1978, compared with 14 percent in Russia in 1985.[26] Moreover, Chinese agriculture (and much of the rest of the Chinese economy) was essentially manual and on a small scale, thus rendering the introduction of private quasi-property rights and small-scale private enterprise easy. In the USSR, management was extremely centralized.

A second cause of difference between the Russian and Chinese experiences was that the longer communism lasted, the more distorted the economy became in a variety of ways. The overemphasis on investment and heavy industry (notably the military-industrial complex) over consumption, trade, and services became ever more pronounced. Enterprise concentration continued. The central planners found it easier to control a smaller number of production units, eliminating small enterprises. Because prices were not adjusted to market conditions, they became increasingly misrepresentative; and to the extent prices mattered, they contributed to inefficient allocation of resources. In particular, energy prices and transport tariffs were notoriously too low, thus encouraging excessive energy use and long hauls of goods. Many decisions were made on purely political grounds, which guaranteed economic inefficiency. The extreme protectionism within both the USSR and the Soviet trading bloc Council for Mutual Economic Assistance (CMEA) led to an irrational structuring of foreign trade. All these structural deformities were far greater in the USSR than in China.[27]

Thus, the longer communism lasted, the greater the need for structural change. Industry had to cut back, while trade, services, and the financial sector had to expand. Many new small enterprises were needed. The dissolution of old trade links was as essential as the evolution of new ties. Finally, the usage of inputs in production had to be reduced sharply. Considering the pent-up needs for structural changes, it would be surprising if the massive disruption required in the USSR and Eastern Europe did not lead to a temporary decline in national income, especially measured national income. The old communist statistics focused on the state sector and tended to neglect the private sector. Thus, less-developed communist economies with a shorter history of communism, such as China and Vietnam, might be able to escape much of the duress other postcommunist countries would inevitably face.

A third reason for differences between reform in the USSR and in China is the political effects of the duration of the communist system. Two processes are at play in this case. On the one hand, the longer a communist dictatorship lasts, the more formal powers are concentrated in the hands of the state. On the other hand, under a communist reign that rules without severe terror, state powers are increasingly devolved or diluted.[28] Josef Stalin was a real dictator; but the ouster of Nikita Khrushchev showed that power had devolved to the Politburo, or possibly even to the Central Committee of the CPSU. Under Leonid Brezhnev, power was delegated to industrial ministries and regional party secretaries. Consequently, when Gorbachev became General Secretary of the CPSU, he turned out to have surprisingly little power. Instead, a multitude of bureaucrats were all dictators within their own spheres of competence. Decisions from above were distorted to the bureaucrats' advantage, which rarely corresponded with a benefit to society. As a result, regardless of his actual intentions, Gorbachev's many decisions contributed to further perversions of the economic system. He did attempt piecemeal sectoral reform in both agriculture and foreign trade, but his attempts showed that such reform could not succeed in the USSR.

The fundamental conclusion is that the USSR was no longer reformable, because the state as an executor of central decisions had withered away. The state controlled too much, but as a result little actual power rested at the summit of government. Furthermore, there was no civil society or democracy that could balance the power of the *nomenklatura*. In China, on the contrary, less power was concentrated in the hands of the state, but the actual power of the state leader was greater. From this perspective, the cultural revolution also increased the reformability of China, because it reduced the autonomy of the bureaucracy.

Finally, China differed from Russia by having a large number of devoted overseas Chinese who were still in East Asia. Many were highly qualified, wealthy, and entrepreneurial. When China opened up trade, they were willing to invest large sums before anybody else. In a way, the overseas Chinese represented an émigré civil society, making up for the lack of one within China itself.[29] This large asset of human capital made it easier for China than for the USSR both to make good decisions as well as to mitigate flawed ones.

Thus, complaints that the USSR or Russia did not try to launch Chinese-style economic reforms are unjustified. Instead, Gorbachev was wrong in trying to follow the Chinese course too closely, because the preconditions were completely different. China was still reformable, but the USSR had long since passed that point. When reform no longer is possible, radical transformation or decay are the only options. The Baltic states and Russia chose a radical path, while most former Soviet republics proved too indecisive and ended up in a state of decay by 1993.

The Author's Personal Involvement as an Economic Advisor

My role as one of several foreign economic advisors to the Russian reform government may require some explanation.

I went to Moscow a fortnight after the abortive coup in August 1991 in the belief that the Soviet Union and Soviet communism were over. I believed that Russia needed a radical and comprehensive market-oriented reform and that there was an opportunity for such a reform. The obvious inspiration was the Polish transition that had been launched in early 1990. Moreover, I was convinced that reform could only be done in Russia and by Russia, not by any broader-based association of former Soviet republics. I went to find out who would become the leading re-former in Russia, as Minister of Finance Leszek Balcerowicz had been in Poland in 1989. Jeffrey Sachs of Harvard University went to Moscow for the same purpose. We joined forces and met with various potential economic policymakers.

Everything seemed to be possible; yet Russia faced a tremendous economic and political crisis. A whole world was falling apart. It had been a terrible world, but the rubble left behind would not be easily fashioned into a well-functioning society. We shared the belief that the economy was in such a terrible mess that a radical, comprehensive, liberal program would be needed to introduce any kind of rational order. Another guiding idea was that the Soviet Union was over; therefore, Russia would have to be the entity of reform.

It was a curious time of vacuum rather than expectation. Initially we tried to work with Yevgeny Saburov and his group. Saburov had just become deputy prime minister of Russia and minister of the economy. After a second trip to Moscow in September 1991 that I undertook with Sachs's collaborator David Lipton, we found that five groups were competing to form the economic kernel of a new Russian government (see chapter 3). However, Saburov hesitated about his aims and seemed more interested in achieving a high position than in launching a serious reform plan, and we were left in doubt. Saburov was sound on radical mass privatization, but he envisaged a far-reaching but gradual liberalization and stabilization. If he were offered a position at a union level, he would abandon the idea of launching reform in Russia. He had sacked 10 out of the 11 old deputy ministers of the economy, but as a consequence the administration of the ministry had effectively broken down.

Rather dispirited after my days with Saburov's group, I was about to leave Moscow on September 20, 1991. At the airport, however, I met my old friend Aleksandr Shokhin, whom I had tried to contact in vain during the week. He had been appointed Russian Minister of Labor in August. Shokhin told me that he, Yegor Gaidar, and others had met that week at a government *dacha* in Arkhangelskoe outside Moscow and were intent on forming a government. They were working with Gennady Burbulis, who was Yeltsin's confidant. They had decided to relinquish the idea of the USSR and to opt for Russia. This time, Shokhin promised me, there would not be any talk of social democracy but of real liberalism. He made it clear that they wanted to pursue a so-called big bang reform of the Polish type. They would continue meeting at the *dacha*, formulating a government program as well as forming a government. Gaidar would become deputy prime minister for economic policy and Shokhin deputy prime minister for social affairs. I told Shokhin that Sachs, Lipton, and I would be happy to work with them. Shokhin accepted my offer, but he said it would be better for us to stand back until they had actually managed to form a government. (It could be compromising to have foreign advisors involved at such an early stage.) We agreed that our new cooperative effort would start immediately after their new government had been appointed.

Time dragged on. Through various channels, we heard that the team at the *dacha* had grown and was becoming even more impressive in terms of size and quality. The best and brightest of Russia's young economists were coming together. Finally, on October 28, 1991, President Yeltsin made his grand speech on radical liberal systemic change in Russia. We were in high spirits. The world, however, paid little or no attention to this great historical event, preoccupied as it was with relics such as Mikhail Gorbachev and the USSR. Soon afterward, on November 6–8, the new reform government was appointed. I was elated to see that the new Russian government had Yegor Gaidar, Aleksandr Shokhin, and Anatoly Chubais in top positions. They represented the cream of Russia's young economists, and they were liberal and democratic.

Since my time as a Swedish diplomat in Moscow from 1984 until 1987, I knew a large number of Russian economists, their institutes, and their weaknesses and strengths.[30] In general, old Soviet economics was Marxism-Leninism rather than economics in a Western sense. Both theory and empiricism were missing. Unfortunately, the middle-aged economic academicians, who had achieved great prominence under Gorbachev, suffered from an excess of professional pride and status consciousness, barring them from seeking insight in modern economics. I knew established academicians, such as Leonid Abalkin and Nikolai Petrakov, better than the young economists. I had even hosted a seminar and a dinner with Ruslan Khasbulatov in Stockholm in May 1990 when he had been professor of international economics. I was therefore increasingly convinced that the old academicians would not go for really radical market reform, which was what Russia needed.

For a long time, I had been looking for young, bright Russian economists, because it seemed clear to me that only the under-40 generation could be sufficiently free from communist ideology to act rationally. Because of all the restrictions under communism that had been imposed by the KGB on foreigners in Moscow, I was not allowed to meet young Russian economists, even in Moscow, until 1987. The first noteworthy young economist I met was Boris Fedorov, at a bank reception in 1986. He was responsible for Scandinavia in the Soviet state bank Gosbank. In June 1987, I first met Aleksandr Shokhin in a meeting with academician Stanislav Shatalin at the Institute of Economic Forecasting. I was amazed to find a young Russian contradicting an older academician. I kept in touch with both, and through Shokhin I met Petr Aven and Vladimir Kosmarsky.

In 1988, young Russian economists started travelling abroad. I met Anatoly Chubais and Vladimir Mashchits at a conference in Verona in September 1990. I first encountered Maxim Boycko in September 1990 at a conference in Davos. Chubais as well as Sergei Vasil'ev, both from

St. Petersburg, visited me in Stockholm. I met Sergei Glaz'ev and Konstantin Kagalovsky at a conference organized by Jeffrey Sachs in Helsinki. I had long wanted to meet Yegor Gaidar, because from 1987 his articles in the journal *Kommunist* were the best Soviet analyses of the Soviet economy. In June 1991, finally, I lectured at his Institute of Economic Policy in Moscow. I realized that Gaidar had mobilized a young brain trust to run the Russian economy, including Andrei Nechaev and Leonid Grigor'ev. I was delighted to see so many of the best and brightest join the Russian government.

Sachs and Lipton flew to Moscow immediately after the new government had been appointed, and I followed later in November. Other Western economists who were involved from the beginning in some advisory capacity included Marek Dabrowski, Jacek Rostowski, Andrei Shleifer, and Richard Layard, but our natural intellectual leader was Jeffrey Sachs. We knew several of the new Russian ministers from various conferences and visits. We all believed that Russia needed a radical change of economic system, and all of the economic advisors involved but Shleifer and me had worked in Poland. We represented various kinds of knowledge. Sachs was the grand strategist; Lipton had mastered monetary and financial matters; Dabrowski and Rostowski possessed the deepest insights into the Polish transition; and Dabrowski was also a most principled liberal, one to whom the Russians listened with great respect. Shleifer worked on privatization, and Layard focused on social aspects and statistics. I was primarily a specialist on the Soviet economy and Russia.

In general, we represented three kinds of relevant knowledge. First, Jeffrey Sachs in particular possessed great knowledge of economic theory. We could thus contribute to a fuller conceptualization of the reforms. Second, all of us had studied other transitions and macroeconomic stabilizations in practice and could offer specific advice on a great range of problems. Third, Marek Dabrowski and I had substantial knowledge of the USSR. We were prepared to spend a lot of time in Moscow to try to be of help. Most of the senior economists and almost all of the junior economists spoke good Russian.

Initially, everything occurred ad hoc. From December 1991 until March 1993, our offices were in the Council of Ministers, formerly the home of the Central Committee (CC) of the CPSU, at the Old Square close to the Kremlin—an extraordinary feat for an old Sovietologist. We foreigners could assist with a great many things, but finding out who decided what and when was troublesome. Frequently, parallel governmental bodies worked on the same issues at cross-purposes or without knowledge of one another's actions. The reform ministers' attitude toward us was open and generous, but their assumption of power was like a hostile takeover. They had seized the top jobs in front of senior bureaucrats who aspired to those jobs themselves, and they mobilized the ministerial administration in adamant resistance to reforms and the reformers. In addition, the reformers were Russian ministers who took over from USSR ministers, and their staffs were sharply reduced. Even so, the ministerial apparatus was intimidatingly large, with more than 30,000 staff.

Today, it is easy to forget how tense and volatile the situation was in December 1991, because so much has been accomplished since. On the evening of December 10, 1991, our group of foreign economic advisors attended a reception at the President Hotel in Moscow with the whole cabinet. I had expected the cabinet to rejoice because of the successful dissolution of the Soviet Union through the Belovezhsky agreement between Russia, Belarus, and Ukraine on December 8 (see chapter 4), but the ministers all appeared tense, for reasons they did not explain. The next day, we met with President Yeltsin in the White House at ten o'clock. The contrast in mood could not have been greater. Yeltsin came in with a beaming smile, and so did his followers. He told us that he had just had a two-hour meeting with the senior military commanders, and they had agreed to swear allegiance to Russia rather than to the Soviet Union, which Gorbachev had tried to persuade them to do. The political independence of Russia and the breakup of the USSR were thus secured, and the threat of a military conflict caused by an imperialist army (as in Yugoslavia) had been averted.

Gradually, both the Russian government and our structure as an advisory group evolved. At the beginning of 1993, after Boris Fedorov had become Minister of Finance, our working conditions became more orderly, though we lost our offices in the Council of Ministers because of new worries about security, which had prompted restrictions on foreigners in government buildings. Jeffrey Sachs and I set up the Macroeconomic and Finance Unit (MFU) at the Ministry of Finance. The unit ultimately had about thirty employees, half of whom were Westerners and half Russians, and we worked directly for Boris Fedorov. When Gaidar and then Fedorov found themselves compelled to leave the government in January 1994, Jeffrey Sachs and I saw no choice but to leave as well, though Anatoly Chubais and several good deputy ministers remained.[31]

Sources and Statistics

Throughout this period of radical transformation, I was continuously involved, registering essential political and economic developments through internal discussions with people in government and by reading Russian government documents, newspapers, and a plenitude of memoranda drafted by our own collaborators in Moscow. Although my original sources are often oral, I can (with few exceptions) verify the facts through public sources. Previously, the Soviet press would have presented one official version of an event, a version that could have been right or wrong. Today, a variety of sources are frequently at hand. The truth is amply publicized, but much that is not true is published as well. At present, Moscow has about 25 daily newspapers. The range of views is vast, and the appreciation of facts varies greatly. I shall in most cases bypass the discussion about wrong versions and simply adhere to the version of events I understand to be correct.

The newspaper I consider most reliable for reports of facts is *Izvestiya*. *Segodnya* is my second preferred source, but it is more opinionated. In 1992, *Nezavisimaya gazeta* was a leading intellectual newspaper, but it declined in late 1992, and its good journalists moved to *Segodnya*. Government documentation is published in many places, primarily in *Rossiiskaya gazeta*, *Rossiiskie vesti*, and *Ekonomicheskaya gazeta*. The first two newspapers also function as legal gazettes. Several Russian sources, especially *Kommersant* and Interfax, I find so unreliable on government policy that I try to avoid them. Yet *Kommersant'-Daily* publishes the best presentations of new legislation, and *Kommersant* functioned as the mouthpiece of the Central Bank of Russia. Communist and nationalist newspapers tend to be inaccurate and mythological. Serious Russian journals have had problems keeping up with events, partly because of slow publication and partly because they are dominated by old socialist economists who do not write concretely about anything. Major program documents are rarely published, though widely circulated as photocopies. A problem is that different versions of a document may exist. Most of the time, multiple sources as well as the original documents are available, rendering checks possible. I shall not bother the reader with verification, and I avoid references to unpublished documents that are not easily available if published sources exist.

Russian statistics are a major headache and merit some initial comments. A great deal has changed in this regard, and what was bad in Soviet statistics has tended to improve, while other problems have emerged. In general, secrecy has diminished. Many statistics that were never published before are now available, and we have a clearer idea of biases. However, data collection has deteriorated. New developments and huge structural changes make it difficult to elaborate on and assess statistics.

The main source of statistics is still the State Committee of the Russian Federation on Statistics (Goskomstat). Until the dissolution of the old parliament in September 1993, Goskomstat was subordinate to the Supreme Soviet. Goskomstat was badly run and constrained by scant resources. It therefore minimized its output and tried to commercialize its information. Goskomstat also presented a parliamentary bias. Since September 1993, the opposite suspicion has arisen—that is, that Goskomstat has adopted a government bias—though it seems to be more professionally run under its new leadership.

Soviet statistics focused on production. The whole production of the state and cooperative sector was likely to have been reported, with some exaggeration. Overreporting might have amounted to 5 percent of recorded production. From 1992, overreporting disappeared, which might have accounted for an immediate fall in registered production of perhaps 5 percent. In parallel, the private sector has grown, but unrecorded private entrepreneurs evade high taxes. Goskomstat makes little adjustment for concealed production. The Goskomstat assessment of Russia's nominal 1992 GDP in rubles varied incredibly. Initially, Goskomstat assessed GDP at 15 trillion rubles; but a few months later, it increased its assessment by one-third to 20 trillion rubles. Finally, it cut it by almost one-tenth to 18.1 trillion rubles.[32]

Strangely, Russia has no regular statistics on the number of enterprises, only irregular censuses. There are at least 1 million small enterprises, but there may be twice as many, and the tax authorities and Goskomstat present very different numbers. Moreover, the numbers of different categories of enterprises are reported from time to time, but never in a standardized series. If enterprises are not even officially tabulated, their production, which is liable to taxation, will certainly not be properly recorded.

An exception is the privatization statistics that are collected by the State Committee on the Management of State Property (GKI). The GKI presents detailed statistics on privatization auctions as well as data on privatization of all enterprises. However, enterprises may split up, thus rendering different privatization data inconsistent.

Unemployment statistics are probably the most mishandled. At one extreme, officially registered unemployment is very low—below 2 percent in 1994. At the other, various "samples" are presented as overall unemployment rates, elaborated on or inspired by the International Labor Organization (ILO). This organization's aim seems to be to both forecast and present the highest unemployment rates possible, thus claiming that unemployment is the overweening problem. The ILO figures for unemployment had already reached 10 percent in 1992. The most plausible assessments are the Goskomstat surveys, which suggest that total unemployment was 6 percent in early 1994.[33]

In the Soviet Union, as few financial and monetary statistics as possible were published. Neither the money supply nor the budget deficit (not to mention the foreign debt) was published. In this case, major improvements have taken place; but the novelty of all these statistics has led to mistakes, corrections, and discontinuities in statistical series. The International Monetary Fund has worked with Goskomstat to improve monetary and financial statistics.[34] The Ministry of Finance provides regular information on the so-called consolidated state budget. This includes both the federal and regional budgets (but not substantial extrabudgetary funds for unemployment benefits, social insurance, medical insurance, and pensions). The budget statistics vary because of unreliable reporting.

The Central Bank is somewhat reluctant to provide information. It does publish many monetary statistics, but revisions are frequent and much of the information is inconsistent.

Goskomstat provides weekly and monthly figures on inflation and the availability of consumer goods based on data from 132 Russian cities. In addition, elaborations are made by the Center of Economic Analysis and the Center for Economic Reform, both with the Russian Council of Ministers. The inflation statistics are revised slightly (at most 4 percentage points for one month—August 1993), but these statistics appear to have become more stable as inflation has fallen. An initial inflation index produced by the weekly magazine *Kommersant* has been debunked.

A large amount of data is available from various exchanges, notably the exchange rates set at the Moscow Interbank Foreign Currency Exchange (MICEX). Commodity prices are established at various commodity exchanges, and these data are published in several business newspapers.

Foreign trade statistics are unreliable because of smuggling and bribery at the borders as well as substandard registration procedures. The problems in underreporting are particularly severe in the "interstate" trade between CIS members. However, even foreign trade outside of the CIS is severely underestimated. Goskomstat has published figures based on data provided by enterprises involved in foreign trade. Only since 1994 has the State Customs Committee gathered foreign trade data. These data coincided with Goskomstat export data; but for the first quarter of 1994, the imports recorded by Goskomstat amounted to about $4 billion, while the Customs Committee registered $6.6 billion, confirming the general suspicion that the size of the Russian trade surplus must have been exaggerated.[35] Foreign debt statistics are now published by Russian authorities; but it has taken time for them to put these data in order, and lacunae remain.

Opinion polls have become a big industry in Russia. The quality of these polls varies, both in terms of questions posed and samples selected. Too many pollsters focus on Moscow. The widely preferred polls are carried out by the All-Russian Center for the Study of Public Opinion (VTsIOM), which has existed for a long time, has long series, and conducts much of its polling outside the main cities.

The IMF and the World Bank have become important verifiers of Russian statistics, and their publications are often preferred sources. The UN Economic Commission for Europe functioned primarily as a provider of data before 1992. In addition, the Russian government publishes the excellent *Russian Economic Trends*. Weekly bulletins from the Center of Economic Analysis and monthly bulletins from the Center for Economic Reform have stable formats. During 1993 and 1994, weekly monetary reports produced by Brigitte Granville at our Macroeconomic and Finance Unit at the Russian Ministry of Finance provided a great deal of data.

In short, the statistics are of poor quality, but the nature of their biases is reasonably certain. Moreover, the scale of the change in Russia has been so great that no hesitation about overall developments is needed.

Structure of This Book

This book's structure follows from the premises I have presented here and concurs with the current literature on transformations from a socialist economy to a market economy.

The second chapter is devoted to the preconditions of economic reform. I assess the legacy of Gorbachev, discuss the transformation of economic thinking, and expound on the depth of the collapse of the state, the economy, and Russian society in 1991.

The third chapter deals with the formation of the reform program, focusing on the political economy of reform. The political premises of reform are discussed, including the program of shock therapy, the formation of the economic reform team, the economic debate they encountered, and the political and institutional problems that impeded their efforts.

The next four chapters are more economic in orientation. Chapter 4 deals with the transformation of Russia's relations with other former Soviet republics (FSRs), especially with regard to the breakup of the ruble zone. Chapter 5 focuses on liberalization of all kinds, both of domestic markets and foreign trade. Although deregulation was quite far reaching, it is striking how much more difficult it was to liberalize markets in Russia than in Eastern Europe. Chapter 6 is devoted to the controversial issue of macroeconomic stabilization. Chapter 7 discusses the seemingly most successful part of the Russian transformation, namely privatization. The eighth and final chapter contains an evaluation of the Russian transformation.

CHAPTER TWO

Preconditions of Economic Reform

DURING THE first half of the 1980s, the Soviet Union was characterized by stability or stagnation, depending on one's preferred perspective. In real terms, the Soviet economy was stagnating; but it was stable, with minimal inflation and no unemployment. Though there was complete political stability, there were also extensive social alienation and apathy. In foreign affairs, the USSR was stronger than ever, with a defense system matching that of the United States. Yet the Soviet defense sector absorbed an ever-increasing share of GDP, and the ongoing war in Afghanistan had proven demoralizing. On the whole, the USSR looked petrified and obsolete. It had not kept up with Western progress—innovations such as microcomputers, the evolution of telecommunications, and the rise of the modern service sector. Isolation, censorship, and repression did not allow Soviet society to evolve. When reform eventually came to the USSR, it started from above, with the ascension to power of Mikhail Gorbachev. However, reform turned out to be fraught with complications, and soon the whole political and economic system began to unravel.

The purpose of this chapter is not to summarize the economic history of *perestroika* (I have done that elsewhere).[1] It is instead to trace the consequences of the essential developments that were required for the real transition to a market economy. In particular, I want to show how severe the political and economic crisis was at that time. Today it is all too easily forgotten, because the deterioration happened so quickly and the recovery was rather swift.

This chapter deals with Gorbachev's legacy with regard to economic reforms, democratization, and institutional development. The fundamental transition in economic thinking, from Marxism to a market economy orientation, is discussed next. The so-called 500-day program of the summer of 1990 marked this transition. I then investigate the depth of the Russian economic crisis of late 1991 and draw some conclusions about the end of the Soviet system.

Gorbachev's Legacy: Institutional Breakdown

Mikhail Gorbachev was elected General Secretary of the Communist Party of the Soviet Union (CPSU) in March 1985. He was one of the brightest *apparatchiki* to emerge from the old Soviet system, but even so was very much a product of that system.

Gorbachev's Aims and Limitations

From the outset, Gorbachev made clear his ambition to undertake substantial economic and political reforms. In a key speech on December 10, 1984, he introduced his reform agenda in vague but strategic terms. Almost all of the catchwords and phrases that he was to make famous were already formulated. Gorbachev called for "revolutionary decisions," "acceleration of social-economic progress," "deep transformation in the economy and the whole system of social relations," "*perestroika* of economic management," "competition," "self-management," "self-government," "democratization," and "*glasnost.*" In February 1986, Gorbachev went further, calling for the establishment of family farms.[2]

At this point, the limits of Gorbachev's desire to reform must also be noted. In his December 1984 speech, a supreme goal was made clear: "Only an intensive, highly developed economy can safeguard a reinforcement of [our] country's position on the international stage and allow her to enter the next millennium with dignity as a great and flourishing power."[3] To Gorbachev, reforms were a means to an end rather than an end in themselves. His aim was to reinforce and revitalize the USSR so that it could maintain its superpower status—a status threatened by its stagnant economy and the arms race with the United States.

Gorbachev wanted to reform the CPSU and its ideology as well as the Soviet economy and political system. His goal was to instill new life in them.[4] The basis for Gorbachev's efforts was his belief that Soviet communism was reformable. This turned out to be wrong; but if he had not believed that reform was possible he would not have been able to destroy Soviet communism.

Gorbachev's outstanding political skill was compromise. Whatever the changes in policy made from 1985 to 1990, Gorbachev appears to have embraced the winning side. The drawback was that he was committed to partial solutions that could not work. Whenever it was necessary to make a clear choice between two sides (or two principles), Gorbachev tried to straddle them. He either made contradictory statements or sought a compromise, even if it was logically inconceivable that one could be found. Boris Yeltsin tellingly characterized Gorbachev:

> He wanted to combine things that cannot be combined—to marry a hedgehog and a grass snake—communism and a market economy, public-property ownership and private-property ownership, the multiparty system and the Communist Party with its monopoly on power. But these things are incompatible. He wanted to retain some of the old things while introducing new reforms. In his latest mistake, he wanted our country to be a single state. That is impossible; that is unrealistic. But he decided to stick to his illusions and bide his time.[5]

It gradually became evident that Gorbachev was firmly rooted in the old communist ideology. His major shortcomings were the result of his refusal to abandon communism, a system that ultimately proved to be both politically and economically inviable. By reacting against many of communism's excesses, he broke the old system without presenting an alternative. This created a deep intellectual void. In the last years of his rule, Gorbachev became popularly known as the chatterbox (*boltun*).

In the end, Gorbachev had little to offer but platitudes, implying that socialism was good by definition.[6] He and his aides considered themselves "children of the 20th Party Congress" of 1956. This was the last generation to believe that socialism was reformable, resisting the influence of younger collaborators or serious international advisors. The reform endeavors Gorbachev made were crushed by the bureaucracy, just as Andrei Amalrik had written in 1970 of earlier reform attempts: "The so-called 'economic reform' . . . is in essence a half-measure and is in practice being sabotaged by the party machine, because if such a reform was carried to its logical end, it would threaten the power of the machine."[7]

Gorbachev's Economic Legacy

The Gorbachev era (1985–91) can be divided into three periods with respect to both politics and economics.[8] During his first three years in power (1985–87), Gorbachev initiated limited reforms of the old system. Over the next three years (1988–90), the reforms were increasingly radicalized, and Gorbachev moved to the political center. After October 1990, everything began to fall apart, and Gorbachev once again embraced the old communist establishment.

From 1985 to 1987, Gorbachev led the reform efforts, but until June 1987 the changes initiated were modest. For example, in 1985 and 1986, the most conspicuous economic measures were neo-Stalinist disciplinary campaigns against alcohol and so-called unearned incomes. The five-year plan for 1986–90 was characterized by the empty slogan "acceleration" of economic growth and called for increased investment for machine-building. In 1986, Gorbachev sponsored technocratic attempts at improving the old system. These included admonitions to enhance shift-work, creation of a new wage system, and development of a system of independent quality control. In addition, there were multiple organizational changes and attempts to improve enterprise incentives. More reformist measures were a partial reform of agriculture in March 1986, which gave more independence to state and collective farms, and a decentralization of foreign trade legislated in August 1986. Because the results of these partial reforms were negative or insignificant, demands for more radical economic reforms increased.

The Central Committee (CC) plenary meeting of the CPSU in June 1987 heralded an attempt at more substantial economic reform. In its immediate aftermath, the Law on State Enterprises was promulgated, coming into force in January 1988. This set the stage for the period 1988–90, when Gorbachev no longer held the radical lead on reforms. In November 1987, he warned publicly for the first time against radicals going too far, with an unspoken allusion to Boris Yeltsin. The Law on State Enterprises was a halfway attempt at economic reform, leaving the economy with neither plan nor market. Officially, compulsory plan targets were abolished; in reality, they remained in watered-down form. Similarly, enterprises were offered more freedom in setting prices and wages. They were given substantial rights but little responsibility. Rather than paving the way for a market economy, the Law on State Enterprises encouraged manipulation of the old rules. The main consequence of its enactment was that wages started rising excessively. Enterprise managers raised prices whenever they were allowed to by the state, while costs and demand were neglected. As a result, relative prices became increasingly distorted; the prices of heavily taxed industrial goods rose, while those of subsidized food stayed low. The aggravated economic crisis prompted fears of hyperinflation from the fall of 1990.

More and more reformers called for a real market economy based on private property. The Brezhnev Constitution of 1977 contained Article 17, which permitted certain private activities: "In the USSR, individual labor activity in the sphere of handicrafts, agriculture, services for the population, and also other kinds of activities, based exclusively on manual work of the citizens and members of their families, are allowed in accordance with law."[9] The promotion of private property had its humble beginnings in the adoption of the USSR Law on Individual Labor Activity in November 1986, which essentially made the constitutional commitment of 1977 operative. A much more substantial step was the promulgation of the USSR Law on Cooperatives in May 1988. Under this law, virtually any private enterprise with at least three owners could be classified as a cooperative. As a result, hundreds of new commercial banks arose as "cooperatives." However, these "cooperatives" became so dynamic that the Law on Cooperatives was amended several times in a restrictive direction. In the winter of 1989–90, USSR laws on leasehold, ownership, and land were adopted, but in reality only the Law on Leasehold had significant impact. In the summer of 1990, statutes on joint stock companies and securities were adopted, as well as a decree on small enterprises. Simultaneously, a State Property Fund was set up to handle privatization. All of this legislation was passed under the jurisdiction of the Soviet Union.

The big Soviet reform debate started in the summer of 1989 and ended in the fall of 1990. Ten major reform programs were worked out and presented. However, in spite of economic deterioration, little happened to the real Soviet economy until the crisis became acute in 1990, and in October 1990, Gorbachev turned his back on all reforms. The remaining reformers departed or were sacked, and Gorbachev joined forces with the communist establishment, the military, and the KGB, whose world he had obliterated. He turned against a more comprehensive notion of privatization. In particular, Gorbachev protested against private ownership of land: "I am in favor of the market . . . but I, for instance, do not accept private ownership of land, whatever you do with me."[10] He envisioned that private ownership would play a rather limited role: "When owners have appeared, private property might emerge; in any case, I imagine that it will be small-scale property. It will be decisive only in certain spheres, where the cooperative and state sectors do not work as necessary."[11]

The last year and a half of Soviet power was characterized by increasingly desperate attempts by the government to reduce subsidies, primarily through price increases. On May 24, 1990, Nikolai Ryzhkov, prime minister of the USSR, announced imminent price increases. This caused a massive run on shops, and Ryzhkov was forced to retract. In January 1991, the newly appointed prime minister of the USSR, Valentin Pavlov, launched a surprise currency reform, demonetizing banknotes of 50- and 100-ruble denominations. Several days of panic and chaos erupted; but in the end, very few banknotes were confiscated, though public confidence in Soviet currency was seriously undermined. Also in January, most wholesale prices were liberalized; but because retail prices stayed fixed, consumer subsidies rose. In April 1991, consumer prices were actually increased substantially, and a growing number of these prices were liberalized. However, the price increases were soon overtaken by increases in wages and social expenditures. A large share of prices were left unregulated, allowing for substantial inflation of free prices. Even so, subsidies were exploding. The Soviet regime was in a state of collapse. The question became how and when it would fall, because it was no longer politically or economically viable.

Gorbachev's Political Legacy

A chronological analysis of Gorbachev's attempts at political reform offers further insight into why the USSR could not be reformed. In addition, this analysis also gives a picture of the state of political institutions at the time of Gorbachev's fall from power.[12]

Gorbachev's political agenda was broad and comprehensive. It included freedom of speech and access to information, foreign policy reform, democratization both of state institutions and the CPSU, extensive organizational changes, and a recasting of the relations between republics within the USSR.

One of Gorbachev's earliest and most persistent efforts was to establish freedom of speech. From the outset, *glasnost* was one of his key slogans. From 1985 on, the sphere of freedom of speech and dissemination of information in the USSR gradually expanded, arousing great popular interest.[13] The process culminated with the First Congress of People's Deputies of the USSR in May and June 1989, whose sessions were televised and attracted huge audiences. For the first time in the Soviet Union, anything could be said in public. What could be said was, and no one was punished. However, as the economic crisis set in, many believed that everything had been said, but nothing had been done. The year of freedom of speech, 1989, also marked the Soviet Union's peak of popular interest in public affairs.

With freedom of information, it soon became evident how badly the Soviet Union had fared in almost every respect, save a strong defense and full employment. All of the problems inherent in a command economy, and its resulting poor performance, were exposed.[14] Similarly, people realized how extensive political and national repression had been. The logical consequence of all this negative information was that, as an ideology, Marxism-Leninism died as a serious political alternative. This opened a vast ideological void, but it was unclear how it would be filled.

One of Gorbachev's greatest and most elaborate successes was his transformation of foreign policy, not only of the USSR but of the whole world. The concept of a bipolar world, divided between capitalism and communism, fell apart. The repercussions of this shattered concept were many. First, the end of the philosophical battle between capitalism and socialism undermined the ideological foundation of the communist dictatorship. Hostility toward the outside world, secrecy, isolation, censorship, and repression were no longer justifiable. Second, Gorbachev abolished the outer empire, comprised of the Council for Mutual Economic Assistance (CMEA or COMECON). Hence, the CMEA and its obsolete trading system, based on bilateral five-year barter agreements, became redundant and could be dissolved at the beginning of 1991. Third, the termination of hostility between the superpowers rendered Soviet defense expenditures excessive, and substantial defense cuts became possible. Fourth, without ideological or superpower competition, Soviet foreign aid to socialist dictatorships in the third world served little purpose.[15] Fifth, Soviet adversity to capitalist organizations (including Bretton Woods institutions such as the IMF and later the World Bank) ceased. Gorbachev appears to have been aware of the possibilities he raised, but he clearly did not realize the extent to which he undermined Soviet rule by calling off confrontation in foreign policy.

At the plenary meeting of the Central Committee (CC) of the CPSU in January 1987, Gorbachev first advocated "democratization," heralding real elections. Gorbachev's political persona was revealed through his attempts at democratization, which was close to his heart. Generally, he aspired to form new and complex institutions with the parliament or Congress of People's Deputies at the center. He wanted to rise above the fray by becoming president. Gorbachev preferred half-measures and wanted some democratization, but not a full-fledged effort. He therefore called for democratic elections of two-thirds of the 2,250 deputies of the Congress of People's Deputies in March 1989, with the remaining third of the deputies to be elected by various political and social organizations controlled by the CPSU. The actual working parliament, the Supreme Soviet, was elected indirectly by deputies of the Congress. Gorbachev did not allow competing political parties. He wanted every election but his own to be democratically contested. In early 1990, Gorbachev was elected the first and last president of the USSR by only 59 percent of the deputies of the Congress of People's Deputies, although he was the only candidate.[16] Rather than urging adoption of a brand new constitution, Gorbachev opted for amendments to the 1977 Brezhnev version.

All of the institutions Gorbachev created were so unwieldy that they were unworkable. They required extensive mediating skills on the part of the president, suggesting that Gorbachev wanted to be the power broker in the major bodies of government. This was true of the Presidential Council, the presidential apparatus, the Congress of People's Deputies, and the Supreme Soviet. Democratic pressures had at long last broken through, but Gorbachev left behind an institutional structure that allowed for no democratic responsibility. In its very design, the sovereign but irresponsible and only partially democratic parliament was a political bomb, and general confusion prevailed over the division between executive and legislative powers. Gorbachev thrived on chaos and left a heritage of institutional disorder in his wake.

Gorbachev dealt with the CPSU in a similar fashion. At the 19th Party Conference in June and July 1988, he pushed through a degree of internal democratization and substantially reduced the power of the central party organs. In effect, the old party apparatus had broken down. Most branch departments of the CC apparatus were merged into one socioeconomic department, and many staff were laid off. The previously powerful CC

Secretariat ceased to meet. In March 1990, the Politburo was effectively replaced with a new Presidential Council. The central party organs that remained were weak and in disarray. Gorbachev had broken down the central policymaking functions of the CPSU and had possibly injured it fatally.[17] After the abortive coup in August 1991 (in which leading CPSU functionaries participated), Russian President Boris Yeltsin could effectively prohibit the existence of the CPSU. By aspiring to revitalize the CPSU, Gorbachev facilitated its death; but presumably he had wanted to see it thrive.

All along, Gorbachev was preoccupied with organizational change. His characteristic approach was to amalgamate state institutions into huge central bodies. The monstrous State Agro-Industrial Committee (Gosagroprom) was a case in point. At the same time, Gorbachev tried to reduce the size of the state administration, especially at the central level. Between 1986 and 1989, the number of employees of Soviet ministries was cut back from approximately 2.4 million to 1.6 million.[18] However, cutting the administration without fundamentally changing its tasks overstrained it and impaired its ability to function.

The administrative disorder Gorbachev generated was paralleled by legal disorder. From the outset, Gorbachev envisioned a rule of law that would have been anathema to earlier Soviet communists. His instincts and mode of politics, however, led him in the opposite direction, and no legal reform was undertaken. Because of Gorbachev's halfhearted democratic reforms, rivalries developed throughout the USSR between the legislative councils at all levels and the corresponding executives. These rivalries were never resolved. Gorbachev wanted to be a go-between everywhere, but he could not possibly have handled all the conflicts he nurtured. The complete confusion of legislative and executive power (which surfaced centrally, regionally, and locally) became his hallmark. Gorbachev took refuge by exacting extensive rights to rule by decree after 1990.[19]

Gorbachev's most stunning shortcoming was his disregard for the USSR's problems regarding nationality issues. His naive statements in his book *Perestroika* are revealing:

> The Revolution and socialism have done away with national oppression and inequality, and ensured economic, intellectual, and cultural progress for all nations and nationalities. . . . If the nationality question had not been solved in principle, the Soviet Union would never have had the social,

cultural, economic, and defense potential it has now. Our state would not
have survived if the republics had not formed a community based on broth-
erhood and cooperation, respect and mutual assistance.[20]

Unaware of the sense of suppression and injustice the various nation-
alities had experienced under Soviet power, Gorbachev was dumbfounded
when one nationality after another called for independence. Initially, Gorbachev treated these efforts as demands for decentralization and offered
some concessions; but when nationalists reasserted their claims, he resisted. He resorted to the use of force in Azerbaijan in January 1990 and
in Lithuania in January 1991. His delaying tactics severely aggravated
these nationality issues, but his understanding of the crisis did not improve. Just before his forced resignation and after the dissolution of the
USSR, Gorbachev insisted: "The process now under way is getting us
back on the track of creating a new union."[21]

The disintegration of the USSR might have been inevitable, given that
only repression and communist ideology had held the country together.
But Gorbachev's neglect and his confused handling of nationality issues
speeded up the process. Moreover, because he had diminished the effectiveness of several union institutions (notably the CPSU) and the government, he rendered republican bodies the only organs left that could fulfil
the ordinary tasks of the state. Not surprisingly, a first declaration of
sovereignty was adopted by the Supreme Soviet of Estonia in November
1988.[22] From December 1989 to March 1990, the union republics held
democratic parliamentary elections to Supreme Soviets. In the case of
Russia, this was a Congress of People's Deputies with 1,068 members,
which in turn elected a Supreme Soviet within itself as at the union level.
These elections were more democratic than those of the Congress of
People's Deputies of the USSR in March 1989. As a result, the republican
parliaments enjoyed greater democratic legitimacy than the Soviet parliament. The stage was thus set for separatism.[23] In March 1990, the
Supreme Soviet of Lithuania went a step further by enacting "the Restoration of the Independent Lithuanian State." By the end of 1990, five
union republics (Estonia, Latvia, Lithuania, Georgia, and Armenia) had
declared themselves independent, while the other ten had issued decla-
rations of "sovereignty," which ambiguously implied autonomy. In 1990,
a "war of laws" over jurisdiction broke out between the USSR and the
union republics and lasted until the union was dissolved in December
1991.[24]

In conclusion, Gorbachev managed to break down a multitude of old communist and Soviet institutions. His outstanding achievements were the dismantling of the outer Soviet empire in Eastern Europe, the introduction of free speech and access to information, the demolition of Marxism-Leninism, the destruction of the totalitarian communist regime, and the initiation of democratization. Gorbachev's capacity for peaceful destruction was truly remarkable, but he left the old bodies of government in tatters rather than definitively finishing them off. The little he actually created, notably the Congress of People's Deputies, became liabilities rather than assets. His legacy was one of institutional chaos.

The Transformation of Economic Thinking

The last years of the Soviet Union saw a complete shift in economic thinking, both within the elite and among the population at large.[25] The Soviet leadership became aware of the mounting economic crisis in the summer of 1989, and in 1990 its severity became apparent to everyone. A fall in the net material product of 4.0 percent was recorded, and shortages grew intolerable.[26] In the fall of 1989 and into 1990, a number of economic programs emerged and one ideological barrier after another was displaced. Marxism-Leninism was no longer allowed to stifle economic thinking. By 1991, overt ideological dogmas were no longer serious concerns, though prejudices lingered. Two other barriers rose instead: limited economic knowledge (both among the old elite and the public), and the vested interests of the old elite. It is worth examining how the dogmas were dismissed.

After the CC plenary meeting in June 1987, Gorbachev paid little attention to economic reform. The first signal of a renewed top-level interest in reform was the creation of the State Commission on Economic Reform at the USSR Council of Ministers on July 5, 1989. It was headed by a senior academic reform economist, academician Leonid Abalkin, who became deputy prime minister. His appointment also signified a new tendency to promote academics to top government jobs. Other economic academicians who joined the administration were Stanislav Shatalin (member of the Presidential Council, March–November 1990) and Nikolai Petrakov (personal economic advisor to Gorbachev, January 1990–January 1991).

In October 1989, the Reform Commission presented its first reform program, popularly called the Abalkin program. This program initiated an official abandonment of fundamental socialist dogmas. The Abalkin program acknowledged that the market must take precedence over the plan, which was one of the first widely embraced economic insights. It established that an efficient market must be characterized by free prices and competition. The value of stock exchanges and a convertible currency, hallmarks of a real market economy, were readily appreciated. No one who wanted to be taken seriously dared call for central planning any longer. The 1987 Law on State Enterprises was replaced by the Law on Enterprises in the USSR, which was promulgated by the USSR Supreme Soviet on June 4, 1990. Judging by its language, this law provided a basis for a market economy. Strangely, this seemingly radical and vital law was ignored by all sides. Yet the market had made a legal breakthrough. A few less reformist government programs followed.

In February 1990, however, a far more radical program was created. Originally called the 400-day program, its authors were three young economists—Grigory Yavlinsky (who headed one department in Abalkin's Reform Commission), Mikhail Zadornov, and Aleksei Mikhailov. The program called for a transition to a market economy within 400 days. Its salient features were rapid, massive privatization through sales; boosting of state revenues to facilitate the financial stabilization of the economy; and swift yet gradual price liberalization. The authors were inspired by the "shock therapy" of economic reform in Poland. They presented their first version of the program with the words: "The time for gradual transformations has been missed, and the ineffectiveness of partial reforms has been proved by the experiences of Hungary, Yugoslavia, Poland, and China."[27]

In the summer of 1990, Yavlinsky and his now 500-day program garnered great public attention and moved to the political center stage. In July 1990, after several political tours, Gorbachev and Yeltsin agreed to form a joint working group to refine the 500-day program. The group was headed by one of Gorbachev's top economic advisors, academician Stanislav Shatalin, member of the Presidential Council. Shatalin was assisted by Nikolai Petrakov, Gorbachev's personal economic advisor. For the rest, the Shatalin group brought a new generation of young economists—the young reform leaders to come—to the political forefront. Apart from Yavlinsky (leader of the party faction Yabloko beginning in 1993), Zadornov (chair of the Budget Committee of the State Duma as of 1994) and Mikhailov (deputy of the State Duma from 1993 on), it included Boris Fedorov (minister of finance and deputy prime minister, 1992–94), Andrei Vavilov (first deputy minister of finance from early 1992 on), Sergei Aleksashenko (deputy minister of finance, 1993–95), Leonid Grigor'ev (deputy minister of finance, 1991–92), Vladimir Mashchits (chair of the State Committee for Economic Relations with Other Members of the CIS, 1992–95), and Yevgeny Yasin (minister of the economy as of 1994).[28]

At the end of August 1990, the Shatalin group presented its elaboration on the 500-day program, a large report with the unequivocal title *Transition to the Market*. However, after a number of political tours, Gorbachev rejected the extended 500-day program in October 1990. Reflecting the reigning political mood, he had turned more communist. However, the political circus Gorbachev instigated to get rid of the 500-day program actually helped to publicize it, and the program remains a liberal landmark. It was in 1990 that the Russian mind-set shifted to support the idea of a market economy, and the idea of privatization became widely accepted. The 500-day program never mentioned the word socialism. Unlike Gorbachev, Yeltsin was prepared to promote young economists within the Russian government. For a few months in 1990, Yavlinsky became Russian deputy prime minister and Boris Fedorov was named Russian minister of finance. However, both resigned when they realized that the time for serious economic reform had not yet arrived.

As Soviet leaders gave up on privatization in 1990, President Yeltsin and the Russian leadership seized the political and legislative initiative. After the Russian declaration of sovereignty in June 1990, Russian jurisdiction effectively superseded that of the USSR. Full-fledged private enterprise was never accepted by the Soviet Union, but it was permitted by the Russian Federation through enactment of its Law on Property in December 1990. This law broached the principle of equal legal treatment of all forms of property—private, state, municipal, and collective alike. The Law on Enterprises and Entrepreneurial Activity enacted in Russia on December 25, 1990, was also a substantial reform law. It gave private enterprises the explicit right to operate and revoked every restriction on private enterprise. All enterprises had to be registered, but registration could not be denied if the proper documents had been submitted. Furthermore, private enterprises could engage in any activity not explicitly prohibited. The legal forms private enterprises could take included individual entrepreneurship, sole proprietorship, general partnership, limited partnership, and joint stock companies. The ordinary Western forms of economic association had thus been introduced.

The issue then became how to carry out privatization. The initial discussion was rather confused and focused on land reform. The first Russian privatization law was the Law on Land Reform, which was promulgated as early as November 1990, together with the Law on the Peasant Farm. Even with the enactment of these laws, no land reform ensued. (A major privatization law was adopted by the Russian Supreme Soviet in July 1991 and is discussed in the context of Russian privatization in chapter 7.)[29] When the Soviet Union came to an end, a broad conviction reigned in Russia that fast, far-reaching privatization was needed. However, there was little understanding of how to carry this out, and serious political and economic interests were involved. The notion of private ownership of land was particularly popular. But the chairs of *kolkhozy* and directors of *sovkhozy* formed a large conservative block in the USSR Congress of People's Deputies and resisted land reform.

Although most people comprehended that marketization was necessary, the politicians were afraid of the social unrest that would ensue if consumer prices were raised or liberalized. They were also politically unable to control expenditures. A widespread dislike of so-called speculation (implying gains from private trade) persisted. There was a prevailing natural unwillingness to accept any social costs, but the economic crisis had already made such great costs inevitable.

A curious reversal of previous dogmas occurred. The more a certain tenet had been disliked by the communists, the keener the popular understanding that it was necessary became. Thus, private ownership of the means of production became as vital a dogma as their socialization had once been. The market replaced the plan as a tenet, although it was more difficult to grasp. A common misconception was that monopolies should be fought through regulation rather than liberalization. However, the concept that proved most difficult to grasp was macroeconomic stabilization; neither the concept nor its components had existed under socialism. The very existence of a budget deficit in the USSR was officially denied until the fall of 1988. Under the old system, money had been passive. Thus no monetary policy had been required or pursued. Concepts such as money supply, interest rates, or reserve ratios had never entered into any discussion of socialist economics. The Soviet currency was not convertible and thousands of exchange rates were in use, rendering exchange rate policy incomprehensible.

From the fall of 1990 on, warnings of imminent hyperinflation were voiced by all sides. But few perceived that this was such a serious crisis that it required decisive action. Gorbachev's reaction in the midst of the crisis was characteristic: "But I want a stage-by-stage, step-by-step process that will not stimulate disintegration and chaos."[30] However, immediately after having disposed of radical measures, he declared his readiness to use force: "It's critical that we not lose control of the situation. Therefore, I'll use my powers as President, first of all as commander in chief of the armed forces."[31]

In the early summer of 1991 in Cambridge, Massachusetts, an effort was undertaken by a joint American-Russian working group chaired by Graham Allison of Harvard University and Grigory Yavlinsky. Its members included top American economists such as Jeffrey Sachs and Stanley Fischer. It went by the name "the Grand Bargain," which suggested a program for political and economic transformation in the USSR supported by massive Western financial aid. Its call for large-scale financial assistance was widely publicized in the West, but similar proposals had been made by Nikolai Shmelev in 1987 and 1988. The great novelty of this program was that it advocated a comprehensive and momentous liberalization coupled with strict macroeconomic stabilization. The Grand Bargain was possibly the first economic program that had drawn serious Soviet participation and that was not gradualist in nature. It also signified a new degree of international collaboration regarding Russian economic reform.[32] However, the Grand Bargain had little impact in Russia because it was not widely publicized there. Yavlinsky limited his domestic propaganda efforts to almost no one but Gorbachev, who did not embrace the program—only its demand for international credits. Moreover, the Grand Bargain focused on the USSR rather than on Russia as the entity of economic reform.

And so, on the eve of the collapse of communism, both marketization and privatization were widely accepted in Russia. Marxism-Leninism was no longer much of a hindrance. However, the problem was that few Russians had any alternative knowledge or understanding of economics. Although the vast majority of Russians wanted a market economy based on private ownership, they did not know what such an economy would entail. The field lay open for both vested interests and populism.

The Depth of the Economic Crisis in 1991

When the Soviet Union broke up in December 1991, the Russian economy was in a crisis as complex as it was profound. The old communist system had proven increasingly inadequate and had caused ever greater wastage and inefficient use of resources. All cheap sources of growth, such as abundant raw materials, had been used up. The ill-conceived reform policies had brought on a macroeconomic crisis, reflected in a growing budget deficit. The excessive issuance of money while prices were controlled and as production plummeted had bred a monetary overhang and had exacerbated shortages, a portent of high open inflation. Gorbachev had drawn extensively not only on Soviet reserves of gold and hard currency but also on international loans. Consequently, at the end of 1991, the USSR defaulted on its international commitments. Finally, the Soviet economy was exposed to a severe external shock in 1991 with the breakdown of the CMEA trading mechanism. Although Russia's terms of trade improved, much of the prior demand disappeared. The Russian economy became subject to a similar external shock in 1992, when the USSR fell apart. Few valuable assets remained aside from human capital and natural resources.

An Inefficient Economic System

When a socialist economic system breaks down, the focus shifts to its macroeconomic imbalances. But the fundamental problem remains the socialist economic system itself. The outstanding characteristic of the Soviet socialist economy was the Leninist primacy of politics over economics. All of the power players, including enterprise managers, tried to maximize their power (and thus their control over resources) regardless of the economic effects. Correspondingly, superiors promoted those people who exhibited complete loyalty, whereas any display of personal integrity was disapproved of, even if its aim was to achieve beneficial economic results.

A second characteristic of the communist economy was its peculiar economic objective, which focused on quantitative production targets rather than efficiency, profits, or future value. As long as unutilized resources remained plentiful, the ability to mobilize all kinds of resources—capital, labor, and raw materials—was an advantage. However, when most resources had become overutilized, excessive costs, low efficiency, and shortages became ever more characteristic of the socialist model, which lacked mechanisms for efficient resource allocation at any level.

Third, regardless of objective function, the socialist order lacked composite standards of value. Prices played a subordinate role; but they still influenced allocation after major allocation decisions had been made in an arbitrary political fashion. Yet existing prices served no useful economic function. Some had been frozen for decades. As economic preconditions altered, prices became progressively more arbitrary. On the rare occasions when prices were revised, it was generally for political reasons or because of administrative loopholes, rather than to meet demand, world market prices, or actual costs.

In the early 1990s, the Soviet price system was in disarray. Certain prices floated freely and rose enormously because of the huge monetary overhang, while most prices remained regulated. For instance, in early 1990, the Soviet wholesale price of one ton of crude oil was 30 rubles, which also happened to be the free retail market price of one package of Marlboro cigarettes. Moreover, enterprises paid one another in noncash (*beznalichnye*) or account rubles, which were legally separated from the cash (*nalichnye*) rubles used on the consumer market. At that time, the black market rate of one cash ruble was three noncash rubles. Hence, with the right connections, it would have been possible to buy three tons of crude oil for one package of Marlboros, or for less than $1, when the world market price of one ton of crude oil exceeded $100. Similarly, the regulated price of a flight from Moscow to Vladivostok was $7, whereas the market price of a cab ride between an airport in Moscow and a downtown hotel was $10. Prices that were less than 1 percent of the world market price were commonplace.[33]

In light of these realities, enterprises had little incentive to improve efficiency, quality, selection, or technology, because they were neither oriented toward making a profit nor subject to competition. Therefore, the rational approach taken by managers of socialist enterprises was to maximize their political clout, by obeying any whim from above. For the most part, managers tried to attain their output targets with a minimum margin. They also attempted to minimize renewal orders while undermining quality, because it was easier and cheaper to produce substandard products. As a natural consequence, the growth rate fell because of declining efficiency, though official statistics did not reflect the deterioration of quality. In the mid-1980s, the annual growth rate in the USSR

Table 2-1. *Average Annual Growth of the Soviet Economy, 1961–85, Net Material Product*

Percent, at fixed prices

Source	1961–65	1966–70	1971–75	1976–80	1981–85
Official	6.5	7.8	5.7	4.3	3.6
Selyunin & Khanin	4.4	4.1	3.2	1.0	0.6

Sources: Tsentralnoe Statisticheskoe Upravleniye SSSR, *Narodnoe khozyaistvo SSSR v 1985 g.* (Central Statistical Board of the USSR, The National Economy of the USSR in 1985) (Moscow: Finansy i statistika, 1986), pp. 38, 409; Vasily Selyunin and Grigory Khanin, "Cunning Figures," *Novy mir*, vol. 63 (February 1987), pp. 194–95.

was probably exaggerated by about 3 percentage points. When Gorbachev became general secretary of the CPSU, the main problem of the Soviet economy was stagnation, as the plausible alternative assessment of Soviet economic growth by Vasily Selyunin and Grigory Khanin suggests (see table 2-1). At the same time, defense expenditures appear to have amounted to about one-quarter of GDP and had risen steadily in real terms.[34]

In 1990 and 1991, state enterprise managers began to adjust to the considerable freedom and security at their jobs as well as to the absurd price relations of the market. Freedom without responsibility amounted to a major principal-agent problem. The principal—the state—had virtually withered away; the agents—the managers—were therefore free to focus on personal gain. Piece by piece, they expropriated the assets of enterprises they managed. Any manager who could sell raw materials abroad did so, at least in part to his own benefit. As a result of both wastage and diversion of resources, supplies of inputs receded and state output slumped; it was not impossible to foresee a virtual collapse in production. The decline in net material product continued apace in 1991 and had reached 21 percent in the last quarter. A far steeper fall seemed feasible.[35]

A Distorted Economic Structure

The combination of politicized decisionmaking, confused objectives, and distorted relative prices resulted in a multitude of structural distortions in the economy.[36]

The structure of the distribution of the GDP was characterized by high expenditures on defense and investment outlays, but low consumption. According to the official statistics for 1985, as little as 47.5 percent

Table 2-2. *Structure of Production: Distribution of GDP, 1991*
Percent (unless otherwise specified)

Country	Agriculture	Industry	Services	1991 GDP per capita (U.S. dollars)
Western Germany	2	39	59	23,650
Italy	3	33	64	18,520
Russia	13	48	39	3,220
Mexico	9	30	61	3,030
Brazil	10	39	51	2,940
Argentina	15	40	46	2,790

Source: World Bank, *World Development Report 1993: Investing in Health* (Oxford University Press, 1993), pp. 239, 243.

of GDP went to private consumption and 32.0 percent to gross accumulation.[37] However, because around 25 percent of GDP devoted to defense was hidden in these statistics, real private consumption was probably less than 40 percent.[38] The large share of GDP reflected that the investment process was especially wasteful, because its plan targets were measured in utilized resources. For production, the plan targets were at least expressed as gross output. As a result, disproportionately large amounts of resources were needed to compensate for minimal efficiency of investment.

In addition, the structure of the economy (both GDP produced and employment) focused too heavily on industry and agriculture and too little on trade and services compared with developed economies. The large agriculture sector was a sign of economic backwardness, while the large industrial and the minimal service sectors reflected systemic distortions. In this regard, Russia had a more backward economic structure than seemingly poorer countries such as Brazil and Argentina (see table 2-2).

Yet another handicap of the Soviet economy was that the industrial structure was petrified—dysfunctional enterprises were hardly ever closed down. The USSR had succeeded in urbanization and industrialization; but it had no mechanism for reallocating resources within the urban sector, because it lacked a capital market. As economic conditions changed, the Soviet enterprise structure grew increasingly obsolete. A typical feature of Soviet cities was the location of old prerevolutionary factories, such as steelworks and electrical power plants, in the city center. (Even the Kremlin faces a power plant on the opposite bank of the

Table 2-3. *Production Per Capita of Selected Products, 1989*

Product	USSR	USA	West Germany	France	Japan	Italy
Electricity (kWh)	5,986	11,964	7,215	7,431	6,092	3,650
Steel (kg)	557	382	691	344	876	436
Mineral fertilizers (kg)	119	101	63	71	12	33
Tractors (per 1,000 people)	1.9	0.4	1.3	0.4	1.3	1.6
Cement (kg)	488	302	489	469	647	690
Meat (kg)	70	120	96	112	32	63

Source: Goskomstat SSSR, *Narodnoe khozyaistvo SSSR v 1989 g.* (The National Economy of the USSR in 1989) (Moscow: Finansy i statistika, 1990), pp. 692–93.

Moscow River.) In the West, such factories were closed down decades ago, as obsolete polluters that made inefficient use of prime land.

Another oddity of the Soviet economic structure was the political nature of allocation, which was done without regard to costs. Enterprises were located anywhere in the country and little or no attention was paid to transportation costs, which led to excessive shipping.

In the end, the inefficiency of the Soviet economic system became staggering. Because of escalating waste, the economy used ever-increasing volumes of materials to produce less final output. Table 2-3 illustrates that the USSR kept pace with leading Western industrial countries in industrial output per capita of products such as electricity, steel, mineral fertilizers, cement, and tractors. In 1989, it was even the world's biggest producer of oil, natural gas, steel, iron ore, mineral fertilizers, sulfuric acid, tractors, and combine harvesters.[39] Notably, the USSR produced almost twice as much steel as the United States. One reason for this was the Soviet emphasis on the defense industry, which consumed vast amounts of steel. Another reason was obsolescence; the USSR had not substituted expensive steel for newer, cheaper materials, such as plastics. A third reason was that the Soviet economy used too much in the way of inputs. High Soviet steel production was thus a sign of wastage rather than welfare.

In general, out of all its production of industrial inputs, the USSR garnered surprisingly little GDP and even less consumption. The Soviet economy required several times more inputs than did Western countries to produce one unit of final output. One of the most staggering examples of Soviet wastage of inputs was in its forestry industry, which consumed seven times more timber than the Finnish forestry industry did to produce

Table 2-4. *Russian Trade With Countries Outside the*
Former Soviet Union, 1990–92
Billions of U.S. dollars

	Exports			Imports		
	1990	1991	1992	1990	1991	1992
Total	78.7	50.9	40.0	72.0	44.5	36.9
Former CMEA countries	34.0	11.7	8.0	32.3	10.9	5.3
Developed countries	28.3	28.8	23.8	28.6	25.9	22.6

Source: Benedicte Vibe Christensen, *The Russian Federation in Transition: External Developments*, Occasional Paper 111 (International Monetary Fund, February 1994), p. 38.

one ton of paper.[40] In addition, the quality, design, and choice of Soviet products were inadequate, and much of what was produced was wasted or inadequately used because of the miserable allocation system.

A fifth dysfunctional characteristic of the Soviet economy was that it was protectionist. This protectionism applied to the entire CMEA block. Trade between the ten CMEA countries was settled in bilateral five-year barter deals that were politically motivated; therefore, trade between the communist countries was probably more distorted than trade within them.[41] With little or no economic rationale behind it, this CMEA-based trade was likely to collapse when free trade was introduced in 1991. (This collapse would have been hastened by the fact that product hauls between CMEA partners were long, and real transportation costs were neglected.) The intra-CMEA trade volumes were much larger than what would have been the case in a market economy, as suggested by the gravity model.[42] Because the trade structure was the result of politicized negotiations, politics rather than economics determined what products were traded. The trade mechanism was perceived as so absurd that it bred contempt for CMEA partners. This led to the attitude that it no longer was necessary for CMEA partners to pay one another after the old CMEA trade mechanism faltered.

In 1991, the CMEA trade system ceased to function, which caused a major external shock. Russia's trade with the former CMEA countries fell by no less than two-thirds in one year, and its imports from them decreased by half from 1991 to 1992 (see table 2-4).[43] Russia gained substantially in terms of trade. Its raw materials and energy had been underpriced in CMEA trade, whereas machinery and other manufactured products (which Russia primarily imported from eastern Europe) had been overpriced. However, the net effect was that both sides reduced

Table 2-5. *Consolidated State Budget Deficit of the USSR, 1985–90*

	Deficit	
Year	Billions of nominal rubles	Percent of GDP
1985	13.9	1.8
1986	45.5	5.7
1987	52.5	6.4
1988	80.6	9.2
1989	80.7	8.6
1990	41.4	4.1

Source: Based on Goskomstat SSSR, *Narodnoe khozyaistvo SSSR v 1990 g.* (The National Economy of the USSR in 1990) (Moscow: Finansy i statistika, 1991), pp. 5, 17; calculations are the author's.

trade with one another. The east Europeans could no longer afford to purchase Russian raw materials after the Russians stopped buying their manufactured goods. When the USSR broke up, similar restructuring was to be expected; an extreme form of protectionism had also prevailed within the USSR.

The Emergence of a Macroeconomic Crisis

Traditionally, the Soviet economy displayed several imbalances, but they were limited. Shortages and a monetary overhang of unsatisfied demand at prevailing fixed prices were permanent features. Producers and sellers prevailed over consumers. A low inflation rate of several percent a year did exist, though it was not recorded in official statistics. Employment was more than full, and labor was in short supply. The state budget usually contained a small deficit, which was financed through assets of the people in the state savings bank. However, with the ascension of Gorbachev, the Soviet macroeconomic balance was completely destroyed in four stages.[44]

The first stage was not at all dramatic. After Gorbachev took over, the traditional Soviet budget deficit of roughly 2 to 3 percent of GDP each year expanded to around 6 percent of GDP in 1986 and 1987 (see table 2-5). On the expenditure side, state investment, consumer subsidies, and social expenditures each increased by almost 1 percent of GDP from 1985 to 1987. On the revenue side, the budget lost about 1 percent of GDP from the foreign trade tax (because of lower oil prices on the world market) and the alcohol tax (the result of Gorbachev's antialcohol campaign). These problems could have been solved in many ways. However (as Gorbachev later explained) when Gorbachev had led the CC Secre-

Table 2-6. *Soviet Wage Increases, 1986–90*

Annual increase in percent

Year	Average national wage	Official net material product, fixed prices
1986	2.9	2.3
1987	3.7	1.6
1988	8.3	4.4
1989	9.4	2.5
1990	14.2	−4.0
1991	70.0	−15.0

Source: Goskomstat SSSR, *Narodnoe khozyaistvo SSSR v 1990 g.*, pp. 7, 36; UN Economic Commission for Europe, *Economic Survey of Europe in 1991–1992* (United Nations, 1992), p. 105.

tariat meetings in 1983, General Secretary Yury Andropov did not allow him or the two CC secretaries who dealt with economic affairs, Nikolai Ryzhkov and Vladimir Dolgikh, to see data on the budget or on military expenditures.[45] The Soviet leaders could not deal with the budget problem, because they were not aware of it. They had cheated themselves with their secrecy. Only in the fall of 1988 was the budget deficit at long last made public.

During a second stage of macroeconomic destabilization (1988–89), the paramount problem was that wages rose more than twice as fast as they had previously (see table 2-6). As a consequence, enterprise taxes declined and the budget deficit expanded. The cause was the USSR Law on State Enterprises, which allowed such enterprises a great deal of freedom without responsibility. Hence, these enterprises rationally raised wages excessively, as it was at the expense of the state.

The third stage that contributed to a macroeconomic crisis took place in 1990, when social benefits were suddenly increased by 25 percent. This was the immediate effect of various populist decisions made by the Congress of People's Deputies of the USSR. Like the state enterprises, the Congress was allowed much latitude but had no real responsibility, because it could not actually oust the government and was only semidemocratic. In parallel with these events, wage increases continued to accelerate. Looking back at the summer of 1990, it was the last time the Soviet financial crisis could have been averted.

In 1991, during the fourth and final stage of macroeconomic destabilization, state finances broke down. The budget deficit skyrocketed to more than 20 percent of GDP. However, if it had been properly calculated (that is, to include semifiscal deficits such as cheap credits and foreign trade subsidies), the deficit would more likely have been on the order of

Table 2-7. *Soviet Foreign Debt and Debt Service Obligations in Convertible Currencies, 1986–91*

Billions of U.S. dollars at year end, unless otherwise specified

	1985	1986	1987	1988	1989	1990	1991
Gross debt	31.4	37.4	40.2	49.4	58.5	61.1	65.3
Net debt	18.3	22.5	26.1	34.1	43.8	52.5	56.5
Actual debt service payments	. .	7.8	8.8	8.4	9.4	2.9	16.7
% of convertible currency exports	. .	29.1	28.1	25.1	26.7	68.2	45.1

Sources: UN Economic Commission for Europe, *Economic Survey of Europe in 1992–1993* (United Nations, 1993), p. 289; Benedicte Vibe Christensen, *The Russian Federation in Transition*, p. 42.

30 percent of GDP. In addition to all these problems, central state revenues began to collapse in the wake of the Soviet republics' refusal to deliver taxes to the union. The republics competed with the union in cutting tax rates instead.

In the second half of 1991, the USSR and Russia faced complete financial ruin. There were grave shortages, and most state shops were nearly empty. Queues were unbelievably long, and people could stand in one line for goods for up to a week. The monetary overhang was enormous, warranting (as it later turned out) a tripling of retail trade prices. Even so, open inflation raged, and prices doubled or tripled in 1991. Statistics are indeterminate for this period, as most goods disappeared from state shops toward the end of that year, although many goods were still available in commercial shops or on the black market, at significantly higher prices.

Foreign Debt Crisis

From 1986 on, international loans were increasingly used to finance the USSR's budget deficit. However, a rising share of the deficit was not financed at all but resulted in more money being put into circulation.

Both gross and net foreign debt rose quickly under Gorbachev. At the end of 1984, the net Soviet debt was assessed at only $14.2 billion; by the end of 1991, it had risen to $56.5 billion (see table 2-7).[46] Substantial Soviet gold reserves had been sold out as well. The debt service ratio (measured as debt service in relation to convertible currency exports) stayed within a reasonable limit of 25 to 30 percent until 1989 but got out of hand in 1990. Table 2-7 shows actual debt service payments, which were much lower than claims in 1991. After late 1989, the USSR started delaying a large number of international payments. As a result, it was offered less international credit with shorter terms, and its backlog of unpaid bills increased to about $6 billion by the end of 1991. At that point, Soviet currency reserves were virtually depleted and hit a low of about $100 million. But this news was left for the reform government to find out.

Human Capital and Natural Resources

These many problems notwithstanding, Russia also had important resources at its disposal. Its natural wealth remained immense despite crude utilization and substantial pollution. Russia had to take little positive action to maintain a substantial flow of exports of oil, natural gas, and other minerals to the world market.

Russia also had substantial human capital: its well-educated work force. The Russians were literate, and the proportion of engineers and scientists among them was large by any standard. Russia was a world leader in several important fields, such as mathematics, alloys, and ceramics. At the same time, there were gaps, the worst being the lack of legal expertise among Russians. Knowledge of all the social sciences was minimal. The inadequate knowledge of economics was evident, the dearth of expertise in political theory less so. Management skills were scarce. Soviet enterprise managers had certainly been impressive as decisionmakers. But they were few in number; all decisionmaking (both in the state and in enterprises) had been extremely centralized, leaving ordinary workers with little sense of responsibility. Language skills were naturally scarce, given the country's history of extreme isolationism. But these were rather specific deficiencies. On the whole, communism left society relatively well educated and fully employed—its two real assets in a postcommunist society.

Conclusions: The End of the Soviet System

Why did the Soviet Union collapse? In the early 1980s, a basic problem was that economic growth had slowed significantly. Economic petrification raised the question of the Soviet system's long-term viability. It remains unclear how long the Soviet economy could have continued to stagnate; but there was certainly no reason to expect it to recover.

Gorbachev shook up the USSR's existing institutional balance in the hope of promoting economic growth. His primary purpose appears to have been to reinforce the Soviet Union's status as a superpower. In his effort to reform the system, Gorbachev made almost every conceivable mistake. In particular, he disregarded finance altogether. His political compromises left the USSR with sadly inconsistent economic policies. The advice he obtained regarding the economy proved inadequate; Soviet economic science had been devastated by political repression and Marxism-Leninism, and advice from economists outside the system was simply not solicited. Gorbachev avoided adopting any clear reform program, and he dismantled most economic policymaking structures without building new ones.

Worse, Gorbachev undermined most Soviet authorities. The central apparatus of the CPSU lost most of its policymaking capacity, while the presidential function was never adequately organized. At the legislative level, amendments to the constitution rendered the parliament both ineffective and unruly. All central authorities were reformed, but none was given a chance to function. The growing chaos in Moscow made it easy for the republican authorities to gain legitimacy, especially through the parliamentary elections in early 1990, which were more democratic than the union elections held a year earlier.

However, many of Gorbachev's flaws now appear to have been inherent. The system could only have been altered from the top down. Therefore, Gorbachev could only have reached the top by subjecting himself to the idiosyncrasies of the communist system, including its self-imposed ignorance of the outside world and of modern social theory. Gorbachev had advanced his career through his supreme ability to compromise; but the crisis he was to face required extraordinary decisiveness instead.

Even if Gorbachev had acted flawlessly, it is doubtful that he could have achieved much greater success. At the pinnacle of society, the many members of the *nomenklatura* were not prepared to collaborate with any reformer. Adamant in their egoistic conservatism, the *apparatchiki* sabotaged any attempt at reform. But society at large had suffered too much and seen too many failed attempts to believe that socialism could be reformed. Cynicism and alienation were rampant throughout the USSR. Gorbachev tried to activate and revitalize Soviet society through *glasnost*, but the many horrifying revelations that followed clarified for the people that socialism had little to offer them. Moreover, the deep structural problems of the Soviet economy rendered any attempt at its reformation too complicated, unpopular, and costly. The petrification of the Soviet communist system had simply gone too far. Substantial destruction of the system had to precede any construction of a new one.

The severity of the acute financial crisis of 1991 can hardly be exaggerated. The Soviet budget deficit had risen to at least 20 percent of GDP, and it had skyrocketed out of control. International financing had been exhausted, and the USSR defaulted on its foreign payments in December 1991. The USSR suffered from a combination of high and rising inflation, and it endured massive shortages and long queues because of a huge monetary overhang. The national income had fallen by at least 20 percent from the last quarter of 1991 over that of 1990 and was accelerating. Fear of famine was widespread. One of the few positive aspects of life in the USSR at this time was the absence of social unrest. After the substantial strikes by coal miners in the summer of 1989, the labor market had remained relatively calm. When Gorbachev finally stepped down as President of the Soviet Union in December 1991, he left behind a country in a state of utter and complete collapse.

CHAPTER THREE

Formation of a
Reform Program

EVENTS IN Russia took a decisive turn with the abortive Soviet coup of August 19–21, 1991. Three big transitions were initiated simultaneously: the emergence of Russia as an independent state, the building of democracy, and the transition to a market economy. Among the Soviet republics, only the Baltic states were prepared for the new tasks. Yet Russia had little choice but a jump start. As Boris Yeltsin put it: "Instead of a gradual transition from the unitarian Soviet Union to a softer, freer confederation, we had a complete vacuum at the political center. The center—in the person of Mikhail Gorbachev—was totally demoralized."[1]

This chapter outlines the chronology of the Russian transformation and then looks at the political situation. The Russian program of radical economic reform is scrutinized, followed by a discussion regarding the formation of the economic reform team. The hostile criticism that erupted after the presentation of the reform program is analyzed, along with a multitude of institutional and political problems hampering economic reform. An analysis of how the radical reform was watered down follows, with a discussion of the major political flaws in (and resistance against) the attempted radical reform.

Stages of the Economic Reform

The chronology of Russian attempts at radical economic reform was entirely determined by political events. Russian politics tends to develop in waves lasting for several months. When one side runs out of steam, counterforces seize the momentum, usually at a spectacular political turning point.

After the failed August 1991 coup, a democratic and revolutionary mood prevailed. However, the euphoria was limited and short-lived. The big push for economic reform was delayed for two months while President Yeltsin made up his mind about what type of government to form and what policy to pursue. On October 28, 1991, Yeltsin made a great speech on radical economic reform to the Fifth Congress of People's Deputies. Immediately afterward, he took the helm of the newly formed Russian reform government. His chief aide, Gennady Burbulis, became first deputy prime minister and his political strategist. Yegor Gaidar became Yeltsin's economic strategist as deputy prime minister and minister of finance and the economy, and Gaidar was allowed to bring his associates into the government. Aleksandr Shokhin was appointed deputy prime minister for social affairs, and Anatoly Chubais was named minister of privatization. The main reform package, which emphasized price liberalization and financial stabilization, was launched at the beginning of 1992 and encountered vehement public criticism even before it was put into effect. The complaints erupted into a political storm at the Sixth Congress of People's Deputies in April 1992, as the Congress increasingly turned against Yeltsin, the government, and radical reform. Even before the Congress convened, Yeltsin sacrificed Burbulis as first deputy prime minister in early April 1992 (though Burbulis stayed on as state secretary, a senior position in the Presidential apparatus).

As a concession to the Congress and the industrial lobby, three state enterprise managers were appointed deputy prime ministers in May and June 1992. Consequently, the reform government was transformed into a coalition between economic reformers and state enterprise managers. The backsliding on the reform program started gradually in early April 1992 with the issuance of subsidized credits to both agriculture and industry. The last important reform legislation promulgated by the Supreme Soviet was the privatization program for 1992, which was finally passed on June 11. Thus the initial push for radical reform essentially lasted from November 1991 until May 1992.

From June until December 1992, not much of a reform policy existed, although Yeltsin had appointed Gaidar acting prime minister in June 1992. (At that time Gaidar's interest in economic reform appeared to have subsided.) Ironically, the IMF concluded a standby agreement with

Russia in July 1992, after the stabilization efforts had ended. On July 17, the appointment of Viktor Gerashchenko as acting chair of the Central Bank of Russia (CBR) by the Presidium of the Supreme Soviet dealt a devastating blow to macroeconomic stabilization. Gerashchenko insisted on letting the money supply explode. Even so, efforts at privatization proceeded. On the first anniversary of the August coup, Yeltsin made privatization (based on the free distribution of vouchers to all) the theme of his speech. Privatization vouchers were hastily distributed to all Russians between October and the end of January. On December 12, the Seventh Congress of People's Deputies ousted Gaidar as prime minister. He was replaced two days later by the deputy prime minister of the energy complex, Viktor Chernomyrdin. By mid-December, reform seemed to have come to an end and Russia appeared to be on the verge of hyperinflation.

Chernomyrdin's appointment appeared to be a victory for the industrial lobby and the Congress. However, soon after his appointment, another young reform economist, Boris Fedorov, entered the political stage as deputy prime minister and minister of finance. Fedorov formulated a program for macroeconomic stabilization and tried to implement it in any way possible. His achievements were sufficient to cap inflation. Yet the Congress became increasingly militant against reform. The political heat peaked in late March 1993, at the Eighth and Ninth Congresses of the People's Deputies. On March 28, the Congress's offensive culminated in an attempt to impeach Yeltsin, but the deputies' votes fell slightly short of the two-thirds majority required. The first four months of 1993 saw a stalemate between the government and the Congress. Within the government, the balance tipped in favor of the conservatives with the appointment of Oleg Lobov, a conservative protégé of Yeltsin, as first deputy prime minister and minister of the economy on April 16. The next ten days were the most critical for the privatization, which slowed down.

The reformers' quandary ended with the referendum on April 25, in which 64 percent of the electorate participated. Of the votes cast, 59 percent expressed confidence in the president. Furthermore, to the great surprise of the government, 53 percent of voters approved of the social policy that had been pursued by the president and the government since 1992.[2] The referendum gave the reformers new momentum on all fronts for almost three months. Privatization geared up to full speed, and important price liberalizations were undertaken. Import subsidies were sharply reduced. The Ministry of Finance reached an agreement with the

CBR on credit expansion, and in May 1993 the two entities concluded an agreement with the IMF on a systemic transformation facility, whose conditions were less stringent than an ordinary standby agreement.

In mid-July 1993, the reform efforts fell apart once again. On July 24, the CBR undertook a confiscatory exchange of banknotes without consulting the Ministry of Finance. As a consequence, public confidence in the president and his government was seriously undermined. In August the Supreme Soviet dealt a decisive blow to any cooperation with the government by adopting a budget with a deficit of about 25 percent of GDP. If adopted, such a budget would have caused hyperinflation. Meanwhile, state credits were allowed to expand far more than had been agreed to for the third quarter. In early September, Gerashchenko instigated a new initiative—"a ruble zone of a new type"—that would further undermine monetary responsibility and discipline. No further reform measures were politically feasible, but privatization surged ahead at full speed. Nevertheless, these were two months of all-out attack against reform.

On September 21, President Yeltsin issued decree number 1400, which dissolved the Congress of People's Deputies and the Supreme Soviet. The immediate cause of his action appears to have been the budget dispute. Yeltsin had exhausted his veto rights. He faced a choice: either violate the constitution by not signing the budget law or by dismissing the parliament, or accept hyperinflation. After the parliament had been dissolved, the most important reform wave since early 1992 erupted. Within the government, radical reformers gained the upper hand; on September 18, Gaidar replaced Lobov as first deputy prime minister and minister of the economy. The agricultural sector was almost completely liberalized, including bread and grain prices. Yeltsin issued a decree allowing private ownership of land. All subsidized credits were abolished, and the refinance rate of the CBR was raised, giving Russia a positive real interest rate from November 1993. The inflation rate began falling significantly, and the ruble's exchange rate stabilized. The peril of a ruble zone of a new type lapsed. At long last, Russia seemed to be on the verge of macroeconomic stabilization, and privatization continued apace. This reform offensive lasted for almost three months.

However, on December 12 the defeat of the democrats in the parliamentary elections brought reforms to a sudden halt. Gaidar and Fedorov found their positions so undermined by Prime Minister Chernomyrdin that they chose to resign. Although the industrialist Civic Union, headed by Arkady Volsky, was the main loser in the elections, the balance within the government shifted in favor of the industrialist center and Chernomyrdin, who was now firmly in charge of economic policy. However, contrary to his public statements, Chernomyrdin chose to preserve the economic policy pursued by Gaidar and Fedorov. Chubais stayed in charge of his privatization program. A market economy had been created; presumably, reform had become irreversible. Yet Chernomyrdin has yet to complete the macroeconomic stabilization, and he did not try to improve the still highly imperfect economic system in any significant regard.

In conclusion, the first reform offensive in Russia lasted from November 1991 to May 1992. It was followed by a period of government passivity from June to December 1992, distinguished by excessive monetary expansion. The first four months of 1993 could be described as a stalemate. The reformers' victory in the referendum of April 25 led to a reform offensive that lasted almost three months. This was followed by a conservative counteroffensive from mid-July to September 21, when Yeltsin dissolved the Supreme Soviet. A radical reform offensive lasted until the parliamentary elections of December 12, which were a severe setback for the reformers. However, no one could really be said to have won the elections. Finally, 1994 has been characterized by a calm stalemate between reformers and conservatives: no new reforms, but no rolling back of prior ones.

A New Political Setting Takes Form

After the democratic breakthrough in August 1991, Russian President Boris Yeltsin faced immense political tasks—namely to administer the dissolution of the USSR and to reform the Russian constitution, the legislature, and the executive branch of the Russian government.

In the immediate aftermath of the August 1991 coup, the Feliks Dzerzhinsky monument outside Lubyanka, the KGB headquarters, was torn down; the headquarters of the Central Committee (CC) of the Communist Party of the Soviet Union (CPSU) in the center of Moscow were sealed off. For a brief moment, anything seemed possible. Boris Yeltsin undertook one major political measure: he prohibited the CPSU by decree. But little happened otherwise.

The dominant political question was how to dissolve the Soviet Union. This presumably absorbed most of Yeltsin's time in the fall of 1991. The previous April, USSR President Mikhail Gorbachev had initiated talks at the estate of Novo-Ogarevo outside of Moscow on the formation of a Union of Sovereign States to replace the Soviet Union. However, the Baltic states had already declared themselves independent and were universally recognized after the August coup. Georgia, Moldova, Armenia, and Azerbaijan withdrew one after the other from the Novo-Ogarevo talks. By the fall of 1991, the talks involved only eight of the Soviet republics—the three Slavic states (Belarus, Russia, and Ukraine) and the five Central Asian republics—and Gorbachev.

In his memoirs, Yeltsin views the abolition of the Soviet Union as a positive choice: "I was convinced that Russia needed to rid itself of its imperial mission."[3] He emphasizes his anti-imperialist role:

> Gorbachev represented the Union, the empire, the old power, and I represented Russia, an independent republic, a new and as yet nonexistent country. Everyone was waiting impatiently for this country to appear. . . . The Soviet Union could not exist without the image of empire. The image of empire could not exist without the image of force. The USSR ended the moment the first hammer pounded the Berlin Wall. . . . I came to the presidency with the idea of making a clean break with our Soviet heritage, not merely through various reforms but geopolitically, through an alteration of Russia's role as a powerful, enduring, long-suffering nation.[4]

In December 1991, the attempt at creating a more loosely joined Union of Sovereign States was abandoned, and the Soviet Union was dissolved. The decisive event was a meeting between the presidents of Belarus, Russia, and Ukraine during a weekend in the Belovezhsky Nature Reserve in Belarus in December 1991. The presidents agreed to dissolve the USSR and form a loose Commonwealth of Independent States (CIS). In effect, Russia abolished the Soviet Union by declaring itself independent. As Yeltsin puts it: "In signing this agreement, Russia was choosing a different path, a path of internal development rather than an imperial one."[5] The immediate reason for the Belovezhsky agreement was that on December 1, the people of Ukraine had voted for independence by an overwhelming majority of 90 percent.

After protests from other republics, the three original signatories agreed to broaden the CIS. On December 21, 1991, at a meeting in Alma-Ata, the capital of Kazakhstan, the CIS was expanded to include eleven of the former Soviet republics (FSRs). Only Georgia and the already independent Baltic states chose not to join the CIS. The Union Treaty of 1922 was abrogated, leaving the remaining Soviet institutions and the Soviet president without a legal foundation.

Multiple bodies of Soviet power had to be reconsidered, and four different approaches were used. Dozens of superfluous Soviet branch ministries and state committees were simply abolished. Then essential central Soviet institutions were merged with their Russian counterparts and subordinated to Russian ministers. In his big reform speech in October 1991, Yeltsin announced that Russia would stop financing about 70 union ministries and other government bodies, effectively abolishing them.[6] At the end of 1991, the Soviet State Bank was dissolved and its assets were divided up among new republican central banks. Next, a single joint CIS command was formed for the strategic forces, a branch of the military. Finally, one important Soviet institution survived— namely the Soviet ruble—but no institution regulated it. (Paradoxically, the Bank for Foreign Economic Relations of the USSR, Vneshekonombank, formally survived as a USSR institution, because it was bankrupt.)

The vital task domestically was to build a democratic state. This called for adoption of a new constitution, holding of parliamentary elections, development of political parties, and possibly reform of the state administration. A constitution should preferably be adopted and parliamentary elections arranged when idealism holds sway.

To write a constitution is technically easy. However, its adoption grows more complicated with time, as political forces learn about their potential strength. The earlier a constitution is adopted, the more equitable and effective it is likely to be.[7] The Russian Federation had an old Soviet constitution from 1978, which was adopted a year after the USSR's "Brezhnev Constitution." The RSFSR Congress of People's Deputies, which was created by Gorbachev in 1990, was empowered to amend the constitution instantaneously with a two-thirds majority vote. Yeltsin did not try to have a new constitution adopted early on. Instead, he settled for a temporary arrangement, legislated through many constitutional amendments. This provisional solution, which Yeltsin managed to exact from the Congress, gave him far-reaching rights to rule by decree for one year beginning November 1, 1991. He was empowered to change government structures, to appoint all ministers, and to adopt a large number of decisions on economic reform by decree.[8] Yeltsin's official explanation was that the situation demanded a temporary solution—a comment revealing little reflection on his part.[9] The main shortcoming of the old constitution, however, was that it did not provide for any division of power; the Congress of People's Deputies remained sovereign. This was not a historically unique situation. Such constitutions were common in

Europe before Montesquieu's ideas of division of power became commonplace at the end of the 18th century. They tended to lead to violent resolutions, such as the partition of Poland in 1772, the royal coup in Sweden in 1772, or the civil war in England under Cromwell in the mid-17th century.

Immediately after the democratic breakthrough in Russia in August 1991, the foremost issue was to safeguard democracy. At the time, the movement Democratic Russia constituted a broad but loosely organized front of democrats. If elections had been held soon after, Democratic Russia would probably have emerged as a political party and won as the Civic Forum in Czechoslovakia did after the velvet revolution. Then democracy would have gained a solid political foundation. However, Yeltsin did not call for new parliamentary elections in the aftermath of the August coup, when the Congress of People's Deputies probably would have complied with such a demand. His explanation regarding regional elections at the time was: "To carry out powerful election campaigns and simultaneously profound economic transformations is impossible! To do that means to destroy everything!"[10]

A dominant belief was that elections arouse conflicts. But they are, on the contrary, a fundamental means of building democratic institutions. Some objected that economic reforms were so urgently needed that nothing must obstruct or delay them. Others observed that too many elections had already been held—one each year from 1989 to 1991, plus a referendum on the preservation of the USSR in March 1991. Thus, moderate technocrats argued: "The state of permanent elections, referendums, voting and re-voting have made the society unreceptive to any ideas of steadiness and stability."[11] Yet another argument against early elections was that, because Lenin had dissolved the Soviets, it was Leninist to dissolve a parliament, even if democrats did it to hold democratic elections. Finally, the prevailing mood was elitist and technocratic, implying considerable contempt for the Russian people as being ignorant and irrelevant—and Yeltsin seemed to be the master of the Congress in any case.[12] Instead, as other issues surfaced on the political agenda, the opponents of authoritarianism naturally parted company. They represented different ideologies and interests, and personal rivalries developed over time. As the democrats became divided, they proved less able to govern effectively. As a consequence, nationalists and old-line communists were soon able to come back with a vengeance.

The Congress and the Supreme Soviet were not especially representative. When the Congress of People's Deputies was elected in March 1990, Russia had not been fully democratized; an overwhelming majority of the deputies had in fact originally been CPSU members. The elections were characterized by negative selection. People voted against known communist party officials without realizing that the candidates they voted for were simply lesser-known communists. In early 1990, the Soviet Union still existed. The Russian parliament appeared to be of such limited significance that most prominent Russian politicians only stood as candidates for the Soviet Congress of People's Deputies. Moreover, the very structure of the Russian parliament was unwieldy. The larger Congress of People's Deputies, with 1,068 deputies, was far too big to serve any orderly function. From within its ranks, the Congress elected a smaller Supreme Soviet, which had an uncertain mandate. Initially, the Supreme Soviet was relatively representative of the Congress; but in 1993, it was elected entirely by the majority of the Congress and was thus politically highly unbalanced.

Finally, the parliament had little political structure; political parties had not been allowed in the elections of March 1990. To begin with, about one-third of the deputies had been democrats and slightly more than one-third had been communists or hard-line nationalists, while almost one-third had occupied the so-called marsh in the middle. Originally, Yeltsin tended to have his way with a small majority of the Congress, if he worked hard at it; but after April 1992, the majority was against him. From December 1992 on, this majority hardened into a disloyal opposition, no longer accepting the legitimacy of the democratically elected President. After the bloodshed of October 1993, Yeltsin acknowledged that he had made a fundamental mistake: "I believe the most important opportunity missed after the coup was the radical restructuring of the parliamentary system. . . . The idea of dissolving the Congress and scheduling new elections was in the air (as well as a Constitution for the new country), although we did not take advantage of it. . . . Meanwhile, without political backup, Gaidar's reforms were left hanging in midair."[13]

With regard to the government, however, Yeltsin showed leadership. First of all, he took the helm during the period of economic reform.[14] Furthermore, Yeltsin forcefully restructured the government, cutting the number of deputy prime ministers to three and the total number of ministers to twenty-one. The central government apparatus was sharply reduced and restructured for reform. Yeltsin also made clear that only the government was to carry out economic reform, thus avoiding conflicts with his own Presidential administration. A large number of old legal acts were declared null and void.[15] Finally, the President appointed a new type of reform government: "When forming [this] government, we discard the priority of political considerations to the benefit of professionals."[16] Yeltsin reached out to young technocrats, who had new insights and expertise ranging outside of the former Soviet Union (FSU).

Yet nothing was done to cleanse Russia's state administration of politically discredited personnel, including KGB and senior party officials. The CPSU was outlawed, and Yeltsin sounded decisive: "A dynamic process is going on to liberate the institutions of power from the heel of the CPSU. We are not afraid of being accused of being undemocratic and we shall act decisively here."[17] But hundreds of thousands of old *apparatchiki* stayed in place. They were demoralized, ignorant of the new tasks facing a democratic society, and frequently corrupt. However, Stalin had made purge a dirty word; as Yeltsin put it: "In seventy years, we have grown tired of dividing people into 'clean' and 'unclean'."[18] Moreover, after the February revolution of 1917, the provisional government, headed by Prince G. E. Lvov, had dissolved the state bureaucracy immediately, which had led to chaos.[19] Yeltsin was aware of that historical precedent and was therefore anxious to maintain order: "It would have been disastrous to destroy the government administration of such an enormous state."[20] As a consequence, the old *nomenklatura* stayed on and waited to exact its revenge. Nor was the KGB abolished, although this was widely demanded by democrats.

At this time, Yeltsin had considerable leeway but chose not to act decisively. The fundamental problem was that he had no real political strategy, which reflected both his lack of knowledge of political theory and of relevant foreign parallels. This dilemma was aggravated by disinterest. The universality of rules on how to consolidate a democracy was not appreciated, because of the general belief in the uniqueness of Russian politics. Russian politicians related to the October revolution of 1917 and tried to do everything differently. As Yeltsin put it: "To break everything, to destroy everything in the Bolshevik manner was not part of my plans at all."[21] Old-line communists exploited this tendency and argued that it was "neo-Bolshevik" to do anything fast, thus impeding the democrats.[22] Yeltsin and the Russian democrats fell into this trap arranged by the old-line communists. Russia's hesitant democratization thus allowed many of the old guard to stay in high positions.

The political dissolution of the USSR was peacefully managed. However, the fundamental issues of adopting a constitution and building a democracy were set aside, while Yeltsin received substantial powers to rule by decree for one year. The unresolved constitutional issue turned out to be a political powderkeg. The government was substantially revamped—but not enough, as shall be seen.

A Program of Radical Economic Reform

Although Yeltsin was ambivalent about reforming Russia's political system, he appeared all the more determined to adopt a program of radical economic reform. There were many reasons for this radicalism and decisiveness. Russia was in the midst of a tremendous economic crisis, with massive shortages and imbalances that augured a collapse in production. So many halfhearted reform attempts had already failed that a fundamental reform seemed the only sensible option to many. Poland had also set an example with its seemingly successful launch of economic shock therapy in early 1990, and in January 1991, Czechoslovakia had followed suit. Many Russians were well informed about the Polish experience. Finally, the cream of the young Russian economists had become convinced that a swift, radical change of economic system was the best solution. This self-confident and well-educated emerging elite was prepared to take over the Russian government under Yeltsin's aegis. Yeltsin thus had access to more sophisticated economic than political advice.

President Yeltsin gave many reasons for radical reform. He realized that the historic opportunity for reform had arrived. He began his big reform speech on October 28, 1991, by stating: "I appeal to you at one of the most critical moments in Russian history. Right now it will be decided what kind of country Russia will be in the coming years and decades."[23]

Yeltsin saw that the problem with previous Soviet reforms and Russia's old dilemma was inconsistency: "Not a single reform effort in Russia has ever been completed."[24] A multitude of reform attempts had failed to fundamentally change anything in Russia, as Yeltsin emphasized: "Russia's trouble was never a shortage or an abundance of reformers. The trouble was an inability to adhere to a consistent reform policy."[25] Therefore, Yeltsin's posture was radical: "I turn to you with determination to stand unconditionally on the road of profound reforms and for support of this determination by all strata of the population. . . . The time has come to act decisively, firmly, without hesitation. . . . The period of movement with small steps is over. . . . A big reformist breakthrough is necessary."[26] In hindsight, Yeltsin reckoned the cure to inconsistency to be a speedy and comprehensive reform program: "The goal I have set before the government is to make reform irreversible."[27] Yeltsin also maintained his belief that radical reform was necessary. "Gaidar's reform had led to macroeconomic improvement or, to be more precise, to the destruction of the old economy. It was achieved with terrible pain. . . . but achieved nonetheless. There was probably no other way to do it. Except for Stalinist industry, adapted to modern conditions and a Stalinist economy, virtually no other industry existed here. Just as it had been created, so must it be destroyed."[28]

Another reason for Yeltsin's choice of a radical program was that he realized how deep Russia's economic crisis was. After August 1991, "the rationing of virtually everything had reached its limit. The shelves in the stores were absolutely bare. . . . The political atmosphere was also quite gloomy."[29] Therefore, he surmised: "Sometimes it takes a sharp break or rupture to make a person move forward or even survive at all."[30] At the same time, Yeltsin thought that Russia was rich enough and strong enough to take such a shock. Although he was convinced of the need for radical market economic transformation, he had only limited understanding of what this would mean in practice. He therefore entrusted Yegor Gaidar (the main author of Yeltsin's speech of October 28, 1991) to formulate the concrete reform strategy.

Yeltsin's reform speech is the central source on the actual reform program. Gaidar insisted on not formulating a proper program; he wanted to present it through actions rather than in words.[31] A list of no less than 70 planned legal acts to be adopted no later than December 15 was approved by government decree on November 19, 1991.[32] Gaidar did write articles and make many public appearances to clarify his policies. Yet the first real economic program that the reform government adopted was the Memorandum on the Economic Policy of the Russian Federation, an IMF shadow program without financing that was passed by the government on February 27, 1992.[33]

For Yeltsin, the central economic tasks were stabilization and economic freedom: "We have a unique opportunity to stabilize the economy within several months and start the process of recovery. We have defended political freedom. Now we have to give economic [freedom], to remove all barriers to the freedom of enterprises and entrepreneurship, to give the people possibilities to work and receive as much as they earn, after having thrown off bureaucratic pressures."[34] Yeltsin's original reform speech is revealing, both for what it contained and what it lacked. Its radical emphasis was an instant transition to free prices and forceful financial stabilization. The speech listed many concrete measures on macroeconomic stabilization, liberalization, and privatization. However, the conceptualization was unclear.

Yeltsin was surprisingly vague on the actual timing of various measures: "The reform goes along a number of directions simultaneously, all-embracing and dynamically."[35] However, the idea of simultaneous liberalization and stabilization was missing. On the contrary, wages of public employees were to be raised one month before prices were liberalized. Although both Yeltsin and Gaidar used the term shock therapy, they took a gradual approach to economic reform, with limited synchronization both in ideas and implementation.[36] Originally, Gaidar did not even envision full liberalization and stabilization before Russia introduced its own independent currency, which he reckoned would require a minimum of nine months of technical preparation.[37] The unofficial working document prepared by the Gaidar team proposed a gradual stabilization and liberalization package to be implemented in one year. Because the only operative program was a list of legal acts, proposals tended to be designed toward solving concrete problems rather than being deduced from overriding principles. This approach prevented a comprehensive program from being developed. The foreign advisors urged as comprehensive a big bang as possible, including wider simultaneous price liberalization, stricter monetary policy, more liberalization of foreign trade, early unification of the exchange rate, full convertibility on current account, and greater efforts to mobilize international financing.[38]

From the outset, Yeltsin made it clear that it was Russia, and not the CIS, that would carry out radical reform: "I am convinced that the Russian Federation must play the decisive role in leading the country out of the deep crisis and return peace and stability to people's lives."[39] Russia was nevertheless prepared to cooperate closely with its neighbors acting as friendly sovereign states in the transformation. Interrepublican organs would only play a consultative-coordinating role; the real power rested with each republic. "We have no possibility to coordinate the terms of the reforms with the conclusion of all-embracing inter-republican agreements."[40] Russia intended to pursue an independent policy based on its national interests. It clarified to the other former Soviet republics what its price liberalization and tax changes would entail. Most republics adopted some (but not all) of the measures. As a goodwill gesture to them, Russia delayed its price liberalization from mid-December 1991 until January 2, 1992.

A spurious issue was whether or not Russia would introduce its own national currency. Yeltsin discussed this at length in his reform speech and presented two options. The other republics could either accept the creation of a unified ruble zone with one central bank and a full-fledged monetary union, or Russia would "introduce a new Russian currency."[41] In a paper written just before he joined the government, Yegor Gaidar advocated "the introduction of a new Russian republican monetary unit."[42] The options were clear. It was evident that the other republics would not accept one common central bank, which would have a Russian majority because of Russia's dominant size. Yet the Russian leadership hesitated, and the vital issue of monetary reform was not resolved in time.

In essence, Yeltsin called for an orthodox macroeconomic stabilization program emphasizing price liberalization and strict budgetary policy. "The deficit of the budget for 1992 should be almost non-existent or minimal."[43] On the expenditure side, major cuts were to be made in subsidies to enterprises, defense, and state administration, and all foreign aid would cease. In addition, price liberalization would lead to a sharp decline in price subsidies. Gaidar clarified that the idea of defense cuts was "to maintain the wage costs, social programs and part of the allocations to military research, but to cut arms procurement with the utmost severity."[44] Thus the armaments industry, rather than the military staff, would be hit. On the revenue side, Yeltsin suggested only that the tax system should be put in order, without tax hikes to citizens. The nominal tax pressure on the economy was already high, and the problem in 1991 was that tax collection for the union treasury was plummeting. Gaidar wanted to replace the old turnover tax, which varied by commodity, with a value-added tax (VAT), and he found it necessary to raise the tax rates.[45] This so-called VAT had been attempted at the beginning of 1991 as an all-union tax, called the president's (that is, Gorbachev's) tax. It was not a pure VAT but was in fact partially a sales tax. In 1991, all the republics opposed this additional union tax, and little revenue was collected. However, tax officials in the Ministry of Finance argued that they were well prepared for the introduction of this tax, and they persuaded Gaidar to go ahead.[46]

Monetary policy received much less thought and attention. Yeltsin spoke vaguely of "preparations of a package of measures on reform of the bank system," including "the introduction of strict mechanisms against uncontrolled emission of money and credits."[47] The prevailing belief was that credits should be rationed, although the President and the government said little about the need for an early introduction of positive real interest rates. Georgy Matyukhin, chairman of the CBR, advocated positive real interest rates with no support from the government.[48] A number of other neglected issues soon aroused serious controversies: subsidized credits, uncontrolled credits to other Soviet republics, the cash shortage, and interenterprise arrears.

Gaidar was anxious to introduce a unified exchange rate and render the ruble convertible on current account. However, the complete exhaustion of reserves and the general disorder prompted Gaidar to delay this until July 1, 1992. Yet the basic exchange rate was allowed to float after January 1, 1992. Gaidar would have preferred to peg the exchange rate, which had facilitated macroeconomic stabilization in Poland and Czechoslovakia, but as he explained: "We have to proceed from reality—we do not have six billion dollars for the creation of the necessary stabilization fund."[49]

It is difficult to assess how great Russian hopes for Western assistance actually were. But in his first reform speech, Yeltsin made strong and extensive exhortations to international organizations and the West for help:

> We turn officially to the IMF, the World Bank, the European Bank for Reconstruction and Development and invite them to elaborate detailed plans in cooperation and participation in the economic reforms.
>
> We appeal to the developed countries and international organizations for technical assistance first of all for the training of personnel, analysis and elaboration of recommendations on principal economic ecological and regional questions. . . .
>
> I appeal to the world community. Russia carries out its reforms in its own interests, and not under external pressure. Help from the world community can facilitate our movement along this road considerably and accelerate the reforms.[50]

At the end of December 1992, Gaidar's hopes for Western support had been raised. As he stated on Russian television: "I am, for all practical

purposes, convinced that if we manage to hang on, if we do not immediately slide back into a new round of price regulation, if we manage to
adhere to tough budgetary guidelines, then by mid-spring, by April, we
should be able to mobilize a hard currency stabilization fund based on
cooperation with international financial organizations."[51]

In his main reform speech, Yeltsin envisioned free wage formation as
one aspect of economic liberty, whereas Gaidar was afraid of excessive
wage increases in the state sector.[52] Therefore, Gaidar was prepared to
accept some kind of incomes policy in principle, but only if the exchange
rate was first pegged, which required a stabilization fund.[53] Gaidar then
accepted the incorporation of a tax-based incomes policy of the Polish
type in the shadow program instigated by the IMF. However, because
no international financing was forthcoming, this commitment was of no
consequence.[54]

Both Yeltsin's speech and the overall reform strategy were surprisingly
vague and inconsistent about liberalization. The concept of economic
freedom was mentioned but was not elaborated on. A variety of separate
elements were discussed instead. The focus was price liberalization, but
it was not put into the wider context of general liberalization. Moreover,
liberalization of prices under conditions of pervasive shortages would
mean massive price increases across the board. After Yeltsin declared
that prices would be liberalized once and for all, various interest groups
chipped away at his resolve.

The prime counterargument against price liberalization was the alleged far-reaching monopolization of the Russian economy. Yeltsin acknowledged this peculiarity. As usual, he promised a "package of measures" to fight monopolies and stimulate competition. The government
was prepared accordingly to start breaking up various large concerns,
and small and medium-size enterprises were soon to offer competition.[55]
Yet the lack of conceptualization was striking.

A major shortcoming of the whole reform strategy was the failure to
broach the idea of free trade. In his long speech, Yeltsin barely mentioned
domestic trade and did not condemn state orders. Freedom of trade was
proclaimed later, in a Presidential Decree adopted on January 29, 1992,
but was not firmly set in the reform framework. Neither did Yeltsin
advocate freedom of foreign trade. He only complained about corruption
and excessive bureaucracy, proposing a number of half-measures, such
as competitive sales of import and export licenses. But Yeltsin did not
see foreign competition as a weapon against monopolies.

The ideas Yeltsin presented on privatization were energetic, vague, and eclectic. He began by declaring: "For impermissibly long, we have discussed whether we need private ownership or not. In the meantime, the party-state elite has engaged in their own personal privatization. . . . Today we have to seize the initiative, and we are intent on doing so."[56] The privatization of small and medium-size enterprises was made a priority; Yeltsin hoped that half could be privatized within three months. The privatization of housing had already started and would continue. Next came the more complicated privatization of large industrial enterprises. Many would remain in state hands, but they should also be transformed into independent joint stock companies, with the shares to be divided between the state and work collectives. State-owned shares would then be sold at market prices to anyone who wanted to buy them. Finally, land reform allowing sales and purchases of land was long overdue.[57]

Yeltsin did not disguise the fact that the transition would have significant social costs, although he made no attempt to quantify them: "I have to tell you frankly: today in the severest crisis we cannot carry out reform painlessly. The first step will be most difficult. A certain decline in the standard of living will take place. . . . It will be worse for everybody for about half a year. Then, the prices will fall and the consumer market will be filled with goods. And toward the fall of 1992, as I promised before the elections, the economy will stabilize and people's lives will gradually improve."[58] However, Yeltsin did not prepare his listeners for a substantial decline in GDP, which was inevitable even if hardly quantifiable. Gaidar stated that production would fall by at least 10 percent in 1992, but the government's uncertain and defensive attitude toward the decline in production provided opponents with good ammunition for the debate.[59] Obviously, no one could have known when the recovery would start. Yeltsin's statement that it would begin as early as the fall of 1992 appears to have been his own opinion. Gaidar harbored a more pessimistic view and did not forsee an early upturn.[60] Yeltsin also promised to provide a new social safety net for Russians, with targeted support for the most needy citizens.

By 1991, before the reform had been launched, crime was already a major public concern. Yeltsin spoke at length about his worries over the rise in organized crime and corruption: "The essence of the mafia is the fusion of private and state structures, from which the worst kinds of monopoly grows. Beside them no free enterprise can survive." He called for an unrelenting struggle against organized crime.[61]

Yeltsin's idea of the capitalism that would arise was similar to that experienced in Russia during the three decades preceding the October 1917 revolution. "There should be only one limitation to profiteering: the law. Unfortunately, the law-enforcement agencies are adapting very slowly and poorly to this new crime phenomenon. That's the typical Russian style."[62] Yeltsin understood that Russian capitalism would have to be messy. His reform speech was both radical and rich in detail, but most of its shortcomings were to have serious consequences for the reform's success.

In conclusion, the emphasis was on balancing the budget and reducing subsidies through price liberalization. If international financing were granted, Russia was prepared to peg the exchange rate, make its currency convertible on current account, further liberalize foreign trade, and possibly introduce an incomes policy. Four major shortcomings that became evident were lack of liberalization of both domestic and foreign trade, poor conceptualization of monetary policy, and vacillation in economic relations with other former Soviet republics. The privatization program was rudimentary but ambitious. For these reasons, the Russian reform program was less comprehensive than the reform programs of Poland and Czechoslovakia, which addressed all these shortcomings. However, unlike Russia, both countries had access to international financial support when they launched their radical reforms.

Formation of the Economic Reform Team

Obviously, neither the old-line Soviet technocrats nor the old school economic academicians could lead Russia into a market economy. In countries that are undertaking a radical change in economic policy, young, well-educated economists (often with foreign doctoral degrees) tend to be drawn to government. President Yeltsin realized that he needed a completely new Council of Ministers to implement radical economic reform: "It was high time to bring in an economist with his own original concept, possibly with his own team of people. Determined action was long overdue in the economy, not just in politics."[63]

A curious process began after August 1991. President Yeltsin had made the strategic decision to sack Russian Prime Minister Ivan Silaev, an old Soviet technocrat and compromise candidate.[64] Yeltsin made it known that he was looking for a new government and encouraged competition over government teams and reform programs. (A similar process had occurred in the summer of 1990, when Grigory Yavlinsky and Boris Fedorov had entered the Russian government with the 500-day program.)

At least five competing groups met at different government dachas around Moscow, formulating their programs.[65] The most conservative group was led by Yury Skokov, manager of a major defense plant in Moscow. Skokov had been close to Yeltsin ever since he served as first party secretary of Moscow City. He represented the interests of the military-industrial complex (VPK) and was against both a market economy and democracy.[66] Another group was headed by Oleg Lobov, an even older friend of Yeltsin who was an *apparatchik* from Sverdlovsk. In 1993, Lobov pushed for the reestablishment of central planning. Both Skokov and Lobov were already deputy prime ministers of Russia in 1991, but neither had much to offer in the way of reform.

In addition to these two groups, there were three liberal teams. All three favored radical economic reform with swift liberalization and stabilization accompanied by mass privatization, and all envisioned a liberalization taking one year. Yevgeny Saburov was already minister of the economy and deputy prime minister of Russia. He had promoted privatization laws that were adopted in July 1991. Saburov had a substantial economic program focusing on privatization. It contained other radical proposals, such as nationalizing the Russian ruble, thus making it a national currency. However, the macroeconomic part of Saburov's program was very weak and suggested a gradual price liberalization with high inflation.[67] Yeltsin disliked Saburov for unknown reasons. Clearly, Saburov had several shortcomings: he was Silaev's protégé, his team was small, he was a poor administrator, and he was a less accomplished economist than Gaidar.

The best known and most popular of the young liberal economists was Grigory Yavlinsky. Yeltsin explains his rejection of Yavlinsky thus: "Harried and harassed over his ill-fated 500-day program, he had already developed a kind of oversensitivity. Besides, psychologically it was difficult to return a second time to the same '500 Days' Program and its creators."[68] Yavlinsky's oversensitivity might have been related to his widely known claim that Yeltsin had betrayed him. Moreover, at this time, Yavlinsky was effectively Soviet deputy prime minister and worked under Gorbachev to foster the survival of the Soviet Union. While working on the Grand Bargain in the early summer of 1991, Yavlinsky had ignored Yeltsin and Burbulis and focused entirely on Gorbachev. Yavlinsky had a relatively small team of mostly junior collaborators. His 500-day program had advocated rapid privatization. However, because it had insisted on sales of property only, it was in practice less radical than Saburov's program, as sales would take longer and lead to a less equal property structure than free distribution of property. The Yavlinsky group put great emphasis on deregulation. Even so, its members foresaw gradual price liberalization and financial stabilization, although the Grand Bargain had embraced economic shock therapy.

The victorious liberal team of Yegor Gaidar was superior to its competitors in most regards, except for his lack of prior prominence and his lack of ability in dealing with the media. It was a large team of economists, potentially involving more than one hundred people, and it contained those who were the best economists from a professional point of view. Gaidar was the group's obvious leader, and he attracted other strong people. Since 1987, Gaidar had published the best Soviet analyses of the USSR's economy as economic editor of the liberal communist party journal *Kommunist*. The Gaidar team also presented the most convincing, radical, and comprehensive reform strategy. Gaidar had studied reforms in Eastern Europe in detail and had concluded that the best economic medicine for Russia was shock therapy of the Polish type.[69] Yeltsin was impressed with Gaidar's confidence, independence, and readiness to fight for his principles. Gaidar spoke plainly and persuasively, and he liked that. "Gaidar's theories coincided with my own private determination to go through the painful part of the economic reform route quickly. I couldn't force people to wait once again, to drag out the main events and processes for years. If our minds were made up, we had to get going!"[70] Another strength of the Gaidar team was that it was supported by Gennady Burbulis, who had been introduced to Yegor Gaidar and Aleksandr Shokhin as late as the fall of 1991. Gaidar and Shokhin had worked together at the Academy of Sciences' Institute of Economic Forecasting in the mid-1980s. Burbulis had emerged as a democratic deputy from Sverdlovsk who had gained prominence in the democratic interregional group in the Congress of People's Deputies. Yeltsin chose Burbulis as de facto prime minister, and Gaidar was Burbulis's man.[71]

On November 6–8, 1991, the new government was appointed. On the advice of Burbulis, Yeltsin decided to head the government himself. Burbulis became first deputy prime minister and in practice was acting prime minister. Gaidar was appointed deputy prime minister and minister of finance and economy.[72] Aleksandr Shokhin had been minister of labor since August 1991. In addition, he was elevated to deputy prime minister for social affairs. Other full ministers from the Gaidar team were Anatoly Chubais, minister of privatization and chairman of the State Committee on the Management of State Property (GKI); Petr Aven, minister of foreign economic relations; Vladimir Lopukhin, minister of fuel and energy; Ella Pamfilova, minister for social affairs; Boris Saltykov, minister of science; and Vladimir Mashchits, chairman of the State Committee for Economic Cooperation with Members of the CIS. Gaidar soon ceded the post of minister of the economy to Andrei Nechaev. In addition to this top layer, numerous deputy ministers, ministerial advisors, and assistants were appointed, and a sizable think tank was built up at the Council of Ministers.

All of these ministers were between the ages of 35 and 40 and were professional economists with doctoral degrees. Gaidar and Shokhin were even professors. None had earned a full degree from abroad, but they had all studied mainstream Western economics, not just Soviet political economy of socialism. They had studied mainly on their own, or together without supervision; few of the older generation of Soviet economists had bothered to talk to their young colleagues or to read international economic literature.[73] Because of the mutual lack of respect between old and young Russian economists, Gaidar, Shokhin, and Chubais had all characteristically set up their own economics research institutes staffed with young scholars. A uniquely sharp generational chasm had thus emerged. Socially, most members of the Gaidar team originated from the Moscow or St. Petersburg intelligentsia. Politically, only a few had significant professional experience (notably Shokhin, Gaidar, and Chubais). All of the senior staff had been members of the CPSU, but they had neither been real communists nor active in Democratic Russia. Their initial attitude toward politics was technocratic; their economic views ranged from the social democratic to those of Friedrich Hayek's school, though they were predominantly of the Western conservative mainstream. What is amazing is that Yeltsin, unlike most of his generation, was able to straddle this generational, intellectual, and ideological chasm.

An Acrimonious Critique

Not everyone could stomach the advance of a new generation, a new professional elite, and a new world outlook from relative obscurity straight into the seat of power. From the very beginning, the young liberal reformers were subject to vicious censure.[74]

The mainstream criticism had three strands: populism, crude Marxism, and vested interests. Leading politicians were the primary sources of populist criticism—notably Vice President Aleksandr Rutskoi and Chairman of the Supreme Soviet Ruslan Khasbulatov, assisted by his chief economist Vladimir Ispravnikov. These politicians were angry that they and the parliament had been excluded from efforts to work out the details of the economic reform program. The same was true of the old school economic academicians, who had been leading reform communists and advisors to Gorbachev. They included Leonid Abalkin, Nikolai Petrakov, Oleg Bogomolov, Yury Yaremenko, and their colleagues. Their outlook was still molded by Marxism, although they had abandoned overt dogma. A third less visible yet powerful group was composed of the associations of state enterprise managers in industry and agriculture. To a large extent, these three strands of criticism of the Russian reform coincided.

Other sections of this book review the reformers' efforts and discuss their outcome. Therefore, this section presents the main arguments of the critics, only briefly outlining the counterarguments. This discussion focuses on criticism in the crucial early period of the reform (primarily February to April 1992), which was when the ferocity of the debate reached its peak and the edge of the radical reform was broken. The problems and causes the critics identified are outlined. What kind of economic system did they envision with regard to the roles of the state and the market, respectively? Moreover, what roles would the budget and monetary policy play? Finally, how did the critics perceive the transformation process, and what models did they aspire to?

One fundamental point of contention centered on the depth and the causes of the economic crisis. The critics did not consider the crisis in Russia to be as serious as the reformers did, and they thought they had plenty of time and many options. In keeping with the Marxist fixation on production, they focused on the decline of production and neglected finances. Characteristically, Nikolai Petrakov gave five reasons for the fall in production in 1991: shortage of hard currency, disruption of economic links with Eastern Europe, blocking of production and investment projects by environmentalists, destabilization of economic links by national and regional conflicts, and structural changes caused by demand.[75] To Petrakov, disruption of the old command economy and the resulting structural changes were problems, not goals. Incredibly, he did not observe that financial imbalances and staggering shortages hampered production.

Though Petrakov discussed the monetary overhang, he failed to mention the budget deficit (at least 20 percent of GDP in 1991), excessive wage increases, or collapsing tax collection as causes of the fall in production. Instead Petrakov blamed Prime Minister Valentin Pavlov's administrative price reform of April 1991, the size of social programs, the exchange of noncash money for cash, and the absence of a consistent credit policy. His discussion lacked any quantitative data.[76] Leonid Abalkin went even further in his disregard of financial imbalances. He even denied that the monetary overhang was a problem: "The starting point here is erroneous, to consider the monetary accumulation as excessive and the rise of incomes in 1991 as inflationary, when the very sphere of investment of incomes was in reality administratively narrowed."[77] To Abalkin, the problem was that the money was not used productively. The academicians' main problem was a complete ignorance of macroeconomics. Moreover, they rarely bothered with statistics. Notably, they discussed state expenditures as if the state could always increase them, and they refrained from any statistical comparisons with other countries in transition (apart from China).

Consistent with their disregard for finances, the old-line Marxists considered the fall of production and investment, but not inflation, to be great problems. They wanted to stabilize production rather than prices. The most extreme position was that the relation between money supply and GDP had been correct before price liberalization and should be reestablished. Viktor Gerashchenko, the new chairman of the CBR, espoused this view: "Could the economy manage with the former money supply when the prices were rising . . . were the previous monetary resources really sufficient to exist at the present price level, when the wholesale prices have risen 16–18 times? According to my view, they were inadequate. That is the cause of the insolvency crisis." Gerashchenko argued that the state should resolve the money shortage by issuing more.[78] To the reformers, the importance of sound finances was paramount, and no recovery of the real economy could be expected until inflation had been brought under control.

But where did the inflation come from? In general, the Marxist critics saw inflation as a result of price liberalization, not of financial imbalances. They ignored the budget balance and monetary expansion, considering them irrelevant to inflation. Alternatively, they claimed the tasks necessary for stabilization could not be achieved. As the first deputy chairman of the CBR, Arnold Voilukov, reckoned: "The task [of achieving] monetary-financial stabilization in the course of the year was unfeasible from the very outset."[79] The economic ignorance among the old school economic academicians was so great that it took some time for pseudo-Keynesian arguments about cost-push inflation to arise. The idea that price liberalization caused inflation was widely embraced.

The Yaremenko group, which had close ties to the military-industrial complex, was particularly opposed to energy price increases: "Liberalization of prices on energy will indisputably lead the economy to open hyperinflation."[80] Based on data for 1991, when production had fallen far more than energy consumption, they concluded: "This means that in spite of the continuing fall of production, the domestic consumption of energy, especially oil, will hardly diminish sharply."[81] They ignored the shift in economic system that had occurred over these two years and the idea that financial stabilization would raise a demand barrier, which would prompt a slump in consumption. Their conclusion was that the government faced the choice "either to abandon the strict monetary policy and satisfy the demand for money in order to preserve production or to allow mass bankruptcy of commercial banks and completely disorganize the monetary circulation."[82] Moreover, so-called independent experts from the Russian Union of Industrialists and Entrepreneurs predicted that the rise in consumer prices in case of a liberalization of oil prices would be 500 to 700 percent, thereby disregarding the effects of monetary policy.[83]

In a step toward modern economics, conservatives focused on inflationary expectations. For instance, Gerashchenko blamed planned liberalization of energy prices for causing inflation by arousing inflationary expectations.[84] He saw state management as a necessity and considered free prices wrong in principle for Russia. He argued that they caused "the pauperization of people, the colossal fall of production, the destruction of all kinds of management mechanisms. . . . We destroy even what has been created and finally lose the management ability, which according to my view was the main cause of the mad tempo of inflation."[85]

Gerashchenko also pointed to what he called nonmonetary causes of inflation. By this he meant inertia of the old system, such as interenterprise arrears, which he sought to cure through additional credits. He defended a monetary expansion of 18 to 20 percent a month during the first quarter of 1993, citing this as a realistic and pragmatic policy to combat unemployment and collapse of production.[86]

For old-line communists, who considered finances to be only a veil, the key problems were administrative disorder and the disobedience of central commands. They thought that the old command model was fine but needed to be applied more vigorously; therefore, they demanded more administrative order. Rutskoi reflected this line of reasoning, persistently advocating energetic administrative control. To him, Gaidar's macroeconomic regulation "in practice means the total absence of management."[87] Similarly, to the Petrakov group, liberalization meant "the government has lost control over the economic processes."[88] In the same vein, Abalkin complained: "In essence management over the economy has been lost."[89]

Although these socialist economists overtly embraced the market, they failed to accept the autonomous functioning of market forces. They did not believe in the ability of market forces to emerge and to balance the market, and they saw any real deregulation as an undesirable loss of state control. As Oleg Bogomolov put it: "I suppose that we should not place great hope in the abolition of the multiple shortages and the appearance in the shops of a surplus of goods."[90]

At the beginning of 1992, the programmatic ideas of the opponents of the reform government were hazy. More or less explicitly, many arguments for some kind of third way or market socialism were circulated, but the ideas were rarely presented as full-fledged alternatives.

Petrakov's group advocated a return to comprehensive state regulation of prices and deliveries during the transition period. They promised many benefits to all conceivable groups, without discussing financing: "What we need immediately is the freezing of prices and wages and the introduction of their state regulation, at the same time as all commitments on social defense of the people are fulfilled (including the increases of wages, pensions, and social transfers)."[91] In their view, the state had to build the market: "Only under the conditions of sufficiently strong state regulation can the transition to the market take place; the most important part of this transition must be a state program for the establishment of a market infrastructure."[92]

Rutskoi went further in his demands for regulation of prices and trade: "The liberalization of prices without the existence of a civilized market requires strict price control. . . . In all civilized countries such strict

controls exist."[93] This last reference was typical of that of many enemies
to reform, revealing an extraordinary ignorance of the outside market-
economic world. In the old communist spirit, Rutskoi abhorred trade
and complained about "the uncontrolled rise of the number of middlemen, exchanges, and commercial banks." He concluded: "As a result, a
dangerous situation of anarchy has been created in the economy." Predictably, Rutskoi saw state control as the solution to this market anarchy:
"The most important part of the activity of the state when the market is
characterized by shortages is the struggle against speculation."[94]

An additional argument for extensive state regulation during the transition was the prevalence of monopolies, whose prices many thought
should be regulated by the state. As Rutskoi put it: "Is the state really
not able to establish control over the prices of monopolized production?
Of course it can, if it wants to."[95] To the Soviet old-liners, it was inconceivable that there were limits to what could be achieved by the state.
The problems were only a lack of will and of discipline and should be
cured through determined action from above.

Similarly, the critics argued that the government should intervene in
the market. This was dressed up as a demand for structural and industrial
policies. The reformers were accused of focusing only on macroeconomics and forgetting about microeconomics. Rutskoi advocated selective tax
breaks as a microeconomic steering mechanism: "The main function of
the state under the conditions of shortages has become tax breaks for
those who expand production of products in short supply."[96]

A legitimate complaint focused on the corruption within the state
administration. However, the socialist critics wanted to fight corruption
with far-reaching regulations. They seemed incapable of comprehending
that more regulation would in fact create ample opportunities for politicians and civil servants to extort bribes, resulting in even more corruption. In other cases (and more so later on), the demand for regulations
was presented by those who would benefit from bribes. The most obvious
examples were the so-called special exporters who enjoyed monopoly
rents from the export of certain commodities.

The real hard-liners argued that the nature of ownership was not
important and privatization was therefore futile. Rutskoi asked rhetori-
cally: "Does the form of ownership have any relationship to the market?
I am convinced that it does not. We cannot transform private ownership
into a dogma."[97]

Strangely, while the socialist critics dismissed financial problem out of hand, they advocated a financial solution to the problem of falling production. A budget deficit was widely seen as stabilizing, as Petrakov's group made plain: "Financial stabilization cannot precede the stabilization of production. . . . As long as the fall of production does not turn into sustained growth, it is necessary to abandon any attempts at the formation of a state budget without deficit. When the volume of production in the country is falling, a budget without deficit can only be accomplished at the price of hyperinflation . . . there are no state budgets without deficits even in well-to-do countries with market economies."[98] Roosevelt's New Deal was invoked as an argument for a budget deficit. The critics rarely discussed the budget and its deficit using actual numbers.

Similarly, Abalkin refuted any attempt to balance the budget. Without any evidence, he made the remarkable statement: "The history of the last two centuries shows that not one single big country has had a budget without a deficit . . . in the conditions of existing inflation it is even theoretically impossible to have a budget without a deficit."[99] An academician specializing in foreign policy, Georgy Arbatov, simply stated that it was impossible to balance the budget, implying that it was stupid to try.[100]

An underlying thought was that enterprises and workers would be stimulated to work better if they earned more. Therefore, the Petrakov group advocated reduced taxes: "The merciless tax policy only aggravates the bankruptcy of the economy and facilitates further price inflation."[101] Notwithstanding that state revenues would fall, they also favored massive agricultural subsidies: "It is necessary to organize assistance at state level to all types of farms with preferential or interest-free credits, budget subsidies, guaranteed purchasing prices. . . . Nobody thinks of modern agricultural production without substantial budget subsidies."[102] These economists patently avoided adding up the accounts for what they proposed. They blatantly favored maximizing expenditure and minimizing revenue, and they advocated a sizable budget deficit in any case.

To the extent that the old academicians thought of monetary issues, they dreamt the problems away by suggesting that Russia should undertake currency reform as Lenin had done in 1921, with the introduction of a parallel hard currency. They omitted the fact that Lenin's currency reform had been based on financial stabilization as well.[103] Rutskoi used monopolies as an argument for a loose credit policy. He wanted to overcome the reaction of Russian monopolies against price liberalization through "the introduction [into] the economy of additional money, which reestablishes the purchasing power of enterprises and helps them to overcome the 'liberalization' shock."[104]

The critics of the reform government did not believe that the West would provide significant financial assistance toward Russian stabilization. Ruslan Khasbulatov took the lead on the issue of Western assistance and stated repeatedly that he did not believe in any billions of dollars to come from the West. Instead, he admonished Russia to rely on its own resources.[105] (This was one of the few instances in which the socialistic critics turned out to be right.)

But how should the transition to a market economy occur? After all, apart from a hard core of old communists, everyone at least gave lip service to accepting a market economy as a goal. All socialist-minded critics advocated a gradual transition. Abalkin in particular disliked the thought of speed: "The transition from the administrative-command system to a market economy cannot be undertaken in one single step but presupposes a sufficiently long transition period of decades."[106] However, Abalkin's arguments for gradualism were little but platitudes: "First, life has again confirmed that it is not possible, even with the best of intentions, to accelerate the transformation, to ignore the lessons of world experience and detach oneself from life. Second, scientific and political extremism, based on the absolutism of monetary methods without consideration of the whole spectrum of contemporary views, cannot lead to success."[107] Because Abalkin could not conceptualize the transition, he apparently did not believe that anyone else could either. This problem was aggravated by the pretense of a theoretical framework when in fact there was none.

The ultimate argument of the critics—and one always used by Arkady Volsky, chair of the Russian Union of Industrialists and Entrepreneurs— was that the government should be "pragmatic."[108] In practice this implied a demand for as minor changes as possible. In the absence of both theory and a desire to transcend one system for another, it was convenient to call for "common sense," "pragmatism," and "moderation," which favored the status quo.

The critics did not welcome structural change, although that was the very purpose of the transition to a market economy. On the contrary, their goal was to minimize and, if possible, reverse any restructuring. Similarly, they wanted to preserve all trade links. Typically, the opposition lamented that instead of stabilization, economic collapse would occur.[109] Curiously, the socialists were more pessimistic about the competitiveness of Russian industry than the reformers. Arkady Volsky stated that only 16 percent of Russia's industrial capacity would be able to hold its own if Russia completely opened up its markets to international competition.[110] One explanation is that the socialists did not believe in price elasticity. They did not understand that a low exchange rate for the ruble would lead to low world market prices for Russian exports, which would stimulate demand. The government had targeted the VPK for downsizing. However, fearful of structural adjustment, Khasbulatov countered that enterprises within the VPK should be exempted from profits tax and import tariffs, and partially from VAT, and should receive "financial means for writing off losses."[111]

The critics also argued that the costs of transition were too high. This is easy to understand, as they did not see the need for structural change. Vladimir Ispravnikov, chairman of the Supreme Economic Council (SEC) of the Presidium of the Supreme Soviet, produced extreme forecasts through simple extrapolations, which he then presented as scientific fact: "According to the forecasts of the SEC, the fall of production can reach 55 percent until the end of 1993 (in comparison with the end of January 1992). Most probably, the standard of living will continue to fall (the consumption of food will diminish by half, and of nonfood goods by four-fifths) and unemployment will increase to half the active population."[112] Petrakov stated that the Russian government had left "over two-thirds of the population under the poverty line."[113] No reference was made to obvious statistical errors.[114]

The sequence of the reforms was a major bone of contention. The starting point of the debate was the 500-day program, which had advocated privatization and far-reaching demonopolization before full price liberalization and stabilization. The government was attacked for trying the opposite approach out of plain ignorance. As the neoliberal economist Larisa Piyasheva observed: "Did the reformers really not know that price liberalization is only possible under one condition: when free commodity producers sell their production at free prices in private shops that compete among themselves for the consumers?"[115] The writer Boris Mozhaev stated categorically: "No market economy and no liberalization of prices is possible as long as land is fully owned by the state."[116] Unabashed old communists put forward such strictures, although they had resisted privatization recently. Georgy Arbatov, a former advisor to Leonid

Brezhnev and Gorbachev on foreign policy, criticized the government vehemently: "There were other ways. Was it really not possible to start [land reform] at least in October [1991]. . . . And why did [the government] not start with a fast privatization and the breaking up of monopolies already then?"[117] Needless to say, Gorbachev (not to mention Brezhnev) had been against all these things.

The order of privatization and liberalization was a real issue. Gaidar responded: "Where has it been the case that market prices were introduced before large-scale and in-depth privatization? Unfortunately, this can be seen everywhere. There has not been and will not be a single example in history where large-scale and far-reaching transformations in ownership relations have successfully been fitted into just weeks and months."[118] Furthermore, Gaidar noted: "In themselves, state regulated nonmarket and unbalanced prices give rise to a continual and permanent monopoly."[119]

Ultimately, with the exception of natural monopolies, Russian monopolies could only be checked by liberalization. Even relatively well-managed Hungary had tried to break up its large state trusts for years but had only succeeded in doing so in weak branches after prices had already been liberalized. In Czechoslovakia, the government waited to enact full liberalization until 1991 in order to demonopolize first, but it achieved nothing because of resistance from strong state enterprises. Only after liberalization do the harmful effects of monopolies become evident, and only then does it become politically feasible to attack the monopolies. Moreover, few private property rights exist if prices, production, and trade are regulated and no property market is allowed. Finally, until substantial liberalization of prices and trade has occurred, the power of the old bureaucracy remains immense, and it is not benevolent. Either it will block privatization or it will usurp public property for its own purposes—or most likely both, as *nomenklatura* privatization tends to take time. The purported need for prior privatization was an excuse for the enemies of free markets to oppose price liberalization, though some thoughtless neoliberals tagged along. The reformers lost the public argument.[120]

Several countries played important roles as models in the Russian debate. The enemies of the Gaidar team referred frequently to the experience of other countries whenever it supported their arguments and were unconcerned with similarities or differences in preconditions. Arkady Volsky referred to Japan, South Korea, Singapore, and China as appropriate models for Russia to emulate. Leonid Abalkin and Oleg Bogomolov focused on European social democratic welfare states, such as Sweden, and Germany was also frequently cited. Despite their limited international knowledge, critics frequently invoked more sweeping references, such as "world experience has proved" or "nothing like that has existed in the history of humanity."[121]

The main line of the critics, however, was that Russia was different from other countries: Neither economic theory nor the experiences of other countries could possibly be relevant to Russia. As Petrakov's team put it: "Our situation is special. It cannot be described by general rules."[122] Khasbulatov argued: "The economic reforms must not be based on abstract and extremely simplified models, but on decisions derived from real life, on considerations of the real situation in the economy, the population of the country, and the experiences of the whole political and socioeconomic history of Russia."[123] With such an argument, anything could be defended. The purported uniqueness of Russia was typically presented as the ultimate argument for why normal reasoning did not apply to Russia.

The Russian reformers tended to cite Poland as the most relevant model—one that their critics dismissed. The critics emphasized the large private sector in Polish agriculture, the roles played by the church and Solidarity, the Poles' longer experience with market socialism, and Poland's even more far-reaching dollarization.[124] In general, the critics were completely uninterested in economic models from Eastern Europe and postcommunist countries in transition. Instead, they turned their attention to those of Western welfare states or dictatorships.

These populist and socialist critiques were by no means the only ones in the public forum, but they dominated it. Gaidar and supporters of the government regularly confronted such criticism. In rebuttal, they pointed out that the policies advocated by their critics would actually cause hyperinflation, that no economic recovery was possible if inflation had not been checked, and that further state regulation would lead to more corruption.[125] The obvious inability of the debilitated state to carry out government functions appropriately generated criticism inspired by Friedrich Hayek. For example, young neoliberal economists suggested that, because of its massive corruption, the government should limit its function to running the legal system.[126]

Grigory Yavlinsky and his EPICenter took a generally liberal position but sharply criticized the government rather than its adversaries. One point of attack was that "the liberalization of the market is far from being completed," which was certainly correct. However, Yavlinsky complained both that "no stabilization has occurred" and that "orientation toward overcoming the budgetary deficit at an accelerated rate has intensified production recession," statements that appear to be contradictory. He declared privatization a failure, because the government had not attained the high targets it had set. However, based on the experience of Eastern Europe, his own insistence on sales only would have led to slower privatization. Moreover, in 1993—after voucher privatization had turned out to be exceedingly fast—Yavlinsky began to argue that the speed of privatization was not important. On the whole, Yavlinsky was primarily critical of the government, but he appears to have favored more liberalization and less stabilization.[127]

The most substantial and far-sighted contribution to this debate was made by the Expert Institute of the Russian Union of Industrialists and Entrepreneurs, headed by Professor Yevgeny Yasin. The institute issued a balanced analysis of the reform strategy in January 1992, and most of its observations hold true today: "In general, the orientation of the Russian reform is correct. Other options are extremely limited." The report noted that "the most vulnerable area of the program is the approach to relationships with former union republics." However, a major complaint was that "the government does not exhibit persistence and consistency" in its "removal of restrictions inherited from the old economic system." Also correctly, the report stated: "Shortly after price liberalization, mass social outbursts are hardly practical." The macroeconomic stabilization program was criticized for being too focused on the short term and too vague on strategy. For the rest, much of the criticism concerned the government's lack of political aptitude.[128]

The prevailing beliefs of the Russian criticism cited here are strikingly similar to the economic populism that for years was characteristic of many Latin American countries. Rudiger Dornbusch and Sebastian Edwards's definition fits the Russian discussion: " 'Economic populism' is an approach to *economics* that emphasizes growth and income redistribution and deemphasizes the risks of inflation and deficit finance, external constraints, and the reaction of economic agents to aggressive nonmarket policies." They emphasize three important features of the populist paradigm:

1. "The populist policymakers . . . are deeply dissatisfied with the economy's performance; there is a strong feeling that things can be better."

2. "Policymakers explicitly reject the conservative paradigm and ignore the existence of any type of constraints on macroeconomic policy. Idle capacity is seen as providing the leeway for expansion."

3. In their policy prescriptions, "the populist programs emphasize three elements: reactivation, redistribution of income, and restructuring of the economy."[129]

For the critics of the Russian government, crude Marxism provided a convenient framework for unabashed populism. The problem was less that the critics knew little of ordinary economics than that they had no interest in learning market economics. If the Russian people had known more about economics, however, this simple populist advocacy would have been too embarrassing for the critics to espouse. The Russian socialists were even worse than the Latin American populists: they opposed restructuring and advocated redistribution of income to the old establishment (the industry, VPK, and agrarian sectors) rather than the people. This reflects the weakness of popular pressure and civic society in Russia, which allowed the political elite to indulge openly in such rent-seeking.

In January 1994, the old economic academicians came back with an extensive program on socioeconomic transformation in Russia.[130] The major authors of the program were Leonid Abalkin, Stanislav Shatalin, Nikolai Petrakov, and Yury Yaremenko. Their criticism of economic shock therapy had not evolved in the least, but now they omitted any reference to the initial crisis altogether. Nor had they elaborated on any real alternative, and they rejected the concept of any ideal model. They continued to avoid concrete data. Because privatization had happened so fast, it was now attacked for having been "artificially speeded up." The program the academicians presented was evidence of a double failure. On the one hand, they had failed to learn anything. On the other hand, because their program became a political event, it showed that the Russian reformers had failed to break the old reform communist paradigm. In Poland, the Czech Republic, or Hungary, such a program would have made laughingstocks of its authors.

With few exceptions, the arguments in this aggressive debate were too weak to be taken seriously. However, the criticism was important in several ways. Through their viciousness, the critics put the government on the defensive and dominated the public debate. The reform leaders were so appalled by this ruthless populism that most of them limited their public appearances and speeches. As a consequence, the deputies felt ignored and were dismayed. In addition, the reformers did not fare well in the battle for the hearts and minds of the Russian people. The debate was an indication of how furious the old privileged class was at having been pushed aside by these young upstarts, reflecting that it was not long ago that gerontocracy had ended. Their disregard for the citizenry and emphasis on the interests of the old elite highlighted the weakness of Russian civic society. The ferocious tone of the proceedings appeared to have divided society even further. Yet despite these failings, quite a few market economic insights were revealed to much of the population. After this debate, with the exception of the citizens of the Baltics, the Russians appeared to have the best understanding of a market economy among residents of the FSU.

Political and Institutional Impediments

From the very beginning, many political and institutional problems hampered the implementation of radical economic reform in Russia. Significant political problems included the problematic relationship between Yeltsin and his government, the weakness of Burbulis, the political isolation and lack of credibility of the government, and the absence of official government programs. Institutional problems proved overwhelming. The sheer size of the old state apparatus was awesome. The reformers had natural enemies in the former institutions of the command economy—the branch ministries, the state enterprise managers, and the bureaucracy in general—but no natural institutional friends as yet. The government was unwieldy, and the constitution needed to be revised.

However radical and resolute Yeltsin sounded, he did not completely commit to reform. Instead, he hedged his bets. After appointing his young reform ministers, he kept them at a distance and gave them no direct access to him: "The ministers would clear all matters requiring [Yeltsin's] involvement through Burbulis."[131] Even Gaidar had little access to Yeltsin. The government was housed in the old CC headquarters at the Old Square, while Yeltsin and his administration sat in splendid isolation in the Kremlin. Yeltsin rarely participated in the weekly meetings of the cabinet, which he officially led. No radical reform would have occurred without Yeltsin's blessing, but his involvement was not sufficiently deep to provide full-fledged political support. His lack of understanding of the requirements of radical reform proved to be a major problem.

First Deputy Prime Minister Gennady Burbulis was the lone link between the president and the reform ministers, and he was too weak. But Burbulis did have advantages. He kept close to Yeltsin, thought of political strategy, was an effective decisionmaker, had found Gaidar, and had convinced Yeltsin of the necessity of radical economic reform. However, as Yeltsin notes: "All of Burbulis's attempts to become a shaper of public opinion were unsuccessful."[132] He failed to work with the deputies or reach out to the Russian people. Nor did he manage his relations with the administration well. In Yeltsin's words, "he hated the bureaucracy as a class." Eventually, Yeltsin also thought that Burbulis "overstepped some boundary in our personal relationship."[133] As early as April 3, 1992, Burbulis was forced to resign as first deputy prime minister, and Gaidar took over as the actual head of government.[134] Without Burbulis, the Gaidar reforms would not have been launched; but Burbulis was neither able to maintain the vital link to Yeltsin nor to provide political support for the reforms.

The reform ministers were isolated not only from Yeltsin, but from politics in general. Initially, the members of the Gaidar team viewed themselves as experts and economists, but not as politicians. Soon their leaders—Gaidar, Shokhin, and Chubais—decided to become politicians, but others on the team were both ignorant and contemptuous of politics. As Yeltsin saw it: "By sophisticatedly refusing to 'dirty their hands with politics' and leaving all political initiative to their chief, the Gaidar team made a tactical error that cost us all a great deal."[135] But the young ministers felt an awesome distance between them and the president. The ministers had been appointed to their posts by presidential decree and therefore did not need to defend themselves before the parliament, but they could be discharged instantly by Yeltsin without appeal. The Yasin group criticized the Gaidar government for working insufficiently "with the parliament, entrepreneurs, trade unions, representatives of the regions, political parties, and movements."[136] Everyone felt excluded from the actions of the government. Yeltsin observed: "Soon it became evident that the Gaidar government, which was rapidly making one decision after another, was in complete isolation. Gaidar and his people never traveled around the country to take the pulse of the nation. From the outset, these ministers perceived the Khasbulatov parliament as an instrument of pressure on them, as a symbol of everything that was reactionary, everything that had to be fought. . . . It was a kind of childish infantile division of people into 'ours' and 'theirs'."[137] The Gaidar team's first priority was to outline a large number of legal changes and have them implemented. They took pride in being professional and in working hard, and they found little time for making or maintaining outside contacts. As a result, they were perceived as exclusive and elitist (which they certainly were). Nor did Gaidar's ministers appear much in the media. The reform government largely abstained from trying to establish a political base in addition to Yeltsin.

A fundamental mistake the Gaidar team made was their decision not to present an economic reform program. As Gaidar stated in December 1991: "We believed that after 11 programs had been adopted and widely discussed in the press and by the bodies of power without exerting any influence whatsoever on real developments, it would simply not be serious to submit a 12th program. We believed that our program must, above all, be implemented via specific economic and political decisions."[138] The lack of an official program had serious consequences. The parliament felt excluded. It had overwhelmingly approved the basic reform ideas in Yeltsin's speech on October 28. Its members might have approved a reform program in November 1991, but when they were not even consulted, they turned against the government. Furthermore, it was difficult to mobilize the Russian people in favor of a program that they had not even seen. The administration also had little idea of what the actual government policy was. The lack of a government program hampered coordination among bureaucrats and facilitated their disobedience. The cabinet itself was heterogenous, and the remaining branch ministers felt free to carry on in their old ways as long as no approved reform program stopped them. Finally, the president needed a clear position paper to make his own actions more consistent.[139]

To carry out a stabilization or economic transformation, the credibility of the government is vital. However, the Gaidar team members jeopardized their credibility by calling themselves a "kamikaze cabinet" and by pursuing "endless talks about [the] short life of the present Government."[140] They were posturing coyly as though they were to be sacked within the month. Because of this behavior, both government officials and state enterprise managers treated the Gaidar team as a temporary phenomenon and consequently refused to adjust. As a result, reforms were sabotaged, and the pressure for cheap credits and subsidies continued unimpeded.

The institutional complications became even more intricate than the political problems. However extensive, the institutional adjustment to a market economy did not go far enough. Central planning had supposedly been abolished, but the State Planning Committee (Gosplan) remained. It had merely been renamed the Ministry of the Economy. There more than 2,000 bureaucrats sat, with nothing better to do than to lobby for the reestablishment of central planning, state orders, and export quotas. (Notably, in the summer of 1993, then Minister of the Economy Oleg Lobov used the former Gosplan as a base to push for a return to central planning.)

Similarly, the State Price Committee was scaled down but not abolished. At the end of 1992, the conservative leadership of the committee persuaded the new prime minister, Viktor Chernomyrdin, to sign a decree reintroducing price controls. The powerful State Committee on Material and Technical Supplies (Gossnab) also escaped being abolished, though as a wholesale organization it adjusted better to the market. One part of Gossnab became Roskontrakt, which had a monopoly on interstate trade. The Ministry of Grain Procurement transformed itself into the Federal Joint Stock Company Roskhleboprodukt. But it maintained its monopoly on grain procurement, for which it exacted huge volumes of subsidized state credits.

A large number of industrial branch ministries and state committees were abolished or merged. However, the few branch ministries that remained proved troublesome—particularly the three headed by conservative technocrats: Aleksandr Titkin, the minister of industry; Stanislav Anisimov, the minister of trade and material resources; and Vitaly Yefimov, the minister of transportation. They continued to rule in the old fashion, issuing state orders and resisting privatization. Worse, old ministries soon began to reemerge in various guises, ranging from "departments," "associations," and "concerns" to directorates of ministries demanding independence once again. Characteristically, the reformist ministers in charge of branch ministries were subjected to the most aggressive criticism. Vladimir Lopukhin never stood a chance against the energy lobby and lost his job after six months. Petr Aven put up a hard fight with the foreign trade lobby and lost his job after thirteen months. Minister of Agriculture Viktor Khlystun had reformist credentials but chose not to resist the conservative agrarian lobby. He survived in his job for three years, until October 1994.

When the reform government was formed, the Council of Ministers had been completely transformed and substantially reduced to only twenty-one ministers, including three deputy prime ministers. Yet the regular Thursday meetings of the Council of Ministers were large, with about 100 attendees. Soon the number of ministers increased. By the end of 1992, the cabinet comprised twenty-nine full ministers (of whom eight were deputy prime ministers), plus seven chairmen of state committees.[141] The idea of a small collegial government had failed. But real "economic" cabinet meetings were held on Tuesday evenings in an informal fashion.[142]

The reform team faced a rather hopeless situation with the old bureaucracy. The government buildings at the Old Square were full of Soviet bureaucrats—the eternally gray, middle-aged men in gray suits, with inscrutable expressions on their faces. Regardless of events, they walked neither quickly nor slowly down the winding corridors. The same bureaucracy (and even the same interior decoration, with red-carpeted floors and eggshell-colored walls with wooden paneling) was reproduced in each regional administration headquarters. In a rare moment of openness, one of these bureaucrats might confide: "I shall tell you frankly. Work was more interesting before. We were building. . . ."[143] The bureaucrat would cautiously stop before the newly prohibited word socialism passed his lips.

In reality, the state apparatus had been subservient to the Communist party. Commands had been passed on by phone, and laws were of limited significance. The old chain of command had been broken, but the old communist contempt for law remained. The bureaucrats gained independence, only to use it to pursue their own interests, and the old state apparatus was made up of communists who were averse to the idea of a democratic society. Moreover, the old officials tended to have the wrong education. They had been trained as engineers rather than as lawyers or social scientists, and they were not well paid. Neither checks nor competence nor ethics stopped them from enriching themselves. So the temptation to do so was great, and corruption became rampant. Yeltsin was not very helpful; he came from the old administration and was convinced of its competence: "Where it was possible to put in experienced 'old' staff, we did."[144]

In the late Soviet administration, there was a steady tendency toward greater disobedience. In effect, every senior bureaucrat was his own dictator, thereby diluting central state power. Gorbachev's attempts to reform the Soviet Union from the top down were futile, because too little effective power remained in the center. In the spring of 1986, Gorbachev issued a decree on agricultural reform. As a foreign diplomat, I went to

Gosagroprom to find out what it meant. However, my questions were met with derisive laughter from senior agricultural officials. They openly declared that nothing would change, and they could not have cared less about decrees passed by Gorbachev.

A mutual, silent hostility prevailed between the reform ministers and the bureaucrats. Rather than opposing the reformers overtly, the old bureaucrats sabotaged them discreetly. The disappearance of important documents became notorious. When Yeltsin appointed the young reformer and Burbulis-Gaidar man Aleksei Golovkov to head the administration of the Council of Ministers, he had to sign the same decree three times, because the first two decrees disappeared in the administration without a trace. (Golovkov was not very popular with the old bureaucrats.) As acting minister of labor in 1992, Vladimir Kosmarsky made three copies of each important document he produced. One copy would be sent through the ordinary official channel, but for unclear reasons it generally vanished. The second copy he would deliver personally to his deputy prime minister, Aleksandr Shokhin; and similarly he would personally bring the third copy to the head of the relevant department in the Council of Ministers.

The burden on the reformers was aggravated by the extraordinary centralization. Soviet ministers traditionally signed a huge number of decisions, most of which they could not possibly have scrutinized. Even officials high up in the hierarchy tended not to take any responsibility. Nor could most of the reformers assess how they ought to recast their jobs when they had just started work. Furthermore, the Soviet administration was extremely compartmentalized. Contacts between ministries were minimal, and an amazingly large share of interministerial communications were handled by the ministers themselves. As a result, some reform ministers were overwhelmed by routine decisions. They had no time for strategic thinking and lost their policy orientation.

The reformers faced an impossible dilemma. Because they knew few of the old civil servants, it was difficult for them to find the right people to appoint and promote. The reformers therefore often selected ineptly, which further demoralized the old staff. When the reformers appointed young colleagues to senior positions, staffers of the old apparatus naturally regretted it. The reformers needed the old administration, but it resisted reform through virtual civil disobedience. No matter what the reformers tried to do with the old administration, they encountered quiet resistance and failed. In practice, the reformers established a stronghold in the Council of Ministers and the GKI (the Ministry of Privatization), but held little sway in the other ministries, including the Ministries of Finance and the Economy. It is noteworthy that the most successful part of the Russian economic reform has been privatization, for which a new state administration was created.

The basic political and institutional problem, however, was that no constitutional or political base for the reforms had been built. No new elections were called, and the parliament operated in loose factions without real political parties. Because the president could rule by decree, the parliament was ignored and circumvented by the government. Political parties played no genuine role and remained rudimentary. As a result of all these complications, a number of political links were too frail: between the president and his reform team, between the government and the parliament, between the government and the regions, and between the government and the Russian people.

With only one legitimate political institution, the presidency, the newborn Russian democracy was weak. Given the parallel weakness of civil society, it would be expected that, in line with Mancur Olson's theory of the logic of collective action, the strongest lobby would consist of large state enterprises. "These industries will normally be small enough to organize voluntarily to provide themselves with an active lobby."[145] Indeed, the state enterprise managers formed the strongest lobby. During the last two years of the Soviet Union, the government's control over state enterprises had loosened to such an extent that hardly any state enterprise managers had been dismissed. The managers had gained control over their enterprises. Moreover, without established rules and norms to curb their efforts, the lobby of state enterprise managers could demand almost infinite resources from the state. The state was an easy victim of this lobby, which was closely linked to the old state apparatus.

At the national level, the state enterprise managers had set up several organizations. The most powerful and high-profile of these was the Russian Union of Industrialists and Entrepreneurs, headed by the experienced but moderate communist *apparatchik* Arkady Volsky. The agrarian lobby of directors of *sovkhozy* and chairmen of *kolkhozy* joined hands to form the strong, militant Agrarian Union. It elected Vasily Starodubtsev (an unabashed hard-liner and one of the instigators of the August 1991 coup) chair as soon as he was released from prison. Both the state and Russian civil society were indeed far too weak to counter the efforts of these numerically small but well-organized and resourceful forces.

The fundamental problem was that the Yeltsin camp had no real political strategy or philosophy. In December 1992, Burbulis was dismissed from the president's administration after intense pressure from the Congress. There were no longer any political strategists and hardly any democratic activists in Yeltsin's inner circle. A postcommunist contempt for anything related to communism prevailed. Parties in general were in disrepute because of the former preeminence of the Communist party. The same was true of propaganda, party discipline, and political participation; even political philosophy was rejected. Modern political science, which was rudimentary in Russia, was completely disregarded. In light of all this, it would have been surprising if important political mistakes had not been made, because politics was just not taken seriously. No strategy for the renewal of the constitution, the parliament, and other political institutions was adopted, nor was elucidating such a strategy a concern. International insights were almost completely disregarded.[146]

However many mistakes were made, the reform ministers were never given much of a chance. As Yeltsin writes: "From the very first days of the reforms, the Gaidar government was operating under terrible mental duress as the press and the parliament let loose a hailstorm of criticism and kept up an incessant drumbeat of protest. Gaidar and his people were cut virtually no slack and were never given even a modicum of freedom to maneuver."[147] The amount of abuse heaped on Gaidar and his team was extraordinary. The actual reason for this vitriolic response was hardly their policies; the old establishment simply remained too strong and united in the early stage of the reform. They were convinced that Gaidar represented only an interlude. From this perspective, the Gaidar team's lack of credibility was probably a more important weakness than its minimal political base.

The Political Undoing of Radical Reform

Political resistance to economic reform arose on all sides. The most serious opposition came from the Congress of People's Deputies and its chairman Ruslan Khasbulatov, who as early as January 1992 had called for the resignation of the reform government.[148] Within the administration, Vice President Aleksandr Rutskoi attacked the reform program viciously on December 18, 1991, before it was even launched. He ridiculed the leading reform ministers as "small boys in pink shorts and yellow boots."[149] The old branch ministries and most of the government administration quietly sabotaged the reforms by sticking to their old routines. From the industrial sector, the well-organized lobby of state enterprise managers, led by Arkady Volsky, skillfully cooperated with all these forces in their efforts to thwart reform policy. The Gorbachev loyalists (notably his generation of the intelligentsia) were vehement in their opposition to reform and appeared regularly in the Russian media. Finally, the communists and hard-line nationalists were outspoken and absolute enemies of reform, but isolated from the fray.

In the face of all this resistance, Yeltsin wavered. Having opted for a radical break with the past, he started to compromise: "To break everything, to destroy everything in the Bolshevik manner was not part of my plans at all. While bringing into the government completely new, young, and bold people, I still considered it possible to use in government work-experienced executives, organizers, and leaders."[150] Yeltsin tried to mitigate criticism of the Gaidar team by granting concessions to four groups: the parliament, state enterprise managers, the old-line bureaucracy, and his close friends.

Before the Sixth Congress of People's Deputies, which opened on April 6, 1992, Yeltsin consulted with congressional factions. He identified four ministers as deficient. Two belonged to Gaidar's team—Vladimir Lopukhin, minister of fuel and energy, and Petr Aven, minister of foreign economic relations. Without discussing this with anyone in his government, Yeltsin "naturally passed this list on to Gaidar through Burbulis, since [Yeltsin] considered it premature to meet with the government at this time."[151] Only afterward did he talk with Gaidar and realize that he was demoralizing his reform team. The Gaidar government won at the Congress (without Yeltsin's support) by dramatically resigning, prompting the Congress to take a moderate line. In the end, Yeltsin sacked Lopukhin at a cabinet meeting in late May 1992 because of grievances among industrialists—again without even having consulted Gaidar. Lopukhin was dismissed because he fought for full liberalization of energy prices, which should have been part of the reform package from the beginning.[152]

At the same time, Yeltsin was putting pressure on Gaidar to add Yury Skokov and Oleg Lobov to the government "for the sake of balance" but was rebuffed by Gaidar. Yeltsin felt "forced to bring in some energetic plant directors."[153] By June 1992, three experienced state enterprise managers had joined the government as deputy prime ministers. Viktor Chernomyrdin, former Soviet minister of the gas industry whom Yeltsin knew from the Urals, took over the energy portfolio. Two defense plant managers were added as well. Georgy Khizha from St. Petersburg was conservative; Vladimir Shumeiko from Krasnoyarsk ended up supporting the reformers.[154]

Yeltsin surrounded himself with close aides and friends who were not in the least reformist or liberal. Two of his closest associates were KGB Generals Aleksandr Korzhakov and Mikhail Barsukov; Yeltsin's chief aide, Viktor Ilyushin, was a former communist *apparatchik* from Sverdlovsk. The most sinister Yeltsin colleague was Yury Skokov, a staunch antidemocrat who was first opposed to a market economy and later in favor of *nomenklatura* privatization. Shokov defended the interests of the military-industrial sector. As Yeltsin himself points out: "Many people were asking what his role was in my inner circle. . . . Skokov was actually the 'shadow' prime minister whom I had always in mind." It is hardly surprising that Gaidar "sensed a latent threat emanating from Skokov," who stayed close by Yeltsin in the Kremlin as secretary of the Security Council.[155] Similarly, Yeltsin's friend Oleg Lobov joined the government as a major conservative force in April 1993. When he was removed from the government that September, he was given another important position as secretary of the Security Council. Lobov tried to build a new Gosplan under Security Council auspices. (From this position, he could attack the economic ministers in government, finally ousting most of them in November 1994.) Until the end of 1992, Yury Petrov, a close party associate of Yeltsin's who was also from Sverdlovsk, was the president's administrative director in the Kremlin. Eventually, Yeltsin dismissed him because communist deputies nominated Petrov as prime minister, who neglected to tell Yeltsin.[156] Yeltsin was anxious to maintain some kind of balance of power within his team. He insisted on having obvious enemies of reform, such as Yury Skokov and Oleg Lobov, around him.[157] Yeltsin was also dissatisfied with the leadership qualities of Gaidar's team: "Not a single one of the deputy prime ministers appointed to positions in the Gaidar team could aspire to leadership."[158] Presumably, he still held to an old communist image of what a big boss should be.

Curiously, Yeltsin appears never to have made a clear choice regarding reform and continuously pursued contradictory strategies. He was the great revolutionary who launched the radical transition to a market economy and carried out the democratic revolution. Yet he was also a traditional Russian ruler who governed by manipulating the state apparatus, the army, and the security forces. These two roles could hardly be reconciled, but both were reflected in his government and his presidential administration. Eventually, Yeltsin's contradictory approach proved self-defeating.

Yegor Gaidar was far more consistent. His government's threatened resignation at the Congress of People's Deputies in April 1992 was an impressive display of resolve, and it won the day. However, Gaidar tended to make the wrong compromises—giving in on strategy rather than tactics, for example, which reflected flaws in his political judgment and negotiating skills rather than in his character. The Gaidar team was politically isolated and needed to reach out for support. Gaidar harbored a certain fear of populism as a cause of excessive wage pressures and rising social expenditures. These problems had been severe in the late Soviet period, but the pressures had been exerted then by Yeltsin and the democrats. Now Yeltsin and his associates ruled. Moreover, much of the apparent "populist" pressure had been brought on by the managers, as it was managers rather than workers who benefitted from more state subsidies. Another reason for Gaidar's acquiescence was that he saw the strong trade unions in Poland as cause for concern. Moreover, the coal miners' independent trade union had played an important political role in the Soviet Union through strikes in 1989. However, the trade unions did not continue to grow, simply because Russia's civil society was too weak. In the spring of 1992, there was much talk about the need to establish a social base for reform policy. The ideal would have been to mobilize real private entrepreneurs for this role, but there were too few of them. Then it was argued that the Gaidar team should forge an alliance with progressive "industrialists," (that is, market-oriented managers of state enterprises) and split the managers' ranks.[159] This notion was a confused mixture of quasi-Marxist class thinking and elitism.

The lesson from Eastern Europe, notably Poland, was that the main opposition against financial stabilization policy came from state enterprise managers. They demanded ownership of the enterprises they managed (which could be partially accommodated) and cheap credits (which ran counter to the efforts toward financial stabilization). On the eve of the Sixth Congress of People's Deputies in early April 1992, the government gave in and decided to issue subsidized credits to agriculture and industry.[160] This credit flow gained momentum and by June 1992 had turned into a flood. Ironically, the subsidized credits were popularly known as "Gaidar credits."

At the beginning of 1992, state enterprises had started to split up into competitive and uncompetitive entities because of a monetary squeeze. Nevertheless, all managers opposed the repeatedly postponed government plan to liberalize energy prices. Had these prices been liberalized in January 1992 as Gaidar had originally intended, the antigovernment alliance that spring would not have been reinforced. The issuance of large volumes of subsidized credits from June 1992 unified the state enterprise managers in their resistance against the government's last remaining attempts at stabilization. Rising inflation increased the enterprises' demand for cheap credits that could help maintain the real value of their working capital. In effect, the state redistributed wealth from the people to state enterprises through cheap credits. Rather than trying to forge a political alliance with state enterprise managers (the natural opponents of stabilization), the government should have reached out to the citizenry to create a democratic political base with a real interest in combatting inflation.

A tragic political miscarriage of the reform government was that it failed to gain control over the CBR. The chairman of the CBR was a middle-aged professor of economics, Georgy Matyukhin, who had been appointed in August 1990 when Ruslan Khasbulatov was nominated as chairman of the Supreme Soviet. Matyukhin was therefore considered Khasbulatov's clone. Moreover, Matyukhin was in favor of gradual price liberalization and a moderately strict monetary policy, and his management skills were not strong. Yet by Soviet standards, he knew a fair amount about money and banking. Initially, the Gaidar team went for an all-out attack on Matyukhin; the government wanted to take over control of the CBR from the parliament. However, on November 22, 1991, the reform government suffered its first serious defeat against Khasbulatov in the Russian parliament. The CBR stayed subordinate to the parliament, and Matyukhin remained its chairman.[161]

During the first half of 1992, public criticism mounted against Matyukhin in the press and the Congress of People's Deputies. The complaints were many, but the main issues were that Matyukhin tried to hold back the expansion of the money supply and to raise the refinance rate of the CBR. Matyukhin defended the CBR's independence. On all these points, the Gaidar team agreed with Matyukhin, who in turn made one of Gaidar's men, Deputy Minister of Finance Sergei M. Ignat'ev, a deputy chairman of the CBR to show his goodwill. Still, Matyukhin allowed excessive credit expansion and insisted on centralization of payments. Rather than forging closer ties with Matyukhin after Khasbulatov had abandoned him, the reformers criticized Matyukhin, taking the opposite point of view.[162]

To the detriment of stabilization, the *nomenklatura* came back with a vengeance. Two alternative candidates for chairman of the CBR were discussed for months. The reformists wanted Boris Fedorov, while the *nomenklatura* backed Viktor Gerashchenko, the former chairman of the Soviet State Bank. Gerashchenko had gone along with the coup in August 1991 and had carried out the so-called Pavlov monetary confiscation in January 1991. However, he was widely considered a competent banker, and he had tried to resist monetary expansion initiated by the republics in 1991.[163] After much consultation, Yeltsin offered Gaidar the choice of Fedorov or Gerashchenko. Gaidar nominated Gerashchenko, justifying his decision by declaring that Fedorov would never be approved by the Supreme Soviet and there were worse candidates in the wings.[164] The Presidium of the Supreme Soviet appointed Gerashchenko acting chairman on July 17, 1992, and the Supreme Soviet confirmed him by acclamation on November 4. Gerashchenko was popular among the old elite because he gave everyone the cheap credits they asked for and kept the refinance rate very low. But he turned out to be the worst choice possible—a guarantor of irresponsible monetary policy and "the worst central banker in history," as Jeffrey Sachs has called him. Meanwhile, Russia was racing toward hyperinflation.

Gerashchenko's appointment also reflected of Gaidar's sincere ambition to co-opt competent Soviet technocrats. Similarly, Gaidar promoted old technocrats in the Ministries of the Economy and Finance. As early as April 2, 1992, he had appointed an old finance official, Vasily Barchuk, as minister of finance to replace Gaidar himself.[165] From that moment, Russia's macroeconomic strategy began to evaporate.[166]

Gaidar's team was severely shaken when he accepted the sacking of Lopukhin, one of his own ministers, without a word of protest. During the second half of 1992, his own associates increasingly believed that Gaidar could accept any compromise to be confirmed as prime minister.

The official excuse for his conciliatory behavior was that privatization was forging ahead and was worth the concessions on stabilization.

Both Burbulis and Gaidar were under so much fire from the parliament from the moment the reform government was founded that they could do little to improve their relation with the Supreme Soviet. Gaidar tried but accomplished little. However, minister of privatization Anatoly Chubais managed to push the Privatization Program through the Supreme Soviet as late as June 11, 1992. But after that, the parliament did not accept anything suggested by the government or the President.

The Russian people, on the contrary, was exceptionally patient. A multitude of analysts had raised the specter of social unrest, strikes, and bread riots like those in the third world.[167] Nothing of the kind occurred; civil society was weak, and most people felt positive about reform, according to opinion polls. The threat to reform did not come from the Russian people, but from the old elite.

Meanwhile, the outside world played a remarkably passive role. It was not until April 1, 1992—five months after radical reform had been announced and President Yeltsin had appealed for international support—that U.S. President George Bush and German Chancellor Helmut Kohl responded, heralding the arrival of a large Western aid package totalling $24 billion. Unfortunately, their offer was not substantiated, and it came too late. The international community had not woken up. During the five months the Russian attempt at macroeconomic stabilization was in full swing, the world had not offered significant support, not even in words.

By June 1992, the reform government was effectively finished. It had been transformed into a coalition government with state industrial managers. Because of large-scale subsidized credits, its stabilization policies were in tatters; soon it even gave up the leadership of the CBR to the enemies of stabilization. The sole exception was the privatization program, which was miraculously salvaged. However severe the criticism against the government, the tragedy is that it fell because of internal compromises that either Yeltsin or Gaidar considered good politics. The most damaging compromise was Yeltsin's submission to the state enterprise managers in his entourage. Ultimately, Yeltsin and the democrats failed to reach out to the Russian people; Yeltsin did not even publicly call for a referendum until December 10, 1992. Still, thanks to a decisive start, an impressive breakthrough toward a market economy had been made.

Conclusions

The launching of radical economic reform in early 1992 was an extraordinary undertaking. What was most remarkable was that such a major concerted policy change could be initiated at all. By doing so, President Boris Yeltsin displayed true political leadership, and he showed great insight into what kind of radical change was called for. Yeltsin's daring ability to find the best economic team available and to let these experts formulate his economic policy was a stunning achievement.

Given the state of the Russian debate and the prevailing political confusion, the actual reform program was surprisingly comprehensive, even if it had not been conceived as a truly "big bang." Its two key elements were a balanced state budget and far-reaching price liberalization. Within the macroeconomic sphere, however, too little attention was paid to monetary policy. In particular, very low real interest rates compromised reform. Moreover, the understanding of economic liberty was limited, and freedom in both domestic and foreign trade was lacking. As a result, price liberalization became vulnerable, and the antimonopoly policy proved regulatory rather than liberalizing. The ideas behind privatization were rudimentary and eclectic but also radical and ambitious. In the end, the general lack of initial comprehension of privatization could be rectified. The implementation of reform policies was highly dependent on the individual ministers, and their performances in office varied greatly, as subsequent chapters of this book make evident.

The reform program's political underpinnings were much worse. The positive elements included a strong political leader who had considerable power to rule by decree, a government with some skillful economic politicians, and a patient citizenry. However, the political base of the reform policy was inherently weak. The old constitution granted the parliament sovereignty, the parliament became increasingly hostile, yet no early democratic parliamentary elections were held. Hence, ordinary political parties did not develop, and the government had no political channels with which to reach out to the Russian people. The government made the situation worse by calling itself temporary and failing to present an official reform program. As a consequence, there was little popular understanding of the reform policies and minimal public education. The government's communication with politicians, the bureaucracy, the people, and the regions was dismal. Because of the lack of credibility, government policy was not taken seriously, which limited its effectiveness.

These political problems were enhanced by a crucial political misjudgment made by both Yeltsin and Gaidar, albeit for different reasons. They threw themselves into the arms of the worst enemies of stabilization: the state enterprise managers. In the traditional Soviet vein, Yeltsin thought too highly of enterprise managers. Gaidar tried to accommodate them because of his misplaced fear of populism, seeking allies against excessive wage demands. However, Gaidar seemed surprisingly unprepared for the managers' push for subsidized credits. It was as though he had been unaware of how harmful the attitude among managers had been in Eastern Europe in the early days of the transition to capitalism. That the government caved in to state managers is all the more surprising, given that both Yeltsin and Gaidar had consistently advocated and then delivered a severe blow to the military-industrial complex, from which they did not retract.

Early on, both Yeltsin and Gaidar expressed high hopes for substantial assistance from the West. In the Russian debate, these expectations were to become grounds for ridicule. Little Western aid was forthcoming, and none of it was given to help stabilization in 1992.

Considering the disarray and confusion at the time, the reform concept was reasonably sound, although it cried out for further elaboration. From the outset, it was not obvious that the macroeconomic policy would turn out so much worse than privatization. Politically, however, the reform process began badly, and the situation grew worse.

CHAPTER FOUR

Relations With Other Former Soviet Republics

IN DECEMBER 1991, the Soviet Union fell apart, and its fifteen former republics became independent countries. The breakup of the USSR was such a remarkable event that its repercussions need to be considered before examining Russian attempts at liberalization and macroeconomic stabilization. In most regards, a special economic regime continued to apply to the other former Soviet republics (FSRs), and open borders compelled FSRs to harmonize on some policies.

The greatest problems were posed by monetary, trade, and payments relations within the former Soviet Union (FSU). This chapter outlines the formation of the Commonwealth of Independent States (CIS) and identifies the specific dilemmas that arose. A review of alternative currency and payment arrangements follows, along with a consideration of what strategies various republics actually adopted toward Russia. The dissolution of the old ruble zone and attempts to construct a ruble zone of a new type are examined. The chapter concludes that economically, the process of dissolving the USSR was a costly failure.

Although the whole undertaking was fraught with uncertainties and complications, the basic issue was whether the CIS was to be an international organization, a confederation, or even a federation—that is, a country. The initial answer was certainly to form an international organization. Then, typical national concerns would have to devolve from the USSR level to the republican level, while ordinary international relations would need to be established between the newly independent states. The breakup of the ruble zone was to be one of the most painful transitions. In this case, there were only two obvious alternatives: either the USSR Gosbank would continue to operate, with full monetary authority; or the ruble zone would be broken up into various areas, each with its own independent national currency. If the currencies were convertible in relation to one another, payments would flow; and once orderly payment relations had been established, it would be easier to maintain relatively free trade.

From the USSR to the CIS

The USSR was formally succeeded by the Commonwealth of Independent States, which was first formed by Belarus, Russia, and Ukraine at a meeting in Belarus on December 8, 1991. They annulled their 1922 treaty on the formation of the Soviet Union. On December 21, in Alma-Ata, the CIS was extended to include eleven of the fifteen former Soviet republics.[1] Only the three Baltic republics (Estonia, Latvia, and Lithuania, whose independence had been recognized by the USSR in August 1991 after the abortive coup) and Georgia chose to stay out.[2] After almost two years of devastating destabilization, Georgia became a member of the CIS in late 1993.[3]

Commonwealth is an appropriate designation for the CIS, as it alludes to the British Commonwealth. The CIS was created for multiple and not very explicit purposes. For Russian imperialists, the establishment of the CIS offered consolation for the loss of the USSR and hope for its rebirth. For those who wanted a definite end to the Soviet empire, the CIS was a useful mechanism to abolish it peacefully. For others, the CIS was a useful international organization for the resolution of common problems among the FSRs. Because the real purpose of the CIS was not more clearly defined, it aroused little political controversy; but its efficacy suffered. The CIS functioned as a universal forum for talks and had no supranational powers. It held numerous meetings at a high level. Many agreements were concluded, but few were implemented. CIS decisions were simply not taken seriously.

The number of participants in CIS agreements varied. Azerbaijan, Moldova, Ukraine, and sometimes Turkmenistan often opted out. The remaining seven countries (Armenia, Belarus, Kazakhstan, Kyrgyzstan, Russia, Tajikistan, and Uzbekistan) formed the core of the CIS.

The breakup of the Soviet Union was remarkably peaceful because Russia, the dominant republic, dissolved the union at the behest of President Yeltsin. Russia was home to 50 percent of the population of the USSR and accounted for about 60 percent of its GDP. Politically, the CIS might have been a convenient arrangement because it was flexible, not supranational, and functioned unobtrusively. A fundamental concern within the CIS was the potentially explosive problem of 25 million ethnic Russians living in other FSRs, primarily Ukraine, Kazakhstan, and Belarus. In Russia itself, 83 percent of the 148 million inhabitants (about 123 million people) were ethnic Russians. Another problem was the presence of 27,000 nuclear warheads in Russia, Ukraine, Kazakhstan, and Belarus—and the large quantity of conventional arms spread all over the FSU.

Economically, the usefulness of the CIS was limited because of its vagueness of purpose and lack of efficacy. Too few decisions were reached, and far too late. CIS agreements were unspecific and rarely enforced. Moreover, there was no enforcement mechanism apart from embargoes, military action, or threats of either. Economics was only one aspect of CIS relations, and it appeared to be subordinate to both political and military concerns. The latter prompted political leaders to tread cautiously; but important economic decisions tended to be made either unilaterally or through bilateral agreements.

At the inception of the CIS on December 8, 1991, the prime ministers of Belarus, Russia, and Ukraine issued a Declaration on Coordination of Economic Policy. This was an agenda for subsequent negotiations, implying far-reaching coordination. However, the declaration was not binding, and its significance was therefore limited. The three countries agreed to pursue "coordinated radical economic reforms" and "to build economic relations and accounts on the basis of the existing monetary unit, the ruble; to introduce national currencies on the basis of special agreements, guaranteeing the observance of the economic interests of the parties." They pledged "to conclude an interbank agreement, oriented toward the limitation of monetary emission, the assurance of an effective control over the money supply, and the formation of a system of mutual accounts."[4] The three governments also committed themselves to coordinate budget deficit cuts, price liberalization, social protection, foreign economic policy, and some aspects of tax policy, and to maintain a common economic sphere. In addition, a settlement needed to be reached on the foreign debt of the FSU. All these issues were supposed to be agreed upon by the CIS within the ensuing three weeks.

This initial declaration displayed the hubris and lack of realism that characterized the CIS. These monumental tasks could not possibly have been resolved so fast. However, Russia did heed the protests of the other CIS members and delayed its price liberalization by half a month, until January 2, 1992. Conversely, the other CIS states undertook limited price liberalization and price adjustments. A significant coordination of changes in tax policy took place, notably the introduction of a value-added tax (VAT) by several CIS states in January 1992. However, no accord was ever reached on economic reform or economic policy in general, and the CIS members were never to agree on such substantive decisions again.

The issues of Soviet foreign debt and claims, as well as Soviet property abroad, led to long negotiations, primarily between Russia and Ukraine. At the end of 1991, in real terms, the Soviet Union had a huge net debt in convertible currencies of $56.5 billion (see table 2-7). It had formal claims on third world countries of up to $150 billion, but these loans were poorly regulated in legal terms, made over the very long term, and at extremely low interest rates (2 to 3 percent a year). Many loans were denominated in rubles, which were to be sharply devalued. But worst of all, most of the loans were owed by chronically insolvent countries, such as Cuba. Therefore, their market value might have been only one-tenth of that nominal value or even less.[5] The Soviet gold reserve was officially declared to be as little as 242 tons in September 1991.[6] The USSR had also held other precious metals and a diamond reserve, about which no information was available, but the total value was assessed at no more than a couple of billion dollars. The USSR had also owned a few banks and many overseas embassies, including real estate. Legally, it would have been exceedingly complicated to divide all these debts and claims, and each claim would have had to be renegotiated.

To simplify matters, Russia proposed taking over all Soviet foreign debts and assets. It would accept a disproportionate debt burden; all FSRs, however, would benefit from a swift resolution of the debt, facilitating their access to new international credits. All of the other FSRs accepted Russia's bid readily, with the exception of Ukraine. Finally, Ukraine conceded, rendering the rescheduling of the Soviet debt possible. On May 17, 1993, the Russian Council of Ministers issued a decree affirming that Russia took the responsibility for servicing the debt of the former USSR as of December 1, 1991, with the FSRs ceding their shares of common assets as of that date.[7]

The important property issue was resolved early on with surprisingly little rancor. Property of the FSU was simply taken over by the country in which it was located.

Dilemmas Posed by the Collapse of the Soviet Union

Much confusion has arisen over the economic implications of the collapse of the Soviet Union. They are easier to understand if the issues involved (of which there were at least six) are first identified:
—Currency area and monetary authority;
—Domestic economic system;
—Foreign trade regime;
—Exchange rate mechanism;
—Payments mechanism; and
—Financing.[8]

The heart of the problem in trying to form a new relationship between the FSRs was a vast inconsistency between currency area and monetary authority. The only remaining Soviet institution was the Soviet ruble, which was used in fifteen different countries. However, the State Bank of the USSR was dissolved at the end of 1991 and divided into fifteen new republican central banks. As Milton Friedman has pointed out: "The key feature of a unified currency area is that it has at most one central bank with the power to create money."[9] The FSU had fourteen central banks too many. Each central bank could expand the money supply by issuing ruble credits. But only the Central Bank of Russia (CBR) could issue cash, for the simple reason that all of the printing presses for Soviet rubles were in the Russian Federation. Nevertheless, credits are also money. This lack of unified responsibility over monetary policy made it next to impossible to begin monetary stabilization. Either the ruble zone had to be broken up, with one monetary authority in each currency area, or the central banks would have to merge into a single monetary authority.

When Russia changed its domestic economic system, all of the FSRs were affected, because of Russia's dominance within the FSU and their long-standing interdependence. Russia had unilaterally decided to liberalize prices and to introduce a new tax system with a high VAT. It encouraged the other FSRs to follow its lead.

Another significant issue was foreign trade between the FSRs, which needed some regulation. When the old command economy collapsed, barter proliferated within the USSR. Quantitative trade barriers were introduced by republics and regions alike. Export barriers sprang up all over, because many goods were sold domestically at low, fixed, subsidized prices. For those republics that had not chosen economic liberalization and a market economy, state monopoly remained the natural foreign trade system. These countries wanted to conclude annual bilateral trade agreements, and domestically they maintained state orders for exports. The free-market alternative was of course free trade, but there was also an intermediate option of protectionist trade policies with quotas and tariffs between the FSRs.

Finding a suitable exchange rate mechanism was yet another issue linked to the breakup of the USSR. The exchange rate must be adjusted to the economic system. The communist choice was multiple, arbitrary, fixed exchange rates, whereas the market option was a unified exchange rate. It can float, or it can be pegged or fixed to a stable currency or currencies. However, in relation to unstable currencies (as new post-Soviet currencies were likely to be), the exchange rate of a national currency should float. Otherwise, if one currency is weak it could destabilize others.

The choice of payments mechanism (which is completely different under socialism and capitalism) also needed to be resolved. Under socialism, money was passive. A payment was essentially a recording indicating the fulfillment of a plan target. If payments were not made, the state paid up one way or the other. A socialist enterprise did not bother to confirm whether it had been paid, and the mechanisms for checking payments were in any case inadequate. But everything changed with the introduction of a market economy. All of a sudden, buyers had an interest in delaying payments, because they could reap profits from the money in the meantime—and they did. Sellers had to start claiming their payments, which turned out to be very difficult, because the payments system was bureaucratic and nontransparent. Therefore, a seller could not easily check whether a buyer had actually paid. Furthermore, it was impossible to claim a delayed payment, as both legislation and the legal system were undeveloped and ineffective. Moreover, with high inflation, delayed payments were inflated away, offering ample incentives to offenders. Significant technical and legal improvements were required.

A final consideration was financing, which was an integral factor of many issues. Most FSRs and Russian state enterprise managers wanted subsidies from Russia. The subsidization took several forms. Under Soviet rule, Kazakhstan and the Central Asian republics received substantial grants from the union budget, on the order of 15 to 20 percent of their GDP. These subsidies disappeared with the breakup of the Soviet Union, putting Central Asia in a precarious financial position. Another financial flow arose from internal Soviet trade. Certain republics (Azerbaijan, Belarus, Georgia, Russia, and Ukraine) had had persistent trade surpluses within the USSR. This had in turn benefitted Kazakhstan and the Central Asian republics, which had total internal trade deficits on the order of 12 percent of their GDP in 1987–89. However, Russia's trade surplus with the rest of the USSR was only about 0.5 percent of its GDP.

A third but implicit price subsidy rose out of Soviet price distortions, because energy prices were relatively underrated. Hence, the energy exporters—Russia, Turkmenistan, and Azerbaijan—were subsidizing the other FSRs. If Russia's interrepublican trade had been valued at world market prices rather than actual domestic prices in 1990, Russia would have gained 37 percent in terms of trade in relation to the other FSRs, according to IMF calculations. The implicit trade subsidy Russia extended to most other union republics exceeded one-tenth of its GDP.[10] A fourth financial flow of massive dimensions materialized as the USSR broke up and inflation rose. Inflation tax, arising from the issuance of money, became an important source of financing. The more credits one country issued, the larger its share of the total GDP of the ruble zone, as long as the other members of the zone did not undertake sanctions. This was a serious free-rider problem.[11] It can also be seen as a form of the prisoners' dilemma. The optimal solution for all would have been monetary restraint, leading to monetary stabilization. However, because the republics distrusted one another, each was prone to issue more credits than was desirable for the common good, driving the ruble toward hyperinflation.[12]

In conclusion, reactions to the economic dilemmas faced by the FSU can be divided into two groups. The reformers emphasized monetary stabilization, liberalization, introduction of new stable economic conditions, and abolition of subsidies, in the hope of a market-oriented restructuring of trade. The conservatives, on the contrary, wanted to minimize both systemic and structural changes in inter-FSU trade, in the hope that the fall in production would be minimized. Because the conservatives focused on production in the short term, the societal costs of subsidies, regulations, and inflation were secondary to them. However, political and national arguments as well as technicalities complicated opinions within the ruble zone, as shall be seen. As Jeffrey Sachs and David Lipton have written: "The monetary problems facing Russia are perhaps the most complex in world history."[13]

Alternative Currency and Payments Arrangements

Among Western economists, there is broad consensus that free prices and free trade are desirable. But there is a wide spectrum of opinion with regard to currency and payments arrangements. When the USSR broke up, there were various options: a maintained ruble zone, a payments union, multilateral clearing, bilateral clearing, barter, payments in hard currency, or payments in new convertible national currencies.

The fundamental problem with the ruble zone, as Jeffrey Sachs and David Lipton argue, was that there was *"no realistic possibility*" of controlling credit in a system in which several independent central banks each have the independent authority to issue credit."[14] Members of the CIS tried to reach consensus on a banking union at the end of 1991. However, Russia and the other CIS countries differed fundamentally on two issues. First, Russia advocated one monetary authority with technical control over the issuing of money (both Central Bank credits and cash): the other CIS republics, while agreeing on credit limits, wanted to maintain their own central banks. Second, Russia demanded weighted votes related to GDP (as in the IMF), but the other states would not accept a Russian majority.[15] It was evident from the outset that it would be impossible to agree on a monetary regime that could control inflation in one common ruble zone.

Even so, many argued in favor of such a maintained zone. Its core supporters were the industrial lobbies both in Russia and the other FSRs. The industrialists were against arduous restructuring to market conditions. They also wanted subsidies from the Russian government, which the ruble zone facilitated. Conservative governments in the other republics had a double incentive to preserve the ruble zone: Both their country and their state enterprise managers—their key constituency—would make money at Russia's expense.

Russian neoimperialists also favored the ruble zone, because they wanted to reestablish the USSR (or the Russian empire). On this issue, they enjoyed uncommonly broad support. Even the otherwise liberal Grigory Yavlinsky has consistently favored a monetary union. Other Russians feared unnecessary disruption or did not want to antagonize the other FSRs by excluding them from the ruble zone. The nostalgia for empire often seemed subconscious.

Ironically, some anti-Russian nationalists (typified by some Ukrainians) also favored maintaining the ruble zone, but only to reap temporary benefits from the inflation tax. Eventually, they aspired to an independent currency as a manifestation of national independence.

What is most ironic, however, is that this position taken by the uninformed, rent-seeking, and irresponsible nationalists was initially also shared by both the IMF and the European Commission. The IMF advocated the maintenance of the ruble zone and threatened that countries that launched their own currencies would not receive any IMF support. At a CIS meeting in Tashkent May 20–21, 1992, the IMF made a formal proposal to the central banks of all the FSRs regarding a system for managing the ruble area: "First, each republican central bank would agree to set a limit on the expansion of its net domestic assets" (that is, credits). "Second, the monetary authorities in all states would agree to set uniform central bank lending rates and reserve requirements; to establish a common, unified exchange system; and to facilitate the settlement and clearance of payments throughout the ruble area."[16] In addition, the CBR "will agree to provide enough ruble currency to the central banks of other states in the ruble area to satisfy the demand for currency in these states."[17]

Under this plan, every central bank would have been permitted to issue rubles, with no effective control on compliance. The IMF memorandum vaguely suggested that the CBR could impose penalty interest rates or suspend the right to obtain ruble currency or other credits.[18] However, with the poor reporting methods, this could only occur after a serious destabilization, and it would mean making a difficult political decision in the face of strong lobbies. Oddly, the IMF proposal ignored financial and economic reform policies.[19] The CBR immediately rejected the proposal as unworkable, because it lacked unified control over emission, allowing each party to act as a free rider.

It is difficult to understand how the IMF could come up with a proposal that would make monetary discipline impossible. The IMF was skeptical of the technical ability of the new states to manage their own currencies. Its main argument was that currency reform should not take place before a country was prepared to pursue credible macroeconomic stabilization. The IMF did not want a new currency to fail, nor did it want to be involved in such a failure. Another reason was that the financial burden of most FSRs seemed overwhelming, and the IMF wanted Russia to carry some of that burden. Moreover, the IMF proposal was politically convenient, because initially about half of the FSRs wanted to stay in the ruble zone.[20] Curiously, Russia had to insist on an arrangement that provided reasonable monetary discipline, in opposition to the IMF.

The European Commission went even further than the IMF in support of the maintenance of the ruble zone. The EC ambassador to Moscow, Michael Emerson, drew far-reaching parallels between the CIS and the European Community, arguing in the Russian press: "Economists argue whether a common market really also requires a common currency. I believe that it does. A single monetary unit more fully uncovers the advantages of economic integration, according to my view."[21]

A substantial (and entirely Western) literature accepted the introduction of independent national currencies but opposed convertibility. A payments union or multilateral clearing was favored instead, in line with the European Payments Union (EPU), which existed from 1950 to 1958.[22] The idea was first presented for eastern Europe, when the Council for Mutual Economic Assistance (CMEA) trade system collapsed in 1991, and it was even more strongly advocated for the FSU. One reason was that CMEA trade had been based on multilateral clearing through one commonly owned bank. The intention was to develop a smoothly functioning payments system and to economize on scarce hard currency. John Williamson has explained the purpose:

> A clearing union is an arrangement in which the member countries agree to accept one another's currencies in payments for exports, deposit their earnings from those exports with the agent of the union, allow the claims to be consolidated and periodically netted out on a multilateral basis, and then settle the remaining imbalances centrally with the union in hard currency. This arrangement permits the establishment or maintenance of current account convertibility while achieving major economies in the need for hard-currency reserves because it is only net imbalances that have to be settled in hard currency, rather than each individual transaction. A payments union has the additional feature that the resulting imbalances

are settled in a mixture of credit and hard currencies, thus further economizing on the need for hard-currency reserves.[23]

Although many Western economists favored a payments union, this view
found little support in the FSU, which knew how badly multilateral clearing
had functioned within the CMEA. Any surplus from one country had been
a cheap credit to countries with deficits. The few local supporters of a payments union appear to have acted for tactical reasons. They were interested
above all in maintaining the ruble zone, and talks about a payments union
fudged the monetary issue and delayed the separation of currencies. To
them, the idea of a payments union was vague and grand enough to
generate long unproductive talks within the CIS.

It is not by chance that a payments union or multilateral clearing has
failed to evolve, either in Eastern Europe or in the FSU.[24] The arguments
for a payments union focus on the shortage of liquidity for foreign trade
transactions and the need to economize on hard currency. But the problems within the FSU were much more profound. The basic problem was
a lack of trust at all levels: between the FSRs, between enterprises in
these states, and between the states and enterprises. This lack of trust
was compounded by the absence of both transparency and legal sanctions. In addition, very high inflation and minimal real interest rates
made the incentives to delay payments overwhelming; under these conditions, it was simply irrational for an enterprise to pay a bill. The essential problem was not financial but moral: how to get anyone—states or
enterprises—to pay when no legal collection mechanisms existed. A huge
and rising structural deficit between Russia and most of the other FSRs
was perceived by the non-Russian FSRs as unjust. The EPU had been a
reflection of the wishes of the West European countries to draw closer
together after World War II. But many FSRs, on the contrary, sought to
distance themselves from Russia. Finally, both the systemic and structural
changes had to be far greater for the FSRs than they had been in postwar
Western Europe. The collapse of old intra-FSU trade flows was both
inevitable and desirable. The focus needed to be on creating a robust
mechanism to facilitate direct contracts between enterprises and the swift
evolution of new, economically beneficial trade. Any clearing agreement
had to make allowances for some credit or delay of payment, and the
prevailing attitude was that any credit was a gift. It was difficult enough
for one enterprise to press another to pay. If the payments were to be
centralized to the state, unnecessary middlemen would appear, obscuring
transparency and further reducing the possibility of payment.

In short, there were few parallels between the FSU and postwar western Europe. Any complexity or shared responsibility had to be avoided in the FSU because of the lack of ethical standards. The only real similarity the FSU had to postwar Europe was that several adjacent countries suffered from a shortage of hard currency, but that would not be a sufficient argument for payments unions in other parts of the world. In reality, the arguments for a payments union became arguments for the ruble zone.

Bilateral clearing was never considered a plausible option by anyone. The problems arising from lack of trust and legal sanctions were the same as with multilateral clearing, but distortions were greater and more financing would have been needed. Such clearing had been attempted among various CMEA countries in 1991, after the collapse of the old CMEA trade system, but invariably it failed in no time. Moreover, talks on trade and payments were pursued within the multilateral framework of the CIS. Payments in hard currency were also not a viable option. Because hard currency was in such short supply, there was too little liquidity to encourage such payments.

In the absence of other payments mechanisms, barter within and between the FSRs developed spontaneously after the collapse of the old command system. One estimate sets the share of sales among Russian enterprises based on barter at 80 percent in January 1992 and even higher in late 1991, but the barter share fell swiftly to 20 percent by March 1992 because of domestic liberalization in Russia.[25] Barter's great disadvantage is that it entails large transaction costs, which limit the number of transactions and bar small deals. But the initial popularity of barter in the post-Soviet period clarifies that it also had important advantages. Barter was one means for an enterprise to hedge against high inflation. It can be considered a primitive form of indexation, because two traded commodities were both likely to rise in price. Through barter, enterprises could also protect themselves against swings in relative prices. Price regulations could also be evaded, if enterprises exchanged commodities that were equally undervalued in relation to market price. Barter facilitated evasion of both taxes and currency regulations; much of the capital flight is explained by underinvoicing in barter deals. It was even easier to secure payments through barter, because money was more elusive than deliveries of goods, which the producer wanted to sell in any case. Finally, in many cases there was simply a need for mutual deliveries between two enterprises, and barter resolved their financing.

The only sensible alternative to the ruble zone was the introduction of independent national currencies that should then be made convertible, at least on current account. Such a solution had all the advantages. It would create the basic precondition for macroeconomic stabilization: one monetary authority responsible for monetary policy in each currency area. The financing and liquidity problem for interstate transactions would be solved, because payments could be made in one of the new convertible currencies. The problem of lack of trust could best be handled between enterprises in different states; under convertibility, they would be able to make direct payments to one another. Convertibility would naturally render trade and payments multilateral and was by no means unattainable. On the contrary, as Jeffrey Sachs has put it: "Convertibility can be achieved with the stroke of a pen, simply by discontinuing the state's role in the foreign exchange market. . . . Convertibility just means a unified market price for foreign exchange, but not necessarily a stable price for foreign exchange."[26]

Another major concern was that one country would suddenly introduce its own currency, without allowing any exchange for ruble banknotes, which would then flood other FSRs. Therefore, Russia demanded that any country that launched its own currency should allow the exchange of old ruble banknotes, which should subsequently be taken out of circulation. The countries that undertook early currency reforms complied with that demand, but in Ukraine, a paltry 0.1 percent of its ruble issue was recovered.[27] In the fall of 1993, the worst flood of banknotes hit the CIS states that had kept the Soviet ruble after it had been annulled in Russia.

The radical Russian reformers, headed by Yegor Gaidar, were in favor of the earliest "nationalization of the Russian ruble" to create the preconditions needed for monetary stabilization. Gaidar had put these demands on record before he took office but worried about practical problems, such as getting new Russian banknotes printed. He reckoned the technical preparation for monetary reform would take at least nine months.[28] In late 1991, all of the foreign advisors to the Russian government advocated a swift separation of the Russian ruble from the other post-Soviet currencies. They contended that if other FSRs wanted to stay in the ruble zone, they should be allowed to do so, but only if they submitted to a united monetary authority. In return, they would receive their due shares of seignorage, credits, and cash.[29]

Many nationalists in other republics were in favor of independent currencies, because they considered them symbols of national independence. The Baltic liberal nationalists combined their wish for independent national currencies with their aspirations for macroeconomic stability.[30] However, there was little understanding of macroeconomic stabilization outside of Russia and the Baltics.

The obvious historical parallel is not the establishment of the EPU but the collapse of the Hapsburg Empire after World War I. Only one country that arose from the former Hapsburg Empire acted appropriately with regard to national currency policy, namely Czechoslovakia. At the earliest instance, over a two-week period in February and March 1919 while the borders were closed, Czechoslovakia stamped the Austro-Hungarian notes circulating within its borders. Its currency was made fully convertible from the outset, and Czechoslovakia pursued highly conservative fiscal and monetary policies. While hyperinflation erupted in the other states that were formed from the Hapsburg Empire, Czechoslovakia pursued deflation. Its economy flourished between the world wars, while those of the other Central European states foundered. Czechoslovakia was also the only country in the region that maintained full democracy until it was occupied by Germany.[31]

Although there are several theoretically possible monetary arrangements, the real choice for the FSU was between the decomposing ruble zone and the introduction of independent national convertible currencies. The ruble zone had no advantage. It generated irresponsible monetary policies and high inflation. It did not provide a proper payments mechanism. The old intra-CIS trade broke down while the ruble zone was in place, and conditions did not stimulate new trade. The longer a country stayed in the ruble zone, the more inflationary its economic conditions were likely to become, given competition in being the most irresponsible and an overflow of currency from other states. Even so, the ruble zone prevailed. The natural outcome of all this was hyperinflation in no less than ten of the fifteen former Soviet republics in 1993. This means that for at least one month these FSRs had a monthly inflation rate of at least 50 percent (see table 4-2 below).[32]

Alternative Strategies of Other Former Soviet Republics

Every FSR had to make a choice regarding monetary regimes. Each faced a variety of concerns. Having a currency was a potent symbol of national independence. A national currency was also a necessary precondition for monetary stabilization. But membership in the ruble zone implied receiving cheap raw materials and credits from Russia. Besides, every FSR needed to manage its relationship with Russia well. Even if the Russian leadership was divided between reformers and conservatives, membership in the ruble zone was generally perceived as doing Russia a favor, and departure would be considered an affront. Although many states altered their stand or were unable to formulate policies, the FSRs can be divided schematically into three groups.

The first group consisted of the three Baltic states—Estonia, Latvia, and Lithuania—who were later joined by Kyrgyzstan. The Baltic states had already attained their independence after the August 1991 coup, and they had chosen to stay outside the CIS. They wanted to introduce their own full-fledged independent national currencies early on, both to symbolize national independence and to undertake domestic stabilization. Their aim was restructuring. They did not care whether they lost inflation tax or subsidies from Russia. They were prepared to take full responsibility for their economic policies and face the ensuing costs.[33]

A second group took the opposite line. It included the countries whose leaders felt closest to Russia: Kazakhstan, Uzbekistan, Tajikistan, Armenia, and Belarus. Belarus had little economic policy or sense of nationality. Therefore, many Belarusians did not mind returning to the Russian embrace. The leadership of Kazakhstan was, for both economic and political reasons, anxious to stay close to Russia, not least because of Kazakhstan's large Russian population. Uzbekistan did not have a highly developed economic policy, so its adherence to the ruble zone appears somewhat accidental and conditioned by its lack of rational economic thinking. Tajikistan was torn by civil war and was the least able to pursue an economic policy. It needed both political and economic support from Russia. These four countries were ruled by old communist elites and minimized their systemic changes. Armenia, in contrast, had a democratic leadership and a reform government, but it was locked into a war with Azerbaijan and crippled by an embargo. It needed Russian support in foreign policy.

The third group of FSRs intended to opt for independent currencies eventually. In the meantime, however, they tried to reap as many subsidies and as much inflation tax as possible from Russia. But most striking was their confusion and lack of responsible economic policies. Members of this group included Ukraine, Moldova, Georgia, Azerbaijan, and Turkmenistan.

The introduction of independent currencies tended to occur in steps. Because of a shortage of cash in the first half of 1992, several republics started issuing a coupon as currency at par with the ruble. Russia retaliated against some republics that overran their technical credits by intermittently cutting them. In a possible third step, either the coupon or a newly issued currency became the single national currency, apart from the Soviet ruble, while account money was simultaneously nationalized. Finally, coupons were exchanged for a national currency. The real currency reform is the third step—when a national currency (both cash and bank accounts) becomes independent, with its own exchange rate in relation to the ruble. However great the importance a nation's people attach to the circulation of a national currency with its own name, this is a mere formality, if the actual currency reform has already occurred and no confiscation takes place.

The Baltic countries introduced their own currencies in 1992. Estonia was first, launching a full-fledged convertible currency, the kroon, on June 20. On July 20, Latvia turned its ruble coupons into an independent national currency, and finally on October 1, Lithuania did the same.[34] On May 10, 1993, Kyrgyzstan inaugurated the som, a fully convertible currency, as its sole legal tender. All these countries introduced their currencies on their own initiative. But they made agreements in advance with Russia on the exchange and disposal of old ruble notes and other relevant issues, and the Russian government approved of their currency reforms.

After having been cut off from technical credits from Russia, Ukraine declared its coupon the sole Ukrainian legal tender on November 12, 1992.[35] The third group of countries was otherwise prompted to introduce their own independent currencies after the CBR had declared old Soviet ruble banknotes invalid, making the Russian ruble a solely Russian currency on July 24, 1993. These remaining countries launched their independent currencies as quickly as possible but were not at all prepared to pursue sensible monetary policies. Consequently, all were thrown into hyperinflation. Georgia made its coupon an independent currency on August 2, 1993. Turkmenistan put its manat into circulation on November 1, and Moldova its leu on November 29.

The loyalist group of FSRs, however, were compelled to leave the ruble zone at about the same time. Belarus had a coupon in circulation as of May 1992 and was subsequently expelled from the ruble zone by Russia. Nevertheless, it tried to use both Russian rubles and its own

Table 4-1. *Introduction of New Currencies*

Country	Currency	Date of Currency Reform
Estonia	Kroon	June 20, 1992
Latvia	Coupon (Lat)	July 20, 1992
Lithuania	Coupon (Litas)	October 1, 1992
Ukraine	Coupon	November 12, 1992
Kyrgyzstan	Som	May 10, 1993
Russia	Russian ruble	July 24, 1993
Belarus	Coupon	July 24, 1993
Georgia	Coupon	August 2, 1993
Turkmenistan	Manat	November 1, 1993
Kazakhstan	Tenge	November 15, 1993
Uzbekistan	Sum-coupon	November 16, 1993
Armenia	Dram	November 22, 1993
Moldova	Leu	November 29, 1993
Azerbaijan	Manat	January 1, 1994
Tajikistan	Soviet ruble	None

Source: International Monetary Fund, *Economic Review: Financial Relations Among Countries of the Former Soviet Union* (Washington, D.C.: February 1994), pp. 42–49.

coupons. After negotiations on a ruble zone of a new type broke down in November 1993, Kazakhstan suddenly launched its tenge on November 15, Uzbekistan its sum-coupon on November 16, and Armenia its dram on November 22. By December 1993, only Tajikistan still used Soviet rubles. All the loyalists were subsequently thrown into hyperinflation.

This is a devastating picture. In the end, only Russia and the four countries that had opted for an early and orderly departure from the ruble zone through unilateral currency reform escaped hyperinflation (see table 4-2). Estonian currency reform was undertaken with the assistance of independent Western experts.[36] The Latvians instigated their currency reform quite independently, and the Lithuanians followed the Latvian example.

The IMF resisted every currency reform until each had already been initiated. Only in Kyrgyzstan did the IMF play an integral role. Otherwise, each currency reform was decided unilaterally, and the IMF was taken by surprise, making little or no contribution to the reform's design. The collapse of the ruble zone in the second half of 1993 was a welcome event, but it occurred far too late. Moreover, although this collapse had appeared inevitable since late 1991, the countries left in the ruble zone were not in the least prepared. The immediate consequences were therefore disastrous. The dissolution of the ruble zone was hardly better managed than the equally destructive breakup of the Austro-Hungarian

Table 4-2. *Annual Inflation in the Former Soviet Republics,*
1992 and 1993

Percent, December over December

Country	1992	1993
Latvia	959	35
Estonia	953	36
Lithuania	1,163	189
Azerbaijan	1,464	810
Russia	2,526	847
Kyrgyzstan	1,771	1,228
Uzbekistan	906	1,514
Kazakhstan	1,165	2,170
Belarus	1,925	2,329
Moldova	2,198	3,222
Tajikistan	732	7,326
Ukraine	1,865	8,940
Georgia	1,465	8,942
Turkmenistan	624	9,952
Armenia	2,028	10,922

Note: The inflation rates are derived from official national statistics. They reflect either the retail price index or the consumer price index.

Source: Joakim Karlsson, "Former Soviet Republics: Widely Differing Performance," *Östekonomisk Rapport*, vol. 6, no. 6 (May 17, 1994), p. 3.

krone zone, although this highly applicable historical precedent was widely discussed. The Baltic and Russian radical reformers (notably Gaidar) showed better understanding of monetary fundamentals than the IMF.

Decay of the Ruble Zone

The demise of the ruble zone was an arduous process. The driving forces were the Russian reformers, who wanted to stop Russian subsidization of the other FSRs; and the recipients, who wanted cheap financing to continue. Everyone had an interest in the flow of payments and trade. During the first half of 1992, no real Russian strategy on the ruble zone had evolved. After July 1992, the Russian reformers tried to stop open-ended technical credits to other FSRs, and they succeeded in doing so in April 1993. From then on, massive cash flows to other FSRs partially replaced the former credit flows. But they were suddenly terminated with the Russian exchange of old Soviet rubles in late July 1993, which effectively ended the ruble zone.

First Half of 1992: One Irresponsible Currency Area

In the first half of 1992, a Soviet-style interstate trade system evolved, and no real currency policy was formed. In January 1992, the FSRs found themselves in dire straits. Output was already falling sharply, and official domestic and interstate trade was collapsing; enterprises simply had no interest in selling to one another at fixed prices far below those of the world market. January 1992 brought four severe external shocks to the FSRs. First, all USSR budget subsidies to the Central Asian states ended. Then price increases and price liberalization changed the terms of trade to the benefit of Russia. The USSR had defaulted on its foreign debt payments in December 1991, which in turn blocked all FSR access to international financing. Finally, the old foreign trade system (based on foreign trade organizations in Moscow) ceased to function. The IMF has assessed the total decline in official transfers from Russia and the deterioration in trade from 1992 to 1994 at more than $15 billion, or about 15 percent of the combined GDP of the other 14 FSRs in 1994.[37] All concomitant problems were to be handled in a ruble zone with fifteen independent central banks, each issuing one nonconvertible currency for which there were thousands of exchange rates. Moreover, noncash money in bank accounts could not even be withdrawn freely. Therefore, exchange rates varied for cash and noncash money, respectively.

Most of the non-Russian CIS members responded by demanding a minimum of change, notwithstanding the fact that several contemplated issuing their own currencies. The CIS members tried to continue to obtain their supplies from Russia as much as possible, at preferential fixed prices and with cheap Russian financing. Because these countries had made few domestic reforms and opted for centralized state-run foreign trade, they wanted minimal changes in the trade system. They therefore insisted on the preservation of state orders issued in Russia by the Russian Ministry of the Economy (the former USSR State Planning Committee, or Gosplan). Interstate deliveries were administered by the Russian central purchasing agent Roskontrakt, which originated with the USSR State Committee for Material and Technical Supplies (Gossnab). The Russian reformers failed to gain control of this complex area, and the conservative Russian officials in the Ministry of the Economy and Roskontrakt were happy to accommodate the other CIS members. In this way, Russia complied with the wishes of the conservative CIS members, and so-called interstate trade became one of the most regulated areas of the Russian economy.

On February 14, 1992, all eleven CIS members signed the "Agreement on the Regulation of Relations Between the States of the Commonwealth in the Field of Trade and Economic Cooperation in 1992."[38] But in reality, little was settled. The parties agreed to use only the ruble for payments made to one another, but individual states were still entitled to introduce their own national currencies. The trade arrangements were thus contradictory, envisioning both free market arrangements and bilateral government agreements regulating trade through quotas and licenses.

In line with this agreement, CIS members concluded bilateral interstate trade agreements for 1992. Their purpose was defensive: to secure traditional markets and supplies. These agreements had essentially three components. The first consisted of what was considered obligatory trade, sanctioned by an interstate trade protocol and covering about 150 so-called strategic goods, such as energy and key inputs. This was traditional communist foreign trade—that is, from government to government. Prices were fixed and governments had to ensure delivery. Obligatory trade was exempt from export taxes and import tariffs but subject to export licenses and quotas. The second component of interstate trade was based on what were called indicative lists of 1,000–1,500 commodities, designated for trade between enterprises; but these commodities were also subject to export licenses and quotas. This was a communist form of decentralization of foreign trade. Finally, the third component of interstate trade comprised the remaining goods, which were assigned for free trade between enterprises, without export licenses or quotas. However, export taxes and import tariffs applied.

The trade agreements for 1992 targeted bilaterally balanced trade. The interstate protocols accounted for only about 70 percent of the 1991 volume off these goods, and deliveries invariably fell short of the targets. On the whole, total interstate trade fell by about 50 percent between 1990 and 1992, and by 30 to 35 percent in 1992 alone. In addition, a chronic trade imbalance arose. All the other CIS countries delivered far less to Russia than they had promised, while Russia came closer to meeting its delivery targets. Without functioning borders or customs offices, statistics on interstate trade are especially unreliable, but the picture is clear enough (see table 4-3). In 1992, Russia had a trade surplus with every CIS state, and in 1993 with all but Azerbaijan and Uzbekistan.

Table 4-3. *Trade Between Russia and Other Former Soviet Republics, 1992 and 1993*

Billions of current rubles

	Trade balance 1992	Russian exports 1993	Russian imports 1993	Trade balance 1993
Ukraine	295.3	7,365	3,647	3,718
Kazakhstan	242.4	2,386	1,414	972
Moldova	12.4	402	112	290
Belarus	64.7	2,205	1,966	239
Turkmenistan	62.7	194	86	108
Kyrgyzstan	17.4	208	112	96
Tajikistan	24.6	97	34	63
Armenia	21.9	69	17	52
Georgia	21.7	42	26	16
Azerbaijan	27.2	167	181	− 14
Uzbekistan	163.7	735	1,026	− 291
Total	954.0	13,870	8,621	5,249

Sources: Goskomstat Rossii, *Sotsial'no-ekonomicheskoe polozhenie Rossii 1993 g.* (The socio-economic situation in Russia, 1993) (Moscow, 1994), p. 91; Pavel Teplukhin and Tatyana Normak, "Trade Between States of the Former Soviet Union (FSU)," *Russian Economic Trends*, vol 2, no. 4 (1993), p. 95.

In 1993, Russian exports to other CIS members exceeded imports from them by 61 percent. (In reality, the Russian trade surplus was probably even greater, because Russia produced more attractive export goods than the other FSRs.) Russians complained more and more frequently that, contrary to common agreement, the other FSRs reexported Russian goods out of the FSU. Furthermore, the Russians protested the smuggling of cheap, price-regulated Russian commodities through other republics (notably exports of metals through Estonia).[39]

The complex and nontransparent CIS trade regime, with extensive state orders and low, regulated prices, was completely different from the normal and much more liberal Russian foreign trade regime. Enterprises had no real incentive to comply with bureaucratic intergovernment trade, and decentralized interenterprise trade was subject to cumbersome restrictions. The stage was set for a severe collapse of mutual trade.

Russia was caught between two contradictory exigencies. Because of its huge trade surplus in intra-CIS trade, Russia was under pressure to check its balance of payments, to avoid financing the trade deficits of other FSRs. Conversely, the CBR was anxious to facilitate payments with CIS members. Eventually, Russia did restrain its exports to other FSRs. Its recorded trade surplus as a share of GDP declined from 5.3 percent

Table 4-4. *Russia's Trade Surplus With Other Former Soviet Republics, 1992 and 1993*

	1992	1993
GDP (trillions of current rubles)	18.1	162.3
Trade surplus (billions of current rubles)	954	5,249
Trade surplus (percent of GDP)	5.3	3.2

Sources: Goskomstat Rossii, *Sotsial'no-ekonomicheskoe polozhenie Rossii 1993 g.*, pp. 7, 91; Teplukhin and Normak, "Trade Between States of the Former Soviet Union (FSU)," p. 95.

in 1992 to 3.2 percent in 1993 (see table 4-4). Moreover, Russia sharply reduced its supplies of attractive and scarce export goods, such as oil, to CIS countries (a 60 percent decrease between 1991 and 1993), while it reduced supplies of plentiful natural gas by much less (8 percent).[40]

Payments and financial flows, however, had a life of their own. They seemed surprisingly unrelated to the recorded trade balance. Table 4-5 shows some startling figures compiled by the IMF. In 1992, the CBR financed no less than 91 percent of Tajikistan's GDP and 49 to 70 percent of the GDPs of Uzbekistan, Turkmenistan, Georgia, and Armenia. These financial flows were larger than total Russian exports to these countries. Thus, these "exports" were sheer gifts from the Russian state,

Table 4-5. *Financing of Other States by the Central Bank of Russia (CBR), 1992*

Year-end 1992 CBR correspondent account position

	Billions of rubles	Percent of GDP
Russia	−2,109	−11.7
Tajikistan	36	90.7
Uzbekistan	292	69.9
Turkmenistan	172	53.3
Georgia	69	51.5
Armenia	34	49.0
Azerbaijan	51	25.8
Kazakhstan	407	25.5
Kyrgyzstan	42	22.9
Ukraine	862	21.7
Moldova	27	11.3
Belarus	102	10.7
Estonia	4	4.0
Lithuania	9	3.2
Latvia	2	1.0

Source: International Monetary Fund, *Economic Review: Financial Relations Among Countries of the Former Soviet Union*, p. 26.

because the credits were either interest free or at rates so low the Russian claims were inflated away. In the case of war-torn Tajikistan and Armenia, this financing appears to have been intentional; but there is no plausible explanation but corruption for the massive financing of Uzbekistan and Turkmenistan.

These statistics reflect that for a long time, the CBR chose a middle way that failed to achieve either speedy payments or financial control. At the beginning of 1992, the CBR converted the interrepublican payments system inherited from the State Bank of the USSR into a set of bilateral correspondent accounts with the central banks of the CIS states. Through these accounts, the CBR and the Russian government hoped to monitor the balance of payments. Every commercial bank was instructed to direct all transactions with FSRs through correspondent accounts at the CBR. However, the CBR had 1,400 payments centers, which could process interstate payments independently and automatically. Given their slow reporting systems, monitoring was impossible. The CBR tried to concentrate interstate payments into its 82 main branches. As a result, payments were clogged in the pipeline and delayed, and reporting remained too slow to allow actual monitoring. Moreover, there were no effective sanctions against violators.[41]

The legal barrier between cash and noncash money was maintained. Although cross rates on exchange markets showed that this barrier was of little significance in Russia, it was important in other republics. A shortage of cash began to emerge in August 1991.[42] The main cause was rising inflation, which increased the nominal demand for cash while the printing of money lagged behind. The massive price rise in January 1992, multiplying prices by a factor of 3.5, caused an acute cash shortage in Russia and the other FSRs, and the share of cash in the money supply fell. Russia delivered currency free of charge to all members of the ruble area but gave itself preference. The CBR first raised alarm about the cash shortage in the fall of 1991, but the USSR Ministry of Finance, which was responsible for the printing of banknotes, did nothing until December 1991. The introduction of new banknotes in larger denominations also had to be approved by the Supreme Soviet, and the prevailing notion was that inflation was caused by money printing. Many did not realize that credits are also money. The Russian Supreme Soviet was therefore reluctant to allow the printing of new banknotes in higher denominations. Finally it did, and the cash crisis was resolved in the third quarter of 1992. In the meantime, six countries in the ruble zone introduced coupons that were circulated along with the Soviet ruble: Ukraine, Belarus, Latvia, Lithuania, Azerbaijan, and Moldova.[43]

July 1992: Russia Attempts to Set Credit Limits

From early July, the Russian government tried to restrict credits to other CIS states. But the CBR under Viktor Gerashchenko, on the contrary, expanded credits. On June 12, 1992, Ukraine announced that it would double its money supply through an enormous credit expansion to settle interenterprise arrears. This was done unilaterally without consulting other governments.[44] Russia responded with unusual swiftness, issuing a presidential decree on June 21, "Measures to Defend the Monetary System of the Russian Federation."[45] This decree offered the other FSRs a choice: They could either leave the ruble zone, introducing a national currency; or they could continue to use the ruble and coordinate their monetary policy with the other FSRs. Russia also set a ceiling on technical credits beginning July 1. The technical credits were offered at the CBR's low refinance rate. The CBR centralized all interstate payments through one Moscow office and created a new system of bilateral correspondent accounts. Under this system, payments from another FSR could not be processed unless that state stayed under its technical credit ceiling. If an FSR exceeded it, its currency would be decoupled from the ruble zone.

In effect, the account rubles of the various countries assumed different market values. They became separate currencies on July 1, 1992, as could be seen on the free currency market in Riga. Meanwhile, the cash ruble remained of equal value in all FSRs. Russia then unified the exchange rate of its ruble, which became convertible on current account. The exchange rate floated and was set at a twice-weekly interbank auction in Moscow. Russia had also prepared its Russian ruble note (and no others) for printing.[46] A reasonable transitional arrangement seemed to have been organized before the full separation of the ruble currencies.

However, this arrangement had little effect. The credit limits of the FSRs were exceeded without public notice. One important reason was that the antireformist Gerashchenko took over as chairman of the CBR in July 1992, and the CBR's working relationship with the Russian reform government ceased. The CBR even expanded its technical credits to other republics (not the least of which was Ukraine), arguing that trade links would suffer otherwise.[47] A massive financial flow opened up. During

Table 4-6. *Financing From Russia to Other Former Soviet Republics, 1992 and 1993*

	1992		1993 (Jan.–Sept.)	
	Billions of rubles	*Percent of Russia's GDP*	*Billions of rubles*	*Percent of Russia's GDP*
Central Bank of Russia correspondent accounts and technical credits	1,545	8.5	1,032	1.1
Government loans	2	—	119	0.1
Commercial bank correspondent accounts	−30	−0.2	−675	−0.7
Enterprise arrears	163	0.9	—	—
Total identified financing	1,680	9.3	476	0.5
(in billions of dollars)	(8.5)		(0.6)	
Currency issue	565	3.1	1,928	2.1
Implicit trade subsidy at 1992 average exchange rate	2,385	13.2	—	—

Source: International Monetary Fund, *Economic Review: Financial Relations Among Countries of the Former Soviet Union*, p. 25.

the first half of 1992, credits of 325 billion rubles (or about 5 percent of Russia's GDP) had been issued by the CBR to the other FSRs. These credits skyrocketed to 1,220 billion rubles during the second half of 1992, although the ceiling Russia and the IMF had agreed to for that period was 215 billion rubles.[48] For all of 1992, total Russian financing of other CIS states amounted to 9.3 percent of its GDP. In addition, the implicit Russian trade subsidy was assessed by the IMF at no less than 13.2 percent of its GDP. Thus, in 1992, Russia gave away as much as 22.5 percent of its GDP to other FSRs (see table 4-6), probably slightly more than it had in 1991. This burden was far too great and also posed a serious moral hazard to the receivers, because it rewarded those who were the most irresponsible.

The limits on technical credits proved ineffective. If a country had exhausted its technical credits, payments were quickly blocked, and there was no other legal way of paying. In general, commercial banks were not allowed to maintain independent decentralized correspondent account relations with commercial banks in other FSRs. After the separation of the noncash rubles in July 1992, all of the non-Russian FSRs saw their noncash rubles devalued in relation to the Russian ruble, because of their balance of payments deficits. However, no legal currency market existed. Soon, markets for noncash rubles from various FSRs developed in some countries (notably in Riga beginning in August), but their capacity was small and access was limited.[49] The natural response of an FSR that had exceeded its technical credit limit was to overwhelm the CBR Moscow office with unfunded payments until the CBR gave up and raised the limit. Gerashchenko did so willingly, anxious to protect commercial links while caring little about monetary stabilization.[50] Even so, payments collapsed and inflation ran rampant.

Despite the severe monetary crisis, the CIS heads of state met in Kyrgyzstan's capital, Bishkek, and concluded their "Agreement on a Single Monetary System and a Concerted Monetary, Credit, and Exchange Rate Policy of the States Which Have Retained the Ruble as Legal Tender" on October 9, 1992. The eventual outcome of this agreement was something quite different—namely an "Agreement on the Establishment of an Interstate Bank," which was signed by ten CIS members at the summit in Minsk on January 22, 1993. Originally conceived as a possible central bank of the ruble zone, the Interstate Bank was transformed into a multilateral clearing center based on the Russian ruble.

The rationale for the Interstate Bank was that it should economize on scarce settlement reserves through multilateral netting. However, as has been discussed, this was not one of the central issues—which included the imposition of monetary discipline and the flow of payments. The Russian reformers resisted the creation of the Interstate Bank, because they considered it another device to diffuse responsibility and diminish transparency in monetary policy, thus facilitating the politicization of credits. In essence, the Interstate Bank would increase pressure for more "technical credits" from Russia and reduce the possibility of withstanding such pressure. Organizing the Interstate Bank cost scarce management capacity, but the bank was superfluous and did not solve any problem. The other FSRs resisted the idea of an Interstate Bank, because it implied closer political ties with Russia. After numerous ineffectual meetings and slow ratifications, the Interstate Bank was finally founded in December 1993, but it is unlikely to take on any real role. It received little support from anyone except for the European Community and the IMF. Yet most CIS states did not want to reject the idea immediately, because they wanted ongoing subsidies from Russia. The CBR saw the Interstate Bank as a means of maintaining the ruble zone. Ultimately, the prolonged discussions about the Interstate Bank delayed finding solutions to the relevant problems.[51]

April 1993: Russia Ends Technical Credits

When Boris Fedorov became deputy prime minister and acting minister of finance in December 1992, the Russian government renewed its attempts to resolve monetary relations between and among FSRs. Fedorov's primary ambition was to put an end to technical credits, which had proved uncontrollable. Initially, he restricted them through the Russian government's Commission on Credit Policy. On April 20, the Russian Supreme Soviet finally decided to terminate technical credits to CIS states and to allow only intergovernmental credits allocated through the Russian state budget. Subsequently, budget limits applied, which were controlled by the Russian Ministry of Finance. From January 1 to April 20, about 850 billion rubles in technical credits were issued, but only 510 billion rubles were disbursed in intergovernmental credits for the rest of 1993.[52] Still, Kazakhstan (the strongest proponent of a unified ruble area) benefitted from unlimited technical credits, and the CBR used these credits as an inducement to the FSRs to stay in the ruble area.[53]

Another important measure taken by the Russian government during the first half of 1993 to put interstate finances in order was the consolidation of interstate balances into long-term state debt. Russia concluded such agreements with all FSRs except for the Baltic states and Azerbaijan. The ruble claims were converted into dollar- or special drawing rights (SDR)-denominated claims valued at $6 billion. (SDR is an artificial currency unit based on a basket of international currencies managed by the IMF.) Interest was set at commercial rates, with specified repayment conditions.[54] These agreements effectively impeded further loans from Russia. The conditions were fairly stringent, but they were meant to be a deterrent.

However, the CBR did not cease with its mischief. Ruble currency continued to be delivered to other CIS states by the CBR, free of charge and without restrictions. After the Ministry of Finance managed to tighten credits, the CBR transferred large volumes of cash instead. During three months (from April 21 to July 28), the CBR shipped 580 billion cash rubles to the other ruble zone countries for free. In fact, cash transfers exceeded technical credits to CIS states in the first seven months of 1993, and much of the cash was used for payments to Russia. The distribution of cash was extremely uneven. For example, during the first seven months of 1993, the CBR issued twice as much cash per capita to

Turkmenistan and 30 percent more per capita to Kazakhstan as it did in Russia.[55]

In 1993, the efficiency of cross-border payments improved considerably, because commercial banks were allowed to deal directly with one another through interstate correspondent banking. In parallel with this improvement, exchange markets continued to develop. The year marked the beginning of capital flight to Russia from FSRs with less stable currencies. During the first nine months of 1993, the net inflow to Russian banks totalled 675 billion rubles. Increasingly, enterprises in other FSRs paid Russian enterprises in Russian rubles from their own ruble accounts in Russian commercial banks.[56]

July 1993: Demonetization of the Soviet Ruble

In July 1993, because of a surprise currency reform in Russia, the ruble zone simply ceased to exist. On Saturday morning, July 24, the CBR suddenly announced that all Soviet and Russian banknotes issued before 1993 would become worthless on Monday, July 26.[57] Russians were permitted to exchange only limited amounts of money. The people reacted by panicking, and their outrage was directed against the Russian government. Everyone rushed to the savings banks, flooding them with crowds for days. This all took place in the middle of the holidays, leaving many Russians stranded without valid legal tender in other FSRs. After an amendment, through a presidential decree issued on July 26, Russians were allowed to exchange sufficient amounts of money, minimizing the confiscatory effect in Russia. Of 5.1 trillion rubles worth of currency circulating in Russia, only 1.7 trillion rubles were supposed to be Soviet and Russian pre-1993 banknotes. The rest were Russian banknotes issued in 1993. According to the CBR, 2.2 trillion rubles of old banknotes circulated in other FSRs.[58] Therefore, this decree was essentially directed against the other FSRs. The official explanation was that Russia was being flooded with cash from other FSRs and had to defend itself by nationalizing the ruble. The Russian government declared that the purpose of the measure was "to stabilize the monetary circulation in the country."[59]

As of July 1993, ten countries still used Soviet rubles, and the demonetization threw their economies into complete disarray. Three countries with parallel coupons (Azerbaijan, Georgia, and Moldova), as well as Turkmenistan, decided on swift currency reforms; but unprepared as they were, they all experienced instant hyperinflation.[60] The remaining six countries in the ruble zone suffered severe cash shortages. The CBR had essentially only provided them with pre-1993 rubles while running the risk of also being flooded with rubles. All six were at a loss.

The demonetization of old banknotes was decided on by the CBR, though Prime Minister Chernomyrdin and President Yeltsin were informed and acquiesced to the decision. The Russian Ministry of Finance, however, was kept in the dark.[61] The currency exchange made no sense. The CBR had insisted on delivering large amounts of cash without conditions to other FSRs until the very last minute, fighting for the preservation of the ruble zone. It had announced a gradual exchange of the old Soviet banknotes on July 6, but without confiscation.[62]

The actual motives behind the CBR's actions remain a matter of speculation, but the most plausible explanation is political. Presumably, the CBR wanted to undermine the president and the government (in collusion with the Supreme Soviet, which protested vehemently and benefitted from not being involved). The currency reform marked the end of a liberal offensive and the beginning of a conservative backlash, which was to last until the parliament was dissolved on September 21, 1993. Another motive might have been the CBR's wish to shock the FSRs that remained in the ruble zone into subordination. A third possibility is corruption. According to CBR data, 2 to 3 trillion more rubles were exchanged than had previously been accounted for.[63]

Ominously, this was a typical Soviet measure, devoid of consideration for both the law and the public. Its instigator, Viktor Gerashchenko, as chairman of the State Bank of the USSR, had previously undertaken an equally disruptive and economically harmful monetary reform in January 1991. At that time, all banknotes in 50-ruble and 100-ruble denominations had been declared void. The USSR had been frozen in its tracks for three days. People had scrambled in panic to salvage their cash; but in the end, little was actually confiscated.

The July 1993 exchange of banknotes also had many negative effects within Russia. The political and psychological impact was probably the worst. Public confidence in the government and state institutions eroded. The mildly confiscatory action of the CBR violated a number of Russian laws, but no legal recourse was taken. Furthermore, Russia defied CIS agreements that it would notify the other ruble zone countries in the event of a currency reform. Consequently, confidence in money was undermined, which made it more difficult for the government to sell bonds to finance the budget deficit and curb inflation. The ruble's exchange rate did not fall because the CBR intervened strongly. In August 1993, monthly inflation unexpectedly reached 26 percent, the high for the year.[64]

A Ruble Zone of a New Type

In spite of the ruble demonetization, six stalwart FSRs tried to re-establish a ruble zone. However, their attempts soon fell through. After July 1993, four FSRs remained undecided on a currency reform and had not introduced any currency coupon. These most ardent supporters of a ruble zone—Kazakhstan, Uzbekistan, Tajikistan, and Armenia—were faced with a desperate monetary dilemma. Once again, they tried to reach an agreement with Russia. Kazakhstan and Uzbekistan rushed to sign a trilateral agreement with Russia on a new ruble zone on August 6. Under the terms of this agreement, the CBR would run monetary policy, and the pre-1993 rubles in Kazakhstan and Uzbekistan would be replaced with new Russian rubles.

This trilateral agreement was swiftly superseded by a multilateral "Agreement on a 'Ruble Zone of a New Type'," which was signed in Moscow on September 7 by six countries: Russia, Armenia, Belarus, Kazakhstan, Tajikistan, and Uzbekistan.[65] The agreement was initiated by the CBR. It was a reflection of a conservative offensive and was resisted by the reformist Russian Ministry of Finance.[66] The multilateral agreement was vague and provided rules for the transitional period with regard to coordination of monetary, fiscal, banking, and foreign exchange regulations. This framework agreement was followed later that month by bilateral agreements between Russia and each of the other five countries.

The goal of these agreements was a reunified currency area. In the meantime, however, the signatories could continue to use their existing currencies or introduce new ones. Although the agreements stated that the ruble would be emitted by the CBR alone, they also declared that "[the other] Side will carry out credit emission within limits agreed to with the Russian Side," thus allowing for multiple emittance centers. The bilateral Russian agreement with Uzbekistan stipulated an incredibly brief transition period of only two or three weeks. During that period, a far-reaching coordination of economic policies and legislation—encompassing money supply, the budget deficit, and interest rates—was to be accomplished. But evidently, no such swift coordination was practicable or politically feasible.[67]

Once again, CIS countries had concurred on a series of unrealistic agreements. The question was only when and how they would come crashing down. A crucial concern was that it was unclear whether the parties could receive new Russian ruble notes before they had fulfilled the stipulated conditions, or only afterward. In its bilateral agreement with Russia, Kazakhstan had managed to include an article (seemingly by a Russian oversight) that Kazakhstan would obtain Russian ruble notes freely as soon as it had ratified the agreement. The crunch came after Kazakhstan's ratification in late October 1993. Russia declared itself willing to supply new Russian banknotes, but only if the other countries provided collateral in gold or foreign exchange corresponding to the value of 50 percent of the new banknotes delivered. Another disagreement concerned the conversion rate for the old rubles in other countries. The Russian government advocated the market exchange rate, whereas the other states (together with the CBR) countered that every old ruble should be exchanged for one new Russian ruble.[68]

The failed attempts to form a new type of ruble zone were victories for the reformers within the Russian government, primarily Boris Fedorov and Yegor Gaidar. In the aftermath of the dissolution of the Russian parliament on September 21, the political wind had once again shifted in a liberal direction. Kazakhstan, Uzbekistan, and Armenia were all compelled to introduce their own currencies, but all were struck by hyperinflation. Tajikistan held on to the old Soviet ruble and was consequently flooded with rubles from other countries, which sent it staggering into severe hyperinflation.[69] For stability and humanitarian reasons, Russia supplied Tajikistan with new Russian rubles through a special state credit.[70]

In the fall of 1993, a further attempt was made to harmonize trade relations among the FSRs, culminating in the signing of a framework treaty for a comprehensive economic union by nine states on September 24.[71] Like most CIS agreements, it was extremely ambitious but not especially concrete. It envisioned a gradual deepening of integration through the progressive establishment of a free trade zone, a customs union, a common market, and a monetary coordination system. Internal tariffs were to be phased out and external tariffs harmonized.[72]

Monetary Union With Belarus

When the political wind once again turned conservative, Russia made a last attempt to restore a ruble area, but this time only with Belarus. The Russian parliamentary elections on December 12, 1993, dealt a severe blow to the Russian reformers. Subsequently, the CBR was emboldened and plotted another attempt at reviving the ruble zone. On January 5, 1994, Viktor Gerashchenko, Prime Minister Viktor Chernomyrdin, and their Belarusian counterparts sprang a surprise. The chairmen of the two central banks signed the "Agreement on the Order of the Unification of the Monetary System of the Republic of Belarus With the Monetary System of the Russian Federation and the Mechanism of the Functioning of the Common Monetary System," and the prime ministers signed a declaration on the impending monetary union.[73]

The most controversial point in the agreement was that the National Bank of Belarus would be entitled to issue credits within a limit it had agreed to with the CBR. This meant that once again there would be no effective, unified control over emission, heralding a return to monetary irresponsibility. Moreover, only the week before, the new Russian Constitution had come into effect. Article 75 clearly stated: "Monetary emission is exclusively carried out by the Central Bank of the Russian Federation."[74] The agreement on a monetary union with Belarus was thus a blatant breach of the newly adopted constitution. Yegor Gaidar and Boris Fedorov cited this as a prime reason for their resignations from the Russian government that January.[75] They also protested the intent to exchange devalued Belarusian rubles at par for Russian rubles, which would imply a substantial transfer of resources. Moreover, the economic policies of the two countries remained completely different. Belarus controlled many prices and had a larger budget deficit and far higher inflation than Russia. The final flaw was that the agreement foresaw the monetary union being concluded by the governments without any ratification by the parliaments, which also contradicted the new Russian constitution. As preconditions for a possible monetary union, Fedorov demanded that the CBR be the single bank of emission, that the exchange of money take place at the market exchange rate, and that any agreement be properly ratified by the two parliaments.[76] In Belarus, the National Bank and some nationalists regretted that their country would lose much of its sovereignty by joining the union.

Although the agreement appeared almost finalized, it was fundamentally revised. On April 12, 1994, the prime ministers of Russia and Belarus signed a new two-part agreement on a monetary union. The first part implied free trade and the lifting of trade and customs barriers between the two countries as of May 1. The second part contained the actual monetary union. The CBR was supposed to be the only bank of emission, with an exchange rate of 1:1 (although the market exchange rate of the Belarusian ruble had slumped to one-tenth of the Russian ruble). The one-time cost of the currency exchange to Russia could raise the Russian price level a few percentage points at worst. (This would be an exact parallel to the West German exchange of East German marks in 1990.) Such an exchange rate, however, would render Belarusian exporters uncompetitive, but that appeared to be of little concern. The new agreement on the monetary union required ratification by both parliaments.[77] The issue of monetary union between Russia and Belarus had been economically and legally contained, and it became a question of Belarusian sovereignty and limited Russian cost. But after the presidential elections in Belarus in July, the whole agreement was just put aside.

Conclusions: A Costly Failure

The peaceful political dissolution of the Soviet Union was impressive. But the economic effects of the dissolution of the ruble zone were disastrous. Three key problems in the economic relations between the FSRs had to be solved. First, the inherited monetary system, with fifteen central banks issuing one currency within one ruble zone, was patently unstable. It pushed the countries within the zone to compete at over-issuing credits, causing high and rising inflation. Because none of the newly independent countries was prepared to accept Russian supremacy in monetary policy, the only plausible solution was to divide the ruble zone into fifteen currency areas, each with its own supreme monetary authority.

In addition, there was no functioning payments mechanism for trade between the FSRs. The problem was manifold. There was no mutual trust. Excessive centralization prevailed. Legal sanctions and incentives for timely and effective payments were absent. Technical channels for payments were weak, and liquidity was scarce. The task was to find the

simplest and most transparent solution to facilitate direct payments between enterprises in different countries. The best means to make such
payments was in convertible currencies with unified, market-adjusted
exchange rates.

Yet another difficulty involved opening up market-oriented trade between the FSRs, which required the liberalization of trade and prices.

All three of these problems called for solutions that were as quick and
clear-cut as possible, to avoid disruption of trade opportunities. Meanwhile, much of the old trade would have to be discontinued as unprofitable and inefficient.

The Gaidar team realized that these were their objectives, as did the
Baltic reform leaders. However, the Russian reformers faced overwhelming resistance from an alliance made up of state enterprise managers,
Russian neoimperialists, conservatives in other FSRs, and the IMF.
Moreover, during the breakup of the USSR, economic concerns had been
subordinate to political and military demands, making caution and gradualism the norm. The old rent-seeking elites, both in Russia and the
FSRs, saw the nontransparency of the CIS arrangements as an excellent
veil for exacting subsidies from the Russian state. Russian neoimperialists
hoped to hold the USSR together. Nationalists in other FSRs aspired to
exact the largest transfers possible from Russia. The IMF also chose this
stand, apparently preferring collective destabilization to the risk of unsuccessful monetary reforms.

The dissolution of the ruble zone proceeded in stages, determined by
the domestic power struggle in Russia. Yegor Gaidar and Boris Fedorov
in particular on the government side fought against the CBR under Viktor
Gerashchenko. Curiously, however, Gerashchenko dealt the death blow
to the ruble zone through the demonetization of the Soviet ruble on July
24, 1993. Further attempts at reviving the zone have proved fruitless.

At first glance, the dissolution of the ruble zone might appear to have
been fast. However, the statistics shatter any illusion of success. No less
than ten of the fifteen countries in the FSU experienced hyperinflation
in 1993. When currency reforms eventually took effect, the countries
concerned were completely unprepared. The window of opportunity for
radical economic reform, which was immediately after independence, had
been wasted in most of these countries. Massive and arbitrary transfers
from Russia to the most perfidious FSRs and to state managers all over
the FSU put a premium on irresponsibility and also destabilized these

economies. Although the ruble zone was maintained, old trade collapsed and little new market-generated trade could develop under such restrictive conditions.

The economic dissolution of the Soviet Union was an intellectually and technically demanding challenge, one for which outside intellectual assistance was potentially useful. The Russian and Baltic reformers did have foreign advisors, who shared their urge for swift establishment of a tenable dissolution that would encourage responsible behavior. However, the mainstream of Western economic discussion was preoccupied with the European Payments Union of 1950–58, focusing on the tertiary problem of liquidity and the choice between bilateral or multilateral clearing. The IMF played a harmful role. It tried to maintain the dysfunctional ruble zone, and it failed to prepare the FSRs for their necessary and inevitable currency reforms. The lessons garnered from the dissolution of the Hapsburg Empire were highly applicable and widely discussed among Western economists. Nevertheless, the West failed to bring these lessons to bear on the all-too-similar breakup of the Soviet empire.

CHAPTER FIVE

Liberalization

A FUNDAMENTAL feature of a market economy is freedom of enterprise.[1] In a market economy, individuals should have the right to create, manage, profit from, and liquidate their private enterprises. Enterprises should have the right to decide what to produce and how to produce it, what to buy and sell, and with whom to do business. Other inalienable rights should include the ability to determine prices freely and to conclude contracts voluntarily. Any state infringes on these rights to some degree, but the rights themselves must be extensive. The crucial difference between a socialist economy and a market economy is whether enterprise managers look more to the state or to the market to earn their money— that is, whether they seek rents (subsidies) or profits. (The state is, of course, also obliged to defend the rights and liberty of enterprises against criminals, as well as to enforce contracts and to provide measures to handle externalities.)

However important it may be, freedom of enterprise is a necessary but insufficient condition for a functioning market economy. An enterprise awash in money—that is, one with a soft budget constraint—has little reason to struggle to turn a profit or to compete with other enterprises, regardless of whether its money comes from the state or a rich uncle. Enterprises with soft budget constraints are in some ways worse than monopolists, because they do not care about what buyers want, and a seller's market prevails. An enterprise must first recognize that money is scarce (and thus be subject to hard budget constraints) if it is to expand its sales and profits. A hard budget constraint is best imposed through strict fiscal and monetary policy (discussed in chapter 6). Only enterprises

137

that are hungry for profits compete and break through barriers to trade, for competition is itself no obvious pleasure. At first glance, it is often difficult to assess a market's shortcomings: is it a monopoly? are there obstacles to trade? does it lack hard budget constraints? Often it is a bit of each, and the question then centers on which one is stronger—the barriers to trade or the enterprises' urge for profits. The Russian debate, however, has focused excessively on the presumed strength of monopoly producers. Risks and high transaction costs upset the functioning of the market. Still, a market can exist even if enterprises are predominantly state owned, as long as those enterprises work for profit. This is known as market socialism, which has existed in several countries, albeit with limited success. For the strategic orientation of enterprises, private ownership is especially important in the longer term.

Liberalization has turned out to be surprisingly difficult to accomplish in Russia in comparison with eastern Europe. One reason is that Russian legislation on liberalization has suffered from lack of coordination and disputes over jurisdiction. At the top, the government or president adopted decrees on fundamental issues, while the Supreme Soviet promulgated laws that increasingly ran counter to government policy. At a third level, branch ministries and other remnants of the command economy made decisions based on old rules, regardless of whether or not those rules had been revoked. At yet another level, regional authorities were explicitly awarded substantial rights to regulate the economy. As a consequence, one government body after another created regulations, and the counterweights against the various regulators were weak. In 1993, almost 48,000 federal government instructions were issued.[2] Entrepreneurs could take the authorities to arbitration courts, and frequently did, but arbitrariness prevailed both in law and legal practice. The legislative system remained biased in favor of regulations. It was difficult enough to adopt liberalizing laws, but to implement liberalization was far more challenging. The heart of the matter was that power—not law—is what truly mattered in Russia. The legalization of liberalization was therefore a moot point.

The first section of this chapter is devoted to the fundamental issue of establishing domestic freedom of enterprise, followed by a discussion of the liberalization of foreign trade. The focus then shifts to particularly problematic areas in the deregulation of the Russian economy: antimonopoly policy, the energy sector, and agriculture. A final section addresses concerns raised regarding whether Russia is failing in its liberalization because of excessive organized crime.

Domestic Liberalization

The domestic freedom of enterprise comprises several different elements: free prices, trade, and production, as well as the freedom to establish enterprises. In Russia, production had already been formally liberalized through the Law on Enterprise and Entrepreneurial Activity in 1990.

The price system was in a state of complete confusion in 1991. The overwhelming aspiration of the last Soviet government was to raise prices to improve the market balance. However, the government was so weak that it tried all kinds of tacit means of doing so, being concerned more with politics than economics. Prices that were not particularly sensitive were raised, regardless of costs or demand. Production prices—but not retail prices—were significantly liberalized in January 1991. Thus, producer prices were allowed to rise, but not consumer prices. Flexible "contractual" prices accounted for 40 percent of the total volume of goods in light industry, 50 percent in machine building, and 25 percent in raw materials. In April 1991, the government at long last revised retail prices, and the general retail price level increased by about 70 percent. The share of fixed prices was reduced to 55 percent of the volume of retail goods, with regulated prices accounting for another 15 percent and "contractual" prices for 30 percent. A free commercial sector also evolved with unregulated and very high prices, as it absorbed some excess demand.[3] As a result, price distortions grew ever greater. The only rationale behind this socialist price system was the political weakness of the government.

The focus of Russian radical reform was on far-reaching deregulation of prices. The reform team was convinced that prices should be free and only natural monopolies should be subject to price regulation. They also believed in a swift, comprehensive decontrol of prices at the start of the transition process.[4] Price liberalization was imposed through a presidential decree of December 3, 1991, "Measures to Liberalize Prices," which solemnly declared that "on January 2, 1992, [the Russian Federation would undertake] the basic transition to free (market) prices and tariffs, formed under the influence of demand and supply" on producer goods, consumer goods, services, and labor. Prices for state procurement of agricultural produce were also supposed to be free of regulation.[5]

Few commodities were excluded from price liberalization. In principle, 80 percent of producer prices and 90 percent of consumer prices were free (in value terms, at 1991 relative prices).[6] Among producer goods, energy and transportation were essentially excluded from price liberalization, and most prices were raised administratively by a multiple of five. Among consumer goods, prices were fixed for a selection of the most basic goods: some kinds of bread, milk, kefir, curd cheese, baby food, salt, sugar, vegetable oil, vodka, and matches, as well as medicine, energy, collective transportation, rent, and public utilities. The idea was to assure the Russian people that these products would be cheap enough to keep them from starving. Most of these prices were raised administratively by a multiple of three and were decontrolled from March to May 1992 without dramatic effect.[7]

In addition, however, regional authorities were allowed to set maximum prices for basic foodstuffs and services as they deemed necessary, though they had to cover any subsidies from their regional budgets. Regional authorities were also entitled to impose maximum markups for consumer goods, and a ceiling of 25 percent became the standard. Although the aim was to liberalize prices, the government decree contained a Soviet-style admonition to various authorities "to reinforce the control of the observance of state price discipline." Instructions on reinforced price control were promptly issued.[8]

The long-awaited price liberalization took place as announced on January 2, 1992. Before, tremendous fear had reigned. People in general seemed to believe the world would go under altogether, or at least fall apart. They thought the sky was the limit for unregulated prices, as existing free prices tended to be extremely high, because of the huge monetary overhang. The authorities, worried about a possible explosion of popular anger, brought in extra police on the day of price liberalization, but nothing happened. No sign of social unrest was reported.[9] Prices rose by about 250 percent immediately—even more than the government had expected. Yegor Gaidar had publicly guessed that prices would rise by about 100 percent a month in January and February.[10] Soon, shortages started to diminish, and one long-unseen commodity after another reappeared in the shops. Meat and sausages, bananas and kiwifruits, and color television sets suddenly appeared. However, the arrival of new commodities in the shops was slow in comparison with what had happened during price liberalizations in Eastern Europe. An important reason was that domestic trade remained so highly regulated.

Curiously, even most Russian reformers did not greatly believe in a swift transition to free trade. On the contrary—in late 1991, they feared that trade would collapse altogether. A quasi-market conviction prevailed: The dominant view was that free prices were necessary, but few believed in the market's ability to allocate goods. Adam Smith's invisible hand was neither known nor accepted in Russia. The argument ran that private commodity exchanges only accounted for about 1 percent of wholesale turnover, and no alternative traders were prepared to replace state intermediaries. Most Russians had the weird idea that a physical market infrastructure had to take the form of an actual building, and many presumed that the state had to erect it. Moreover, the old Marxist devotion to production and contempt for trade and everything connected with it held sway.[11]

These perceptions were formed by the existing distribution system for producer goods, which were apportioned through three channels: through the old centralized allocation system with the State Planning Committee (Gosplan) and the State Committee for Material and Technical Supplies (Gossnab), directly between enterprises, and through new commercial structures. Formally, the government planned that in 1992, the old centralized allocation system would purchase 50 to 55 percent of the production of state enterprises through state orders. In reality, however, in the first half of 1992 it turned out to be barely 40 percent, because purchases were voluntary and prices remained free.[12] Not surprisingly, the hundred wholesale companies that had arisen out of the Gossnab system gradually lost market share. The system of state orders withered away, and though no straightforward deregulation had taken place, little of it remained by the end of 1993. Direct deals between producers became the dominant form of trade in producer goods instead, accounting for 60 to 70 percent of volume in 1992. Independent intermediaries were insignificant, although there were more than 20,000 independent wholesalers in June 1992.[13]

The old Gossnab structures split up and adjusted relatively smoothly to market conditions, but several other wholesale organizations continued to fight to maintain their monopolies. Rosnefteprodukt, the former State Committee for the allocation of petroleum products, still insisted on allocating gasoline. Gazprom, the former USSR Ministry of Gas Industry, reinforced its legal monopoly on the production, transportation, and sale of natural gas. The Federal Joint Stock Company Roskhleboprodukt, the former Ministry of Grain Procurement, monopolized trade in grain. The Foreign Trade Organization Exportkhleb enjoyed a monopoly on the importation of grain, and trade in timber was also monopolized. Interstate trade with other CIS countries was controlled by Roskontrakt, which arose out of Gossnab. To the detriment of consumers, the wholesale trade of food tended to be monopolized at the regional level. These regional wholesale monopolies were blamed for the sluggish improvement in the supplying of goods to retail shops, and they were popularly believed to be cooperating with organized crime.

Because of a reaction to the unsatisfactory degree of liberalization, Yegor Gaidar managed to push through a presidential decree on freedom of trade on January 29, 1992. It read: "Enterprises, regardless of their form of ownership, and citizens are granted the right to engage in trade, intermediary, and purchasing activities . . . without special permission. . . . Enterprises and private citizens may sell things . . . in any place of their convenience."[14] The purpose was to let trade develop from the bottom up, boosting competition and thus overcoming monopolism in retail trade. Prices were completely free and unregulated. The inspiration for this decree came from Poland, where retail trade had developed successfully from the streets to the shops, providing Poland with the most competitive trade sector in eastern Europe.

The popular reaction to this decree was extraordinary. Central streets and squares in big Russian cities became crowded with street traders. Anyone could engage in street trade, and anything could be bought in the street. However, public resistance soon arose against such trade. Well-to-do Russians reacted against the disorder and dirt of these disorganized "bazaars," which they held in contempt as lower-class phenomena. They wanted elegant shops. Moreover, street prices were initially higher than those of state shops, which did not adjust prices to the market, partly out of monopolistic inertia and partly because of the 25-percent legal limit on their markup. Furthermore, because anything was sold in the street and everything was in demand, quality was uncertain. People did not understand that efficient allocation of goods was a value in itself. They reacted against private traders who were primarily reselling commodities bought in state shops. Politically more important, however, was the regret felt by municipal authorities, who did not receive any revenue, legal or illegal, from the disorganized street trade. Finally, few

Russians realized that markets develop best with a maximum of liberty and competition, or that racketeers were at a loss in truly free street markets, with thousands of temporary peddlers. As soon as hawkers were registered, limited to a restricted area, or (worse still) to kiosks and shops, organized crime would assume control.[15]

Soon, revenues, bribes, and demands for order got the upper hand. Street trade in Moscow was regulated through municipal orders at the end of April 1992. The reformers in the government were already too weakened to offer much resistance. Such local mandates were given a legal underpinning through a presidential decree in late June 1992 restricting freedom of trade.[16] In obvious attempts at extortion, the police engaged more energetically in their campaign against street trade than against anything else. Such trade did not altogether disappear but did diminish sharply. Street traders were compelled to pay either the police or racketeers. In sensitive areas, such as subway stations, only trade controlled by organized crime (notably flower sales) was seen. Yet a large number of kiosks emerged. Initially, these concentrated on high value-added commodities, such as alcohol and cigarettes, but eventually they sold virtually anything. Unfortunately, kiosks developed so slowly and in such a restricted way that organized crime seemed to acquire complete control over them.[17]

Corrupt officialdom, communist prejudices, and organized crime had won over free enterprise. Consequently, shortages persisted for a surprisingly long time. In the spring of 1994, the mayors of Moscow and St. Petersburg proceeded to prohibit all street trade, restricting the number of kiosks and the commodities they were allowed to sell to the old paltry Soviet assortment.[18] Although blatant shortages had essentially ended, trade was far too restricted to permit real market saturation.

Prices were supposed to have been liberalized. Yet the old State Price Committee survived, although in a somewhat scaled-down version, and it was as communist as ever. The first deputy chairwoman of the USSR State Price Committee, Lira Rozenova, had been rejected as its chairwoman by the former USSR Congress of People's Deputies for her orthodox communist views in 1989. Strangely, at the beginning of 1992, Rozenova was appointed chairwoman of the Russian State Price Committee by Gaidar. Completely unreformed, she advocated extensive regulation of prices to combat inflation: "Exploiting their dominant position on the market, many enterprises reduce their production, creating additional shortages of production for which there is demand."[19] In short,

Rozenova wanted to fight the distortion caused by any regulation with even more regulations, in the old communist fashion.

Rozenova's moment seemed to have come in December 1992, when Viktor Chernomyrdin replaced Yegor Gaidar as prime minister. The State Price Committee presented Chernomyrdin with a long-prepared draft decree, "State Regulation of Prices of Certain Kinds of Products and Commodities," and he signed this renewed comprehensive price regulation on December 31, 1992. Fortunately, it was revoked on January 18, 1993, under the influence of the new Minister of Finance, Boris Fedorov, who described the initial signing as a "bureaucratic mistake."[20] Yet Rozenova remained at her post.

The original December 1991 decree on price liberalization had granted regional authorities the right to regulate the prices primarily of food in their region. In mid-1992, such regional restrictions were reported in 23 out of 89 regions, and a year later, in more than 50 regions.[21] Certain regions regulated prices more than the decree permitted (notably Ulyanovsk *oblast,* which was popularly referred to as "Soviet power in one *oblast*"), but the transgressors were not disciplined. Even in Moscow, gasoline prices remained under local control, prompting hour-long queues outside gas stations, even in 1994. This led to a highly criminalized black market for gasoline. Because of lingering price controls on a few commodities, queues were not abolished. Moreover, regional price regulations disrupted the national market. Any region with local price controls was prone to check the outflow of price-controlled goods; and because there were police posts at all regional border roads, this was easily done.

Freedom of enterprise received little attention. Admittedly, the Russian Law on Enterprises and Entrepreneurial Activity of December 1990 had formally done away with all restrictions on private enterprise, but these were mere words. Increasingly, local authorities demanded licensing, officially stating the need to impose order but in reality demanding more bribes. On May 27, 1993, the government gave in to these demands and issued a decree requiring regional authorities to license virtually all kinds of economic activity. The decree was sponsored by two conservative deputy prime ministers, Yury Yarov and Oleg Lobov. Formally, freedom of enterprise was seriously violated. In practice, however, little changed, as private enterprises were troubled by local executives in any case, and actual liberalization had a momentum of its own. The most disturbing aspect of this decree was that the government introduced licensing to provide local authorities with opportunities to exact more bribes.[22] It was also a blatant violation of the enterprise law.

Although local authorities interfered improperly with emerging private enterprises, they failed to collect even elementary statistics on them. For example, the State Committee for Statistics (Goskomstat) and the Ministry of Finance had different, completely incompatible series on the number of new enterprises. Because no one knew what was happening to private enterprises at an aggregate level, the concerns of such enterprises were disregarded. Ultimately, what is not measured is neglected. The reformers would have done private enterprise a good service if they had started collecting relevant essential statistics, making the development of private enterprise an important indicator of successful performance among regional authorities. However, the reformers worried that such information would be used by local authorities to control, extort, and suppress private businesses.

The liberalization of prices and domestic trade was a much slower and more arduous process in Russia than in eastern Europe. Yet gradually decontrol (or rather, the spontaneous collapse of regulations) caught on. By the end of 1993, regulations persisted in only two sectors, energy and agriculture, whose intricacies merit further discussion.

Liberalization of Foreign Trade

Foreign trade was a formidable area of liberalization.[23] (Only foreign trade outside of the CIS is discussed here.) The interests involved were particularly strong, and the stakes were high. At the end of 1991, the Russian economy as a whole was in a state of crisis, but foreign trade represented the worst expression of that crisis. All conceivable complications arose, and all were severe.

Russia's exports officially fell by $20 billion or 28 percent between 1990 and 1991. One cause was the dramatic decline in domestic production. Pervasive domestic shortages also minimized incentives to export, because anything could be sold with ease within the USSR. In addition, the abolishment of the CMEA trade system in 1991 prompted a collapse of trade between Russia and the other CMEA countries. Moreover, in December 1991, the USSR defaulted on its international debt and the inflow of foreign credits stopped. As a consequence, Russia's imports plummeted by $37 billion or 46 percent between 1990 and 1991.[24] The sharp reduction in imports was largely allocated by administrative fiat, causing acute shortages and disruption of production, which contributed to the drastic decline in GDP.

The foreign trade system was distorted and completely out of control. The old communist state monopoly on foreign trade had effectively been abolished in late 1986, when various branch ministries were given the right to pursue foreign trade independently. Soon, large state enterprises had also gained foreign trade rights, and more and more enterprises got involved. The state tried to control exports through licensing, but export licenses were easily acquired through bribery. All incentives were perverted, because of arbitrary restrictions, a multitude of so-called currency coefficients (or individualized exchange rates for various commodities and enterprises), and completely different foreign and domestic prices for goods. At that time, major export items, such as oil, cost less than 1 percent of the world market price, and the price structure was thus utterly deformed. The USSR had no unified exchange rate but hundreds of currency coefficients. In principle, these currency coefficients were supposed to equalize world prices with regulated domestic prices, but they were fairly arbitrary. The free exchange rate was extremely undervalued, with the average monthly wage in Russia at $6 in December 1991. Imports were controlled through the centralized allocation of hard currency at an unrealistic exchange rate of 1.6 rubles per dollar, or 1 percent of the market rate. This caused import subsidies to grow to 20 percent of GDP. The deformities were of such magnitude that it was difficult to imagine the effects of abolishing them, which caused uncertainty and apprehension.

In the reform government, Minister of Foreign Economic Relations Petr Aven and Yegor Gaidar himself determined the policy on foreign trade during the first year of reform. They wanted to make the ruble convertible, with a unified and market-oriented exchange rate; to liberalize foreign trade; and to replace quotas and licenses with tariffs. Through deregulation, the government hoped to alleviate distortions and rent-seeking and stimulate economic efficiency and structural change. However, the acute crisis raised several concerns. The government was anxious to maintain exports but was also afraid that export revenues would not be repatriated or that foreign trade taxes would not be collected. Underinvoicing and capital flight pursued by irresponsible state enterprise managers were worrisome. At the same time, the government wanted to alleviate shortages of essential goods, such as food and energy.

The government faced strong vested interests of the old system. Domestically, there were few main producers of vital export items, such as oil, natural gas, and metals, and they therefore possessed strong bargaining power. The same was true of energy exporters and the food import monopoly. The Ministry of Foreign Economic Relations (MVES), with its powerful foreign trade enterprises, was a force in its own right. The Ministry of Finance and the Central Bank of Russia (CBR) monitored Russia's financial interests, but a variety of interest groups (such as Russian traders) influenced decisionmaking as well. Moreover, the other former Soviet republics (FSRs) had a say in many issues that also concerned them; and without functioning borders between them, the FSRs were highly interdependent. Finally, foreign banks and governments (whose financial claims Russia was unable to service) had compelling demands, even as these same foreign governments offered new commodity credits.

Despite these complications, a substantial liberalization of foreign trade went into effect in January 1992, but it was far less than the reformers wanted. Foreign trade was the sphere in which reforms were the least radical. As a result, inconsistencies abounded, necessitating frequent legal changes in foreign trade regulations. Excessive restrictions bred instability; virtually every month, the foreign trade system was amended. To some extent, these alterations were also connected with political cycles. Sergei Glaz'ev, who succeeded Aven as minister of foreign economic relations from December 1992 to September 1993, aggravated the instability. Although Glaz'ev was young and had a doctorate in economics, he was trapped in the mold of old Soviet thinking. His main objectives were to recentralize foreign trade to the MVES (which in any case carried out one-third of foreign trade through its foreign trade organizations) and to protect Russian industry through high import tariffs.[25] Fortunately, his power was too limited for him to do much damage. Yet clear dominant trends prevailed (which shall be examined) and after Glaz'ev's resignation, foreign trade regulation stabilized.

From the outset, all enterprises were given the freedom to engage in foreign trade. Although convertibility was a high priority with the reformers, they did not dare to introduce it at the beginning of 1992. Their great fear was that hard currency revenues of Russian exporters would be kept abroad. This was a serious problem, especially because Russia's reserves of foreign currency were depleted. In principle, all export earnings were supposed to be repatriated to Russia, but that stipulation was

widely disregarded with impunity. A mixed system of surrender requirements was instigated, based on hopes of capturing hard currency earnings
in one way or another. It was therefore exceedingly complex. Although
the system of multiple currency coefficients was abolished for exports,
three new exchange rates were introduced. Exporters were obliged to
first surrender 40 percent of their hard currency earnings to the CBR at
a fixed rate of 55 rubles per dollar. Then an additional 10 percent had to
be surrendered at what was supposedly the "commercial rate," which
was fixed at 100 rubles per dollar. The free market exchange rate, set at
biweekly currency auctions in Moscow, became the official exchange rate.
This vacillated but averaged 155 rubles per dollar in the first half of 1992.
On the import side, however, so-called centralized imports persisted for
vital goods, with a multitude of highly subsidized currency coefficients.

In July 1992, the exchange rate was essentially unified (with the exception of centralized imports) and the ruble made convertible on current
account. At the same time, the surrender requirement was altered.
Twenty percent of hard currency earnings had to be sold on the Russian
currency market through commercial banks, and another 30 percent to
the CBR. Because the CBR delayed payments by one or two months,
the surrender to the CBR implied a discount of about 20 percent due to
high inflation. In July 1993, the 50 percent of hard currency earnings
exporters were required to exchange into rubles could be exchanged on
the currency market without any CBR involvement. The relaxation of
the surrender requirement reflected a growing confidence on the part of
the government and the CBR in Russia's ability to attract hard currency.

Petr Aven argues that in January 1992, the government was not powerful enough to unify the exchange rate, but this was much easier to do
after extremely low exchange rates had been abolished.[26] The auctions
for foreign exchange steadily gained volume, which inspired confidence
in the ruble. After all, people bought it voluntarily, and the ruble exchange rate remained fairly steady during the first half of 1992 despite
high inflation, which implied a substantial real revaluation. The Moscow
Interbank Foreign Currency Exchange (MICEX) became a daily exchange. Beginning in July 1992, currency exchanges were set up in other
cities—first in St. Petersburg, and later in Yekaterinburg, Vladivostok,
Novosibirsk, and Rostov.

Because the dominant economic concern in Russia was domestic
shortages (especially food), a complete liberalization of imports in
early 1992 did not arouse controversy. During the first half of 1992,

Russia had no import quotas or tariffs. However, despite the continuously low exchange rate, protectionist pressures from Russian producers soon emerged. An additional argument for tariffs that was advanced by the Ministry of Finance and the IMF focused on fiscal needs. In July 1992, Russia introduced a low unified import tariff, which rose to 15 percent in September. In January 1993, import tariffs were diversified and then adjusted in March, June, and August 1993 as part of Glaz'ev's attempts to fine-tune administrative regulations. Since Glaz'ev's departure, only one general revision of import tariffs has been made (in July 1994). The current trend is toward increased protectionism, but the degree of differentiation varies, reflecting the strength of Russian lobbies. However, the protectionism of producers is increasingly being countered by trade lobbies in the big cities, whose trade suffers from import tariffs that raise prices. The average import tariff still hovers around 15 percent—not high by international standards—and import quotas or licenses are not used.[27]

A major problem inherited from the USSR was heavily subsidized centralized imports. Essentially, the government bought goods on the world market and sold them to a Russian enterprise at a small fraction of the world price. The Russian enterprise, in turn, sold the merchandise at the domestic market price, pocketing most of the subsidy and using the rest for bribes. This system was indefensible from every point of view. Reportedly, monopolistic domestic traders threatened to provoke food riots if their subsidies were cut. Moreover, most import subsidies were neither transparent nor regulated through the state budget, because they were incorporated in foreign commodity credits. In 1992, 45 percent of Russian imports were centralized and thus subsidized; in fact, subsidies covered as much as 94 percent of this portion of the import bill. According to IMF figures, total import subsidies corresponded to an extraordinary 17.5 percent of Russia's GDP in 1992. Most of this was not budgeted but financed (and in fact caused) by $12.5 billion in commodity credits and exports extended by Western countries to benefit their own farm lobbies.[28] In the spring of 1993, Boris Fedorov and the IMF joined forces to reduce both the volume and the degree of subsidization of centralized imports to a few percent of GDP in 1993, and to abolish subsidization of such imports in 1994. Fedorov succeeded in blocking any other harmful commodity credits. These unjustified import subsidies, which only enriched corrupt middlemen, are a telling example of the unintended large social costs that arise from hesitant deregulation.

Surprisingly, Russia's export policy has been far more complex and bureaucratic than its import policy. The foreign trade policy evolved during a time when incredible shortages raged and the dominant export commodities on the Russian market were priced at about 1 percent of the world price. It was therefore considered outrageous to deprive the domestic market of its few goods or to allow prices to rise to the free market level all at once. Another concern was that rogue traders were depriving Russia of its national wealth by selling raw materials cheaply abroad. Underinvoicing was chronic, often because the exporters did not own the products they exported to their own benefit. The call for strict export controls was overwhelming.

Much of the old regulatory system persisted for more than 70 percent of Russian exports, including oil, oil products, gas, coal, metals, fertilizers, certain other chemical products, timber, fish, and weaponry. The old system required the licensing of exporters, export quotas, and export licenses. First, the Ministry of the Economy would issue quotas for the export of particular goods. Then the exporter would conclude a contract with a foreign partner and the Ministry of Foreign Economic Relations would issue an export license, essentially to check that the price was correct. A novelty for 1992, however, was that exporters of regulated items had to pay export tariffs, which were set in European Currency Units (ECU). The export tariffs were supposed to tax most of the difference between the domestic price and the world price, but these tariffs met with vehement opposition. Exporters sought exemptions and evaded export taxes on a broad scale. The export control system was simply unworkable: The number of exporters was too large to be monitored. At the same time, many exporters were so powerful that they could blackmail the government into exempting them from export taxes by threatening to stop exporting. The government tried to improve its monitoring by introducing a category of "special exporters," restricting the right to export strategic goods to a limited group, but this device did not work either. The MVES was bogged down because of pressure from enterprises demanding to become special exporters, and their numbers multiplied quickly. Leading special exporters also exploited their clout by lobbying members of government for tax exemption.

Centralized exports were another bureaucratic device. State exporters of oil, natural gas, and oil products were exempt from export taxes, because their revenues went straight to the treasury. In this way, they were supposed to cover the country's costs of centralized imports and foreign debt service. In 1993, the planned volume of centralized exports was one-quarter of total exports, though revenues fell short of this goal by one third. Still, the reformers and the Ministry of Finance were reluctant to give up centralized exports, whose large state revenues accrued straight to the Ministry of Finance.[29]

The only solution to this muddle was to liberalize the domestic prices of export goods. These prices rose gradually, which facilitated liberalization of the export plan. In small increments, the number of strategic items had been reduced, export taxes lowered, and the significance of special exporter status played down. In 1992 alone, export tariffs were adjusted five times and were primarily lowered.[30] Export quotas are only in the interest of the few who are granted them, because they are effectively a lever for exacting exemption from export taxes. Such quotas are ostensibly distributed by administrative fiat (and in practice through bribes). Auctions of export quotas have repeatedly been attempted, but they have been hindered by resistance from the corrupt beneficiaries of the old nontransparent system. Since 1994, export quotas have been limited to oil and oil products, natural gas, coal, electricity, nonferrous metals, cellulose, wheat, liquor, fish, and timber, but these goods account for about 70 percent of Russia's exports.[31] Repeatedly, export quotas for timber and oil have supposedly been abolished, but at the last minute these commodities have been returned to the list.

Predictably, tax evasion had all along been particularly great in the sphere of foreign trade, where tax rates are high, the tax base very narrow, and the number of controllers small (and thus easily bribed). In short, the preconditions for bribery in the sphere of foreign trade were excellent and the opportunities well utilized. In the medium term, the only sensible solution is a complete liberalization of exports, which the Russian government envisions for 1995; but a necessary precondition is the liberalization of domestic prices.[32] From his experience, Petr Aven has formulated this dictum: "Any obstacle to economic activity, especially one which assumes the existence of a discretionary choice, will be circumvented in Russia, and therefore this country has to be more liberal than any other."[33] That is, in general terms, strong states can liberalize slowly, weak states cannot.

For less attractive export items not subject to domestic price control, Russia liberalized its export regime fully in January 1992 without backtracking. This liberalization aroused no controversy.

Table 5-1. *Size Distribution of Soviet Industrial Enterprises as of January 1, 1988*

Number of employees on enterprise staff	Enterprises	Employees (thousands)	Share of all employees (percent)
1–200	20,152	1,823	5.3
201–1,000	15,990	7,336	21.4
1,001–5,000	5,991	12,410	36.2
Over 5,000	1,187	12,751	37.1
Total	43,320	34,319	100.0

Source: IMF, IBRD, OECD, and EBRD, *A Study of the Soviet Economy*, vol. 2 (Paris, February 1991), p. 37.

With the important exception of exports of strategic raw materials, Russia has introduced a foreign trade system that conforms with the General Agreement on Tariffs and Trade (GATT). The ruble is convertible on current account, and its exchange rate is market-determined. Imports are not subject to nontariff barriers, and tariffs are reasonable (around 15 percent). Within the sphere of foreign trade, there are hardly any subsidies left. In the fall of 1993, Russia applied for accession to GATT. Already the application has functioned as a limit on protectionist tendencies.

Antimonopoly Policy

The Russian conventional wisdom insists that the Russian economy is unique in being completely dominated by gigantic industrial monopolies. It would therefore follow that the transition to a market economy would be far more difficult in Russia than elsewhere.

It is true that the Soviet economy was distorted through the domination of relatively large enterprises, because small enterprises barely existed. The reason for this concentration was a combination of exaggerated belief in economies of scale and the planners' desire to limit the number of production units to allow for better oversight. In Soviet industry during 1988, 73 percent of the employees worked in enterprises that were classified as large (that is with more than 1,000 employees), while as little as 5.3 percent of the industrial workforce were in small enterprises with less than 200 employees (see table 5-1). Still, the total number of enterprises in each branch was substantial. In 1992, Russia had 23,776 industrial enterprises, 25,600 *sovkhozy* and *kolkhozy*, 5,000 road transportation enterprises, and 170,000 retail trade enterprises.[34]

The prevailing Russian view of monopolies centered on three tenets. First, Russia was considered uniquely monopolized. Second, a widespread belief held that monopolies were generated from production rather than trade. Therefore, the objective was to combat production monopolies; meanwhile, trade monopolies were neglected. Third, most Russians wanted to fight monopolies with price regulations rather than through competition. As will be seen, all these points were misconceived. Unfortunately, they were to dominate antimonopoly policy, which was largely outside the control of the Russian reform government.

This conventional wisdom regarding monopolies had three foundations. The first was that Soviet statistics on monopolies were highly disaggregated. For example, two screws of different dimensions would be considered different products, thus classifying the two producers of the screws as monopolists, although they could easily compete by producing the same screws. The second reason for the belief in far-reaching monopolization of Russian industry is statistics from Gossnab. For instance, of 5,884 specific machine-building products supplied to Gossnab, 87 percent came from only one enterprise. However, Gossnab was merely responsible for some centralized distribution. This was a reflection not of production capabilities, but of Gossnab's inclination to order from only one supplier. In addition, distribution took place within scores of branch ministries, regions, and enterprises. Because the market or horizontal allocation functioned miserably in the socialist economy, branch ministries and enterprises alike resorted to autarky. As a result, contrary to official intentions, specialization in the Russian economy was limited. The problem was not a shortage of producers but, on the contrary, a dearth of market relations.[35] The third reason is simply that people confused the monopolization of trade within the command economy with the monopolization of production, presumably inspired by the usual Marxist fixation on production.

In fact, the monopolization of Russian industry was largely a myth, as Anette Brown, Barry Ickes, and Randi Ryterman have shown in their analysis of the Soviet industrial census of 1989.[36] Their statistical study offers overwhelming evidence to refute this myth. At the national level, there was little aggregate or industry concentration. Monopolies and oligopolies accounted for an unusually small share of national employment and production in Russia. The researchers observed that Russia's largest enterprises were actually smaller than those in many countries in the Organization for Economic Cooperation and Development (OECD).

The total number of employees in the top twenty enterprises in Russia was less than in the twenty biggest enterprises in the United States, Japan, western Germany, the United Kingdom, and France, even in absolute numbers. The average enterprise size was large only because there were so few small enterprises. In addition, the hundred largest enterprises in terms of number of employees were by no means dominant. On the contrary, they accounted for as little as 14.3 percent of total Russian employment. There were also extremely few national monopolies in Russia by Western standard definitions. Brown, Ickes, and Ryterman found that only 43 of 21,391 civilian manufacturing enterprises constituted monopolies at the national level, representing only 0.2 percent of civilian employment. Finally, enterprises with at least 35 percent of the national market share accounted for less than 4 percent of all employment. In short, by any international standard, apart from the important absence of small manufacturing enterprises, the Russian industrial structure was unusually competitive. A more significant problem is that Russia is full of company towns. Almost half of all Russian towns have only one industrial firm. Still, although three-quarters of all the towns have no more than four firms, these towns account for only 12.2 percent of all civilian employment in industry.[37]

The overwhelming Russian opinion, however, held that Russia was paralyzed by industrial monopolies, and the reformers simply failed to transcend this conviction. Antimonopoly policy was widely perceived as crucial to the success of economic reform in Russia. Hence, in the fall of 1990, one of the first Russian reform measures was to set up a State Committee for Antimonopoly Policy and the Support of New Economic Structures (henceforth, the Antimonopoly Committee). Subsequently, in March 1991, the Law on Competition and the Restriction of Monopolistic Activities in Commodity Markets was promulgated. In October 1991, on the eve of the radical reforms, the Antimonopoly Committee was ordered to establish a register on monopolistic enterprises and then regulate them. Although this was intended as a reformist effort, it was entirely regulative. Moreover, in late 1991, the Antimonopoly Committee was transferred from the government to the Russian Supreme Soviet, and the reformers in the government lost control over it. Subbranches of the Antimonopoly Committee were set up in each region and many localities, forming a large new administration.[38]

The definition of monopolies was far from stringent—that is, enterprises whose "share of the corresponding product market for a certain product exceeded 35 percent," or any other limit that the Antimonopoly Committee chose. Neither product differentiation nor the geographic extension of a product market was specified. Enterprises could also be labelled monopolistic if their "actions (inaction) violate the antimonopoly legislation."[39] The focus was on producers, not traders. As a consequence, inclusion in the register of monopolists was fairly arbitrary. In February 1992, the register listed about 2,000 enterprises suspected of being monopolistic in some undefined fashion. On June 1, 1993, the federal register of monopolists contained 641 enterprises and associations and the regional lists around 5,000.[40]

The presidential decree on price liberalization in December 1991 instructed the Russian government to regulate the prices of products from monopoly enterprises. Subsequently, a set of legal guidelines were issued on the regulation of monopolies, focusing on old administrative measures such as compulsory deliveries. However, the essence of antimonopoly regulation became price control, including fixed prices, maximum prices, maximum rates of profits, and notification of free prices. In practice, indirect price regulation came to the fore. The markup allowed suspected monopolists was restricted, usually to 25 percent. Regional and local Antimonopoly Committees could rule arbitrarily. They tended to control prices with the food industry for the dubious benefit of the Russian people.[41] In many regions, price regulation and antimonopoly policy became enmeshed. These arbitrary regulations (enforced primarily at the regional level) harmed the development of a national market, reinforced regional market segmentation, and incited officials to extortion. The "antimonopoly" policy was in fact an antimarket policy, and its price regulation was used by conservatives to impede reform. To contain its damage, the reform government shrewdly instigated a presidential decree in August 1992, which limited the staff of the Antimonopoly Committee to 350 and its regional organization to a total staff of 2,500.[42] The best that can be said about this antimonopoly policy is that it probably had little effect.

The predominant Russian criticism of the antimonopoly policy was that it failed to break up enterprises. However, that was hardly a primary concern. Production was not monopolistic, and the Russian privatization process produced significant deconcentration by privatizing individual enterprises rather than associations. The privatization authorities also encouraged units to break away from existing enterprises. Attempts by conservative branch interests to form large financial-industrial holding companies were worrisome, but the privatization authorities defeated most of these forays.[43] Another criticism was that price controls on monopolies were ineffective. But how could they possibly have worked, and why should they have?

The essential problems revolved instead around regional market segmentation and a shortage of small enterprises. Among the key tasks were opening up markets and encouraging domestic and international competition. For these purposes, it was vital to liberalize the market and stop state officials from interfering with enterprises. Another essential task was to make money scarce through a strict monetary policy. Russian enterprises would then face hard budget constraints, compelling them to expand sales to other regions and divest themselves of unprofitable workshops. A final effort was to facilitate formation of new small enterprises by simplifying the legal system and keeping it stable. Regional regulations should largely be prohibited.

Actual natural monopolies were relatively insignificant and limited to public utilities, for which prices in any case were regulated. In the fall of 1993, plausible complaints were registered about monopolistic pricing, as Russian railway tariffs rose above the Canadian level despite lower costs.[44]

The monopoly register and its accompanying regulations had limited legal authority until the end of 1993, and in 1994, the legal framework for antimonopoly policy was completely redrawn. With the dissolution of the Parliament in September 1993, the Antimonopoly Committee became subordinate to the government. It began to cooperate well with the State Committee for the Management of State Property (GKI) without undergoing a change in leadership. In March 1994, the government adopted a "Program for Demonopolization of the Economy and the Development of Competition." The old regulative measures were abolished, and the emphasis shifted toward pro-competitive efforts, ranging from better information systems to measures designed to alleviate market barriers. Only natural monopolies were to be restricted through regulations.[45] The document was somewhat vague, and it remains unclear whether the new policy regarding competition will have any significant effect; but at least the old, harmful ideas had been abandoned.

Problems With the Deregulation of the Energy Sector

From the outset, energy was a major bone of contention in the Russian political debate on reform. A complex web of interlocking problems hindered liberalization of the energy sector, which turned out to be the most difficult branch of the economy to liberalize.

The basic problem was that Russian energy prices were ludicrously low—less than 1 percent of world market prices. (Notably, in December 1991, the oil price was only 0.4 percent of the world price.)[46] Energy inputs were perceived as vital to all production; therefore, a great fear of energy shortages reigned, although the amount of energy utilized per unit of Russian production was enormous by any standard and actually needed to be drastically reduced. Moreover, energy production was declining, though at a rate less than that of industrial production in general; oil extraction, for example, plummeted by 10 percent in 1991 and 13.4 percent in 1992.[47]

Many of the problems in foreign trade deregulation were energy related. Exports were falling sharply, and energy accounted for about half of Russia's exports outside the FSU. Furthermore, the other CIS countries demanded sustained deliveries from Russia primarily of oil and natural gas, insisting on low prices and deliveries made through the old centralized trade system. Energy was also perceived as a price standard. State industry leaders as well as the general public believed that energy prices determined the rate of inflation. Therefore, they advocated low, regulated prices.

Finally, the energy industry was a strong lobby, deeply intertwined with the state. It was conservative and rent seeking. The coal industry harbored the only strong independent trade union, and because it had turned Russian politics to Yeltsin's advantage in the summer of 1989, it had great political clout. Low domestic energy prices had necessitated rigorous export controls, but these were circumvented illegally, generating enormous fortunes for the corrupt culprits.

As a consequence of all these special demands on the energy sector, the government was encumbered by too many objectives. Basically, the reform government believed in free energy prices but feared that measures that were too radical would disrupt production. At the same time, the government was also anxious to maintain exports to the West. It wanted to increase efficiency both in energy utilization and within the economy in general, and it aspired to stimulate energy production. The energy sector had proven to be too great a claimant on state subsidies, although it had the potential to be a major generator of tax revenues if energy prices were allowed to rise.

The key issue was energy prices. Initially, the reform government only administratively raised all energy prices fivefold, with the intention of freeing these prices by March 1992. (In hindsight, Gaidar considers it one of his greatest mistakes that he failed to convince President Yeltsin to support a full liberalization of energy prices from the start of the reform in January 1992.)[48]

Soon, the antireformers found energy prices to be fertile ground for a political pitch, and all of state industry (including the energy sector) joined in. Extensive criticism, primarily from state enterprise managers, convinced President Yeltsin not to allow any liberalization of energy prices.[49] The first target date, March 1, 1992, passed without any change in energy prices; so did the second, April 1. In its IMF shadow program signed on February 27, 1992, the Russian government committed itself to liberalizing domestic prices for fuel before April 20, but that date also passed with no action taken because of President Yeltsin's opposition.[50] Moreover, Yeltsin sacked Gaidar's reformist minister of fuel and energy, Vladimir Lopukhin, because he advocated free energy prices.[51] Instead, the foremost representative of the Russian energy industry and former Soviet minister of gas industry, Viktor Chernomyrdin, joined the government as deputy prime minister for energy.

Yeltsin's veto against the decontrol of energy prices left the reformers in a bind on energy policy. Energy prices remained fixed while high inflation raged, so real energy prices fell even further. The government managed at least to raise energy prices administratively on May 18, 1992. The price of oil rose by 471 percent, natural gas by 419 percent, and coal by 316 percent, but these prices remained fixed for the next three months.[52]

In September 1992, the government renewed its attempts to raise energy prices. It was aware that it would be impossible to do so during the winter, because of the prevailing popular conviction that the economy could not take a Russian winter and energy price rises simultaneously. The nominal oil price was almost doubled, and the coal price was increased by 90 percent, while the natural gas price stayed fixed. This price decree allowed for a wider free market for oil in which prices rose gradually. These prices were still far below world market prices, but a domestic market price of oil had evolved and had risen to about one-sixth of the world price. The real regulator of the oil price had become export quotas.[53]

With Chernomyrdin's appointment as deputy prime minister, natural gas became a matter that was considered separately from the rest of the energy sector. First, a huge gas monopoly was created. All enterprises dealing with natural gas—ranging from producers to pipelines, a foreign trade company, research institutes, and construction companies—were incorporated into one big concern with about 400,000 employees. This became the Russian joint stock company Gazprom. Oil production, to the contrary, was divided among a score of Russian oil companies. Curiously, the natural gas price was kept very low at the insistence of Gazprom. By January 1993, the price of natural gas had fallen to 3 percent of the world price. This was raised to at least 8 percent of the world price in February 1993. Gazprom presented low natural gas prices as a public service; but gas production remained high, and Gazprom needed to keep the price low if it was to sell all its output. Gazprom kept up its deliveries to customers in Russia and the CIS long after they had ceased to pay, far longer than any other enterprise in Russia. Presumably, the management of Gazprom was convinced that Chernomyrdin would guarantee them state subsidies for their deliveries, and it was the last enterprise in Russia with soft budget constraints.

Yet another idiosyncracy of the Russian gas industry was that Gazprom, which was probably Russia's wealthiest company, received extraordinary subsidies, tax exemptions, and other nontransparent state transfers. Investment in the gas industry was financed through tax exemption of gas exports, which was worth more than $4 billion in 1993. By the end of 1993, after extensive liberalizations in other branches of the economy, the gas industry remained the most monopolized and regulated industry in Russia. Gazprom enjoyed production, gas pipeline, and export monopolies. Its exports were subject to licenses and quotas, but Gazprom itself was exempt from export tax, some import tariffs, and VAT. Price regulation and price discrimination persisted. This lack of transparency helped Gazprom to become presumably the most successful rent-seeker in Russia.[54] The only plausible explanation for the truly exceptional treatment Gazprom received is that Prime Minister Chernomyrdin rewarded his old colleagues at the expense of the state.

Russian energy policy changed considerably in 1993 as Boris Fedorov took charge of price policy. His prime objectives were to cut state subsidies to the energy sector and to raise state revenues, primarily through excise taxes on energy. Because of Russia's inability to receive payment for its energy deliveries to most CIS countries, it had cut back on its deliveries, rendering the Russian market much more balanced, notwithstanding a continuing decline in energy production. After the winter of 1993, Fedorov tried to raise (and preferably to liberalize) energy prices. He differentiated among the energy types, dealing with each kind of energy separately and investigating various solutions. In addition, excise taxes were raised intermittently on various kinds of energy.

The easiest undertaking was to liberalize the retail price of gasoline. Only the Russian people were affected, and they lacked clout in Russian politics—even though the President thought this decision would be unpopular and postponed it until after the referendum of April 25, 1993. The price of gasoline was officially liberalized on May 25, but local price regulation remained common.[55]

The liberalization of coal prices on July 1 was a much more daring step. The coal industry was unenthusiastic; its major customer, the metallurgical industry, was furious. The metallurgical industry feared it would find its inefficiency exposed, and the coal industry feared falling demand and rising arrears. The pressure from these two industries and the Supreme Soviet, complemented with the threat of strikes, compelled the government to continue subsidizing the coal industry. The size of the coal subsidies vacillated with political cycles and remained at 1 to 3 percent of GDP. Deregulation brought on great differentiation in coal prices between different coal fields, breaking up the alliance of the entire industry. The informal coal monopoly had been crushed, and the price of coal started rising faster than the rate of inflation.[56]

In the summer of 1993, the government took on the price of natural gas. On July 20, this price was raised by 123 percent to 10 percent of the world price, and more importantly, it was indexed monthly to the industrial wholesale index. The gas price started to climb in real terms and surpassed 20 percent of the world price by December 1993. It continued to rise faster than inflation, exceeding the supposed indexation, although it remained regulated by the state.[57]

Similarly, electricity tariffs were finally raised almost 20-fold on August 1, 1993. Like natural gas delivered through pipelines, electricity is a natural monopoly; therefore, the state should regulate the price. Because local conditions and costs can vary greatly, electricity was regulated regionally. Electricity tariffs stayed relatively low due only to low costs.[58]

The crucial issue in the battle over deregulation of the energy sector was price decontrol. Failure to liberalize energy prices at the beginning of the reform process was an important opportunity lost. Politically, it cost the reformers a great deal. Instead, the energy price adjusted gradually, contributing significantly to inflation, and exposing the government each time to sharp public criticism. Still, after two and a half years, price deregulation had taken hold in the oil and coal industries. Although the prices have not reached world levels, they have come a long way. In July 1994, the domestic Russian prices of natural gas and oil were 36 percent and 38 percent of the world market prices, respectively, though they fell toward the end of 1994, when the oil price was only 27 percent of the world price.[59] The market price of energy should be relatively low in Russia, given its abundance of energy resources and despite its high transportation costs, but hardly less than 80 percent of the world price.

The behavior of the energy industry appears to be contingent on its degree of monopolization. Characteristically, the oil industry, with its competitive enterprise structure, was the first energy industry to accept price deregulation. Despite resistance from managers and strong trade unions, the government managed to force the coal industry, which was not fully monopolized, to liberalize prices. Conversely, the thoroughly monopolized gas industry has insisted on keeping the lowest prices. It might appear strange that the energy industry was not in the least enthusiastic about price hikes. However, because it was rent-seeking and not profit-seeking, it focused on exacting rents from the state, not on making profits. Moreover, the managers were in charge of the enterprises and were probably able to channel more rents than profits into their own pockets, considering that rent-seeking minimized transparency. In the spring of 1992, as head of the Russian gas industry, Chernomyrdin did not advocate higher or free energy prices. Nevertheless, in 1994, he stated that a fundamental mistake of the first reform government was its failure to liberalize energy prices at the beginning of the reform.[60]

Agriculture: Intertwined Rent-Seeking Monopolies

The political attention devoted to agriculture in 1991 and 1992 focused on land reform, leaving the economic functioning of agriculture relatively neglected. The minister of agriculture, Viktor Khlystun, had advanced in his career through the Association of Peasant Farms and Agricultural Cooperatives of Russia (AKKOR), which promoted family farms. Although he was sympathetic toward reform, he was neither strong nor effective. Khlystun left the reform government without an agricultural policy, yet still survived politically until November 1994. Russian agrarian policy took shape haphazardly under the influence of a variety of pressures. With the beginning of reform, the manifold large budget subsidies to agriculture were simply abolished in an attempt to balance the budget. This was an impressive show of political will by Yegor Gaidar, but it went almost unnoticed. However, without any actual policy, and with the old communist structures still in place, agriculture soon fell into a conservative trap.

The regulative drive took shape in a decree on January 4, 1992, regarding compulsory deliveries of food to the state. It stated that a volume of grain corresponding to 35 percent of the average harvest between 1986 and 1990 should be delivered to the state. This reflected the Russian government's anxiety to acquire enough food to feed those in the big cities and in the north, but it also showed the government's lack of belief in market allocation. It felt compelled to take responsibility for the distribution of food by formulating quantitative delivery targets. In line with the December 1991 decree on price liberalization, compulsory deliveries of agricultural produce were supposed to be paid for at market prices, but the government was compelled to obey its own delivery targets and raise prices as high as the farms wanted. The government's line was overtly market oriented, but the underlying thinking was still stuck in the old command economy.[61]

Furthermore, state and collective farms were tightly organized in the strongly antireform Agrarian Union, led by Vasily Starodubtsev, one of the leaders of the August 1991 coup. The leaders of both the Agrarian Union and AKKOR had their offices in the main building of the Ministry of Agriculture, and ministerial officials showed more loyalty to the Agrarian Union than to their own minister. AKKOR was no less rent-seeking than the Agrarian Union and demanded huge subsidized credits for each new family farm.[62]

Because the state had accepted major responsibility for the distribution of food, it needed agents to carry out the relevant tasks. As in the old system, the Ministry of Trade and Material Resources and the Ministry of Agriculture were the main agents. The natural choice as overseer of the most sensitive commodity, grain, was the former Ministry of Grain Procurement. This had briefly been the Committee of Grain Products of the Ministry of Trade and Material Resources, but it soon gained independence as the Federal Joint Stock Company Roskhleboprodukt. In

1993, it began privatizing itself through sales of shares to insiders and related enterprises and became a fairly independent monopoly for the state procurement of grain.[63]

An alternative source of grain was through imports, and in 1992 no less than 26 million tons of grain were imported. Here, too, a monopoly—the foreign trade company Exportkhleb—ruled. Despite its name, which means "export of grain," this company only imported it. It did so through centralized imports at an exchange rate of only 1.6 rubles per dollar, or about 1 percent of the market exchange rate during the first half of 1992. These imports were financed with so-called humanitarian Western commodity credits, which subsidized grain producers in Western countries. In Russia, the difference between the price of the imported grain and the market price was largely absorbed by shady grain traders, and as a result this assistance hardly benefited the Russian people at all.[64]

The financial market was also monopolized. An important government decree on subsidies and subsidized credits to "stabilize the economy of the agroindustrial complex" was adopted as early as April 4, 1992, on the eve of the Sixth Congress of People's Deputies. This signalled the government's weakening resolve regarding stabilization policy. By July 1992, subsidies and subsidized credits had become a flood. Agricultural credits were offered at a nominal annual interest rate of only 8 percent, whereas inflation exceeded 2,500 percent in 1992 and no ceiling was set for the volume of grain credits. The cheap credits were distributed through the old state bank Rosselkhozbank, which was unable to do much else. As the summer drew to an end, the government felt compelled to procure as much grain as possible. The farms called for (and received) a much higher procurement price than the state had intended.[65]

During the second half of 1992, the reform government seemed to have given up on financial stabilization. In the face of its apparent lack of policy on agriculture, the government had put itself in a hopeless bargaining position, squeezed among four interlocking monopolies: the Agrarian Union, Roskhleboprodukt, Exportkhleb, and Rosselkhozbank. It was pressured through three levers: the procurement price, subsidized credits, and budget subsidies. The pressures varied with the season. In the spring, the farms wanted subsidized credits that would allow them to afford to sow crops. In the summer, they asked for subsidized credits for harvesting, and Roskhleboprodukt wanted subsidized credits to purchase the harvest. Next, Roskhleboprodukt sought cheap credits to buy grain from itself for its bakeries. The government had put itself into this bind by focusing excessively on land reform (which could not have been accomplished at the time), rather than liberalizing trade in agricultural produce, which was in fact doable. The predominant but flawed belief was that no agrarian market could function without dominant private ownership. In the meantime, nothing checked the flow of subsidized credits to the agricultural industry.

The cost of agricultural policy in 1992 was high. Centralized credits to agriculture alone amounted to 7.7 percent of GDP; and given the highly negative real interest rates, these credits were virtually gifts. Half of the subsidized credits were allocated to the procurement of 29 million tons of grain. However, as it happened, to procure this volume of grain Roskhleboprodukt received twice the necessary amount in so-called centralized direct credits, which were obviously used for other purposes. Everything was wrong. The procurement price had been higher than the free market price; subsidized credits had been far too large and cheap, were not controlled, and were used for illicit purposes; and centralized imports had been both more than was necessary and extremely costly to society. All kinds of budget subsidies had been given, but the main beneficiaries were rent-seeking middlemen in agrarian businesses. The entire situation had become financially and morally untenable.[66]

In early 1993, the easiest and most urgent measure for Boris Fedorov to undertake was to reduce centralized, heavily subsidized imports of grain sharply and to eliminate them entirely in 1994. At the same time, Fedorov managed to block harmful commodity credits from the West. Russia's total grain imports were almost halved to 14 million tons in 1993 and fell sharply again in 1994. The agrarian lobby did not care much about Exportkhleb, which made this task achievable.

The agrarian lobby, however, gained strength by colluding with the Supreme Soviet majority. On May 14, 1993, the Supreme Soviet promulgated a blatant antireform law, the Law on Grain. The grain trade was to be monopolized (under Roskhleboprodukt) and procurement prices were to be both regulated and indexed. Similarly, exports and imports of grain were to be monopolized (under Exportkhleb) and deliveries regulated by state orders. The state was to maintain a large stock of grain and would provide a wide range of subsidies, subsidized credits, and tax exemptions to agricultural enterprises.[67] This was the low point in Russian agricultural policy.

In the summer of 1993, there was new conflict over procurement prices, and farm representatives managed to exact higher prices than the government wanted. However, substantial free trade in grain had now developed on commodity exchanges. The procurement price exceeded the market price by 40 percent, and it was to be indexed monthly by 10 percent. Roskhleboprodukt pressed for and received large credits at an interest rate of 10 percent per annum. As in 1992, Roskhleboprodukt began pressuring the government for ever-larger subsidized credits. It did so by not paying the farms, claiming that it had not obtained promised funds from the government and that it was really the government that owed the farms money. Conservatives in the government, including deputy prime ministers Alexander Zaveryukha (who was responsible for agriculture) and Oleg Lobov (who was minister of the economy), urged the government to buy 40 million tons of grain, because the harvest had been so good. They wanted the government to pay larger subsidies accordingly to collect more grain when there was no danger of a shortage. The Ministry of Finance protested, but there was a conservative offensive in the late summer of 1993, resulting in larger state expenses than had been intended.[68]

With the dissolution of the old parliament on September 21, 1993, political fortunes were swiftly reversed, and the agrarian lobby was politically discredited. First of all, Boris Fedorov and Yegor Gaidar, who replaced Lobov in the government on September 18, abolished all subsidized credits by September 25. They then stopped the state procurement of grain and liberalized grain trade and prices. Next, by October 15, the prices of bread and baby food were liberalized, which hardly endeared Gaidar to the voters in the December elections. Finally, the Law on Grain was effectively revoked on December 21. As a result, foreign trade in grain was also liberalized. At the same time, the right of private ownership of land was granted by presidential decree. Agriculture in Russia was formally and completely deregulated and subsidies minimized. In no time at all, reports on the overproduction of grain started to appear.[69]

The parliamentary elections in December 1993 once again reinforced the strength of the agrarian lobby. The Agrarian Party, an outgrowth of the Agrarian Union, received 8 percent of the popular vote and won 12 percent of the seats in the Duma.[70] It immediately started lobbying Prime Minister Chernomyrdin to adopt an omnibus decree, "Economic Conditions for the Functioning of the Agro-Industrial Complex of the Russian Federation in 1994." Eventually, Chernomyrdin signed it on February 23, 1994, after significant cuts in the regulations and subsidies demanded. The decree was unabashedly rent-seeking, with plenty of measures implying either direct subsidies or regulations that could reinforce future demands for them. Large centralized credits were designated for numerous purposes. Initially, the interest rate was at the market level, but later the agrarians managed to get some subsidization. Plan targets were introduced for ten major agricultural product groups, which gave the agrarians some standards to use in bargaining with the state. Certain entities were given monopolies on state orders for various products (notably Roskhleboprodukt for grain), but planned state purchases were much smaller than they had previously been. Again, state procurement was supposed to take place at market prices, permitting the agrarians to use their collective clout to boost prices.[71]

The decree reintroduced much of the old regulative system, but the regulations were not as strict as before and the monopolies not so extensive. Many of the stipulations were merely empty words, and much remained ambiguous. Out of an initial demand for 35 trillion rubles in subsidies, by July the agrarians had obtained concrete budgeted promises for about 18 trillion rubles, or some 3 percent of projected GDP. However, disbursements were further reduced because of a shortfall in state revenues. Interestingly, the agrarian lobby altered its policy on foreign trade. Instead of associating themselves with Exportkhleb and its demands for subsidized imports, the agrarians wanted higher import tariffs and no food imports. Finally, substantial import tariffs were introduced on July 1, 1994. Gradually, the relationship between the farm lobby and Roskhleboprodukt also soured. The agrarians were remarkably slow to realize that Roskhleboprodukt cheated them, exacting state subsidies meant for farms while not paying those farms for deliveries made.[72]

The controversy over agriculture in the summer of 1993 and throughout 1994 shows that the agrarian lobby holds its own as the most potent lobby in Russia, though its policy has been modified. Middlemen (primarily Exportkhleb, but also Roskhleboprodukt and Rosselkhozbank) have lost their standing with the farm lobby. Since these intertwined monopolies have faded, the agricultural market has developed. Liberalization has gone far, and subsidies have shrunk to a low level by international standards. In only two years, Russia overcame its chronic grain shortage, although the liberalization was timid and gradual. At long last, a reasonably broad and attractive assortment of foods are available all over Russia, although several superfluous regulations remain. The state procurement of food serves no function in a market economy and should be abolished. Regional price regulation of essential foods and regional prohibitions against export of certain foods should be prohibited, because they disrupt with the national market.[73]

Economic Crime as a Threat to Liberalization

The most worrisome development in Russia in the 1990s has been the rise in crime, particularly murder, robbery, and corruption. A feeling of lawlessness has spread. People in general are worried about run-of-the-mill criminals and hooligans, while business executives have been pestered by racketeers and forced to bribe officials to be able to stay in business. Crime in Russia has clearly been more intimidating than in eastern Europe. It has led to extremely high transaction costs and high thresholds for starting new businesses. Racketeers have often created local monopolies (for instance, in construction), leading to outrageous prices. Crime has become a major impediment to liberalization of the Russian economy.

The total number of reported crimes increased 50 percent between 1990 and 1992, and the number of premeditated murders increased 80 percent between 1990 and 1993, to 29,200. The statistics for Moscow are particularly shocking. In 1987, at the height of the antialcohol campaign, the murder toll hit a low of 172; but in 1993, it had risen to 1,404. (Yet that is still less than the murder rates in large American cities.)

However, a tendency toward leveling off is noticeable. The total reported crime rate rose by 27 percent in 1992, stagnated in 1993, and fell by 6 percent in 1994. Presumably, this was the result of people improving their personal security. Most Russians do not go out as late as they once did and tend to stay away from dangerous areas. Many have put bars on their windows, steel doors outside their apartments, and sturdy locks on their doors. The increase in the murder rate slowed in 1994. Murders had still increased by 11 percent, but in 1992 they had increased by 42 percent. Reported burglaries and robberies fell sharply in 1994, but this might be because many victims no longer cared to report such crimes. Yet these statistics suggest that the worst may be over, although crime has intensified in certain regions, notably Moscow.[74] This development corresponds to earlier trends in eastern Europe, where crime rates first surged for a few years after communism. (They fell in Hungary and the Czech Republic in 1994.)

Not only the sharp rise in serious crimes but also the nature of organized crime itself have evoked public apprehension. The Ministry of the Interior estimated in 1994 that there were 5,691 criminal groups with about 100,000 members. Organized crime is widely perceived to be in a mutually beneficial relationship with the government, and opinion polls among Russians have revealed a general sense of insecurity and lawlessness. Organized crime was said to control 40,000 Russian enterprises. In large parts of the country (notably Moscow and St. Petersburg), many believe that no enterprise could be run without settling its relations with crime syndicates, primarily by paying protection money.[75]

Organized crime has three types of members. First, historically, Russia had a large number of hard criminals, many of whom had been released on amnesty. Their ranks were expanded with the addition of veterans of the war with Afghanistan who could not adjust to civilian life, professional sportsmen used to the high life but now laid off from their jobs, and KGB officials tempted by higher earnings. A second group comprised the corrupt former elite, joined by some members of the new political elite who fell for the temptations of corruption. A third group was made up of ruthless new business owners involved in organized crime. Many of the criminal gangs had a particular ethnic character.[76]

There were numerous causes of the sharp rise in crime. A basic precondition was the old communist contempt for law. In the old days, virtually everyone stole from the state whenever possible. Corruption had been widespread, even endemic in many places, and the party apparatus itself had often operated as a mafia.[77] But now the old party hierarchy had fallen apart, together with party norms and threats of terror, while all that was left was alienation and demoralization. Moreover, the new legislative framework in Russia was highly rudimentary, and its construction was delayed and complicated by the ongoing strife between the president and the old Supreme Soviet. The law enforcement apparatus remained large, but its members were demoralized, and many were corrupt. In addition, they endured new public criticism, low salaries, and poor education. The legal system was inadequate, and lawyers were scarce. And finally, in a market economy there is more wealth to steal; and anything can be bought for money.

Crime, criminal revenues, and corruption were exacerbated by the lingering inconsistent and discretionary regulatory system, which stimulated massive rent-seeking. Major fortunes were made early on through the export of oil and metals, which were exceedingly cheap on the domestic market. The trick was to acquire both the commodity and an export permit through contacts and bribes. In 1992 and 1993, the principal source of corrupt revenues was through subsidized credits issued by the CBR. The banking system became a criminal bonanza. In 1993, 35 bankers (many of them prominent) were murdered.[78] Banks still suffer from the inability of the legal system to exact payments from debtors. There is little property that can be used as collateral. Property registries are missing, and purported collateral may be owned by someone else or used to secure several other loans. In the end, legal procedures can barely put collateral in the effective custody of a claimant. Therefore, banks take recourse to using gangsters, who force people to pay under threat of physical harm. A lasting source of illegal income has been protection money and extortion, which were reinforced by the licensing of enterprises. The central bodies of government most prominently accused of corruption typically included the Ministry of Foreign Economic Relations, the Ministry of Fuel and Energy, the Ministry of the Economy, the Ministry of Agriculture, the Ministry of Defense, and the CBR, from which large rents could be exacted.[79]

The transformation of the economic system fundamentally altered the preconditions for criminal activity. As a result, the nature of such activity should also change. Most of the original sources of illegal revenues tend to disappear with deregulation (notably revenues from illegal exports, currency exchange, and subsidized credits). Protection fees and extortion are undoubtedly important sources of criminal revenues but comparatively labor-intensive and probably overexploited by racketeers. Conversations with Russian business owners make clear that a standard rate for so-called protection or alternative security arrangements is 15 to 20 percent of their total turnover, which is already high. However, sometimes this protection rate is pushed toward 40 percent. Many enterprises are subject to extortion from competing gangs, who behave like robbers rather than like a local mafia with an interest in the survival of local enterprises.

As a result, Russian entrepreneurs often find it impossible to collaborate with gangster syndicates. One-third of bank employees are security guards, as banks either are infested with the mafia or reckon that it is more profitable to fight gangsters than to pay them off. The steadily rising rate of serious crime and the murders of gangland godfathers indicate the instability of Russia's criminal world. It is true that many criminals venture into ordinary business activities (notably real estate); but why should they keep their criminal status if they are moving into the legitimate business sector?[80] However, as long as the Russian legal system is too weak to assure the collection of payments due, people in business need to resort to strong-arm methods to exact payments.[81]

Contrary to common perceptions, there are many reasons to believe that the Russian crime wave might be approaching its peak. The criminal revenue base has been eroded. Criminality succeeded inflation as the top public concern of 1994, and Russian voters are demanding to be represented by politicians who take crime seriously. Moreover, the Constitution of December 1993 provides a new and proper foundation for legislation. Legal reform is under way as new lawyers are being trained. The law enforcement forces are huge and are being expanded quickly, and many elite troops in the police force evidently fight organized crime seriously.

In 1994, the government undertook numerous measures against crime. A number of new laws were adopted, including a federal program for fighting crime. The budget for 1994 contained a large increase for law enforcement, which should suffice both to double the real wages of police officers and to purchase modern equipment. The police are no longer ill-equipped and underpaid. On June 14, President Yeltsin signed a decree regarding the fight against organized crime. The government's sense of urgency in taking effective measures was evident. Yet the Duma refuted many of these anticrime measures as unconstitutional (notably arrests for up to 30 days, searches of offices and flats without warrants, and the scrutiny of bank accounts).[82] The respect for and understanding of law remain slight. These measures are not likely to solve Russia's crime problems, but they are indicative of crime's new political significance.

The crime hazards in Russia are serious, and their solution will require many measures and will take years. First of all, a much more radical liberalization is necessary. After capitalism had first made its forays into Western Europe in the 1840s, the legal system was still rudimentary. The response was far-reaching deregulation and *laissez-faire,* which lasted for about thirty years, until the legal system had gained strength. A similar approach would be advisable for Russia. In particular, the tax system must be simplified so that it becomes possible for entrepreneurs to comply with it. After all, Russia has a huge law enforcement apparatus; there are laws against corruption, even though loopholes exist. Although many officials are corrupt, others are not, and much can be done, even at present. The share of crimes solved actually rose from 47 percent in 1992 to 60 percent in 1994.[83] The crucial missing factor is the will of Russian leaders to clamp down on top officials who are evidently corrupt. If no serious action is taken, the legitimacy of democratic rule will be undermined. The government's lack of credibility in fighting crime was a major drawback in the elections of December 1993. With regard to criminality, Russians draw parallels with Italy or Latin America, alluding to collusion between organized crime, state enterprises, state officials, and politicians.[84] Yet a wide range of options appears possible, depending on what the Russian leaders decide.

Conclusion: Accomplishing Liberalization, However Slowly

The liberalization of the economy in Russia has been more arduous than it was in Eastern Europe, but it has proceeded and was essentially accomplished in two years. Russia has an index reflecting the availability of 98 basic commodities in 132 cities. In February 1992, it stood at only about 35 percent, but it has risen steadily and reached 92 percent in October 1994. The price structure has become much closer to what is considered normal in the West. Price differentials between different regions remain abnormally large, although the gap appears to have narrowed slightly in the summer of 1994.[85]

Russian liberalization was gradual, primarily because the government thought the market could set prices but not allocate goods. However, to liberalize prices while maintaining monopolistic trade links, the government encouraged monopolistic pricing, which was a costly misconception. Fortunately, the initial price liberalization went far enough to force relatively fast market liberalization. Another cause of the gradual liberalization was the power of the old establishment's entrenched interests, particularly in foreign trade and energy. To maintain their monopolies, regulations, and accompanying subsidies, members of the old guard exploited the government's fear of a collapse in supplies of essential goods, such as food and energy. Yet the power of both the foreign trade and energy lobbies has been checked as normal economic and political institutions have evolved. The agrarian lobby, however, is a different story. It benefits from broad grassroots representation and has therefore not succumbed to marketization and democratization. On the contrary, it has been integrated into the democratic process (as in most Western countries), demanding regulations and subsidies with significant success.

Monopolies have played an important role in the Russian economy, but their nature has been widely misunderstood. The predominant conviction that Russian production is utterly monopolized lacks any empirical foundation. There are serious monopoly effects in Russia, to be sure, but they arise from formal or informal regulations on trade. These effects should be fought with decontrol and marketization, opening up and unifying the national market.

The aspirations of Russian monopolies have also been misconceived. The general conviction has been that monopolists wanted to raise prices to boost their profits and cut production. The energy monopolies, at least, did the opposite, particularly in 1992. They insisted on low regulated prices and resisted both price increases and decontrol. At first glance, this behavior may seem irrational, but that is a misperception. These monopolists had not made the transition to a market economy. Therefore, they were not profit-maximizing but were actually rent-seeking entities, which was rational in the old state-regulated paradigm. They wanted a maximum of regulations so that they could maximize their rents. Each regulation offered enterprises an opportunity to claim state compensation, as they could argue that underpriced services and goods implied public utility. Moreover, regulations clouded transparency. In hindsight, the rationality of the monopolists' approach is proven by the large subsidies and tax exemptions they exacted from the government. Contrary to its overt purpose, the Russian antimonopoly policy reinforced monopoly effects with its regulations. Furthermore, the rights of both ministries and regions to regulate trade continue to disrupt the national market.

The overall conclusion that can be drawn is that the initial liberalization effort comprised a sufficiently big bang for the liberalization to eventually succeed. However, it was far more timid than was optimal, with serious economic, intellectual, social, and political consequences. Virtually every regulation implied state subsidies, the loss of potential state revenues, or both. Therefore, the effect of tardy liberalization on the balance of the state budget was immense—on the order of tens of percent of GDP. As is seen in the next chapter, insufficient liberalization was a major cause of high inflation.

To a remarkable extent, the Russian intellectual paradigm was not transformed. Many Marxist prejudices, such as irrational devotion to production, disbelief in market allocation, and belief in regulations, were not crushed. Too many regulations remained in place, and each served as an argument for the retention of still other regulations.

The combination of a lack of real stabilization and distorted prices delayed restructuring. The state enterprises in the greatest need of restructuring did not use this time to prepare themselves; on the contrary, they steeled themselves against any systemic and structural changes. The tardiness of liberalization bred parasitic behaviors, and the rents caused by inertia and inconsistent deregulation generated criminality. Any regulation was an argument for one bureaucrat or another to indulge in extortion.

High inflation and rising criminality were major arguments raised against the reformers in the parliamentary elections of December 1993, which show that late liberalization was also politically costly. From the Russian experience, the arguments for a liberalization that was as comprehensive as possible at the start of the systemic change appear overwhelming.

CHAPTER SIX

Macroeconomic
Stabilization

THE ESTABLISHMENT of a stable, convertible currency is one of the foremost prerequisites of successful capitalism. Currency stability implies stability of both the domestic price level and the exchange rate. It does not, however, imply stability of production. On the contrary, the transition from socialism to a normal market economy should facilitate structural transformation. This inevitably means a decline in total production, when gross distortions have accumulated for a long time while free reserves have been exploited.

In this chapter, I consider why macroeconomic stabilization is so important for postcommunist economic transformation and then examine to what extent Russia is unique in these respects. The discussion in the next section suggests how inflation should be fought in Russia. The five ensuing sections review various attempts at macroeconomic stabilization between 1992 and 1994. I then examine the peculiar problem of inter-enterprise arrears and scrutinize the role of the West in the Russian stabilization efforts.

Why Macroeconomic Stabilization Is So Important

Much of the discussion and the academic literature on systemic transformation has focused on macroeconomic stabilization.[1] It is, of course, a dominant part of mainstream economics; and at least for short-term

174

phenomena, macroeconomics provides a convenient unifying framework. However, this framework is not merely a matter of convenience; it is vital to an understanding of the Russian economic transition.

It is true that Stalin controlled inflation and even lowered prices in the USSR after World War II. But he did so through price controls, which resulted in enormous shortages. Price liberalization is an intrinsic part of a move to a market economy; but when prices are liberalized, they invariably rise. Initially, prices rise primarily because of large unsatisfied demand, or a so-called monetary overhang. However, a number of additional factors can then contribute to inflation. At the microeconomic level, enterprises are subject to soft budget constraints; that is, they are used to getting the money they need from the state and will not adjust to demand until they are forced to do so. At the macroeconomic level, budget deficits have prevailed at the end of communism. The state budget has provided large subsidies to state enterprises, which has kept their budget constraints soft. Macroeconomic stabilization and microeconomic adjustment are thus closely correlated. Moreover, after overt fiscal deficits have been controlled, semifiscal deficits (such as covert import subsidies or subsidized credits) have spurred inflation. Neither theoretical nor empirical arguments support a soft, or hesitant, approach to combatting inflation.

Controlling inflation is a litmus test of the short-term success of systemic change: Society will either face a single price adjustment or a high and lasting inflation. A swift adjustment is preferable from all points of view. The empirical record from five years of systemic change in postcommunist countries of the former Soviet bloc is abundantly clear. Those countries that underwent more comprehensive reforms (Poland, the Czech Republic, Estonia, and Latvia) have done better than those that took a more hesitant approach (notably Romania and the former Soviet republics [FSRs]). The radical reform countries have endured a smaller total fall in production, though more of it occurred early on. Their production has turned upward sooner, and hard budget constraints have forced enterprises (both private and state-owned) to restructure early. Finally, both investment and consumption have benefitted from the early upturn.[2]

A frequently made critical argument is that too much attention has been paid to macroeconomics and too little to microeconomics. However, this view is misconceived. A focus on macroeconomics is a precondition for microeconomic improvement—that is, structural change at the enterprise level. Enterprise managers will only rarely attempt to restructure their enterprises before they are convinced that money has become scarce and that the government will not bail them out. Only a credible macroeconomic stabilization can make money scarce and break the managers' expectations of being saved by government intervention. Managers of state-owned as well as private firms will then have to adjust to the market and its demands. To slow down or delay structural changes means lowering the standard of living more than is necessary. A major lesson learned from the attempts at stabilization in Russia is that every possible measure must be undertaken to make stabilization credible. Many Soviet managers have simply refused to believe that the times and the economic system have completely changed until their enterprises have gone under.

Nor are there any social grounds to advocate a hesitant stabilization policy. The level of unemployment does not appear to be related to firmness of stabilization or speed of restructuring, but rather to wage levels, wage flexibility, and creation of new jobs. The Czech Republic has maintained a low rate of unemployment (less than four percent of the labor force), although its rate of restructuring has been impressive.

High inflation is the most regressive of taxes. It is caused by subsidies and subsidized credits paid by the state to a small rent-seeking elite; the inflation tax, on the contrary, is paid by the society as a whole. Moreover, the destabilizing state subsidies are often exacted through bribery. Through inflation, the state thus redistributes wealth from the populace to the wealthy few. Perpetrating such a blatant injustice can easily delegitimize a regime and undermine democracy, as has frequently been the case in Latin America. In short, there is no plausible social argument for so-called soft stabilization policies.

As was discussed in chapter 1, a major problem with the Russian transition to a market economy that is unlike what is being experienced in China is that official production in Russia is bound to fall. Part of the decline is a statistical illusion, but a significant portion represents a real decline. Moreover, the resulting structural change will be great. This will be unsettling and will increase the sense of risk even for those who will benefit materially from the transition. Income distribution will change considerably, and the gap between rich and poor is bound to increase. The actual size of the fall in GDP depends on the accumulated need for restructuring in a particular country, the alteration in its terms of trade, and the economic policies pursued. Assessing the relative weight of these factors is hardly possible, given the paucity of available statistics. With regard to Russia, the accumulated need for structural change will likely be enormous, because the communist system (with all its distortions) lasted for so long. Russia has faced a serious external shock, although its terms of trade have actually improved considerably. An important conclusion to draw from this experience is that the costs of such an economic transition are inevitably high; but if inflation is allowed to rise, they will be even higher.

Is Russia Unique?

The preconditions for macroeconomic stabilization can be categorized into three groups: general problems of countries with high inflation, predicaments specific to transitional postcommunist economies, and particular difficulties faced by FSRs.

The preconditions of systemic change in Russia were discussed in chapter 2. In late 1991, Russia faced severe financial imbalances of all kinds. Its budget deficit was completely out of control, with a consolidated state budget deficit in 1991 on the order of 30 percent of GDP. Public expenditures (notably social benefits) as well as wages were skyrocketing. The Soviet government had borrowed excessively abroad (eventually defaulting on its international debt in late 1991) and was subject to a triple external shock. In 1991, the CMEA trade system fell apart; in the same year, the USSR was precluded from obtaining international financing because of its default; and in 1992, trade with other FSRs collapsed. The external shocks caused a sharp reduction in imports, which hit both production and exports. The nonconvertible ruble was substantially devalued on free markets. But multiple exchange rates provided ample rents to those with access to hard currency at the official exchange rates, and as a result the USSR experienced sizeable capital flight in 1991. Still, these are problems typical of countries in severe financial distress.

In fact, most problems Russia confronted were common to all countries in transition from communism to capitalism (although they tended to be worse in the former Soviet Union [FSU]). Massive shortages were characteristic predicaments. They were caused by low fixed prices for an insufficient supply of goods and services, coupled with a monetary overhang of unsatisfied demand or forced savings. In 1991, the Soviet shortages grew so devastating that they brought on a drastic slump in production. The initial fall in production was entirely induced by shortages of supply and was largely unrelated to demand.

All communist countries shared monetary and fiscal similarities that needed to be amended when they became market economies. In all of them, money was passive. Their monetary systems were rudimentary and monetary policies almost nonexistent. For instance, in 1991, Soviet interest rates stayed at 6 percent per annum. No reserve requirements applied to commercial banks, and no credit policy was pursued. At least big enterprises benefitted from soft budget constraints—they could exact more state money if they needed it. Enterprises did not care whether or not they were paid by their final customer, because they received money from the bank in any case. The state netted out debts between enterprises at the end of the year and offered cheap loans to cover those enterprises that had deficits. Velocity of money was low; money did not have much value for businesses, so why economize on it? There was little collateral, because of the scarcity of private property and the weak legal system, which did not allow for collection of debts. No bankruptcy or other mechanism was in place to eliminate poorly performing enterprises, so the state was compelled to keep them afloat. Capital markets were rudimentary and thin. In short, virtually all means of imposing fiscal discipline on state enterprises were missing. In this regard, Russia was worse off than Eastern Europe, but not more so than other post-Soviet countries.

The fiscal systems of communist states shared several characteristics. Public expenditures were high (around 50 percent of GDP in the USSR). Most taxes were collected from three sources: enterprise profits, turnover taxes, and taxes on foreign trade. Profits that remained in an enterprise at the end of the year and that had not been allocated to some enterprise fund were expropriated by the state. Turnover taxes were individualized for each commodity, with the state seizing the difference between the fixed wholesale and fixed retail prices for a commodity. The large foreign trade taxes isolated domestic prices from international prices and implied great protectionism.

The FSRs also had common peculiarities caused by inadequate reform, the breakup of the USSR, and a relatively severe economic crisis. Unlike much of Eastern Europe, cash and account money in the FSRs had not been unified but circulated in separate cycles. As was discussed in chapter 4, the collective irresponsibility of the ruble zone complicated any monetary policy and aggravated payment problems between enterprises. The poor delineation of state functions left the Russian Ministry of Finance without the authority to exercise proper financial control, and both tax collection and state expenditures were outside its purview. The combination of complex regulations and a severe financial crisis brought the market exchange rate of the ruble to an extreme low in December 1991, when the average Russian wage was just $6 a month. As inflation rose because of the excessive issuance of credits, the printing presses could not keep up with the demand for cash, which led to a cash (not money) shortage. This has happened in other big inflation crises, but the cash shortage in Russia was prolonged because of a dispute over who was responsible for printing money.

Milton Friedman has observed that inflation is always a monetary phenomenon. When inflation is as high as it has been in Russia, the quantity theory of money is most illuminating; that is:

$$MV = PY$$

where M is the stock of money in circulation, V is the velocity of money, P is the price index, and Y is the national income. In a Russian context, it is important to remember what money is. In this discussion, M2 will be used as a measure of money. It is defined as currency in circulation, demand deposits, and time deposits in commercial banks. Thus, M2 includes both cash and account money, but not interenterprise arrears or interenterprise debts. (Interenterprise arrears are far from being money by any definition, because they are not liquid and their value is dubious.)

The crucial variable to observe is the expansion of the money supply, which falls into four categories. The Central Bank of Russia (CBR) can issue credits to the government to finance the budget deficit, or to the enterprise sector, or to the other FSRs. The domestic money supply can also expand if the CBR buys hard currency on the market for rubles. These four sources of money must all be kept under control. An expansion of the money supply does not immediately lead to higher inflation, because it takes some time for the effect to filter through the payments system. For Russia there seems to be a lag of three to four months between the expansion of the money supply and the onset of inflation, though this relationship may not remain stable as payment routines change.

Although the money supply is the central variable, the demand for money is also a factor. Before price liberalization, it was impossible to assess the demand for money, and the attempts made heavily overestimated the Russians' desire to hold ruble assets. As a result, the initial price hike was greater than expected. It was equally difficult to know if and to what extent Russians and Russian enterprises preferred to hold liquid assets in Russian rubles or in hard currency (notably dollars). Rudiger Dornbusch has observed that dollarization usually starts much later than expected but proceeds much faster than anticipated.[3] If demand for domestic money decreases, the velocity of money increases. The remaining demand for money then shifts from bank deposits to high-powered money (cash), which allows faster transactions. Savings are put into dollars, and dollarization begins. When inflation rises, confidence in the currency falls further and the velocity of money increases even more, giving additional impetus to inflation. But on the contrary, when inflation falls, people start hoping for stabilization and dare to hold more money (which is certainly more convenient), and the demand for money rises, which further reduces inflation.

A standard Russian argument against applying the quantity theory of money to the Russian economy is that the theory cannot hold, because the Russian economy is uniquely monopolized. (The idea of extraordinary monopolization has already been refuted in this book.) However, even if the Russian economy were indeed that monopolized, profit-maximizing monopolies would only raise their prices to the optimal level and keep them there. They would not continue to raise prices, because a monopoly has no dynamic effect if the money supply is kept constant. In fact, the strongest Russian monopoly, Gazprom, has not raised its prices above a competitive market level; on the contrary, it has kept them below the market-clearing level to boost sales. (Gazprom has chosen to maximize its gains from the state budget rather than from the market.)

Another argument for the uniqueness of the Russian economy is that enterprises create their own money by not paying one another, creating what are known as interenterprise arrears. However, there is nothing uniquely Russian about this phenomenon; it is common to all postcommunist economies. Nor have Russian interenterprise arrears been especially high in comparison with those of Romania or Ukraine. However, the complexities of the problem justify devoting a later section of this chapter to interenterprise arrears.

Still, it must be remembered that Russia also enjoyed important advantages. Although it endured external shocks, Russia benefitted greatly from improving terms of trade. The country possessed a wealth of highly marketable natural resources, such as oil and natural gas. Its population was well educated. As a big country, Russia had a large domestic market and considerable clout in international affairs. Unlike other newly independent states, Russia had reasonably well-developed national institutions and a large elite. The country was peaceful, with a notable lack of social strife and strikes. In most regards, Russia was indeed better off than other FSRs.

In general, fighting inflation in former communist countries has turned out to be difficult, and it has proven to be more arduous in the FSU than in Eastern Europe.[4] Still, however complex and severe Russia's financial and monetary difficulties, they were hardly unique. They needed to be fought by ordinary means, but their very nature rendered them more difficult to resolve. Therefore, resolute action had to be taken, despite possibly diminished hope both for resolution and success. Even so, because of a synergism of poor payment systems and asocial enterprise behavior, there was no alternative.

How to Fight Inflation in Russia

In principle, the tasks and instruments of macroeconomic stabilization are the same in Russia as elsewhere. The consolidated state budget needs to be reasonably close to being balanced, and monetary policy must be sufficiently strict. Other options to be considered include an exchange rate policy, an incomes policy, and international financing.

The most self-evident aspect of a financial stabilization policy involves bringing the consolidated state budget under control. All the instruments to pursue fiscal policy were in place, and it was easy to understand what expenditures to cut. In the case of Russia, three big expenditure items could be substantially reduced. First, the risk of major wars and the ambitions of expansionism had faded away, which meant military expenditures could be cut sharply. Second, wasteful enterprise subsidies could be eliminated through price liberalization. Third, enterprise investments no longer would be financed through the state budget. These cuts could be so substantial that no changes in social expenditures would be necessary. The state administration could also be trimmed, although the direct savings in the budget would not be large. Cutting back on the administration would prevent it from sabotaging reform and pilfering from the state. In more general terms, public expenditures could be substantially reduced, because the state functioned poorly and used funds inefficiently. Furthermore, public expenditures were quite high given the actual level of Russian economic development. In addition, in a postcommunist transition there are normally semifiscal deficits that are beyond the control of the Ministry of Finance, and budget revenues would be likely to fall later on. Therefore, the budget should preferably show a surplus.

On the revenue side, substantial changes were required. First, the individualized turnover tax would have to be either evened out or replaced by a value-added tax (VAT). Foreign trade taxes would then need to be changed to ordinary, limited fixed tariffs. However, profit taxation had already been altered. In 1991, confiscatory taxation had been abolished and the tax on profits lowered to 30 percent. There was no need to alter a long-standing flat payroll tax of 38 percent. Income taxes were low, and it made no sense to raise them, because the state was unable to collect them.

Monetary policy was much more difficult to implement, because the tools of monetary policy simply did not exist. Previously, interest rates had been of no economic significance; but now they were needed to restrain demand. They had to be raised sharply, but most of the elite understood little about monetary policy and did not accept higher interest rates. With deliberate ignorance, enterprise managers compared the Russian nominal interest rates with those in the West. They argued that interest rates were far too high in Russia, omitting that Russian real interest rates were extremely negative. The whole concept of commercial borrowing was alien to the socialist mind. In the old system, credits had been fairly automatic for big state enterprises, and much of enterprise investment had been funded through the state budget. The CBR wanted to maintain its authority to lend directly to enterprises (which would be alien to an ordinary central bank), and its big customers preferred to go to the source of the money rather than through an intermediary. Reserve ratios of the commercial banks, which would be held with the CBR, were introduced. Such a decision was readily accepted, because it was in line with the old command economy mentality. The alteration of the payments system was immensely complex, and enterprises resisted any attempt at making payments less automatic. Payments and credits to other Commonwealth of Independent States (CIS) members created other major complications. It was clear from the outset that it would be difficult to impose a strict monetary policy, but it was nevertheless necessary.

To fix or peg the exchange rate and use it as a nominal anchor during the initial stages is generally advantageous for a macroeconomic stabilization. However, Russia's reserves of hard currency were virtually exhausted, and it could hardly fix its exchange rate before it had received substantial international credits. Yet the IMF did not want to provide any stabilization fund before the Russian exchange rate had stabilized (that is, when it was no longer needed). The Russian exchange rate was also extremely devalued. If Russia had fixed the exchange rate in December 1991, it would have imported an inflation rate of almost 2,000 percent until December 1993, because the real revaluation of the Russian ruble would take the form of inflation with a fixed exchange rate (see tables 6-1 and 6-2). Russia could either let the exchange rate float upward for a while or boldly start a revaluation, but the latter would have required substantial foreign reserves, which were not at hand.

Another common instrument of macroeconomic stabilization is incomes policy. Considering the power of the managers and the powerlessness of the workers in Russia, the need for an incomes policy seemed limited. The real worry was that managers would use their workers to press for more state subsidies. However, as soon as enterprises (whether privatized or only corporatized) became independent of the state budget, managers began withholding funds from their workers to their own benefit, as state funds were no longer freely available.

International financing was required for several purposes. First, Russia had run out of international reserves; international credits could replenish them, giving Russia an opportunity to build reserves in an orderly fashion. Foreign credits were also needed to finance any possible budget deficit or semifiscal deficit, to stabilize the domestic price level. Russia also craved balance of payments support to raise its collapsed imports to a reasonable level once again, thus salvaging falling production and reducing the social costs of the collapse of communism. Furthermore, the conditional nature of an international agreement on stabilization would be an important lever for the Russian reform government to use in defending its reform program domestically.

Given that the monetary overhang in Russia was so large that prices rose 245 percent instantly in January 1992, it has been argued that currency reform would have successfully eradicated the monetary overhang. However, no preparations had been made, and undertaking a currency

Table 6-1. *Monthly Inflation and the Expansion of the Money Supply,*
1992–94

	Increase in CPI (percent)	Increase in M2[a] (percent)	M2 velocity[b]
1992			
January	245	12.3	
February	38	11.9	
March	30	13.7	
April	22	10.0	
May	12	9.0	
June	19	27.5	
July	11	27.5	0.47
August	9	28.3	0.41
September	12	31.9	0.36
October	23	26.7	0.35
November	26	5.5	0.37
December	25	17.8	0.39
1993			
January	26	19.4	0.56
February	25	10.0	0.60
March	20	17.0	0.61
April	19	22.9	0.70
May	18	19.0	0.64
June	20	1.5	0.76
July	22	37.0	0.71
August	26	13.7	0.57
September	23	3.3	0.67
October	20	10.6	0.71
November	16	8.3	0.75
December	13	11.2	0.93
1994			
January	18	5.3	0.69
February	11	6.1	0.85
March	7	9.2	0.86
April	8	16.9	0.90
May	7	11.3	0.88
June	6	13.0	0.74
July	5	10.2	0.73
August	5	12.0	0.73
September	7	5.7	0.79
October	15		
November	14		
December	16		

a. M2 equals currency in circulation, demand deposits, and time deposits in commercial banks.
b. M2 velocity is defined as GDP at the price of that month divided by M2.
Sources: Government of the Russian Federation, *Russian Economic Trends*, vol. 2, no. 4 (1993), pp. 116–18; Brigitte Granville, Weekly Monetary Report 60, June 8, 1994; *Russian Economic Trends: Monthly Update*, May 31, 1994; Institute for Economic Analysis, *Rossiiskie ekonomicheskie reformy: poteryanny god* (Russian economic reforms: a lost year) (Moscow, December 1994), p. 75; Goskomstat Rossii, *Sotsial'no-ekonomicheskoe polozhenie Rossii 1994 g.* (Russia's socioeconomic situation, 1994) (Moscow, 1995), p. 84.

Table 6-2. *Wages, 1985–93*

	Average wage (rubles per month)	Change (percent)	Real wage index (1985 = 100)	Wage in U.S. dollars per month
1985	201		100	
1986	208	3.2	101	
1987	216	4.0	104	
1988	235	8.8	113	
1989	259	9.9	117	
1990	297	14.8	128	
1991	516	73.9	114	
1992	6,011	1,065	77	
1993	58,234	885	81	
1992				
January	1,438	51.4	67	6.8
February	2,004	39.4	67	10.8
March	2,726	36.0	70	18.2
April	3,024	10.9	64	19.6
May	3,672	21.4	70	30.5
June	5,067	38.0	81	40.2
July	5,452	7.6	79	38.1
August	5,870	7.7	78	34.9
September	7,379	25.7	87	33.5
October	8,853	20.0	85	25.0
November	10,576	19.5	81	24.8
December	16,071	52.0	98	38.7
1993				
January	15,690	−2.4	76	32.4
February	18,672	19.0	73	32.8
March	23,559	26.2	76	35.5
April	30,562	29.7	83	39.9
May	37,505	22.7	86	39.7
June	47,371	26.3	91	43.9
July	55,995	18.2	88	54.7
August	65,400	16.8	82	66.3
September	80,900	23.7	82	75.4
October	93,000	15.0	79	78.3
November	101,495	9.1	74	85.0
December	140,650	38.6	91	113.9

Source: Government of the Russian Federation, *Russian Economic Trends*, pp. 33, 119. The last column has been calculated from CBR data by Alla Gantman, Microeconomic and Finance Unit at the Russian Ministry of Finance.

reform was practically impossible. Yegor Gaidar estimated that nine months would be needed to prepare for any such reform. Moreover, Soviet Prime Minister Valentin Pavlov's currency exchange in January 1991 was still fresh in everyone's memory. It had led to three days of chaos and had no advantageous effects. A currency reform was therefore considered hopelessly unpopular. After two currency reforms within a year, popular confidence in the Russian currency would not likely return easily.

There were abundant reasons for undertaking radical, comprehensive economic reform in Russia. The financial and economic crisis was devastating and called for immediate action. The government's ability to make policy was scant, necessitating that policymakers focus on the most important issues and choose solutions simple enough to be implemented. The bureaucracy not only disobeyed but also sabotaged reforms; therefore, only simple and consistent policies could be implemented. Information was both scarce and highly distorted. Policymakers had to act on principle rather than facts, which made any kind of fine-tuning of reform impossible. Finally, there was no coordinated economic policymaking. The government, the CBR, and the Supreme Soviet steered their own independent courses in different orbits, though the President enjoyed substantial rights to rule by decree. Everything in this setting pointed to the need for a hard and (of necessity) rough stabilization policy.

The most important reason for a radical approach, however, was the asocial behavior of the state enterprise managers—an outstanding peculiarity of the FSRs. At the start of reform, there was hardly any mechanism for ejecting Russian state enterprise managers. They felt no threat to their positions and were buoyed by their almost boundless power. The managers enjoyed the freedom of a market economy coupled with the irresponsibility of a command economy. Their budget constraints were soft; they were confident that the state would eventually pay them whatever they considered necessary. They could high-handedly neglect all demands both from the state and the market, not to mention the banks and their own workers. When it was convenient, they refrained from paying wages or for deliveries. Nor did they care to collect payments from their customers. Although production fell sharply, state enterprises continued to make deliveries, regardless of whether or not they had received any orders for the goods, believing the state would be obligated to pay them in the end. A major task of the transition to a market economy was introducing elementary business ethics to enterprise managers. Therefore, it was necessary to hit them hard and break their ties through strict macroeconomic stabilization. The managers needed to undergo true economic shock therapy. However, they were bound to collude with old allies throughout much of the Russian elite (including those in the government, the Supreme Soviet, and the CBR) to ease the pressure of working for money, demand, and the market. Enterprise managers formed the most formidable vested interest of the transition period.

Considering the power balance in Russia as reforms began, the reformers were probably only able to deliver a sufficient shock briefly. Their assignment was to maximize the blow to the state enterprise managers, to introduce political and economic institutions capable of sustaining that pressure, and to convince everyone of the credibility of the new policies.

Radical Reform: January–May 1992

The year 1992 started off with a big bang. With the subsequent relaxation of the stabilization policy, it is easy to forget how great the change actually was. Yegor Gaidar led the charge with intelligence and decisiveness. He focused on two major measures: far-reaching liberalization of prices and balancing of the consolidated state budget.

An extraordinary improvement in the budget balance—a textbook example—was accomplished. Arms procurement was initially cut by 85 percent, while military salaries were kept high. Many subsidies were cut and state investments minimized, but social expenditures were maintained. The old Soviet government administration had also been radically reduced through its merger with the Russian government.

On the revenue side, the foremost novelty was the introduction of a unified VAT of no less than 28 percent. This was not a pure VAT but was in part a turnover tax. In addition, new excise taxes were instituted. Gaidar was anxious to let the state enterprises that were big producers be the mainstay of budget revenue. (He presumed that a small-scale trade sector would soon emerge, and it would be extremely difficult to collect taxes from these enterprises.) The three main taxes were profit taxes (basically at a 32-percent rate), payroll taxes (unchanged at 38 percent of the wage fund), and the new VAT. All these taxes would primarily be paid by big state enterprises; the old tax collection system would continue to function. In effect, state enterprises paid taxes in advance each month through automatic deductions, giving the state a positive Tanzi-Olivera effect (that is, with the treasury reaping the gains from inflation). Personal income taxes remained very low—12 percent of official income for most people, and a maximum of 30 percent for the very rich, who in any case did not pay income taxes. The liberalization of imports meant that all import taxes were eliminated, while new export tariffs were introduced for strategic goods.[5]

The CBR introduced ordinary reserve ratios of 20 percent of commercial bank assets, to be held at the CBR without interest. CBR chairman Georgy Matyukhin tried to raise the refinance rate gradually but faced strong resistance. The refinance rate was only 20 percent per annum at the beginning of 1992. It was raised to 50 percent per annum that April and to 80 percent per annum in June.[6] The CBR was therefore forced to ration credits in the face of enormous demand. To get control over payments both within Russia and with other CIS states, Matyukhin centralized the system, which meant that payments were slowed down. Even so, the CBR lacked the capacity to monitor all payments.[7]

The exchange rate floated and was not subject to any particular policy, because no international financing was being offered. Nor was there any incomes policy; Gaidar reckoned it was impossible to control incomes without a pegged exchange rate. In practice, Russia pursued a so-called orthodox stabilization policy based only on fiscal and monetary policy. However, this was conducted not on ideological or theoretical grounds but because of the lack of international financing.

Despite the profound economic crisis at the end of 1991, the stabilization policy got off to a decent start. Gross shortages disappeared, and inflation fell month by month. The initial price jump in the consumer price index (CPI) in January 1992 was 245 percent. This was followed by monthly inflation rates of 38 percent in February, 30 percent in March, 22 percent in April, 12 percent in May, and finally 9 percent in August (see table 6-1).[8] Still, the fall in monthly inflation was insufficient. Even in August 1992, annualized inflation was 181 percent. The ruble appreciated significantly in real terms, and the exchange rate was relatively stable, notwithstanding the high inflation. Hence, the average monthly wage, measured in U.S. dollars, rose from $7 in January to $40 in June 1992. Contrary to many predictions, no social unrest erupted. Real wages fell steeply in statistical terms to about two-thirds of their precrisis level in the mid-1980s (see table 6-2). This primarily reflected that the monetary overhang had been eliminated and said less about the actual standard of living. Moreover, wages started shrinking as a share of actual income as people increasingly earned money on the side. Because shortages had disappeared, cash could be used again, and barter in the Russian economy was swiftly reduced. However, all bank savings had been eaten away by inflation, which turned many people (especially those who were elderly and well-to-do) against the reform government.

Initially, the government was more successful in balancing the budget than hardly anyone had expected. Tax collection recovered considerably. Even according to IMF statistics (which tend to present a more accurate but bleaker picture than domestic sources), the general government balance on a cash basis was a budget surplus of 0.9 percent of GDP during the first quarter of 1992, succeeding a deficit of about 30 percent of GDP in 1991. Yet the IMF also provides a much higher figure (− 8.0 percent of GDP) based on government commitments; however, that is not particularly relevant, as government commitments are not binding in Russian practice. The difference thus reflects not government arrears but ad hoc cuts by the government.[9]

The CBR came under extraordinary pressure. When the monetary overhang was eliminated, the real money supply (M2) fell from 77 percent to 25 percent of GDP between December 1991 and January 1992.[10] Enterprises found their real money balances severely devalued because of the price jump and ongoing inflation. They were not prepared for this shrinking of their working capital. Rather than making adjustments and economizing on this capital, state managers vehemently demanded additional credits. When they had failed to exact money from the Ministry of Finance, they turned to the CBR with their demands. Money and time had suddenly become valuable, though penalties for delayed payments remained minute, rendering it profitable to delay payments. There was no effective threat—neither job loss nor bankruptcy—to use in disciplining managers. As state enterprises stopped paying each other, arrears mounted up. The lack of adjustment to inflation implied that the velocity of money did not accelerate as fast as it would have in an ordinary market economy. By May 1992, enterprises started demanding prepayments from one another. It was a positive sign, because it showed that they had begun to care about collecting payments. Because the legal system was so weak, the only effective collection mechanism was to demand payment before delivery.

The reform efforts were greeted with a mounting outcry from all branches of the old establishment. Their prime concern was that industrial production was collapsing. In reality, however, the decline in official industrial production eased. In 1991 as a whole, industrial production had dropped by 14.7 percent and the decline had accelerated during the year, compared with a slump of only 13.5 percent in the first half of 1992.[11] For the start of a systemic change, this was minor. Nor was there any unemployment. By ordinary standards, the Russian economy was actually overheated. A more justified concern would have been that the monetary squeeze was too loose, prompting too little structural adjustment.

The primary problem was that the money supply (M2) had expanded by as much as 11 percent a month on average from January to May 1992 (see table 6-1). Therefore, monthly inflation barely fell below that level. The firm correlation between the increase in M2 and the inflation rate (with a lag of three to four months) showed that inflation in Russia was a monetary phenomenon—the quantity theory of money functioned normally in Russia once the monetary overhang was eliminated. Russia's true predicament was that it had not experienced any real economic shock therapy, because CBR chairman Georgy Matyukhin tried to pursue a moderately strict monetary policy. As a consequence, he made enemies of everyone—both those who demanded credits as well as those wanting reform—and failed to control inflation. All the lobbies attacked him for having too strict a monetary policy, whereas the reform government criticized him for promoting too loose a monetary policy.

A number of predictable problems built up during the first half of 1992 as a result of an insufficiently credible stabilization policy. Inter-enterprise arrears mounted, and Russia suffered from an acute cash shortage. Credits leaked to the other CIS states, which paid Russia back with its own credits. Finally, the government's failure to liberalize energy prices gradually undermined the budget.

A more curious predicament arose when Russia was flooded with international commodity credits during the first quarter of 1992—credits that were meant primarily for food imports. These centralized imports of grain were subsidized 99 percent; the exchange rate used was just 1 percent of the market exchange rate, but it was financed by commodity credits. As a consequence, the IMF assessed Russia's "enlarged fiscal deficit" on a cash basis at 25.3 percent of GDP during the first quarter of 1992, although the domestic budget showed a surplus.[12] Ironically, foreign credits designated as humanitarian aid disqualified Russia from IMF support for macroeconomic stabilization.

The attempt at stabilization began to unravel in early April 1992. The government tried to cover its back in anticipation of the expected anti-reform onslaught at the Congress of People's Deputies later that month. First, Yeltsin sacrificed Gennady Burbulis as first deputy prime minister, and Gaidar took his place. Although this seemed to strengthen the position of the economic reformers, it had quite the opposite effect, because it disengaged Gaidar from focusing on economic strategy. Worse, Gaidar appointed in his stead an old Soviet technocrat, Vasily Barchuk, as minister of finance, and Barchuk followed the path of least resistance. Consequently, price liberalization of energy was postponed indefinitely. The government made a number of compromises with the barons of communist agriculture and industry, offering massive subsidized credits (colloquially called Gaidar credits). This initial ambitious attempt at macroeconomic stabilization was definitely broken by June 1992, with the unleashing of a flood of cheap credits from the CBR. The main resistance against reform had come from state enterprise managers and the Supreme Soviet, but both President Yeltsin and the CBR showed weak resolve. Gaidar could hardly have impeded these forces, but he can be criticized for agreeing to stay on as acting prime minister after his stabilization policies had been abandoned.

Backsliding: June–December 1992

The reform government had become a coalition government with the inclusion of three industrialists as deputy prime ministers. In June 1992, the macroeconomic stabilization policy of the government evaporated. The government's only rationale for remaining in office was that privatization was proceeding. In the following months, all the news was bad. Wages rose sharply in June, although that appears a natural readjustment after an excessive fall of real wages. Most damaging was the appointment of Viktor Gerashchenko as chair of the CBR on July 17. Soon thereafter, it was decided to net out interenterprise arrears and cover the balance with state credits.

In June, credit started flowing in all directions: to agriculture and industry; to the other FSRs; and to the budget, because of increasing subsidies. The domestic budget deficit peaked during the third quarter of 1992 at 14.6 percent of GDP on a cash basis.[13] The money supply (M2) increased by no less than 28 percent per month during the five months from June to October 1992 (see table 6-1). With such monetary expansion, velocity of money was bound to rise, which would increase inflation more than the expansion of the money supply, and hyperinflation (or inflation of more than 50 percent a month) could easily follow. Destabilization was rampant. Curiously, in early July 1992, after Russia's efforts at stabilization had ceased, the IMF deemed it ripe for a full-fledged standby agreement. The board of the IMF decided to give Russia a first tranche of $1 billion in August 1992.

Russia had inherited a few extrabudgetary funds from the USSR, but in 1992 new extrabudgetary funds mushroomed. They were used to guarantee the financing of top-priority projects. Key funds included pension, social insurance, and employment funds, which were financed out of the payroll tax, which was the most reliable. The pension fund and the social security fund were controlled by the Supreme Soviet, and the trade unions ran the social insurance fund. In addition, a multitude of extrabudgetary investment funds was set up by old branch ministries. The very purpose of these funds was to deprive the Ministry of Finance of fiscal power and flexibility, and their founding was instigated by the enemies of radical reform. In 1992, the total revenues in the funds amounted to 18 percent of GDP, and they ran a surplus of several percent of GDP. Information on extrabudgetary funds was hard to obtain, presumably because a substantial part of their revenues was spent illicitly. These funds were (and are) not included in the consolidated state budget. If they are included in the government finances, the public deficit falls by a few percent of GDP. Hence, total tax collection in 1992 amounted to 51 percent of GDP, which makes the persistent concern with the collapse of tax revenues seem somewhat exaggerated.[14]

The new, loose monetary policies were popular with the old elite. However, contrary to what Russian industrialists and conservatives had argued, production did not recover when ample credits were provided. In the third quarter of 1992, the economy was flooded with credits, but industrial production fell by 24.2 percent compared with the already low level in the third quarter of 1991—that is, almost twice as much as in the first half of 1992.[15] The argument that the economy needed monetary stimulation had been tested, and it did not hold water.

Capital flight appears to have gained momentum, because there were few investment opportunities in Russia. A standard estimate is that capital flight amounted to about $1 billion a month in 1992. The exchange rate fell sharply from 135 rubles to the dollar on June 30 to 309 rubles to the dollar on October 1, 1992. Dollarization gained momentum, as dollar deposits in Russian banks grew from 34 percent of M2 at the end of April to 119 percent of M2 at the end of November 1992.[16] The most stunning statistic is that gross accumulation amounted to as much as 34.6 percent of GDP in 1992. Fifteen and a half percent of GDP went into an increase of stocks. This presumably reflects both increased hoarding of goods by enterprises (because of soft budget constraints and high inflation) as well as capital flight. Meanwhile, investment fell from a still high 24.4 percent of GDP in 1991 to 19.2 percent of GDP in 1992, which presumably is an exaggeration.

Yet as the monetary policy became looser, tax collection improved, because enterprises had plenty of money. There was no evident wage pressure, and social peace reigned. The weakness of labor was manifested by the continued absence of wage indexation despite lasting high inflation. The average wage in U.S. dollars fell from $40 in June to $25 in November 1992 as confidence in the ruble diminished (see table 6-2).

As a result of the credit expansion from June to October, monthly inflation reached 25 percent during the last quarter of 1992. Because the velocity of money was bound to rise, inflation would increase even more. As Russia raced toward hyperinflation, one significant improvement finally occurred. On October 7, 1992, the president issued a decree on the formation of a Government Commission on Credit Policy. The commission was headed by Gaidar and dominated by reformers. Before, there had been no government coordination or control of credits, although these credits frequently included state subsidies. Empowering this commission probably saved Russia from hyperinflation.

Stalemate: January–September 1993

On December 12, 1992, Gaidar was ousted as acting prime minister by the Congress of People's Deputies. Two days later, Deputy Prime Minister Viktor Chernomyrdin was promoted to prime minister as a compromise candidate, with strong support from the industrial lobby. This aroused great fear that reform had come to an end. During the week of New Year 1993, a time of buoyant consumer demand before the main holiday of the year, weekly inflation rose to 10 percent. This corresponded to a monthly rate of 50 percent, the commonly acknowledged threshold to hyperinflation.

Faced with this precarious situation, the leading economic reformers remaining in the government, Anatoly Chubais and Aleksandr Shokhin managed to convince the president and the prime minister that the young, liberal economist Boris Fedorov should be appointed minister of finance and deputy prime minister. Fedorov, who was a professor of economics, had been Russian Minister of Finance during the second half of 1990 but had resigned in protest against populist financial policies. He then joined the European Bank for Reconstruction and Development (EBRD), and he had been the reformers' candidate for chair of the CBR. In the fall of 1992, Fedorov became Russian executive director of the World Bank. Beating all the odds, including the strong resistance of the parliament and most of the government, Fedorov took a strong stand on macroeconomic stabilization. He managed to steer Russia from the brink of hyperinflation and prepare the way for stabilization. Fedorov formed a full macroeconomic strategy with a multitude of measures and energetically engineered breakthroughs wherever possible.[17]

In early 1993, the prime macroeconomic task was to control credits. Fedorov activated and reinforced the Commission on Credit Policy, which had been instigated by Gaidar. The commission had to approve frames for credit allocation, thereby enabling Fedorov to rein in the loose credit policy of the CBR. In the aftermath of the referendum of April 25, 1993, which approved economic reform policies, Fedorov brought about a joint "Declaration on the Economic Policy of the Government and the Central Bank of Russia," which was signed by Prime Minister Chernomyrdin and Chairman of the CBR Gerashchenko in May 1993. This was a brief but substantial agreement that established quarterly credit ceilings.[18] Fedorov also pushed the CBR to raise its interest rate. The CBR committed itself to raising the refinance rate to not more than 7 percentage points less than the interbank lending rate. The CBR honored its commitment and started to raise its refinance rate, but the interbank market rate was still highly negative, because there was so much money on the market (see table 6-3). These conditions were part of an agreement with the IMF on a Systemic Transformation Facility (STF). A first tranche of $1.5 billion on an IMF STF credit of $3 billion was disbursed to Russia.

Another major concern was extensive cheap credits to the other CIS states, which had been spearheaded by the CBR. As discussed in chapter 4, Fedorov managed to block the flow of unregulated technical credits

Table 6-3. *Interest Rates and Inflation, 1992–94*

Percent per month

	Central Bank of Russia refinance rate	Interbank lending rate	Real interbank lending rate	Increase in consumer price index
1992				
January	1.6	2.6	−242	245
February	1.6	3.0	−35	38
March	1.6	3.3	−27	30
April	4.2	4.0	−18	22
May	4.2	5.8	−6	12
June	6.7	6.8	−12	19
July	6.7	7.7	−3	11
August	6.7	8.3	−1	9
September	6.7	8.3	−4	12
October	6.7	8.6	−14	23
November	6.7	8.9	−17	26
December	6.7	9.6	−15	25
1993				
January	6.7	9.9	−16	26
February	6.7	10.8	−14	25
March	6.7	11.0	−9	20
April	8.3	11.3	−8	19
May	8.3	11.7	−6	18
June	11.7	12.1	−8	20
July	14.2	14.5	−7	22
August	14.2	15.4	−11	26
September	14.2	15.8	−7	23
October	17.5	17.1	−3	20
November	17.5	17.9	2	16
December	17.5	17.9	5	13
1994				
January	17.5	17.5	0	21
February	17.5	17.8	7	11
March	17.5	17.6	10	7
April	17.5	17.0	10	8
May	16.9	15.0	8	7
June	14.8	12.3	6	6
July	12.9	11.7	6	5
August	11.9	10.4	6	5
September	10.8	10.0	2	8

Sources: Government of the Russian Federation, *Russian Economic Trends*, pp. 24, 117–18; Brigitte Granville, *Monetary Report 65*, November 1, 1994, Moscow, pp. 19–20.

that were essentially free of charge. He did this through a decision by the Supreme Soviet on April 20, 1993, against the wishes of the CBR. Then the CBR took to delivering cash; but this flow ceased after the CBR's currency reform that July. Ultimately, Fedorov succeeded in regulating financial relations with other CIS states, and after August 1993, only limited and properly regulated state credits were issued.

Fedorov's third macroeconomic concern focused on huge import subsidies (which were discussed in chapter 5). Dealing with them was a comparatively easy task. Fedorov managed to reduce these subsidies by about half their volume between 1992 and 1993, and they were to be abolished in 1994. At the same time, their subsidization was also halved. Total import subsidies therefore fell from 17.5 percent of GDP in 1992 to about 4 percent of GDP in 1993, and Fedorov succeeded in putting an end to destabilizing foreign commodity credits.[19]

Another important group of macroeconomic measures undertaken by Fedorov centered on raising or liberalizing energy prices. As reviewed in chapter 5, petroleum and coal prices were liberalized. The prices of natural gas and electricity were raised significantly in the summer of 1993, and energy taxation through VAT and excise taxes rose.

Meanwhile, Fedorov fought to keep the budget deficit under control. Tax revenues fell substantially between 1992 and 1993—that is, by 8 percent of GDP, three-quarters of which was attributed to falling VAT revenues (see table 6-4). One explanation was that the VAT had been reduced from 28 percent in 1992 to 20 percent in 1993; another was that unjustified tax exemptions had been awarded as privileges to strong industries. The expansion of the private sector complicated tax collection. Fedorov tried to include all semifiscal deficits (such as subsidized credits and import subsidies) in the budget so that the budget deficit would reflect the real fiscal situation. As a result of this increased transparency, the public budget deficit appeared larger, which raised concerns.

Finally, ordinary short-term state bonds were introduced on March 18, 1993, and a new issue was added each month. Initially only three-month bonds were issued, but 1994 saw the introduction of state bonds with a duration of six months. To begin with, the total bond amounts were small, but their volume gradually increased, as market demand rose. The Ministry of Finance adjusted the supply to how much they thought the market would absorb rather than to what financial needs actually were.[20] A base had been laid for an ordinary state bond market.

Table 6-4. *Consolidated State Budget, 1992 and 1993 (Outcomes)*
Percent of GDP

	1992	1993
Revenues		
Total revenues	33.6	25.8
VAT	12.9	6.9
Excise taxes	1.2	1.3
Profit tax	10.1	10.3
Household income tax	2.8	2.7
Foreign economic activity	3.0	1.4
Tax on natural resources	1.4	0.7
Expenditures		
Total expenditures	39.0	35.3
National economy	12.5	9.9
Education, health, and culture	10.1	8.8
Defense	5.8	4.4
Foreign economic activity	2.0	1.7
Law and order	—	1.6

Sources: International Monetary Fund, *Economic Review: Russian Federation* (Washington, D.C., 1993), p. 96; Government of the Russian Federation, *Russian Economic Trends*, p. 13.

On most measures, the CBR under Viktor Gerashchenko actively advocated policies leading to macroeconomic destabilization. Against all the evidence, Gerashchenko alleged that the issue of large subsidized credits to old state-owned industries and agriculture and the other CIS states would stimulate production. Fedorov publicly and repeatedly called for Gerashchenko's ouster. However, Gerashchenko stayed put because he enjoyed solid support from Prime Minister Chernomyrdin.

Although no real stabilization occurred in 1993, positive changes emerged. A highly visible development was the sudden and unexpected rise of not only the real but also the nominal exchange rate from mid-June to August; in fact, the real exchange rate more than doubled during the second half of 1993. In June, Fedorov made himself famous by betting with anyone who wanted to that the nominal exchange rate would not fall more than 10 percent by September 1.[21] In fact, the rate rose, but few believed Fedorov at the time. His very statement reinforced confidence in the ruble. The rising interest rate was probably the main cause of the steadier exchange rate, but Russia was also developing a large trade surplus.

Inflation fell slightly during 1993, but its monthly average from January through September 1993 remained at a disappointing 22 percent. Although the expansion of M2 was limited to 267 percent during the first nine months of 1993, the CPI rose by almost twice as much—500 percent. The velocity of money was rising, as big enterprises at long last began to adjust to inflation, reducing the real balances of money they held. The monthly M2 velocity (that is, monthly GDP at current prices divided by M2) almost doubled between December 1992 and June 1993 (see table 6-1). Another explanation was the price liberalizations that took place in the summer of 1993. Dollarization remained high until June but diminished significantly in relation to the Russian money supply during the second half of 1993. The real interest rate in Russia climbed considerably, and the real exchange rate also rose. Wage pressure was not a serious problem, and real wages averaged slightly over 80 percent of their mid-1980s level (see table 6-2).

Boris Fedorov's tenure in office was just over a year. His record is striking evidence of how much one forceful individual in a key post can accomplish in such a volatile situation, despite the lack of a genuine political base. Still, some macroeconomic measures remained out of reach. It had proven impossible to abolish subsidized credits or even to diminish the degree of their subsidization. Agriculture had resisted any attempt at deregulation or lowering of its subsidization. In late July 1993, Gerashchenko sprang the unpleasant surprise of a disruptive and harmful currency reform (discussed in chapter 4). This lowered confidence in the Russian ruble and speeded up the velocity of money and inflation. Meanwhile, the credit ceilings for the third quarter were broken under pressure from the agricultural and northern lobbies. The Supreme Soviet adopted a budget for 1993 with a deficit on the order of 25 percent of GDP. Fedorov refused to abide by such a budget. A political stalemate over economic policy had been reached. A political explosion appeared inevitable.

The Second Reform Wave: September–December 1993

On September 21, 1993, President Yeltsin made the long overdue decision to dissolve the old predemocratic Supreme Soviet and Congress of People's Deputies and to call for new elections and a referendum on a new constitution. Suddenly, the tables were turned. Just before, Gaidar had returned to the government as both first deputy prime minister and minister of the economy. His appointment was pivotal to tipping the balance within the government in favor of reform. For the first time since early 1992, a major reform offensive was possible.

Fedorov focused on two important macroeconomic measures. First, as early as September 25, 1993, he abolished all subsidized credits via government decree.[22] Most centralized credits, notably those to agriculture and to the northern territories, had been subsidized with an interest rate of 10 or 25 percent per annum. Second, through a number of decisions, he succeeded in deregulating agriculture, and the prices of bread, grain, and baby food were liberalized. The state stopped procuring food, leaving its trade to the market. Large potential subsidies were preempted. Fedorov also reinforced budgetary policy, keeping the planned budget deficit constant at a somewhat high 9.5 percent of GDP. He did this by refusing to pay out new expenditures, which were continuously being authorized by government officials who lacked the authority to do so.[23]

The reformers made a new attempt to oust the conservative chairman of the CBR, but Chernomyrdin saved him.[24] Nevertheless, Gerashchenko adjusted to the reformist pressure. In October 1993, the monthly refinance rate was raised to 17.5 percent. As a consequence, in November it rose above the interbank lending rate for the first time, and Russia experienced a positive real interest rate. From then on, monetary policy became the major instrument of monetary stabilization.

An important change made at the beginning of 1994 was the introduction of a new system of fiscal federalism. Previously, the allocation of tax revenues had been fairly arbitrary. This led to long, unstructured negotiations between the Ministry of Finance in Moscow and the 88 regional authorities. Basically, the new system introduced clear rules. A certain share of taxes were to go to regional authorities and another share to the federal treasury. The responsibility for expenditures was correspondingly clarified. Transfers from the center to regions in need were supposed to amount to a couple of percentage points of GDP. However, complaints arose that transfers were based more on political considerations than actual needs, and strong regions demanded that taxes be redistributed to their advantage.[25]

By the end of 1993, Russia was prepared to adopt a full-fledged stabilization policy. The necessary institutional changes had been undertaken. At long last, Russia's monetary policy had become a responsible one. Russia had a positive real interest rate and credit ceilings, and the ruble was the national currency. Fiscal controls were in place. For monetary stability, the main remaining task was to reduce the budget deficit to 6 percent of GDP so that it could be financed in a noninflationary, nonmonetary way—that is, through domestic bonds and international credits. This could be done by targeting one of three lobbies. One possibility was to abolish the completely unjustified tax exemption granted Gazprom. A second option was to abolish export restrictions for oil. This would lead to a doubling of the oil price, and much of the price increase would be taxed. A third possibility was to eliminate subsidies to agriculture. Any of these options could reduce the budget deficit by 3 to 4 percent of GDP. In addition, if it were pegged, the exchange rate would serve an important function as a nominal anchor.[26]

However, for the reformers the results of the parliamentary elections on December 12, 1993, amounted to a vote of no confidence. Turnout was low—only 54.8 percent of registered voters. The liberal party Russia's Choice, led by Yegor Gaidar, received only 15.4 percent of the vote in the proportional part of the election for the State Duma, the lower chamber of the new Russian Federal Assembly. The other liberal party, Yabloko, headed by Grigory Yavlinsky, got a paltry 7.8 percent. Instead, the apparent election winners were the hard-line parties—the ultra-nationalist Liberal Democratic Party (Vladimir Zhirinovsky), with 22.8 percent of the vote; the Communist Party (Gennady Zyuganov), with 12.4 percent; and the Agrarian Party (Mikhail Lapshin), their partner in the countryside, with 7.9 percent. Another 20.4 percent of the vote was cast for centrist parties.[27] Half the seats, however, were distributed through majority election in one-person constituencies. Therefore, the parliament was divided into three almost equal shares of liberals (30.1 percent of the seats), centrists (28.7 percent), and a red-brown communist and nationalist block (39.5 percent), though some deputies changed factions and party discipline varied (see table 6-5). However serious the setback was for the reformers, they had not lost out altogether.

A Policy of Passivity: January–October 1994

After the elections in December 1993, it was unclear what would happen to both the government and its economic policy. The formation of a new government took time. Prime Minister Chernomyrdin, who had not run in the election, simply remained in office. Gradually, the actual outcome of the elections emerged. On January 16, 1994, Gaidar resigned from the government, and Fedorov followed suit on January 20. Gaidar

Table 6-5. *Party Factions in the State Duma, June 1994*

Party factions	Number of deputies	Share of seats (%)
Russia's Choice (liberal)	74	16.5
December 12 Union (liberal)	32	7.1
Yabloko (liberal)	29	6.5
PRES (centrist)	31	6.9
New Regional Policy (centrist)	60	13.4
Russia's Women (centrist)	23	5.1
Democratic Party of Russia (centrist)	15	3.3
Agrarian Party (communist)	55	12.3
Communist Party (communist)	45	10.0
Russian Way (nationalist)	13	2.9
Liberal Democratic Party (fascist)	64	14.3
Independent	7	1.6
Total	448	100.0

Source: "On Whom Does the Government Rely in the State Duma?," *Izvestiya*, June 16, 1994.

cited two specific causes: the wasteful and unauthorized decisions by the president's administration to construct a new parliamentary building for $500 million, and the monetary union concluded with Belarus on January 5, 1994, which was supported by Chernomyrdin.[28] Moreover, on January 20, Chernomyrdin held a press conference at which he said that the time for "market romanticism" was over. Instead, he advocated "nonmonetary measures" for fighting inflation, by which he implied wage and price controls, as well as state support for investments. Chernomyrdin insisted on keeping Gerashchenko, and he appeared supportive of giving huge state subsidies to the agricultural sector.[29]

The most telling reflection of Chernomyrdin's aspirations was the composition of the presidium of his new government. He himself represented the oil and gas lobbies and saw to it that they would continue to be given favorable treatment. First Deputy Prime Minister Oleg Soskovets was another original enterprise manager and branch minister, but from the metallurgical industry, and he took the military-industrial complex under his wing. A third member of the presidium was Deputy Prime Minister Aleksandr Zaveryukha, who had been elected a deputy in the duma for the pro-communist Agrarian Party. Deputy Prime Minister Yury Yarov was most noticeable for being completely inconspicuous. Finally, President Yeltsin had appointed Chubais deputy prime minister and chairman of GKI before Chernomyrdin formed his new government. Although all these men had held these posts before the elections, five reformist deputy prime ministers (Boris Fedorov, Yegor Gaidar, Sergei Shakhrai, Aleksandr Shokhin, and Vladimir Shumeiko) had been left out. With the exception of Chubais, the new government looked like a government of Russia's strongest industrial lobbies.[30]

In reality, however, Chernomyrdin perpetuated Fedorov's policy, although he did not move it toward the full stabilization Fedorov had aspired to. After having criticized Fedorov for sequestering state expenditures when state revenues did not reach the planned level, Chernomyrdin cut these expenditures even further. Consequently, the budget deficit stayed fixed at 9.5 percent of GDP. The new constitution of December 1993 worked. Although it took until June 24 for the new parliament to approve the 1994 budget, the State Duma showed great responsibility and did not significantly increase the budget deficit. The Duma was disciplined by political parties. The less important upper chamber, the Federation Council, showed much less responsibility. It was elected entirely in one-person constituencies and worked without political parties. In practice, most of its members were regional governors and other prominent representatives of the old elite.

In the first quarter of 1994, M2 expanded by approximately 7 percent a month. The refinance rate remained high, and in March 1994 the real positive annualized interest rate peaked at an incredible 200 percent (see table 6-1).[31] The CBR satisfied a long-standing demand from liberals and began conducting monthly credit auctions on February 28, 1994.[32]

Russia was experiencing a real stabilization effort. Monthly inflation fell from 18 percent in January to 7 percent in March and then to a low of 4.6 percent in August. The restriction of demand had effects on the real economy. During the first half of 1994, official industrial production fell by 26 percent, twice as much as during the first half of 1992, but this time the protests against this decline were much milder. Russians had increasingly come to realize that there was no viable alternative to financial stabilization; though transitional costs were substantial, a market economy would eventually work.

Restructuring gained momentum.[33] As a combined result of increased stabilization and the successful voucher privatization, foreign portfolio investments began pouring into Russia, peaking in August at an estimated $500 million.[34] The Russian stock market experienced a great boom from the beginning of the year until September. Savings increased greatly. Russia went through a spree of popular speculation, which resulted in a large number of new private fortunes as well as financial scams, notably the MMM pyramid game scandal involving millions of Russian savers.

However, the real exchange rate of the ruble did not appreciate, and the nominal exchange rate continued to depreciate approximately at pace with inflation. The apparent reason was that the government did not create any expectations of stabilization as it had in 1993; on the contrary. In a speech on July 15, 1994, Prime Minister Chernomyrdin declared that while it was good that inflation had fallen to 5 percent a month, it had been unacceptable to pursue a financial and monetary policy so hard that inflation would have been squeezed to 2 to 3 percent a month or even less. According to Chernomyrdin, that would have harmed the investment climate.[35]

But many problems with macroeconomic policy remained. First of all, the government did not really aim at a full stabilization but appeared satisfied with an annual inflation rate of about 100 percent. In addition, after Fedorov's departure from the government, macroeconomic policy was left in weak hands. No new minister of finance was appointed, and Fedorov's first deputy minister, Sergei Dubinin, was left as acting minister of finance, giving him little authority. Dubinin aggravated the situation further by appearing more like a civil servant than a policymaker. Aleksandr Shokhin had become minister of the economy and soon became deputy prime minister once again, but he no longer pushed for any particular policy. Instead, he played a passive role and focused on debt renegotiations. At the CBR, Gerashchenko continued advocating subsidized credits to industry to revive production. In effect, Chernomyrdin himself took over responsibility for economic policy, and he neither asked for nor accepted serious economic advice.

A first step, and an unrealistic one, was to raise the consolidated state budget as a share of GDP. The so-called consolidated state budget included the federal and regional budgets, but not the extrabudgetary funds (about 15 percent of GDP). Although actual revenues of the consolidated state budget had been 25.8 percent of GDP, Chernomyrdin raised the budgeted state revenues by almost 5 percent of GDP, to 30.7 percent for 1994. This was completely unfeasible, and for the first quarter of 1994, revenues stayed at 20.2 percent of GDP.[36] As a result, Chernomyrdin had to sequester expenditures far more aggressively than Fedorov had done in 1993, and the whole budget became a sham. It is difficult to get a full picture of expenditures, which fall into three categories: federal budget, regional budgets, and extrabudgetary funds. Most of the time, only expenditures of the federal budget are discussed. They are cut when revenues fall; the extrabudgetary funds have the safest financing, and the regional budgets appear to have priority over the federal budget.

Considering the extrabudgetary funds (for which little recent data are available), total state revenues remained reasonably high by international standards at around 35 percent of GDP. The widely anticipated collapse of state revenues had not taken place, even as they fell to a more reasonable level for a country with Russia's modest economic development. Part of the decline in state revenues was simply an effect of stabilization policies, squeezing enterprise profits, sales, and ability to pay taxes. Another reason was privatization and the emergence of new private enterprises that were much more difficult to tax. Finally, the tax system as a whole was a problem.

The Russian tax system had been an inconsistent patchwork all along, and it grew worse over time. Basic tax rates were quite high, and allowances for depreciation were far too small. Ordinary Russian enterprises suffered from the high costs of corruption and extortion (according to anecdotal evidence, on the order of 15 to 20 percent of their turnover), and most of these costs could not be legally deducted. Regional authorities also added a variety of taxes, primarily for social purposes. For instance, one enterprise reported that it had to pay a basic profit tax of 38 percent. This was in addition to a municipal tax of 1 percent of the profit, 3 percent for garbage collection, 2 percent in property tax, and 10 percent in ecological tax, amounting to a total tax of 54 percent of its profits. In other cases, the basic profit tax could be much higher. Taxes were collected by tax inspectors as well as by independent tax police, both of whom worked on commission. In practice, enterprises found it difficult to defend themselves legally against the tax authorities, and taxation became confiscatory. As a defense, enterprises increasingly evaded taxes. Thus, excessive tax rates, lack of legal protection, and an overblown tax collection apparatus led to the breakdown of tax morale in early 1994.[37]

During the first half of 1994, a battle raged over military expenditures. All the top military brass were agitating for military expenditures to more than double. Chernomyrdin kept quiet in public, but he managed to hold sway. When the State Duma finally adopted the 1994 budget on June 24, military expenditures had been raised insignificantly, from 4.4 percent of GDP in 1993 to 5.1 percent of GDP in 1994. Moreover, sequestering hit the defense sector harder than before. Only 74 percent of the means allocated to defense for the first half of 1994 was actually paid out by the state.[38]

For the rest, however, the composition of the budget was swiftly becoming less socially oriented and all the more focused on the interests of major industrial lobbies. The share of GDP devoted to education, health, and culture continued to shrink, while the allocation for the national economy (essentially subsidies) started to rise. For instance, centralized investments were supposed to increase as a share of GDP from 1.7 percent in 1993 to 4.8 percent in 1994. The subsidies to agriculture increased gradually over the year, and no attempts were made to tax the gas and oil industry effectively. Meanwhile, expenditures on state administration increased substantially.[39] This policy could be described as paying off the state administration, the gas and oil industry, and the agriculture sector while fighting the military-industrial sector and neglecting the people. The problem with economic lobbies, however, is that they are never satisfied but only demand more and more.

After a rocky start during the first quarter of 1994, Chernomyrdin's grasp began to slip. The federal budget deficit rose from 9.4 percent in 1993 to 11.0 percent in 1994. The halfway stabilization policy started to unravel. The supply of money increased by 14 percent a month in the second quarter of 1994, paving the way for rising inflation.[40] In the third quarter, the government issued large credits to the agriculture sector and the northern territories, exactly as it had in 1992 and 1993. Strangely, the prime minister appears to have been taken by surprise. The CBR had gradually lowered the high real interest rates in April, and by the end of September it approached zero. In September, the exchange rate started falling faster, and the CBR announced that it was losing international reserves through large interventions in support of the ruble. The fall accelerated in October. Finally, on October 11, "Black Tuesday," the exchange rate of the ruble collapsed and fell 27 percent in one day. Admittedly, it recovered the following day; but the exchange rate collapse amounted to a major political crisis. With a slight margin of victory, in the aftermath of the currency crisis the government survived a vote of no confidence in the State Duma on October 27.[41]

That an exchange rate crisis could almost bring the government down shows that Russia had really become a market economy. A drop of 19 percent in the exchange rate during one week in January 1994 after Gaidar's demise was possibly the first time the market had played a role in Russian politics, but this was a real shock. The mistakes made were many and obvious. First of all, the government had not pursued a real stabilization policy, with an excessive budget deficit and no apparent effort at genuine stabilization. Moreover, monetary expansion had been excessive, and the real interest rate had become negative in October. Worse, however, was the irresponsible short-term behavior of the CBR. In September, Gerashchenko had argued strangely that the ruble's exchange rate was too high. The leadership of the CBR, which usually said little about CBR reserves, repeatedly stated in September that the CBR had intervened for billions of dollars and that reserves were down. In early October, Deputy Chairman of the CBR Aleksandr Khandruev declared that the CBR would stop intervening. On "Black Tuesday," the CBR did not intervene at all in support of the ruble, and there were even allegations that it had sold rubles.

As a consequence of the ruble crisis, acting Minister of Finance Sergei Dubinin and CBR Chairman Viktor Gerashchenko were sacked by President Yeltsin, and Aleksandr Shokhin was forced to resign soon afterward. The result was a major transformation of the government, spearheaded by Yeltsin, which left Chernomyrdin a bystander. Anatoly Chubais was promoted to first deputy prime minister, beside Soskovets, with responsibility for economy and finance. Under him, Vladimir Panskov, a former deputy minister of finance of the USSR and Soviet technocrat, became minister of finance, and the old liberal reformer Yevgeny Yasin became minister of the economy. Deputy Chairwoman of the CBR Tatyana Paramonova became acting CBR chairwoman. Chubais swiftly appointed a government reform commission.[42] All these changes appear to have been improvements, but a number of other personnel moves in the government may have weakened the reformers' position.

The currency crisis suddenly shook Russian policymakers out of their complacency with the halfway stabilization effort, leaving inflation at 100 to 200 percent a year. Moreover, monthly inflation rose to 15 percent in October 1994 as a result of prior monetary expansion and rising velocity, and it stayed that high in November and December. Foreign portfolio investment fell from $500 million to $100 million from August to November.[43] The dollars that had been turned into rubles had been exchanged once more.

On October 27, Chernomyrdin spoke to the State Duma again. This time he no longer belittled genuine financial stabilization, instead stating: "If we seriously want a real stabilization of production and a renewal of economic growth, then we are obligated to attain a monthly inflation of not more than 1 to 2 percent. A macroeconomic stabilization must not be drawn out for long."[44] The essence of the new government program was to limit the budget deficit to slightly less than 8 percent of GDP, to finance the deficit fully with international credits and domestic state bonds, and (possibly) to peg the exchange rate.

However, Chernomyrdin, Soskovets, Zaveryukha, and other representatives of the industrial lobbies wanted to shield the interests of their constituencies while happily sacrificing social concerns. The key dispute became the liberalization of oil exports. During 1994, the domestic wholesale price of oil had fallen from 42 percent of the world level in the first quarter to 27 percent in the fourth quarter.[45] The domestic market was flooded with oil, while export quotas blocked exports. This was in the interest of those who could buy oil at domestic prices and export it at world prices. If oil exports were liberalized, the domestic oil price would probably rise to 80 percent of the world price, because transportation costs should warrant a lower oil price in Russia. Much of this price increase could be taxed, and the additional tax revenues could amount to as much as 4 percent of GDP, which would be sufficient to achieve stabilization. Even so, in the Russian government only Chubais and Yasin advocated liberalization of exports, indicating how deeply entrenched corrupt interests remained in the leadership.[46] Yet, at least initially, Chubais and Yasin did have their way with ardent support from the IMF and the World Bank.[47] The vested interests of the gas industry and the agrarian sector were too strong to allow these to be cut. In their stead, health, education, and culture were sacrificed even more.

The year 1994 departed Janus-faced. Russia was edging closer to real macroeconomic stabilization, and only a minor show of political will was required to achieve a stable currency. No technical problems block the road any longer. Moreover, the exchange rate crisis showed that the market had gained real political clout. Yet the unsavory and corrupt industrial lobbies continued to display such strength and self-interest that they were both ready and able to sacrifice vital social interests to their own benefit.

How to Deal With Interenterprise Arrears

A peculiar problem of postcommunist economic transition has been the accumulation of interenterprise arrears, which arose as many enterprises failed to pay for deliveries from other enterprises. This has generated great confusion. One reason is that a number of different problems have been labelled as arrears. In addition, there are several causes of arrears, and this is one of the more sophisticated complexities of a market economy. Strong real interests have hidden behind this veil.

The Russian word *neplatezhi* (nonpayments or arrears) is used for a number of different phenomena. The first and central problem is interenterprise arrears—that is, unpaid invoices between Russian enterprises. Another phenomenon is wage arrears by enterprises, and a third is the government lagging behind with budget disbursements. These three problems have been the focus of the arrears discussion. However, other issues have also been raised. Enterprise arrears to banks, for example, have generally been quite small by Western standards. With high inflation, banks have been cautious, and most bank credits have been extremely short term (up to three months). Moreover, old bad debts have been inflated away. Another issue is enterprise tax arrears, which rose considerably with stricter monetary policy in 1994. And finally, arrears to Russian enterprises from enterprises in other CIS countries were substantial, especially in 1992. The following section focuses on interenterprise arrears, which have inspired substantial discussion.[48]

Arrears have routinely been exaggerated. They have been spoken of in absolute figures without reference either to national aggregates or international standards. The old system did not tolerate arrears: The state-controlled bank system netted them out and then issued credits to eliminate them. The absence of arrears is thus evidence of the absence of a market economy. Interenterprise arrears rose sharply during the first half of 1992 and peaked at 3.2 trillion rubles at the end of July 1992, corresponding to 120 percent of M2 or 24 percent of GDP at current prices.[49] Then the CBR pushed through the netting out of existing arrears and covered the rest at highly subsidized interest rates. Fortunately, the exercise took more than four months. Most of the arrears were thus inflated away, offering little relief to incautious creditors. The total net debt amounted to about 450 billion rubles.[50]

However, financial discipline was limited, and interenterprise arrears began mounting up again, albeit more slowly. Much of the drama had been dispelled after central registration of the arrears had ceased on July 1, 1992. The discussion is further confused by varying definitions. As of October 1, 1994, the surveyed creditor indebtedness of Russian enterprises in industry, agriculture, construction, and transportation had risen to 147.4 trillion rubles. However, of this only 71.8 trillion rubles were for overdue creditor indebtedness or real arrears, corresponding to about 12 percent of GDP at current prices.[51] This would be a perfectly reasonable level of creditor indebtedness by Western or East European standards, showing that the problem is under control.[52] On October 1, overdue debts owed by enterprises to the budget amounted to only 14.6 trillion rubles, and overdue bank credits of enterprises totalled 4.5 trillion rubles, far less than what would be normal in the West. The overdue indebtedness of enterprises in the FSU to those in Russia was minimal at 1.9 trillion rubles, while overdue payments to Russian enterprises from those outside the FSU was significant at 8.8 trillion rubles.[53]

The most striking observation about Russian concern over arrears is that Russians were not used to this feature of a market economy. Arrears have been surrounded by a number of myths in Russia that first need to be dispelled. Contrary to frequent allegations, this is not a uniquely Russian problem. Interenterprise arrears have arisen in all postcommunist countries, although their levels have varied greatly. Moreover, they exist in all market economies, where trade credits are a standard feature. Interenterprise arrears are proof of the emergence of a market economy. The problem is not that they exist but that they continue to rise to excessive levels.

Another common claim is that monetary stabilization does not function in Russia because enterprises simply stop paying one another, creating their own money. However, arrears are not money by any standard definition; they are not transferable and hold no certain store of value and no unit of account. They reflect that money has become scarce and thus that there is a demand for money, but they lack the standard properties of money. The issue is to block the monetization of arrears so that they are not allowed to contribute to inflation. Another argument that has been made is that enterprises will not start paying one another until severe bankruptcy procedures are introduced. However, this has been empirically disproved. The East European countries (apart from Romania) have gotten interenterprise arrears under control, whereas only Hungary has had a large number of bankruptcies. The issue is indeed financial discipline, but there are many other means to impose it.

Yet interenterprise debts involved several real problems. The prime issue is to establish which one is most fundamental. Essentially, three alternative explanations have been presented. One is macroeconomic, arguing that there was too little money in the economy. Another is technical, focusing on the payments system, which functioned poorly. A third is microeconomic, observing that enterprises had little incentive to collect their payments and even less to pay their debts. My emphasis lies heavily on the microeconomic nature of the problem of moral hazard, which holds that if enterprises only have the right incentives, they will press for a solution to technical problems.

Russian state enterprise managers, communists, and Gerashchenko argued that the real problem was too little money in the economy. They noticed that prices in 1992 rose several times more than the money supply. They then advocated replenishment of the money supply, neglecting the previous existence of a monetary overhang or that demand for money fell with inflation, prompting the velocity of money to rise. They proposed different ways the CBR should direct credits to cover the arrears.[54] However, one outstanding characteristic of a market economy in contrast with a socialist economy is that money is scarce. The real problem was that enterprises had to adjust to that new reality, but they protested and demanded that money should be as abundant as before.

The real struggle was between the reformers, who wanted state enterprises to adjust to the market and to a demand barrier, and the enterprise managers, who did not want to adjust, but just sought unlimited amounts of money from the state. The enterprises tried to exact money in various ways. The most obvious was to not pay their suppliers. Moreover, during the first half of 1992, enterprises could not really check on whether or not they had been paid so that they could stop deliveries. Worse, the delivering enterprises did not care much about being paid. Cash and noncash money were then still distinct from one another, and wages were paid with cash that circulated independently of the noncash money paid for deliveries. Furthermore, in mid-1992 it was impossible to establish who was a net debtor or a net creditor, because enterprises had both creditor and debtor indebtedness. The buildup of arrears raised a cloud of impenetrable nontransparency around the creditworthiness of enterprises. The mountain of arrears facilitated collective action of state enterprise managers against the state, and they all demanded the state must pay. In this way, the microeconomic moral hazard was transformed into a macroeconomic problem. However, this problem was not a shortage of money but the collusion of state enterprises to exact more cheap credits from the CBR—an endeavor facilitated and even blessed by Gerashchenko, who favored such a destabilizing policy.

The technical problem—the poor payments system—was of vital importance for this collusion of state managers. It was difficult to effectuate payments, and delays were notorious. Rather than facilitating a solution, the CBR overcentralized payments in a vain attempt to monitor them. As of April 1, 1992, all payments had to be processed through CBR cash settlement centers, which slowed settlements further and instantly tripled arrears.[55] These problems could be resolved through decentralization, which would allow commercial banks to clear payments freely among themselves. Improvements had already occurred by July 1992, though the CBR policy remained overly restrictive. The banks, in turn, exploited this sluggishness to hold onto the money longer, reaping the interest. During the first half of 1992, arrears amounted to the cheapest credits, but that problem was amended in the summer, with the introduction of a rather high penalty rate for arrears.

A major problem was that the legal provisions were so weak that arrears could hardly be collected. There were many reasons for this. Legislation was poorly developed, lacking a commercial code or a bankruptcy law. There was little collateral at hand and no registries of property. The courts were weak, and there was no effective collection system. Hence, the only way of securing a payment from a little-known customer was to demand prepayment, a practice that proliferated beginning in May 1992 and was legally facilitated that July. Typically, small enterprises were the first to demand prepayment; the energy enterprises, especially Gazprom, were the last to cut deliveries if they were not paid, because they counted on Chernomyrdin's help. By the end of 1993, prepayment had become the standard for almost all enterprises, with the notable exception of those in the energy sector. On October 1, 1994, the fuel industry accounted for one-third of all overdue debtor indebtedness.[56] Cash payment was an alternative that had been used in Poland. However, the CBR maintained the distinction between cash and noncash money, even if there were many ways to circumvent it.

The central issue in all of this is credibility. The greater the belief that the state will pay interenterprise arrears, the greater the arrears will be; and the more often the state does pay, the longer the arrears will last.

The central problems of interenterprise arrears are twofold: accumulated interenterprise debts and future enterprise behavior. The second issue is easy in principle: The state must convince enterprises that it will not finance their arrears. However, a favorable treatment of the old interenterprise debts may detract from the government's credibility.

In principle, there are four different methods for dealing with the problem of the stock of arrears. The first is that the state could try to cover interenterprise debts by simply issuing more gross credits. That would lead to massive inflation and undermine all credibility regarding the state's monetary restraint.

The second method is netting out of interenterprise arrears, with the state covering the outstanding net balance. This would involve less credit emission than the first alternative; but even so, credits would explode. In this way, Ukraine doubled its money supply in June 1992 and moved on to hyperinflation. Russia decided to net out its arrears in July 1992, which contributed to high inflation. However, the effect in Russia was mitigated in several ways. The net balance turned out to be relatively limited. The reformers also managed to delay the issue of credits by more than four months, so that the bulk of the arrears was inflated away and the neglectful sellers thus punished. The tax authorities vetted the disbursed credits first, collecting substantial tax debts. Still, the state bailed out the worst enterprises, which were unable to sell their output for ordinary money.

A third possible approach is to transform arrears into securities. This procedure was preferred by the Russian reformers. A first decree allowing such a procedure was issued in June 1992 in Russia. However, it never caught on, because the CBR took over in July with its netting out of arrears, which the enterprises preferred for obvious reasons. In general, the Russian market for securities was rudimentary, and these securities would hardly be the most attractive. Moreover, because of the difficulties in collecting debts, their value to outsiders would be small. Still, it would have been advantageous if enterprises had been entitled to net out their mutual debts on a bilateral basis, and if trade in secondary debt (with or without securitization) had been allowed.

The best solution, as argued by Jacek Rostowski, is simply for the state to do nothing at all. Enterprises would then be forced to take responsibility for their own payments, because otherwise they would receive no revenues, and they would therefore allow few new arrears to arise. But the enterprises that do not pay would also be punished, because they would not be able to purchase anything without prepayment in the future. The practice among state enterprises of delivering to other state enterprises that have not placed orders would stop. Then enterprises would face hard budget constraints and demand barriers, compelling them to adjust to demand and undertake the necessary structural changes. Otherwise, they should be allowed to perish. Old arrears will gradually inflate away. As enterprises get to know each other, they could resolve many of the payments issues on their own, if only trade in secondary debts is allowed. In short, by interfering the state can only undermine enterprise morals, so it should stay out.

In effect, the Russian government has chosen the last option, after the netting out in the summer of 1992. However, the problem has not gone away. Increasingly, arrears have been connected through illicit or illegal activities by both debtors and creditors.[57] In the summer of 1994, a high-level government committee was formed to deal with interenterprise arrears. Its chairman, First Deputy Prime Minister Oleg Soskovets, described the situation as a dangerous crisis, although total arrears were relatively limited. His statements must have detracted from the credibility of the government's financial firmness. A government decree of September 26, 1994, announced the securitization of interenterprise arrears into promissory notes, which would be tradeable.[58] On December 20, 1994, a presidential decree was issued declaring that the maximum period of payments was three months. If an invoice had not been paid within that time, the debtor enterprise had to write off the claim as a loss. The claim on the creditor enterprise would then be transferred to the State Bankruptcy Agency. The purpose of this decree was to pressure both purchaser and supplier.[59]

Interenterprise arrears are often confused with government arrears. In late 1993 (and more so in 1994), large budget arrears arose. State revenues fell short of their targets, and the Ministry of Finance was forced to reduce expenditures to keep the budget deficit constant. In late 1994, the accumulated budget arrears for 1994 were estimated at 4.5 percent of GDP.[60] Moreover, the government has been blamed for not disbursing many expenditures that unauthorized officials had promised. For instance, the Ministry of Defense ordered arms whose purchase had not been granted by the Ministry of Finance.

A particularly nasty practice that proliferated in 1994 was the refusal of state enterprise managers to pay their workers wages earned, although the enterprises possessed the necessary means to pay these wages. These managers argued that the state had not paid them. In this way, state enterprises simply used their workers as blackmail hostages against the state. Occasionally, state enterprises and local former communist officials even organized demonstrations against the government, demanding what they considered their due payments.[61] According to the Federation of

Independent Trade Unions, accumulated wage arrears surged from 0.7 trillion rubles in January 1994 to 5.9 trillion rubles in October, corresponding to 14 percent of monthly money incomes.[62] As stabilization began to take hold in 1994, arrears to tax authorities and commercial banks became more common because of a real shortage of money. By late 1994, nonpayment of credits had put about 100 commercial banks in a critical situation.[63]

Interenterprise arrears also caused statistical distortions. One effect was that wholesale prices rose much more than retail prices in 1992. This was because they reflected invoice prices (which enterprises frequently did not pay), while ordinary consumers had to pay immediately for goods they bought.[64]

The ultimate problem of interenterprise arrears is low morale, though this is aggravated by the weakness of the payments and legal systems. Initially, interenterprise arrears surged far higher in Russia than in Poland or Czechoslovakia, because the resolve of the Russian government in its financial restraint was much less credible.[65] Rather than punishing debtors for their lack of caution, the CBR undertook a netting out of mutual debts, giving a premium in subsidized credits to the least creditworthy enterprises. Even so, in the meantime the solution has been the proliferation of prepayments until legal standards and mutual trust facilitate ordinary trade credits. Still, the state has not shown the right moral resolve. It has stated that interenterprise arrears reflect moral hazards of the enterprises concerned; but it appears prone to intervene again, reinforcing destabilizing expectations. Instead, the state should improve collection and bankruptcy procedures. The poor credibility of the Russian government in its determination to solve the problem of interenterprise arrears has contributed to a delay in enterprise restructuring and thus to the decline in production.

The Role of the West

The demise of the Soviet Union was possibly the most important event of the twentieth century. The West had won the cold war, which turned out to be one of the most peaceful big wars in history in its main theaters of operations. Essentially, the United States had consciously pursued an arms race that the USSR could not keep up with, neither economically nor technologically. In response, the USSR had been compelled to try to reform, only to realize too late that it was not reformable.[66]

When the abortive Soviet coup collapsed on August 21, 1991, the Soviet dictatorship was basically finished, and the West could have proclaimed victory. However, the West was confused and tried to hang on to the defunct Soviet Union and its president, Mikhail Gorbachev. The two months after the August coup were certainly befuddling; but by the end of October, everything became clear. In his extraordinary reform speech on October 28, Russian President Boris Yeltsin discussed, at length and in detail, the need for Western assistance and cooperation and promised the West whatever information and collaboration it could desire.[67] This was a unique moment in Russian history. Never before had a Russian leader appealed to the West so openly.

What was most striking about the response of Western governments to the economic and political transformation in Russia and the rest of the FSU (with the exception of the Baltic states) was their unwillingness to make any major commitment. The first act of the Group of Seven (G-7) leading industrialized nations in response to President Yeltsin's offer of cooperation was to send their deputy ministers of finance to Moscow to secure claims to the Soviet foreign debt. In mid-November 1991, the G-7 officials gathered top-level representatives from the USSR and all the FSRs (except from the Baltic states) in Moscow. The G-7 representatives then asked them to promise to take "joint and several" responsibility to service the Soviet foreign debt in return for a minor debt repayment deferral. The FSRs agreed, because the new national ministers were inexperienced and saw this as a matter of honor. Besides, they wanted to show goodwill to the big Western nations. However, their promise was completely unrealistic. The Soviet currency reserve fell below $100 million in December 1991, and the FSRs and Russia could do nothing but default on their foreign debt. Officials of the G-7 nations unfairly concluded that the new Russian reform ministers were unreliable. This meeting lasted four days, but economic reform (or its financing) was not even on the agenda. Like Georges Clemenceau at Versailles, the lowly G-7 financial officials had only come to appropriate money due to them. Ironically, this money had once been given freely to the communists who had bankrupted the USSR.[68]

The leading Western governments seemed unable to comprehend that the Soviet Union was gone. For instance, on November 5, 1991, the *Financial Times* concluded: "All the main Western industrialized countries are making efforts to shore up the crumbling centre of the Soviet Union." The most extreme supporter of maintaining the Soviet Union was French President François Mitterrand, who had even acknowledged the erstwhile government of the attempted Soviet communist coup in August 1991.[69] After the initial CIS agreement, CIA Director Robert Gates expressed baffled skepticism typical of the U.S. administration at the time: "Russian President Yeltsin has articulated bold economic reform plans, but it remains to be seen whether he can carry them out. Market reform will be accompanied by inflation and unemployment that could generate a social explosion, endangering the stability of fledgling democratic governments."[70] In February 1992, Jim Hoagland concluded that U.S. President George Bush considered Boris Yeltsin a transitional figure.[71]

These attitudes could not be defended as resulting from a lack of reliable information. The major newspapers published it all and drew sensible conclusions. For instance, in November 1991 the *New York Times* urged in an editorial: "The challenge for the West is to encourage Mr. Yeltsin's real, radical program by giving attentive assistance now."[72] In December 1991, an editorial in the *Financial Times* stated: "Now is the first and, perhaps, the last chance for the west to promote radical economic reform in the former Soviet Union."[73] What was lacking among the Western governments was political will.

As if to conceal the lack of American interest in supporting radical economic reform in Russia, U.S. Secretary of State James A. Baker saw the post-Soviet dilemma as a humanitarian emergency. This obscured the real nature of the problem, which was a need for systemic transformation and macroeconomic stabilization. Baker sought to build a U.S.-led coalition of donor countries, inspired by the Gulf War alliance, to meet "immediate and dramatically increasing Soviet humanitarian needs." His declared aim was to ensure that the Soviet people "take the right steps this winter, spring, and summer to ensure a better situation next winter."

A large number of ministers for foreign affairs held two international meetings on humanitarian aid to Russia, one in Washington, D.C., in January 1992 and the other in Lisbon in May 1992. More than 60 countries and a dozen international organizations participated in the Lisbon meeting. The Washington meeting was tightly organized and divided into sectoral issues of humanitarian aid. Its obvious purpose was to avoid any substantive discussion of systemic change and macroeconomic stabilization. Strangely, the intended recipients of this aid were not invited to participate in the Washington meeting. There was no humanitarian emergency in most of the FSRs, but humanitarian aid is cheap and generates good publicity. The real issue of providing substantial financial support to help Russia move to a market economy was avoided. In the meantime, not only the communist opposition but also representatives of the reform government started to ridicule the small amounts proffered in the much-publicized Western humanitarian aid. It was all too evident that the Western governments did not take the Russian attempt at economic transformation seriously.[74]

Finally, on April 1, 1992, U.S. President George Bush and German Chancellor Helmut Kohl issued statements on behalf of the G-7 nations announcing that a package of financial assistance totaling $24 billion would be disbursed to Russia in 1992. The announcement was politically well timed—it preceded the opening of the important session of the Russian Congress of People's Deputies five days later. Curiously, the German and U.S. statements contained contradictory figures on how the financing would be subdivided. The bulk of the package—$11 billion in the U.S. statement and $13 billion in the German statement—was supposed to consist primarily of bilateral food credits. The IMF and the World Bank were to provide $4.5 billion according to the U.S. statement and $5.5 billion according to the German statement. The U.S. statement specified a multilateral currency stabilization fund of $6 billion to bolster confidence in the Russian ruble, as well as $2.5 billion of debt payments deferral. Japanese protests followed, because the package had not been cleared with Japan.[75]

The entire package depended on an agreement regarding an adjustment program between the Russian government and the IMF. The IMF and Russia had already concluded a shadow program on February 27, 1992, which looked like an ordinary standby agreement. However, it was not accompanied by any financing, because the West was not politically prepared to provide any. Russia, together with the other FSRs, was accepted as a member of the IMF on April 27, 1992.[76] Even so, the negotiations on a standby agreement became increasingly complicated as reformers gradually lost ground in Russia. Petr Aven complained that the IMF was delaying an accord by paying too much attention to minor details, when the important thing was that Russia was embracing sweeping reforms to create a market economy.[77]

The IMF completed a standby agreement with Russia in early July (ironically, when the bold Russian stabilization program had been crushed under the combined pressures of the Supreme Soviet and industrial lobbies). The manner in which the IMF agreement was concluded was to become a pattern. Michel Camdessus, managing director of the IMF, flew to Moscow for a weekend after negotiations between the Russian government and the IMF staff had broken down. Nevertheless, Camdessus secured a political settlement. As a result, the Executive Board of the IMF decided one month later to issue a first tranche of $1 billion out of an envisioned standby credit of $4 billion. The World Bank followed suit and decided to loan Russia $600 million. However, the Russian government had to promise not to use the IMF standby credit but to keep it as a reserve. The IMF opposed the formation of a stabilization fund, because it demanded that the exchange rate be stabilized *before* it would commit to any stabilization fund. Thus, the Russian reformers undertook commitments they approved of but no longer had the political strength to fulfil. Immediately afterward, the G-7 nations had their annual summit in Munich. Camdessus emerged as the star of a lackluster meeting, momentarily saving face for the West because he had concluded an agreement with Russia.[78] By in mid-September the IMF realized that Russia had issued excessive amounts of credits since June 1992.[79]

Western countries did offer Russia $12.5 billion in commodity credits in 1992, most during the first half of the year. As has been previously discussed, the credits resulted in large unbudgeted import subsidies. Therefore, the IMF could not support the financing of Russian stabilization. The absurdity of this reasoning is blatant, as Jeffrey Sachs has shown. Western governments did not want to finance Russian financial stabilization; on the contrary, they provided financing that undermined Russia's finances and did so for the benefit of their domestic farm lobbies. The IMF supported and lauded the Western assistance provided to Russia, although it knew that these commodity credits were harmful to the Russian economy. The IMF then disqualified Russia as a recipient of stabilization financing, because it had received such large amounts of detrimental commodity credits. Fortunately, Boris Fedorov managed to put an end to this tragic farce in 1993.[80]

Another important Western contribution was the IMF's insistence on maintaining the ruble zone, as discussed in chapter 4. It was important for several reasons. First, this was a technically complex issue, and the IMF could be expected to possess unique competence in this area. Naturally, the IMF view on the ruble zone would be considered credible by inexperienced governments in the FSU. Second, without the assistance of the IMF, many governments did not have the technical expertise to act independently in monetary policy. In some countries, the IMF was effectively in a monopoly position. Third, the IMF initially made adherence to the ruble zone a condition for concluding standby agreements and providing financing. Fourth, many political forces were mobilized for and against the ruble zone. The IMF therefore possessed a swing vote that could tip the balance for or against the introduction of independent national currencies. In the end, the IMF had little or no effect on currency reforms in the FSRs (with the exception of that of Kyrgyzstan). Ten countries subsequently ended up in hyperinflation. The record could hardly be worse and the effects have been horrendous, demonstrating a serious flaw in the functioning of the IMF. The secrecy the IMF imposed meant that few among the specialists knew what a faulty stand it had taken on the ruble zone, and those within the IMF who knew could not protest effectively. The government members of the IMF do not appear to have taken the dissolution of the ruble zone seriously enough.

The most important Western support of the economic transition in Russia has been more or less private in nature, though often financed with public technical assistance money. Myriad exchanges have proven useful. Top-level economic and legal advice has certainly been of significance. Russia's privatization could not have been carried out without substantial Western technical assistance. The education of young Russians at Western universities has been too limited but, even so, has generated ample returns. The beneficial publication of textbooks in Russian that has been supported from abroad appears to have been sponsored largely by George Soros rather than by governments.

For half a year before the brave Russian attempt at financial and monetary stabilization fell apart, Russia openly called for Western assistance. However, in the crucial first half of 1992, the West did not make any financial contribution to Russian stabilization at all. The IMF had ambitiously taken the political lead, but it was slow in making any agreement with Russia. Its priority appeared to be to avoid risking money, in the manner of a private banker rather than an institution defending a major public interest.[81]

The Western contribution had thus essentially been negative. Western behavior during this time was reminiscent of the period after World War I, when no nation led or took any international responsibility and while each looked to its own national interests, in the most narrow sense and to the detriment of all. None of the idealism and broader outlook of the Marshall Plan days was present. Notably, at the height of the Marshall Plan in 1948–49, U.S. donations totalled 2.1 percent of U.S. GDP; for 1995, the U.S. budget request for aid to the whole FSU amounts to 0.01 percent of GDP.[82] The many unsubstantiated Western promises have bred cynicism about the West in Russia.

Why was the West so impotent? An obvious answer was that all the major Western countries were ruled by weak and shortsighted political leaders. No one showed international leadership. Therefore, the IMF gained more prominence in the post-Soviet transition than it had capacity for. An important explanation was that the collapse of the Soviet Union was not sufficiently dramatic for the world community to realize that a fundamental postwar crisis loomed. If the war had been hot rather than cold and had left millions of corpses behind, the world might have woken up. None of the fundamental lessons learned in the aftermath of World War II was applied—notably, that a postwar transition requires the focus of world leaders, political will, substantial financing, and a new institutional framework. It was logical that the Soviet breakup was more reminiscent of the breakup of the Hapsburg Empire than of the Marshall Plan days. One can only hope that Russia is strong enough to manage on its own.

Conclusions: Money Is Money in Russia, Too

The macroeconomic stabilization policy Russia has actually pursued has been neither extreme nor consistent. It has been a stopgap policy that has changed about twice a year, and most of the time it has been either incomplete or too soft, or both.

However heroic Gaidar and Fedorov's attempts at financial stabilization, their packages were incomplete and too brief. Initially, the major problem was the lack of financial support from the IMF and the international community. Another fatal problem was the maintenance of the destabilizing ruble zone. But the main and lasting reason for high inflation in Russia has been that the CBR has not believed in the quantity theory of money. It has insisted instead on issuing too much money, and it has colluded with state enterprise lobbies. The evidence is clear: the quantity theory of money is applicable in Russia, too. As has been shown, inflation can be explained by the increase in money supply and the velocity of money.

An additional and related problem has been that Russian stabilization policies have lacked credibility. The Gaidar team's talk of a brief kamikaze cabinet convinced state enterprise managers that there was no point in adjusting to the new policy, because it would not last. Soon persistent opposition from the Supreme Soviet undermined the credibility of the government. In 1994, Chernomyrdin's refusal to clearly state any stabilization policy meant that people did not expect it, and right they were. All along, public explanations have been scant and insufficient. The only example of a positive effect of credibility was Fedorov's bet on exchange rate stability in the summer of 1993.

Nothing suggests that the economic tenets of the reformers were wrong. They were instead forced to concede too much to the old establishment, which seized the opportunities offered to them to pursue extraordinary rent-seeking. Because of the strength and ferocity of the old elite, Russia needed a more stringent and simple stabilization program than had the East European states. Therefore, it was particularly important to eliminate any opportunity for rent-seeking, such as centralized imports, subsidized credits, or price controls for energy and grain. Furthermore, the reformers could only win against the old rent-seekers if they acted swiftly and hit hard. The resistance was formidable, and whatever was achieved was accomplished because of a big push. The initial big bang had been big enough to provide a lasting momentum for reform. The relative achievements of 1994 were the result of the radical policies implemented by Gaidar and Fedorov in the fourth quarter of 1993, and Chernomyrdin failed miserably in his attempts to reach a quiet stabilization.

The whole policy of macroeconomic stabilization circles around three names: Gaidar, Fedorov, and Gerashchenko. Gaidar and Fedorov stand as the courageous protagonists of stabilization and introduced virtually all the positive measures that were undertaken. Gerashchenko, on the contrary, stands as the historic nemesis of swift stabilization in Russia, with Chernomyrdin as his savior.

The record of 1994 is contradictory. The exchange rate crisis in October left the legacy of a new political importance of stable money in Russia. A constituency of private business interests made its presence felt. Finally, a great many Russians had learned what a market economy is and what is required to live in it.

The key issue of stabilization was, and remains, to bring down inflation so that the old elite cannot exploit inflation by transferring money from the people to its own use through the inflation tax. There is nothing socially beneficial about high inflation and its accompanying corruption.

A number of much-touted dangers associated with stabilization have never appeared. There was never any serious risk of social unrest (apart from limited strikes, primarily in the coal industry). Nor was there any significant wage pressure, because labor was so weak. State revenues have not collapsed. Initially, they remained far too high (at about half of GDP, if huge extrabudgetary funds are included), though new confiscatory tax rates and lawless collection methods pose new threats to tax revenues. Unemployment has remained low, as could be expected when people are highly educated and real wages remain extremely flexible. Russia did have, and still has, a fairly extensive social safety net. The prime problem was that the old communist system produced too few resources and also allocated them ineffectively with regard to the public welfare.

As stabilization has proceeded, it has primarily been based on a monetary squeeze. Meanwhile, fiscal policy has remained far too loose. Production and investments have been crowded out by extremely high real interest rates, causing unnecessarily high social costs. The gradual stabilization has led to a long-lasting decline in production, while investment and recovery have not been possible with such high inflation. The absence, so far, of an effective nominal anchor has left stabilization incomplete, and the task of instilling public confidence in the ruble remains.

CHAPTER SEVEN

Privatization

PRIVATIZATION appears to be the most successful aspect of the Russian transformation. The idea of privatization had been anathema to Soviet communism. It was one of the last communist dogmas to go, but all of a sudden it was widely accepted. The 500-day program of the summer of 1990 broke the ice, as discussed in chapter 2. The emphasis on privatization has been great ever since. The reason seems to be a prevailing reverse Marxism, which implies that no market can exist before private property has achieved hegemony. Initially, the dominant domestic criticism from both the right and the left against the Gaidar reform was that privatization was not carried out before price liberalization.

In this chapter, I examine the late Soviet view of private enterprise, early Russian ideas of privatization, and the leading ideas on privatization held by Russian reformers in power. Their ideas are contrasted with those of the general debate, and this discussion is followed by an outline of the privatization program. I then scrutinize the administration of privatization, small-scale and large-scale privatization (including voucher auctions), housing privatization, land reform, and the development of new private enterprises, and then draw conclusions.

Private Enterprise at the End of the USSR

One of the most fundamental communist principles had been the nationalization of the means of production to abolish the exploitation of man by man. In practice, this meant that the only private economic

Table 7-1. *Russian Employment by Ownership, 1991*

	Thousands	Percent of total
Total employed population	73,809	100.0
State sector employees	57,188	77.5
Leased enterprise employees	5,590	7.6
Joint stock company employees	1,068	1.4
Economic association employees	795	1.1
Social organization employees	679	0.9
Joint venture employees	141	0.2
Collective farm workers	3,945	5.3
Cooperative workers	2,901	3.9
Individual labor	342	0.5
Private subsidiary agricultural workers	1,078	1.5
Private agricultural workers	83	0.1

Source: The World Bank, *Statistical Handbook 1994: States of the Former USSR* (Washington, D.C., 1994), p. 492.

activity communists could ideologically accept was individual work, possibly involving a whole family but no hired labor and little capital. Private trade was long abhorred as "speculation."

However, most of these old Marxist ideas were swept away under *glasnost* and *perestroika* (as discussed in chapter 2), with the promulgation of the Law on Individual Activity in November 1986 and the Law on Cooperatives in May 1988. A great variety of private enterprises began to emerge under the heading of cooperatives, but full-fledged private enterprise was never introduced in the Soviet Union.

Instead, the initiative on private enterprise moved to the republics. The Russian Law on Enterprises and Entrepreneurial Activity was adopted on December 25, 1990, and allowed for all kinds of enterprises. Their legal forms included individual entrepreneurship, sole proprietorship, general partnership, limited partnership, and joint stock companies. Joint stock companies could be open or closed. The shares of closed companies could not be traded publicly, and they became a popular device of insider privatization. The shares of open joint stock companies, however, could be openly traded without restrictions.[1] All these enterprises were vaguely referred to colloquially as "commercial structures." All kinds of private enterprises were allowed for more than a year before the transformation to a real market economy started in Russia. Employment in various forms of private enterprises in 1991 is presented in table 7-1.

This liberalization proceeded with foreign enterprises as well. In 1991, Russia adopted a Law on Foreign Investment. This was followed by the presidential decree of November 15, 1991, "On the Liberalization of

Foreign Economic Activity on the Territory of the Russian Federation," which was part of the very first wave of radical reform decrees. The Law on Foreign Investment allowed foreigners and their enterprises to invest through both joint ventures with Russian enterprises and wholly owned enterprises. In principle, foreign enterprises were allowed to conduct business in any area not prohibited by law, though there were exceptions. Foreign banks required a license from the Central Bank of Russia (CBR), whereas companies with foreign participation had to be registered with the Ministry of Finance or other authorized state agencies.[2] Despite the effort to treat foreign companies and domestic enterprises equally, inequalities arose in a number of practices. For instance, foreign enterprises were rarely allowed to participate in small-scale privatization.

Similarly, state enterprises were given more and more independence from the branch ministries, first through the Law on State Enterprises of June 1987 and later through the USSR Enterprise Law of 1990. Inspired by market socialism, these laws introduced the concept of workers' self-management, with a general meeting of the labor collective and enterprise councils with some elected members. These institutions were retained in the Russian Enterprise Law of December 1990.[3] At the end of the 1980s, many managers were sacked by the work councils; but everything soon reversed quietly, and rudimentary self-management by workers dwindled. Instead, the power of managers expanded. The branch ministries lost the actual power to remove them with the promulgation of the Russian Enterprise Law of 1990, and the managers were effectively left without masters.[4]

Leasing was one late Soviet attempt to make state enterprises more independent and their workers better motivated. It was introduced by a Soviet decree on leasing in April 1989. In practice, a work collective leased the state enterprise where its members already worked. Leasing of state enterprises by employees gave insiders such a degree of control that privatization through cheap employee buyouts was the natural next step. The Russian reform government tried to stop this form of inside privatization and forbade new leasing agreements in 1992. However, the leasing sector was already quite large. By the end of February 1992, 9,451 state enterprises were leased, accounting for 8 percent of total employment.[5] At the end of 1992, 3,485 leased industrial enterprises generated 11 percent of industrial production.[6]

Between 1989 and 1991, a plethora of "associations," "concerns," and "corporations" were set up. Frequently, the name plate of a branch ministry was simply replaced with that of a concern with the same specialization. A subdivision of a branch ministry or a group of state enterprises could form associations on its own initiative, on the basis of 1989 amendments to the USSR Law on State Enterprises and the Russian Enterprise Law. These new associations combined the interests of the old federal branch organizations (which wanted to survive and to reinforce monopolistic practices in supply and financing) with those of enterprise managers (who sought to privatize their enterprises to their own benefit through so-called *nomenklatura* privatization). By the end of 1991, there were 3,076 associations, 227 concerns, and 123 consortia. With their complex cross-ownership, the associations were difficult to sort out. At the end of 1991, the reform government tried to reassert control over all privatization, but the associations remained, despite their uncertain legal status.[7] *Nomenklatura* privatization later took the form of financial-industrial groups and holding companies to make it sound more market oriented and sophisticated.

Early Russian Ideas on Privatization

Although many Russians favored private ownership, ideas on how to privatize remained vague. The 500-day program from the summer of 1990 set an early standard. It envisioned three means of mass privatization that were somewhat contradictory. First, some shares should be given away for free to workers at the enterprise that was being privatized. Second, all citizens or adults should receive some share of state property for free. Third, property should mainly be sold, not given away for free. A variety of forms of privatization was anticipated (albeit with little elaboration), and there was a heavy emphasis on an early breakup of monopolies. Enterprises showing initiative were to be given priority. Potential revenues from sales of state enterprises were considered a significant contribution toward balancing the budget and financing macroeconomic stabilization.[8] The 500-day program established the need for fast, massive privatization. However, the program's emphasis was on sales—recalling the not very successful Hungarian privatization strategy, which gradually lost its attractiveness. Nevertheless, several authors of the 500-day program, notably Grigory Yavlinsky, continued to insist on sales rather than free distribution of property.

Through the influence of discussions in eastern Europe, the idea of free distribution of property gained popularity. It became obvious that Hungary did not privatize as quickly as it had wanted to through sales. Moreover, the people who had money tended to belong to unpopular social groups (such as the old *nomenklatura*) or to be foreigners, black marketeers, or *nouveaux riches*. Their stunning new wealth tended to arouse resistance to privatization. The Polish failure to privatize because of attempts to make discrete sales was illuminating, while the Czechoslovak attempt at voucher privatization looked promising. Increasing anxiety about the need to speed up privatization and the distribution of enterprise property prompted the Supreme Soviet of the Russian Soviet Federated Socialist Republic (RSFSR) to adopt the Law on Privatization of State and Municipal Enterprises in the RSFSR[9] and the Law on Personal Privatization Accounts in the RSFSR on July 3, 1991.[10] These laws had been promoted by the liberal Russian Minister of the Economy Yevgeny Saburov. The privatization law was the most substantial reform law that had yet been adopted. It was widely believed that privatization should precede the transition to a market economy. The government finally managed to persuade the Supreme Soviet to amend the privatization law on June 5, 1992, to make the law more efficacious, but many of its initial principles were maintained. It singled out enterprises for privatization and thus provided a supply of property. A maximum of 20 percent of the shares was to remain with the state.

The Law on Personal Privatization Accounts was supposed to provide a demand for property to be privatized. By law, every citizen of Russia would receive a certain, equal, annual amount in a personal privatization account with the state savings bank. Such privatization accounts had already been introduced in Lithuania. They could be used for purchases of all kinds of state property to be privatized throughout the Russian Federation and had to be spent within three years. This law aimed at quick mass privatization, without giving insiders any advantage. The main problem with the law, however, was that it called for highly complex privatization procedures that were not likely to work. Its lasting contribution was that it established the principle of free distribution of property to the people.

Unlike the Russian Federation, the Soviet Union never managed to adopt a privatization law. However, a draft Law On the Fundamental Foundations of Destatization and Privatization of Enterprises was put forth in June 1991, in competition with the Russian law on privatization.[11]

228   PRIVATIZATION

Its principles largely ran counter to the Russian privatization law, and its ideas were to recur as an alternative in the Russian debate. Essentially, the law stipulated that the work collective should decide the form and order of privatization, and social security should be guaranteed. The draft Soviet law said nothing about how fast privatization should be implemented and little about what methods of privatization should be used, and the resulting property rights appeared limited. Moreover, the law emphasized several reasons for impeding privatization. It called for limited free distribution of property; and like the Russian privatization law, it argued that all citizens should have an equal right to receive property shares. Presumably, the lack of clarity in the draft law was motivated by a desire to let the branch ministries retain full control over the privatization process.

The Russian Reformers' Ideas on Privatization

When the reform government was formed in November 1991, Anatoly B. Chubais was appointed minister of privatization and chairman of the State Committee for the Management of State Property (Goskomimush-chestvo or GKI), as the actual Ministry of Privatization was called. Chubais started his ministry with an almost clean slate, lacking either an administration or a policy. The general mood was expressed by President Boris N. Yeltsin in his reform speech on October 28, 1991: "For impermissibly long, we have discussed whether private property is necessary. In the meantime, the party-state elite has actively been engaged in their personal privatization. The scale, the enterprise, and the hypocrisy are staggering. The privatization in Russia has gone on for [a long time], but wildly, spontaneously, and often on a criminal basis. Today it is necessary to grasp the initiative, and we are intent on doing so."[12]

A strong sense of urgency prevailed, because of a widespread understanding among the people that what was not privatized would be taken—legally or illegally—by the old elite. The concept of *prikhvatizatsiya* (which means "grabbing," but sounds like it should mean "privatization" in Russian) was already commonplace. An approximate synonym was *nomenklatura* privatization, meaning that the old establishment privatized state property by dubious means to its own benefit. Therefore, public demands for quick privatization were strong. Alternative approaches to privatization were scrutinized according to the criteria of whether they could be practically implemented and would lead to quick privatization. Privatization had to be real, leading to individual (not collective) property rights. But both communists and members of the old *nomenklatura,* on the contrary, favored diluted property rights to retain control and have time to appropriate property for themselves.

An important understanding in Russia was that public property was not truly public. Usually, hidden quasi-property stakeholders rights existed.[13] If the state was to play a role, it essentially had to renationalize property, which would be a major undertaking. The pragmatic view of the Russian privatizers was that various stakeholders had to be given an acceptable deal so that they would go along with the privatization. The reformers therefore conceded that the distribution could not be based on strict rules of distributive justice.

The Russian decisionmakers looked at privatization in Poland primarily to learn what pitfalls to avoid and at that of Czechoslovakia to learn how to do it.[14] At the same time, they were acutely aware of Russian peculiarities, such as the highly corrupt state administration. Corruption was a recurring theme in any discussion of privatization in Russia. The reformers' main concern was to avoid any kind of direct negotiated deal between officials and purchasers. Instead, auctions and public tenders were called for, which would provide for competition, transparency, and market prices.[15]

However, Russia also had helpful characteristics. Because nationalization had occurred so long ago, few claims for restitution were lodged, which greatly simplified privatization. Nor did people think that any exact justice was possible. Therefore, it was comparatively easy for the reformers to focus on overreaching goals and to avoid excessive detail.

An initial step, which had already been announced by Yeltsin in October 1991, was to transform large enterprises into joint stock companies.[16] At the same time, the nominally public enterprises were in effect renationalized, because the bulk of the shares were supposed to be transferred to the state (that is, to the privatization authorities and not to branch ministries). The purpose was to stop spontaneous *nomenklatura* privatization of public enterprises and to impose a reasonably regular privatization process.[17]

Several alternative ideas circulated about who should benefit from privatization. The 500-day program had focused on budget revenues. The Russian privatization law of July 1991 had discarded the idea of privatization as a means of reaping state revenues, but it still lingered. On

December 29, 1991, a presidential decree on "Basic Provisions of a Program of Privatization of State and Municipal Enterprises in the Russian Federation in 1992" was adopted.[18] This rudimentary privatization program reflected the new views of privatization, but much remained unclear. It contained explicit revenue targets from each of the next three years (1992–94). The targets turned out to be easy to meet because of unexpectedly high inflation. However, they lost all political significance, and privatization revenues merely became a measure of the scope of privatization rather than having any import in themselves.

In his speech of October 28, 1991, Yeltsin initially stated that enterprise shares would be divided between the state and the work collectives or employees.[19] The transfer of property rights to the work force remained a high priority. Hardly anyone opposed it; the question was only how much should be given and in what form. A first authoritative answer was provided in the preliminary privatization program of December 1991. The "members of the work collectives" were to obtain shares in enterprises that would be transformed into open joint stock companies. The workers would receive 25 percent of the company capital for free as preferential shares, but this was not the last word.[20]

The purpose of giving a substantial share of the ownership to workers in enterprises that were to be privatized was not based on any ideology or concept of justice, but simply on a desire to facilitate quick privatization. The workers (frequently including their managers) were swiftly transformed into active advocates of privatization. As Chubais explained the decision at the time: "If we didn't accept that, the work collectives would hardly support privatization. But now they have 'suddenly' shown an interest in the law and started egging on the administration."[21] This scheme was shrewdly designed. The workers would receive stock only after their enterprise had been transformed into a joint stock company, so they would not only push for privatization but also for corporatization. The shares given to workers would be individual property, thereby excluding the dangers of collective property and Yugoslav-type worker self-management, with its attendant collective irresponsibility. The government also harbored the hope that workers would keep illicit privatization by managers in check. In particular, the government was afraid that its decision to in effect nationalize enterprises would encounter resistance. Therefore, it was anxious to have the workers on its side from the very beginning.

The decision to initially give stock to workers in enterprises that were to be privatized meant that workers received preference over all potential outside owners. The privatization program of December 1991 canceled the distribution of privatization accounts to all Russian citizens in 1992. Still, the idea of mass privatization was not abandoned. The privatization program rather loosely prescribed that preparations should be made for the opening of privatization accounts before the end of 1992.[22]

The privatization policy included free distribution of a certain amount of shares to workers, managers, and the population at large, but there was no clear concept of how much should be given to whom and of what was considered just. This left a lot of room for negotiation and compromise. However, there was a firm conviction that the people should be involved and that mass privatization should take place. Moreover, there was also an urge to both achieve a reasonably broad ownership of shares and to facilitate the emergence of strong owners. In effect, the initial distribution of shares to workers and managers gave them more preference than the policymakers intended or realized at the time.

Foreign investment did not play a major role in the privatization strategy, though initially it received more attention than it did later on. At the time, no foreign takeovers of Russian enterprises were possible without government approval. The government lacked the capability to attend to such matters, although foreign investment (both in joint ventures and wholly owned enterprises) was allowed. The privatization program of December 1991 contained passages regarding "utilization of foreign investment in privatization." However, this phrase is telling. Foreign investors were requested to do what Russian enterprises failed to, notably to take over enterprises that were operating at a loss or to complete unfinished construction projects.[23] The proponents of quick privatization opposed privileges for foreign investors, because they believed in the liberal principle of equal treatment of foreign and domestic investors. Discrimination against domestic enterprises was unjust and had proved ineffective elsewhere, and it would spur resistance to privatization as such. Conversely, the reformers opposed discrimination against foreign investors. They defeated a proposal that would have introduced a discriminatory exchange rate against foreign investors. Such demands were vocalized in early 1992, when the Russian ruble was extremely devalued. Still, the government worried about foreign investors buying big Russian companies for almost nothing, because that would arouse public hostility to privatization.[24] In addition, key liberals realized that little foreign investment could be expected given Russia's unstable conditions. Why take a risk for nothing?

In general, the Russian privatizers tried to avoid controversy and focused on what they believed was doable. Therefore, the privatization program for 1992 prohibited or limited privatization of anything that would cause a public outcry, notably natural resources and sources of cultural heritage.[25] Nor did the reformers specify how far privatization should go, although they made clear that it would be far-reaching. An eventual privatization of 70 percent of the economy was vaguely mentioned.[26]

The Russian privatizers never forgot that the ultimate purpose of privatization was to create a market. Therefore, a number of restrictions were always present. Prices of property should preferably be set through a market, and the best rudimentary market is an auction. An auction price is by definition always a market price, if several independent participants have been admitted to bid. Another market-related principle is that markets should be open and transparent. A related idea was to use the privatization process to develop markets, notably capital markets. That is, whenever open competitive trade could be generated, it should be. Monopoly was to be avoided, but that concept had to be sacrificed in many cases. The internal resistance against the breakup of large enterprises was great. This left the privatizers with the choice of either leaving an enterprise alone for years or privatizing it as it was. The idea that excessive concentration of ownership was harmful led to the splitting of privatization into different blocks of shares.

The Great Privatization Debate

During the first half of 1992, an intense and rancorous debate raged over privatization.[27] Although Russia already had a privatization law and a preliminary privatization program, this was when the Russian privatization actually took shape.

The prime question was, naturally, who was going to own the enterprises. The debate concentrated on the work collectives: How much should they receive, and should their shares be individual or collective? The directors wanted as much as possible for themselves, but they frequently hid behind the work collectives. A third group of claimants was the branch ministries, which wanted to retain their old prerogatives as far as possible. Other forces included regional authorities, new entrepreneurs, the general population, and the state itself. As Chubais described it: "The pressure is extraordinary every minute. The regions resist the branches, the work collectives the directors, the directors together with the work collectives the entrepreneurs, and parties pressurize from various sides."[28] At the time, the debate appeared of poor quality, disorganized, and overly aggressive; but in hindsight, it seems to have been surprisingly productive.

The government banner was held by the Minister of Privatization and Chairman of the State Committee of the Management of State Property Anatoly B. Chubais; his deputy, Dmitry Vasil'ev; and Petr Fillipov, chairman of the Subcommittee on Privatization in the Supreme Soviet.[29] Incidentally, these three men were newly arrived from St. Petersburg, where small-scale privatization had taken off in 1991 under Chubais's aegis.

Evolution of Privatization Options

The government's starting point was that 25 percent of the shares should first be distributed free of charge to the employees as preferential nonvoting shares. In addition, employees could buy 10 percent more of an enterprise's statutory capital as voting shares at 70 percent of the (very low) book price. The management could then buy 5 percent of the shares at the book price. In the privatization program for 1992, this was to become option one. Chubais argued for the principle of sales even as he envisioned some free distribution, without elaborating on his view. To him, real individual property rights were of fundamental importance, whereas workers' collective self-management of a Yugoslav kind was to be avoided.

The loudest public attacks against Chubais and the government were launched, curiously enough, by a group of liberals led by Larisa Piyasheva.[30] They believed that the state should transfer all property freely to the work collectives to ease growing social tensions and to undertake the speediest privatization. It was also a question of justice: The state should return the property to the people. However, these liberals were initially oriented toward collective ownership. They were against auctions, and they happily accepted closed joint stock companies. Chubais responded that they had forgotten all the people who did not work in enterprises—teachers, physicians, military personnel, pensioners, and students, among others. The Piyasheva group then added a proposal that citizens who were not employed by organizations undergoing privatization should be given tradeable privatization checks for free with which to buy shares. Piyasheva introduced her model of privatization of shops in Moscow, giving away the shops to their employees. Unfortunately, this resulted in great uncertainty. The employees were not informed of (or did not believe in) their property rights, and their managers tried to assume total control. Thus, purportedly privatized shops were run virtually the same, while new private shops assumed a much more market-oriented character.[31]

Managers and workers exerted strong pressure for more property for the work collectives. This resulted in a second option in the privatization program for 1992. All of the employees of a privatized enterprise would be granted the right to buy voting shares representing 51 percent of the authorized capital at 1.7 times the book price, leaving insiders with a majority of the votes. This ran counter to Chubais's conviction that control by employees would deter both domestic and foreign investors from considering an enterprise. However, he conceded in order to salvage the privatization program in the Supreme Soviet.[32]

The lobby representing directors mounted the strongest resistance against the government's privatization program. It was represented by the Russian Union of Industrialists and Entrepreneurs and in the Supreme Soviet by the strong centrist faction known as the Industrial Union.[33] The general directors were effectively in control of the state enterprises. In 1992, few general directors of Russian state enterprises lost their jobs. The state left them alone, and the workers were disorganized. The managers wanted to consolidate their proprietorships. They could best do so through tacit deals and slow privatization, and they abhorred early distinct property rights and transparency. One of their proposals was ESOPs (employee share-owning programs).[34] In particular, they were hostile to early Western investment, fearing that Western companies would oust them.[35]

The government was compelled to accommodate the managers. The second option was quite attractive to them, but the government added a third option—privatization limited to medium-size companies with more than 200 employees and fixed assets of more than 1 billion but less than 50 billion rubles. It entitled a group of managers to buy 20 percent of the voting shares of an enterprise at book value if two-thirds of the employees agreed. Later on, the management could purchase an additional 20 percent of the shares at a discount of 30 percent of their nominal value. However, the reformers designed this option ingeniously so that few enterprises were eligible. The first privatization option was therefore formed by the government, the second option through pressure from the work collectives, and the third as a bone tossed to the managers.

The Idea of Privatization Vouchers

In the summer of 1992, President Yeltsin chose to make privatization vouchers a centerpiece of economic reform. They became the theme in his speech on the anniversary of the August 1991 coup. He advocated a kind of people's capitalism, arguing that "we need millions of owners rather than a handful of millionaires." Yeltsin stressed equality of opportunity and freedom of choice: "Everyone will have equal opportunities in this new undertaking, and the rest will depend on ourselves. . . . Each citizen of Russia and each family will have freedom of choice. The privatization voucher is a ticket for each of us to a free economy."[36]

The idea of vouchers had arisen relatively late. They were not referred to in any legal context until a presidential decree in April 1992 announced that they would be distributed to the people in the fourth quarter of 1992, but this remained preliminary. In connection with Yeltsin's August speech, a presidential decree, "On Introducing a System of Privatization Checks in the Russian Federation," was issued that contained the necessary specifications.[37]

The voucher scheme was designed to be simple, equal, comprehensible, and market-conforming.[38] The vouchers were meant to form demand for all kinds of property to be privatized. The basic principle was that each Russian citizen should be entitled to receive one privatization check or voucher with a nominal value of 10,000 rubles. It was thus a system of free distribution, available equally to all with no differentiation between people. Nor were there vouchers for different purposes. They were all of one kind. The idea of privatization accounts had been abandoned in lieu of vouchers printed like securities, because these were simply easier to handle. In Poland, the government had intended to send vouchers by mail. This had caused an uproar not only over the possibility of theft, but also because people would be granted ownership without any effort whatsoever, with the state having to pay for giving away its property.

Therefore, Russian vouchers had to be picked up at a branch of the State Savings Bank for a nominal fee of a mere 25 rubles.

The system was similar to the Czechoslovak voucher scheme, although it was more populist. The administrative fee was smaller, even children could participate in the Russian scheme, and everyone got one voucher. In both countries, the intention was to let voucher privatization be massive enough to make it worthwhile and to undertake several issues of vouchers. An important difference was that the Russian vouchers were not personal but fully transferable and tradeable. This was seen as a matter of freedom of choice. As Yeltsin put it: "It is possible that some citizens do not want to become owners. Then they will be able to sell their vouchers."[39] The government also saw the voucher market as a rudimentary market for securities. The accumulation of blockholdings was considered something positive, because there was a concern that ownership would be too diluted to produce strong owners. Chubais hoped that the voucher price would rise on the market and render voucher privatization popular.[40]

Some worried that vouchers would be used as money and would thus contribute to inflation through an increase in the quasi-money supply. Therefore, state-owned firms were formally prohibited from receiving vouchers as payment. The nominal value of vouchers was also set relatively high, and they were valid only until the end of 1993.

The approach was *laissez-faire* and from the ground up, letting citizens use vouchers however they wanted. They could participate in voucher auctions or (according to option two) use vouchers for buying out a share of the enterprise where they worked through closed subscription. They could also invest their vouchers in investment or voucher funds or simply sell them. The voucher funds were formed spontaneously from below on private initiative exactly as in Czechoslovakia; but because of widespread fraud in the Russian economy, the authorities insisted on the licensing of voucher funds. Even so, almost 650 of them were soon formed. Because the government was afraid of outside corporate raiders behaving irresponsibly, voucher funds were not allowed to possess more than 10 percent of the shares in any enterprise.

Fears that people would not bother to pick up their vouchers proved unjustified. In fact, 144 million Russians, or almost 97 percent of those eligible, collected their vouchers after the deadline had been extended one month to January 31, 1993.

The Balancing of Various Stakeholders

Traditionally, branch ministries had stood against regional governments. Under Nikita Khrushchev, the regions had briefly taken over the economy, but the branch ministries had come back with a vengeance. They dominated industry completely in the Brezhnev period beginning in 1964, while the regional party committees had controlled agriculture, trade, and consumer services. The privatization program redressed this balance to the benefit of the regions. Regional privatization authorities were actually carrying out the privatization of even federal property. All revenues from small-scale privatization went to the regional budgets. Some enterprises, such as water and other public utilities, became long-term local government assets. Finally, the regional property committees retained voting control posts in privatized enterprises of usually 15 to 20 percent of the shares to be privatized later.

A big problem, however, was that regional governments were also in the best position to take bribes. An inevitable effect of the decentralization of privatization was that substantial bribery arose at the regional level. Regions with large assets also refused to allow people from elsewhere to have access to their privatization.[41] Yet both these factors tended to encourage regional governments to support quick privatization. It was worse if regional authorities believed they were so strongly entrenched that they wanted to settle for long-term control and reap the rents of the property they have seized. The most obvious example has been the city of Moscow. Mayor Yury Luzhkov became a major critic of the government privatization program, because it did not generate state revenues. Therefore, Luzhkov insisted on sales rather than privatization for vouchers, although his real concern appeared to be to maximize the flow of bribes. Luzhkov, like Chubais, was considered close to Yeltsin; therefore, Chubais could not use Yeltsin's support to win over Luzhkov. On the contrary—Yeltsin sided with Luzhkov, who soon changed his stance and insisted on voucher privatization only in Moscow, to the obvious benefit of him and his cronies.[42]

The branch ministries were entirely hostile to privatization, because they had been the actual owners of big enterprises in the Brezhnev era. They argued that enterprises were too important to society to be privatized, that no private individuals would be able to raise sufficient capital, and that it would be dangerous to have foreign owners. Yet the branch ministries had been scaled down considerably and lost most of their powers under *pere-stroika*. They no longer had any right to issue commands to enterprises and their allocation of state orders and investments was limited, but they still made their interests felt in the massive federal bureaucracy.

The branch ministries realized their weakness and settled for a second line of defense. Rather than opposing privatization, they argued for a false privatization through the free distribution of shares—not to individuals or private enterprises, but to state enterprises within the same industry. As a result, enormous holding companies with interconnected ownership would emerge. State enterprises would own each other in a complex web without clear responsibility or transparency. In reality, the holding companies were supposed to replace branch ministries. The official justification for this was to maintain the technological links and supplies between enterprises that could break down with the onset of privatization. Stability rather than competition and restructuring was the aim, which ran counter to the widespread concern with excessive monopolization of the Russian economy. The prime spokesman for the branch ministries in the spring of 1992 was Minister of Industry Aleksandr Titkin, but Deputy Prime Minister Vladimir Shumeiko was also their advocate just after having joined the government in June 1992.[43]

Although these plans ran counter to government policy, it was a hard job for the liberals to block them, and they reemerged under new guises.[44] In a couple of branches of industry, they won support from managers and could therefore be implemented. Subsequently, special legislation was drawn up for holding companies. Managers have typically sided with branch ministries in two cases: First, when enterprises have operated chronically at a loss and could only survive with substantial subsidies (notably in the military-industrial complex), holding companies can obscure financial flows and provide a convenient veil for subsidization; and second, when managers cannot afford to buy huge enterprises, such as oil companies, holding companies offer a maximum of power and control.[45] Otherwise, managers have usually sided with regional authorities rather than with branch ministries. Still, branch ministries have some say about the privatization of very large enterprises, and some holding companies have been created through discretionary government decisions. Yet on the whole, branch ministries remain the big losers.

The central state bodies were either passive or loyal to the GKI. But in the summer of 1993, the Ministry of the Economy—formerly Gosplan—tried to recover its former influence under the leadership of Oleg

Lobov, an old conservative friend of President Yeltsin. His proposals included raising the book value of the enterprises so that vouchers could buy less and reducing the share of property given away and demanding payment. However, Chubais managed to defeat this serious attack.[46] The Ministry of Finance did not really enter into the discussion, as it was on the reformist side, and federal state revenues were left aside.

The Supreme Soviet opposed the government's privatization program but did not present much of an alternative until early 1993, when it proposed a fourth option: Ten percent of an enterprise's shares should be sold on the stock exchange, and the enterprise should receive the revenues. The remaining 90 percent should be given to the employees, formally paid for by retained profits over 3 to 5 years, of which 10 percent should remain collective property over which the managers would have voting rights.[47] This was an attempt to turn both workers and managers against the government's program. The scheme would delay privatization, although its supporters presented it as a means of speeding it up. The property would remain ambiguously collective, and outside ownership would be minimized. The government managed to block the adoption of this alternative on the grounds that it contradicted the original privatization law of July 1991. In the end, the Supreme Soviet tried to sabotage the privatization program through fairly meaningless proposals. These included replacing vouchers with privatization accounts—merely a different technique of mass privatization, but one that would impede privatization and presumably halt it because of technical complications.[48]

The sympathies of the Russian people were investigated through a large number of opinion polls. Their results varied remarkably and greatly over time, allowing for few generalizations. However, the smaller and more personal an object, the more popular its privatization. One poll established the decreasing order of popularity among objects of private property as follows: houses or apartments, plots of land for a house or *dacha,* farms, cars, and shops or businesses. Each enjoyed an approval rating of at least 75 percent.[49] The privatization of big industrial enterprises was much less comprehensible and was approved by no more than half the people.[50]

Several groups were not truly represented in the privatization debate. Trade unions and workers councils, which should have been formed according to the Law on State Enterprises of 1987 and sometimes did actually exist, were barely heard from. Yet the old trade unions advocated free distribution of ownership to work collectives. One group that lost out altogether in this first round was outside investors—that is, rich Russians not employed in the administration or enterprises undergoing privatization. They were labelled "shadow capital" in the debate. Similarly, foreign investors were excluded, and foreign countries wisely undertook only limited efforts to express their concerns.

Although foreign advisors did not represent any economic interests, they shared current Western and academic insights into Russian thinking on privatization. The main inspiration at the time was the successful privatization in Czechoslovakia, while the mistakes in Poland had been well learned.[51]

Many practical issues had been sorted out. All ideas of complex evaluation had definitely been thrown out. Either the nominal book value that had been inflated away was used, or some kind of auction or competitive price was substituted. Yet in the name of flexibility, the government was forced to accept not only open joint stock companies but also some closed ones, as well as some negotiated prices of property. The idea of collective ownership had been dealt a serious blow, and holding companies had taken a beating, but they were to reappear. Because privatization accounts were impractical, vouchers of a much simplified Czechoslovak type was chosen. Unlike Czechs and Slovaks, not only adults but all Russians received vouchers, but only one each.

Perhaps the most sophisticated aspect of the Russian privatization program has been its politics—how various stakeholders have been considered and co-opted. The approach could either be described as pragmatic or unprincipled. Yet fundamental principles have been adhered to, and the policy has been deliberate and flexible; compromises have been tactical rather than strategic. When Chubais presented the government privatization program for 1992, he stated that the chief task during the document's preparation had been giving the fullest possible consideration to all interests.[52] His top advisors, Andrei Shleifer and Maxim Boycko, have described privatization as a redistribution of existing control rights over assets between a company's stakeholders.[53] In the end, the workers got the most, followed by managers. The local government gained quite a bit, and even the people got something, but the branch ministries (with a few exceptions) got next to nothing. For Chubais, the main goal of privatization increasingly became "to form a broad stratum of private owners."[54] Yeltsin liked this idea and made it the main theme of his speech in August 1992 on the anniversary of the failed coup.

In the public debate, hardly anyone questioned privatization as such, even though it was obvious many were against it. Most proposals—even the fourth option put forth by the Supreme Soviet—were presented as attempts at speeding up privatization. A broad political consensus had evolved in favor of rapid privatization.

A Radical Privatization Program

The main outcome of the privatization debate in the spring of 1992 was the adoption by the Supreme Soviet of the "Program of Privatization" for 1992.[55] It contained substantial alterations in both the privatization law of July 1991 and the provisional privatization program of December 1991. This was to be followed by annual privatization programs for 1993 and 1994, but its principles survived only until July 1994. The privatization program for 1992 covered all state and municipal property except for state farms (*sovkhozy*), land, and housing.

The program clarified the main aims of privatization:

—to form a stratum of private proprietors interested in the creation of a social market economy;

—to raise the efficiency of enterprises;

—to improve the social safety net with proceeds from privatization;

—to concur with financial stabilization;

—to create a competitive environment and demonopolization;

—to attract foreign investment; and

—to prepare for further privatization in 1993–94.

Enterprises were categorized by administrative level, branch, and size. First, state property needed to be divided into federal and municipal property. In principle, that was done through a decree adopted by the Supreme Soviet on December 27, 1991.[56] Enterprises were then divided into five categories by branch—those that must be privatized in 1992; those that must not be privatized in 1992; and those that could be privatized only by a decision by the GKI in consultation with a branch ministry, or by the Russian government alone, or by local authorities. For more than 30 percent of the property of Russia, privatization was prohibited. Thirty-one percent could only be privatized through permission of the government, 20 percent required the permission of the GKI, and 17 percent could be privatized freely by local authorities.[57]

The enterprises subject to compulsory privatization were in wholesale and retail trade, public catering, consumer services, construction firms, construction materials, state agricultural enterprises other than *sovkhozy*, firms in the agroindustrial sector, food and light industrial enterprises, enterprises operating at a loss, factories that were still standing, and unfinished construction projects. The idea was to start with what was technically easy and politically popular to privatize. Most of these enterprises were subject to small-scale privatization.[58] The prohibition from privatization was limited to 1992. The reformers thereby avoided a futile discussion about the eventual limits of privatization before it had even started.

In a third step, enterprises were categorized as small, medium-size, or large. Small enterprises were defined as enterprises with no more than 200 employees and a book value of less than 1 million rubles. Large enterprises had more than 1,000 employees and fixed assets of more than 50 million rubles, while those in the intermediate group with 200 to 1,000 employees were considered medium-size. The double definition based on both employment and capital offered the enterprises choices regarding their classification and thus their privatization.

In principle, small enterprises were supposed to be auctioned off or sold through public tender, large enterprises were to be transformed into open joint stock companies, and medium-size enterprises could be privatized either way. However, additional methods of privatization were permitted, notably employee buyouts of leased property. The transformation of state enterprises into closed joint stock companies was explicitly proscribed; but many did so in any case, and the state failed to stop them.

The privatization program for 1993 was ready in December 1992, but it was severely criticized by the Congress of People's Deputies. The criticism delayed its adoption, and the privatization program for 1992 remained in effect instead. The main opposition to privatization then came from branch ministries that insisted on ownership of 51 percent of the shares in a large number of enterprises. The GKI exploited the impatience of local authorities and demanded a far-reaching decentralization of how privatization proposals would be authorized. Moscow could no longer order the regions around, and the GKI adjusted its tactics accordingly, playing down the threat of central sanctions while putting more emphasis on incentives.[59]

In hindsight, the period around April 20, 1993, appears to have been the time of gravest threat to the Russian privatization program. The president, together with the government, faced a political stalemate with the Supreme Soviet, which advocated its fourth option and tried to block the privatization program. However, these actions were revoked through presidential decisions. The branch ministries were making their last big offensive, and the regional authorities also took their most critical stance on privatization. Several regions had stopped privatization altogether. Small-scale privatization almost ground to a halt, while voucher privatization proceeded under a cloud. The voucher price had fallen well below par for political reasons. On April 16, 1993, Oleg Lobov had been appointed minister of the economy and first deputy prime minister. One of Lobov's main ideas was to block voucher privatization. Mayor Yury Luzhkov of Moscow took the same line. The appointment of Lobov suggested that Prime Minister Chernomyrdin was of the same opinion and that President Yeltsin wavered in his support of privatization. At the same time, public criticism of the privatizers reached a peak, and Chubais was on the verge of being ousted from the government. In the end, however, both the privatization program and Chubais were salvaged by unexpected popular support for the economic reforms in the referendum of April 25, 1993.

Considering the broad political onslaught on privatization, it is remarkable that the privatizers did not give up on their principles. As Chubais stated early in 1993: "We are categorically against any principal changes in the approach to privatization and no such changes occur. . . . The current course has been adopted, and now things are progressing completely normally. To change the course now would simply mean to cheat millions of people who have believed in it. . . . We shall insist till the end on the fundamental, basic principles of privatization."[60] He maintained this stand and did not change policy, nor did he sacrifice any of his collaborators.

After the referendum, privatization regained its momentum, and it never fell into such dire straits again. The privatization program for 1994 was adopted by presidential decree on Christmas Eve 1993. It maintained the same principles while being more specific and elaborating on incentives, redressing the balance between inside and outside owners to the benefit of outsiders.[61] Beginning in July 1994, a new postvoucher privatization program was adopted. Because the intended free distribution of ownership had taken place, the government could now opt for decentralized competitive sales for money. State revenues, strong owners, and investment were emphasized, but speed remained important.[62]

Skillful Administration

A vital precondition for the success of Russian privatization was political arrangements. In stark contrast to Poland, which did not even have a Ministry of Privatization during most of the first year of its economic transition, Russia established one federal state authority that was responsible for privatization, the GKI. Moreover, within the government one man was in charge of privatization, namely Minister of Privatization and Chairman of the State Committee for the Management of State Property Anatoly B. Chubais. (It helped that Chubais managed to hold on to his position throughout the first two years of reform and that he was promoted to deputy prime minister, while retaining his previous job, in June 1992.)

More than any other economic reform minister, Chubais succeeded in convincing President Yeltsin of the importance of his domain. Chubais appears to have enjoyed frequent access to Yeltsin, and it is striking how many presidential decrees were issued in support of Chubais's privatization policies.

Although there was no official reform program, Chubais worked out a comprehensive privatization program at breakneck speed. The first provisional program, "Basic Provisions of the Privatization Program," was adopted at the end of December 1991. Chubais continued to elaborate on fully fledged programs for the consecutive privatization also.

However controversial privatization appeared, Chubais managed to gain a full political mandate for it. As soon as the first provisional privatization program was ready, Chubais induced President Yeltsin to contact Ruslan Khasbulatov, the chairman of the Supreme Soviet. The Presidium of the Supreme Soviet swiftly and unanimously adopted the program at a joint meeting with the government on December 27, 1991.[63] A presidential decree of January 29, 1992, "On the Acceleration of the Privatization of State and Municipal Enterprises," introduced the necessary regulations to keep the privatization process moving. However, parliamentary approval of a full-fledged privatization program was needed.

In late March 1992, a draft privatization program was ready for adoption by the Supreme Soviet, but its political mood had turned much more negative. Even so, Chubais worked hard to try to convince the deputies, with valuable support from Petr Fillipov, chairman of the Subcommittee on Privatization in the Supreme Soviet. They made real concessions to benefit both workers and managers. After months of vigorous debate, the Supreme Soviet finally adopted the key privatization program for 1992 on June 11, 1992. As it later turned out, this was the last major reformist decision the Russian Supreme Soviet was to make. Chubais had exploited a window of opportunity that was just about to close and obtained the necessary legal base for privatization. Henceforth, important decisions on privatization were made through presidential decrees, while less significant decisions were made by the government or the GKI itself. In 1993, the Supreme Soviet made one decision after another to impede privatization, but these were invariably revoked by presidential decree.

During the first half-year in office, Chubais built up the GKI at the center, through a State Property Committee in each of the 88 regions as well as local property committees in cities.[64] This organization was essentially new and thus not as marred by communist practice and thinking as other state organs. It was created for the very purpose of privatization and was not confused by previous opposing tasks. Moreover, its organization was highly decentralized, with about 400 employees at the GKI in Moscow compared with about 100 at each regional Property Committee.

Although the GKI had been created under the reform government, an entity called the Property Fund had been established under the old regime for the purpose of privatization and was subordinate to the Supreme Soviet. The Russian Federal Property Fund was retained under the new scheme and developed a regional organization parallel to the GKI. The idea was that the regional branches of the GKI should prepare for and implement privatization as well as manage assets during its implementation. However, property rights would reside with the regional property funds, which were the legal sellers. Yet the property fund administration was both smaller and weaker than the GKI. The scheme was complicated by the GKI's subordination to the government, whereas the Property Fund was under the aegis of the Supreme Soviet, which saw the Fund as an instrument to seize administrative control over privatization.[65] Therefore, conflicts between the government and the Supreme Soviet were to recur between the property committees and the property funds at all administrative levels, which complicated all efforts toward privatization.

In November 1991, a Committee on Foreign Investment was set up to promote such investment. It was headed by a Gaidar confidant, Leonid Grigor'ev, who became deputy minister of finance. In February 1992, the American investment bank Goldman Sachs became an official advisor to the Russian government on foreign investment. Goldman Sachs tried to boost Grigor'ev and his committee. However, neither the committee nor foreign investment took off. Grigor'ev clashed with Chubais over fundamental policy principles. Grigor'ev wanted to allow Goldman Sachs to negotiate individual discretionary deals with its Western clients, but Chubais abhorred any nontransparent deals with foreign companies that would arouse political opposition to privatization in general. Similarly, Grigor'ev opposed voucher privatization and decentralization of privatization, because they would preclude the government from selling enterprises to foreign businesses. Chubais countered that foreign enterprises were welcome to buy vouchers and participate in voucher auctions or to buy shares from Russian individuals or enterprises after voucher privatization had taken place. Chubais won, and Grigor'ev left his job in the fall of 1992. The Committee on Foreign Investment was essentially abolished.

Privatization legislation was federal, but the execution of privatization was regional. The capacity for privatization therefore became much greater than if it had been centralized, and the process could not be stopped by temporary upsets in Moscow. Even major political crises caused only moderate fluctuations in the volume of privatization. Ardent adversaries of privatization, such as the old branch ministries or their remnants, were highly centralized. The privatizers could frequently mobilize regional authorities against adversaries of privatization in Moscow, and because regional authorities greatly extended their powers at Moscow's expense, privatization benefitted.

The privatization officials astutely exploited the mechanisms of both the old and the new systems. The provisional privatization program of December 1991 contained so-called compulsory plan targets (usually around 50 percent) for the privatization of enterprises in 1992 in ten specified branches in all regions. This would keep old Soviet officials working for privatization. Monthly statistical reports replete with tables were also requested from each region to encourage all of them to compete over quick transfers of property. These techniques gave rise to jokes about liberals resorting to Bolshevik methods, but they worked.

Another method was to activate various government bodies by requesting that they produce privatization programs. The GKI centrally fostered an annual privatization program, and in each region, the property committee was obliged to produce its own program. Most important, each enterprise singled out for compulsory privatization had to elaborate on its own privatization proposal. Thus, exactly as in Czechoslovakia, enterprises in selected sectors were compelled to privatize, but they were given a choice on how to go about it. Other enterprises were encouraged to propose their own means of privatization with permission from privatization authorities, although certain sensitive branches were initially excluded from privatization.[66] The Russian reformers carefully avoided the situation that had been created in Poland, where the privatization law of July 1990 gave several interested parties the right to veto privatization.[67] The strategy thrived on grassroots initiative taken by enterprising managers, who saw that they could secure a fair amount of both ownership and support through privatization.

To formalize all sides of privatization, the state needed to adopt hundreds of legal documents. However, Russia has an acute shortage of lawyers, and the entire legal system is in a deplorable state, because of its small size, extreme shortage of qualified staff, and widespread corruption. This has been a seemingly permanent dilemma of Russian privatization. The reformers' main approach was to simplify as much as possible. A surprising number of legal acts were written by Jonathan Hay, an American lawyer employed by the GKI. Another element was great tolerance toward the violation of central regulations, for either benign or malign purposes. The underlying assumption was that what was not privatized would be stolen. Therefore, a somewhat irregular privatization was preferred to a halt in privatization.

In few areas has the Russian need for foreign intellectual assistance been as great as in the case of privatization. A large number of Western lawyers and economists have been involved.[68] Complaints have focused on how much they were paid rather than on the utility of their work, which proved to be great. For such tasks it is crucial to have few but highly qualified staff. It would be foolhardy for aid agencies not to pay market-adjusted remuneration for such services. Still, the main explanation for successful Western assistance to Russian privatization is that the leading Russian privatizers, Chubais and his deputy Dmitry Vasil'ev, knew what kind of policy they wanted. They instructed their advisors about the policy framework, and the advisors were not permitted to act as an interest group. Their job was to provide the government with useful advice within the parameters of the government policy. This was in stark contrast to the situation in Poland. A number of Western advising companies had initially advocated an excessively complicated, expensive, and slow British approach to privatization there, which turned out not to work. Consequently, large-scale privatization in Poland failed. The foreign technical assistance provided to Russian privatization is likely to stand out as some of the most effective Western aid in support of postcommunist economic transition.

Ordinary Small-Scale Privatization

Small-scale privatization in Russia was neither innovative nor complicated. The lesson from eastern Europe was clear: Let the local authorities sell small enterprises at auction for money, and encourage them to do so swiftly.[69] Experimental sales of shops had taken place in St. Petersburg in 1991, but only a few dozen small state enterprises had actually been privatized.

First, state property had been divided between the state and municipalities. Enterprises next had to be properly delimited as legal entities, specifying what property belonged to a particular enterprise. For trade this was done through the presidential "Decree on the Commercialization of the Activity of Trade Establishments in the RSFSR," which also set out the terms for commercialization. The legislation also called for the splitting up of large trade establishments.[70] Regional and local property committees had to be organized, which was accomplished during the first half of 1992.[71] Rules then had to be adopted regarding how privatization should occur, which was done through a presidential decree on January 29, 1992. Competitive sales (either auctions or public tender) open to all locals were requested, though in practice small enterprises could also be leased with the right of employee buyout. Moreover, some rather small enterprises were transformed into joint stock companies.[72] Finally, the authorities in charge of privatization were to be given strong incentives for speedy privatization. Revenues from auctions were to be kept by the local authorities that carried out the sales. Plan targets for small-scale privatization for each region and branch (usually ranging between 40 and 60 percent) had been set in the provisional privatization program. Monthly privatization reports containing some fifty tables were requested from each region—a truly Russian trick conceived by Dmitry Vasil'ev. Chubais threatened slow privatizers with the loss of their jobs, although in practice he was lenient.

Everything seemed primed for rapid small-scale privatization. An additional ingredient was a bold pioneer attracting much publicity—Nizhny Novgorod, which was ruled by young democrats. In early February 1992, the first 21 shops were auctioned off at a highly theatrical televised auction in Nizhny Novgorod in the presence of both Yegor Gaidar and Anatoly Chubais.[73] One by one, other regions felt exposed as laggards and speeded up their small-scale privatization. As in eastern Europe, small-scale privatization soon accelerated. The decisive push seems to have been the adoption of the privatization program in June 1992.

Small-scale privatization had reached full speed in August 1992, and on average 5,000 to 6,000 enterprises a month were privatized between August 1992 and April 1993. By the end of 1992, 46,815 enterprises had been privatized (see table 7-2). Characteristically, the peak month (with almost 12,000 enterprises privatized) was December 1992, which showed that the traditional *shturmovshchina* or annual production spurt of the command economy was at work. The regional bosses were still anxious to fulfill their annual privatization plan. Russia was supposed to have privatized 35 percent of its municipal firms in 1992.[74] The goal for 1993 was to complete the small-scale privatization, and it continued despite Gaidar's departure in December 1992. However, beginning in April 1993, the number of enterprises privatized was only measured in an even number of thousands per month, implying an extremely inexact measurement. The government's attention had shifted to large-scale voucher privatization, and statistics are too inexact to allow any certain judgment. Moreover, because of the heated strife between the president and the Parliament in late March, small-scale privatization slowed down in the spring of 1993. Several conservative regions even prohibited further privatization.[75] This appears to have been the last serious impediment to privatization, which was disposed of by the referendum on April 25. By the end of 1993, about 89,000 enterprises had been privatized, including more than 70 percent of all small enterprises.[76] The pace of privatization fell

Table 7-2. *Number of Enterprises Privatized, March 1992–August 1994*

Month	Total number of firms privatized	Total number of firms privatized each month	Small firms privatized each month
1992			
March	1,352		
April	2,995	1,643	1,643
May	5,855	2,860	2,860
June	8,933	3,078	3,078
July	12,015	3,082	3,082
August	17,230	5,215	5,215
September	22,572	5,342	5,342
October	29,235	6,663	6,663
November	34,932	5,697	5,697
December	46,815	11,865	11,883
1993			
January	54,243	7,428	7,323
February	57,989	3,746	3,555
March	59,495	1,506	1,071
April	66,000	6,505	5,900
May	68,000	2,000	1,411
June	72,000	4,000	3,142
July	78,000	6,000	5,144
August	81,000	3,000	2,223
September	82,000	1,000	72
October	83,000	1,000	159
November	86,000	3,000	2,133
December	89,000	3,000	1,957
1994			
January	91,000	2,000	1,332
February	93,000	2,000	1,295
March	95,000	2,000	1,068
April	98,000	3,000	2,134
May	99,000	1,000	162
June	102,000	3,000	1,645
July	104,000	2,000	
August	106,000	2,000	

Note: Column 3 is the total number of privatized firms minus the number of firms sold in voucher auctions (see table 7–3). The rounded figures indicate the imprecision of the statistics.

Source: Government of the Russian Federation, *Russian Economic Trends*, vol. 2, no. 4 (1993), p. 68; "Russian Economic Trends: Monthly Update," October 17, 1994, Table 11.

from about 3,500 enterprises a month in 1993 to about 2,000 a month in 1994. By September 1, 1994, the number of privatized enterprises had risen to 106,000.[77]

Quantitatively, small-scale privatization almost complied with the ambitious goals set for it. The targets had intentionally been set high to press the local property committees to speed up privatization.[78] Key consumer sectors became predominantly private in 1993. For instance, by May 1, 52 percent of retail trade establishments, 47 percent of restaurants and bars, and 55 percent of consumer service establishments had been privatized, and small-scale privatization had spread throughout almost the entire country.[79]

Qualitatively, however, privatization did not work out quite as intended. Auctions and public tenders did not become the dominant methods used. By May 1, 1993, only 13.6 percent of enterprises privatized in retail trade had been sold at auction and 36 percent through public tender. However, 40.4 percent had first been leased and then bought out by employees, and 13.6 percent had been privatized by being transformed into shareholding companies, which usually amounted to employee buyouts as well. The impression of a lack of transparency and predominance of insider ownership is reinforced by data on the new owners. Employees had bought 69.9 percent of all privatized retail outlets by May 1, 1993, whereas 22.3 percent belonged to legal entities, and only 7.9 percent to outside individuals.[80]

One reason for the mass acquisition of enterprises by their employees was that they were offered excellent purchasing conditions. If a work collective submitted a winning bid in an auction, it received a discount of 30 percent on the final price up front. In addition, the collective would have to pay only 25 percent of the real purchase price within a month. The remaining payments were interest free and could be made over a three-year period, thus in effect being inflated away. A private bidder would, on the contrary, have to pay the whole purchase price within a month.[81] Even so, work collectives overwhelmingly preferred buyouts under even better conditions. Frequently, a buyout was undertaken by the enterprise itself. Retained profits were used as payment, and the real beneficiary tended to be the management rather than the workforce.

In eastern Europe (particularly in Poland), the contrast between state-owned shops and private shops was enormous in terms of style, supply, and service. In Russia, however, the difference between privatized shops and state-owned shops was slight. An *Izvestiya* journalist depicted privatized Moscow shops at the end of 1992 thus: "The shop shelves are empty as before. The salespeople-owners have not become more polite. The cheating of purchasers continues."[82] This was an exaggeration, because commodities had returned to the shops; but progress had not been satisfactory. It was even more striking that, when asked, salespeople frequently did not know whether their shop had been privatized or whether they owned it. In fact, much of the privatization of shops was gradual *nomenklatura* privatization to the benefit of the shop managers. As Chubais frequently pointed out, an auction produced a turnaround of a shop, whereas an employee buyout (as in Moscow) brought little or no change.[83] Stifling regulations contributed to the inertia. Private property rights had not been reinforced. But newly established private shops and kiosks could immediately be spotted as being private because of their far more affluent appearance.[84]

An eastern European success story was state sales of trucks at local auctions, notably in Poland and Albania. As a result, many small private truck companies emerged, and a decentralized and competitive road transportation system had been created. Chubais found this idea attractive and tried to execute it, but this proved exceedingly difficult to do in Russia. The conservative minister of transportation refused to endorse his scheme. He argued that the huge Russian truck companies were efficient, although it was only too evident that all productivity measures for these firms were abysmal, with most trucks driving empty and with extremely low utilization rates. After repeated failures, Chubais turned to military trucks instead, because the military was to be scaled down; but an argument ensued that demobilized officers should be allowed to buy surplus trucks at a low price. Because this view gained in popularity, nothing happened.[85] Finally, at the end of October 1992, 195 trucks from a local company were sold at auction in pioneering Nizhny Novgorod. These were the first privately owned trucks in Russia.[86] But this auction did not garner much of a following. By January 1, 1993, only 302 road transport enterprises—6 percent of the total—had been privatized. This rate improved a bit, and by January 1, 1994, 1,475 road transport enterprises (30 percent of the total) had been privatized, but in relative terms road transport continued to lag behind.[87]

Large-Scale Mass Privatization

The greatest challenge for Russian privatization was privatizing 25,000 large and medium-size industrial enterprises that had constituted the very fabric of the Russian economy. Small-scale privatization had served as the first test of the privatization administration, and it was ready for greater tasks in late 1992. The division of state property between various administrative levels had already taken place, and privatization options had been set. What remained was to transform state enterprises into joint stock companies, to generate more demand for privatized property for which vouchers would be issued, and then to carry out the actual privatization.

Corporatization

From the very beginning of the privatization discussion, it had been widely agreed that large enterprises and some medium-size ones should be transformed into joint stock enterprises. However, the process was impeded by considerations regarding the creation of boards of directors.

With the adoption of the privatization program in June 1992, the time had come for the mass creation of joint stock companies. A presidential decree to this purpose was issued in early July 1992.[88] The aim of corporatization, or commercialization, was to make enterprises independent of state administration and to delimit their property. This was therefore a means of both hardening the budget constraints on enterprises and allowing them more freedom of action.

The corporatization decree prescribed that all enterprises to be privatized be transformed into open joint stock companies. The time limits were rigid, and all mandatory conversions had to be completed by November 1, 1992. After corporatization, the property committee in question had to transfer all shares to the relevant property fund. As long as the state owned all the shares, the board of directors would consist of representatives of the GKI, the managers, the workers, bankers, and perhaps other parties involved in the corporation. After privatization, the board would be elected by the shareholders, as in any private company.

As could be expected, corporatization was not undertaken as quickly as had been intended, but it was relatively fast. By April 1994, about 80 percent of the 20,000 large and medium-size enterprises eligible for privatization had been converted into joint stock companies.[89]

For corporatization to be carried out, a general meeting of a workers' collective was held to select one of the three privatization options. By the end of 1993, 79 percent of the collectives had selected option two, with 51 percent of their shares bought cheaply by insiders; approximately 17 percent had selected the first privatization option, with 25 percent of the shares being given free to employees; and only 1 percent chose option three, with management buyout. However, an additional 3 percent of enterprises (comprising those that had previously been leased) were bought out by their employees. This had not been intended as a legal option.[90] The selection was logical. Insiders were in a strong position, and they took as much ownership as possible. In some enterprises (notably very rich ones), employees could not afford to buy all the cheap shares offered them in option two. To them, option one appeared to be more favorable, because it implied a giveaway. The third option was intentionally designed to resist blatant attempts at cheap management buyouts, and it worked.

Voucher Auctions

The actual privatization of an enterprise involved several steps. First, soon after corporatization, privatization commissions were formed for each enterprise to be privatized. They organized closed subscriptions among employees to allocate shares in accordance with the chosen privatization option. In a second round, a voucher auction was held. Then an ESOP could be formed out of remaining shares in the property fund. Some shares (about one-tenth) would be retained by the property fund until their distribution was determined.

Although most shares were given away for free or sold cheaply to insiders, voucher auctions became the definitive event in the privatization process. A voucher auction concluded the privatization process by raising private ownership above the 65-percent limit that was the defining line for an enterprise to be considered private. The transparency and unique character of an auction reinforced this sense of a definitive event.

The auctions were technically as simple as possible. Anyone could participate in a voucher auction—employees, locals, voucher funds, outsiders, and even foreigners—but only vouchers were allowed as payment. However, outsiders were excluded by illicit means, primarily through withholding of information about voucher auctions. Voucher auctions were usually local affairs, dominated by employees, related locals, and possibly one or two blockholders (usually voucher funds). Individuals were often crowded out at voucher auctions, where the ratio of individual to institutional investors tended to be 1:4.[91] Property committees at all levels tried to counter this tendency by advertising extensively, including on television. They also encouraged large enterprises to undertake national voucher auctions to boost their prestige, which after a sluggish start turned out to be a hit.

Because voucher auctions did not involve money, they did not offer local authorities much. Later on, local property committees were given an important incentive: They were entitled to sell some shares for cash *after* a voucher auction. Although 35 percent of the shares were supposed to be sold for vouchers, an average of about 20 percent was put up for auction. A presidential decree on the rights of Russian citizens to participate in privatization was issued in May 1993. It established that not less than 29 percent of all shares should be sold at voucher auctions within three months after an enterprise had been corporatized.[92] However, the share stayed at around 20 percent, because enterprises continued to resist voucher privatization, preferring to keep the stocks for their employees. (Notably, oil companies released less than 10 percent of their shares for voucher auctions.)

The first 18 voucher auctions took place in eight regions in December 1992. Some of them were trendsetters, boosted through massive publicity. The number of voucher auctions and regions involved grew steadily until June 1993, when almost 900 enterprises were sold at voucher auctions conducted in 79 out of 88 regions. This high level of auctions was maintained until June 1994. The number of voucher auctions peaked in December 1993 and June 1994, showing that the old communist tradition of final spurts held sway. Almost 14,000 large and medium-size enterprises were sold at voucher auctions altogether (table 7-3).

The Russian people had rather differentiated attitudes toward voucher privatization. One VTsIOM poll in December 1993 asked what people had done, or wanted to do, with their vouchers. Twenty-six percent chose the easiest option of buying shares in a voucher fund, while 25 percent preferred to sell their vouchers and 7 percent opted for giving them away. Fifteen percent bought shares in an enterprise where they, family members, or friends worked, but only 8 percent wanted shares in other enterprises. Twenty-five percent did not know what to do with the vouchers.[93] The eventual outcome was not all that different, according to the polling organization Mnenie: 30 percent had bought shares in a voucher fund, 26 percent had sold their vouchers, and 13 percent had given their vouchers away, though only 8 percent had exchanged their vouchers for shares in the enterprises in which they worked and 6 percent in other enterprises.[94] By June 30, 1994, 144 million out of 148 million Russians (97 percent) had invested their vouchers.[95]

As a result, 14 percent of the population or 21 million Russians enjoyed direct ownership of shares, and an additional 30 percent or

Table 7-3. *Results of Voucher Auctions, December 1992–June 1994*

Month	Enterprises sold each month	Total number of enterprises sold
1992		
December	18	18
1993		
January	107	125
February	197	322
March	446	768
April	614	1,382
May	577	1,959
June	909	2,868
July	915	3,783
August	902	4,685
September	814	5,499
October	964	6,463
November	962	7,425
December	1,043	8,468
1994		
January	668	9,136
February	705	9,841
March	932	10,773
April	866	11,639
May	838	12,477
June	1,355	13,832

Source: Statistics from GKI/Russian Privatization Center.

44 million had indirect share ownership. These numbers are truly impressive. Even so, in August 1993, 56 percent of the population agreed with the statement that the distribution of vouchers was "a show that does not change anything in reality."[96] Clearly, most people realized that they did not benefit much economically from voucher privatization. There were many reasons for this. Most shares had gone to insiders, and many of the most valuable enterprises evaded voucher privatization. The rights of outside shareowners were weak, and people did not believe in their rights as shareowners; many were also disappointed that they had failed to purchase shares in concrete enterprises. The limited public trust in the vouchers was reflected in their price, which did not rise with inflation but even stayed below par for most of 1993. The voucher price was influenced more by political events than by the supply of property for privatization. Still, people did not actively react against voucher privatization.

Despite the many privatization auctions, fewer vouchers than anticipated were initially used. In the fall of 1993, the government decided to prolong the validity of the vouchers until June 30, 1994, declaring that all future privatization would be for money. There would not be any second or third tranche as had originally been intended. There was a strong supply effect in the spring of 1994, as many big enterprises that had not been interested in voucher privatization before (notably energy companies) suddenly decided that it would be their best option. The managers of these rich enterprises had delayed privatization because they did not have enough money to acquire sizeable ownership. Yet they reached the conclusion that they would obtain more ownership through voucher privatization, with its low evaluation of fixed capital, than through ordinary sales. On the demand side, in the spring of 1994 the offer of new, rich enterprises led to a sharp increase in the price of vouchers to several times their nominal value.

Although voucher auctions thus only privatized one-fifth of the shares of 14,000 large and medium-size enterprises, voucher privatization was the towering event in the privatization process. The distribution of vouchers attracted extraordinary attention and was the theme of much government propaganda and information. A representative VTsIOM poll indicated that to Russians, this was the second most important event of 1992, after the liberalization of prices in January.[97] Voucher privatization served to redress the imbalance between insiders and outsiders in the privatization process. Otherwise, people would have felt excluded from privatization, and their dissatisfaction could have blocked the process. Moreover, information about voucher auctions from the privatization authorities and advertisements of voucher funds came to dominate television advertising. They helped to explain what privatization meant and brought people into the process. The transparency of the auctions undoubtedly helped to limit corruption, *nomenklatura* privatization, and public distrust. Finally, because of their conclusive character, voucher auctions transformed enterprises qualitatively in a way that neither corporatization nor closed subscription for insiders accomplished.

Undramatic Housing Privatization

Housing privatization started early on, because the idea that people should be able to own their own homes was popular. It generated a large number of owners. The obvious conclusion was that tenants should be allowed to purchase their apartments for a low or negligible sum, because they enjoyed quasi-property rights to their quarters. Rented apartments were frequently inherited, and rents were negligible. Because large apartments were rare, the distribution of housing was rather egalitarian. Nor did any former owners cause complications, apart from those in a few historic buildings.

The first Soviet decree on the selling off of state housing, which was rather ineffective, was adopted as early as December 1988, and in 1989 the first state apartments were privatized. In July 1991, a more serious attempt was launched with the promulgation of the Russian Housing Privatization Act. It constituted the legal basis for the privatization of housing and was accompanied by a large number of detailed regulations on its application in October 1991.[98]

The essence of the legislation was that Russian citizens and families living in state-owned apartments could acquire legal title to their apartments if they wished. This implied full property rights, including the right to sell, lease, and bequeath their flats. A minimal area was given for free, while additional space was available at limited cost. Local authorities were put fully in charge, and privatization of housing ceased to be a national issue. The speed of privatization varied greatly depending on relevant local authorities, and it is therefore difficult to provide an overview.[99]

Initially, people were hesitant to acquire title to their apartments. They were sure of their possession in any case, and rents were low, while rumors of new property taxes ran rampant. Those who privatized their apartments tended to be old people who wanted to facilitate the inheritance of their homes or migrants who wanted to sell their apartments. Yet a housing market emerged in no time, and privatization caught on. By the end of 1992, 2.8 million apartments had been privatized, and in 1993, an additional 5.8 million. By October 1, 1994, a total of 10.4 million apartments (31 percent of the housing subject to privatization) had been privatized. As much as 91 percent of these apartments had been given away free. The housing privatization continued on a broad front, but it peaked in March 1993, when 729,000 apartments were privatized and then fell to about 150,000 apartments a month in the summer of 1994 (see table 7-4). In this sphere, Moscow took and maintained an early lead because of the energetic efforts of local officials.[100]

The privatization of commercial real estate was much more complicated and was left till the end. The legal situation was highly complex. Property rights between enterprises and local governments were often confused. Frequently, one enterprise controlled premises but was not

Table 7-4. *Privatization of Apartments, 1989–94*

Thousands

	Privatization	Total
1989	10	10
1990	43	53
1991	122	175
1992	2,613	2,788
1993		
January	555	3,343
February	630	3,973
March	729	4,702
April	640	5,342
May	519	5,861
June	490	6,351
July	408	6,759
August	357	7,116
September	356	7,472
October	308	7,780
November	319	8,099
December	493	8,592
1994		
January	307	8,899
February	339	9,238
March	184	9,422
April	200	9,622
May	201	9,823
June	190	10,013
July	151	10,164
August	135	10,299
September	152	10,451
October	140	10,591
November	143	10,734
December	241	10,975

Source: Goskomstat Rossii, *Sotsial'no-ekonomicheskoe polozhenie Rossii 1994 g.* (Russia's socioeconomic situation, 1994) (Moscow, 1995), p. 83.

allowed to receive rent from them, which had to be paid to the local authorities.

Stalled Land Reform

According to a multitude of opinion polls, land reform was by far the most popular kind of privatization. Private ownership of a farm enjoyed a popular approval rating of 75 percent or more.[101] There were many explanations for this popularity. For one, Soviet mismanagement in agriculture was particularly striking. *Kolkhoz* was used as a popular synonym for chaos. About 50 million Russian families (almost all) have private agricultural plots and enjoy working the land. A certain rural romanticism has held sway, as evident from the success of the Russian village prose writers in the 1980s. Consequently, when President Yeltsin finally issued a decree introducing private ownership of land in October 1993, it was perceived as the fourth most important event in that eventful year.[102]

These popular aspirations were countered by the mighty agrarian lobby, composed of the heads of some 25,000 *kolkhozy* and *sovkhozy*. These agrarian barons had no interest in the privatization of agriculture. On the contrary—they wanted to maintain their *kolkhozy* and *sovkhozy,* as well as a maximum of regulations and subsidies.

It was a technically and economically complex assignment to privatize agriculture. The whole sector was huge, with state and collective farms staffed with hundreds of workers. Agrarian monopolies controlled sales to and purchases from farms. Distances were long and the infrastructure poor. The population in the countryside tended to be older, as the young had left for the cities. Land registries were missing, as were land inspectors to establish them. Single farms that were split off from large state collectives lacked security, because they could easily be vandalized or burned by jealous neighbors who believed that they had not received their due.[103]

Nevertheless, family farming began as one of the forms of lease under Gorbachev at the beginning of 1990, but the scale was limited. At the end of 1990, there were 4,400 private farms.[104] The Russian reformers took on land reform at the Russian Congress of People's Deputies, which adopted the Law on the Peasant Farm and the Law on Land Reform as early as November and December 1990. The Law on the Peasant Farm gave individuals the right to leave collective and state farms with their shares of communal land and assets. However, the Russian Congress of People's Deputies refused to adopt the law before it was amended with the stipulations that no land could be resold within ten years. In addition, the farm's general meeting should decide what assets would go to a peasant farm.[105] The number of peasant farms increased by about 45,000 in 1991.[106] However, property rights to land remained limited and private ownership of land was not recognized by the RSFSR Constitution, although it was accepted in the Law on Land Reform of December 1990.

Full-fledged property rights to land and real land reform became pet issues of the democrats. At the same time, however, the agrarian lobby gained support in the Congress of People's Deputies. By April 1992, a solid majority of the Russian Congress of People's Deputies voted against allowing private land ownership. This strong opposition made it impossible for the reformers to amend the constitution. Consequently, land privatization became one of the top political issues of the fall of 1992. Before the Seventh Congress of People's Deputies in December 1992, the Democratic Russia movement carried out a campaign to gather signatures for a referendum on land reform. The campaign was successful; 1.9 million signatures were collected, although only 1 million were needed to force a referendum. But the Congress of People's Deputies dodged the issue by giving limited rights to sell land.[107]

The agrarian question was complicated even further when Yeltsin assigned the task of carrying out agrarian reform to Vice President Aleksandr Rutskoi from February 1992 to April 1993. Rutskoi patently caused mischief and joined forces with the agrarian lobby. He soon decided that the country could not afford to set up more family farms. Instead, he preferred large agroindustrial companies with massive inflows of state subsidies, as though he had been inspired by Nikita Khrushchev.[108]

In the face of this complex and difficult situation, the government adopted a three-pronged approach. The first was to move carefully with the mass of *kolkhozy* and *sovkhozy*. The government adopted a decree on December 29, 1991, ordering that they be reorganized into any ordinary form of association.[109] Most of them transformed themselves into a similar kind of partnership, but at least they became real enterprises. The direct link to the Ministry of Agriculture was formally cut. By the end of 1993, 95 percent of these farms had actually undertaken their required legal transformation.[110] Similarly, enterprises trading with the countryside were included in the small-scale privatization, but here too the agrarian lobby resisted forcefully.

Time and time again, the president and his government tried to introduce a law that would at long last allow private ownership of land. Unfortunately, the Supreme Soviet opposed it until the bitter end. On October 27, 1993, Yeltsin finally issued a decree, "On the Regulation of Land Relations and the Development of Agrarian Reform in Russia," which gave full approval of private ownership of land.[111] A land registry was instituted at the same time, and it became permissible to buy and

Table 7-5. *Expansion of Private Farms, 1990–93*

Year	New private farms (net)	Total number of private farms
1990	NA	4,432
1991	44,581	49,013
1992	133,774	182,787
1993	87,213	270,000
1994	9,000	279,000

Sources: Government of the Russian Federation, *Russian Economic Trends*, vol. 2, no. 4 (1993), p. 69; Goskomstat Rossii, *Rossiiskaya Federatsiya v tsifrakh v 1993 godu* (Moscow, 1994), p. 40; Goskomstat Rossii, *Sotsial'no-ekonomicheskoe polozhenie Rossii 1994 g.*, p. 54.

sell land as well as to use it as collateral. This decree prepared the road for the breakup of *kolkhozy* from below, which had been tested in Nizhny Novgorod and later approved by Chubais and Prime Minister Chernomyrdin.[112]

The second approach to land reform was to continue trying to establish family farms. Legally, family farms were either leased or (increasingly) private. Their expansion continued after the demise of the USSR. A net of 134,000 new family farms were set up in 1992 and 87,000 in 1993, raising the total to 270,000 (see table 7-5). The average area was 42 hectares. In 1992, only 5,100 family farms were abandoned, though in 1993 this number had risen to 14,100, which implied a more reasonable survival rate. Yet during the second half of 1993, only 12,000 new family farms were added, and a mere 7,000 in 1994. As the general hotbed conditions in agriculture with highly subsidized credits disappeared, family farms were squeezed by larger state and collective farms in their areas, on which they were highly dependent. As a result, the conditions of peasant farms were uncertain, their access to resources limited, and their productivity unimpressive.[113]

The third approach to land reform was to expand the time-tested use of private plots. Officially, they had traditionally comprised 2 percent of agricultural land, accounting for 24 percent of gross agricultural production in 1990. From 1991 to 1993, the area of private plots more than doubled to 5 percent of agricultural land in 1993, when they accounted for 36 percent of gross agricultural production. New legal provisions introduced full private ownership of the plots. Their total appears to have reached 50 million in 1993—that is, one private plot for every third Russian, or one plot for every household.[114] Anyone who so desired could have a private plot. Because private plots were supposed to be privatized to their tenants, a base had been created for broad property ownership.

Besides, the private plots produced a great deal and were social shock absorbers.

It might appear unfortunate that the most popular privatization was among the slowest. However, several countries (such as Albania, Bulgaria, and Lithuania) started with early land reforms because they were popular. But the results were devastating. Land reform is sensitive and easily leads to a drastic drop in agricultural production, if farmers feel insecure or if markets for agricultural products are not sufficiently free. The popular emphasis on land reform was, in fact, a reflection of reverse Marxism—that is, placing a heavy emphasis on ownership and production while neglecting the importance of free trade and the legal sanctity of property rights. At least in the sensitive years 1992 and 1993, Russia avoided such hardship. It also appears to have been wise to avoid a head-on clash with the agrarian lobby over land reform until agricultural trade had been liberalized.

Development of New Private Enterprises

Statistics on the development of new private enterprises are particularly poor and do not allow for much comparison over time. It is evident that many new private enterprises have been formed. Goskomstat states that there were about 700,000 small enterprises accounting for 11.5 percent of all employment on October 1, 1993.[115] However, the real number must have been at least twice as large, given widespread evasion of taxes and registration. Still, by any East European comparison, this is a very small number, and it is obvious that new small private enterprises have not developed as quickly in Russia as in eastern Europe. One reason is that small enterprises in Russia have been far more suppressed both by criminals and corrupt state officials.

Of these small Russian enterprises, 58 percent were in trade. That, however, is low in comparison with Poland, where the share of trade swung between 60 and 80 percent of all new enterprises in 1990 and 1991, immediately after its so-called big bang. It appears as if the unstable legal situation in Russia has particularly damaged private trade. Even so, private trade (including consumer cooperatives) is estimated to have accounted for 75 percent of Russia's retail trade sales in 1993.[116] In manufacturing, small private enterprises have developed fairly dynamically, doubling in 1993 to 75,000 and providing 10 percent of industrial employment.[117]

One of the early capitalist developments in Russia was the emergence of 300 commodity exchanges, which functioned as precapitalist commodity exchanges. They auctioned everything off with little order or specialization. With the great price liberalization in January 1992, the commodity exchanges entered a crisis. They had lived primarily on artificial arbitrage—their brokers bought goods at low state-controlled prices and sold them at high free-market prices. (Little wonder that they made fortunes.) By the summer of 1993, the number of active exchanges had fallen to 150, and only 40 of those operated steadily. Forty percent of their turnover had been concentrated in six commodity exchanges, four in Moscow and the others in Saratov and Omsk. For major commodities, such as oil (Moscow), grain (Saratov), coal (Novosibirsk), nickel (Moscow), aluminum (Moscow), and lumber (Moscow), most of the trade had been concentrated in one specialized exchange. A few developed into real stock exchanges; operations with money and securities rose from 3 percent of the exchanges' turnover in 1992 to 46 percent in 1993.[118]

After ordinary private wholesale trade had been permitted, the anachronistic commodity exchanges thus scaled down on their own. In the meantime, however, they had made a valuable contribution to the establishment of all kinds of markets. The rise and fall of the commodity exchanges provide good support for the idea that a market spontaneously develops the best market structure if it is allowed to be free, even if it goes through premodern phases. If the precapitalist exchanges had not been allowed to evolve freely, the increasingly sensible exchange structure that currently exists could not have emerged. Without the free exchange prices of, for instance, grain, deregulation would have been much more difficult to accomplish.

In addition to commercial banks and investment funds, insurance companies became a market fad in 1993. About 1,000 of them were established, mostly as closed joint stock companies.[119]

Tardy Bankruptcy

If a market economy is to function and be renewed, the destruction or reconstruction of enterprises is vital, and bankruptcy is therefore a helpful tool. A bankruptcy law was an early aspiration of the Russian reformers. A draft law was presented as early as 1990, but the Supreme Soviet repeatedly refused to adopt it. The industrial lobby posed the primary opposition to bankruptcies, arguing that they could lead to widespread closing of enterprises.

President Yeltsin countered the intransigence of the Supreme Soviet by issuing a decree "On Measures to Support and Rehabilitate Insolvent State Enterprises (Bankrupts) and the Application to Them of Special Procedures" on June 15, 1992. This decree empowered property committees with the right to declare enterprises bankrupt, and these committees were given the option of reorganizing or liquidating bankrupt enterprises.[120] In reality, however, hardly any enterprises were declared bankrupt.

On November 19, 1992, the Supreme Soviet finally adopted the Law on Insolvency (Bankruptcy) of Enterprises.[121] This law put the main responsibility for declaring enterprises bankrupt in the hands of existing arbitration courts. The full legal basis for bankruptcies finally existed, and a few bankruptcies occurred. Yet until March 1994, only about 50 bankruptcy cases went to court, and only ten enterprises were declared bankrupt.[122] The deeper problem was that within the existing institutional structure, few had an interest in forcing an enterprise into bankruptcy.

In May and June 1994, the government undertook new efforts to speed up bankruptcies. A number of legal documents were adopted to introduce strict criteria for when bankruptcy had to be declared. A State Bankruptcy Agency had also been created. By December 1994, it had grown to a staff of 1,000. However, the Bankruptcy Agency did not see its role as one promoting bankruptcies, but rather as instructing enterprises, and it became an additional hindrance.[123] As a result, the number of bankruptcies remained small, although large fixed assets were caught at a standstill in thousands of enterprises that had effectively ceased operation. Unfortunately, in the former communist world only Hungary has managed to undertake a large number of bankruptcies of medium-size and large enterprises. It would have been surprising if Russia had been able to impose more bankruptcies early on.

Conclusions: A Successful Privatization

In March 1994, Anatoly Chubais could make the proud statement: "I am happy to announce officially that the promised crash has not occurred

Table 7-6. *Employment by Ownership, 1990–93*
Millions

	1990	1991	1992	1993
Total employment	75.3	73.8	72.0	71.0
State and municipal sector	62.2	55.7	48.2	41.5
Enterprises of mixed ownership	3.0	7.5	8.3	12.1
Social organizations	0.6	0.7	0.6	0.5
Joint ventures	0.1	0.1	0.2	0.3
Private sector	9.4	9.8	14.7	16.6

Source: Goskomstat Rossii, *Rossiiskaya Federatsiya v tsifrakh v 1993 godu*, p. 82.

and it can no longer occur. More than half of our gross national product is already produced outside of the state sector."[124] The transfer of half the economy from the state to private hands in just two years was an extraordinary achievement. It is hard to imagine a more speedy and extensive transfer of complex property on the scale that Russia success-fully carried out. Tens of millions of new owners emerged.

Measurements of privatization vary greatly, and as a result only an approximate picture of the relative share of the private sector in various branches can be assembled. At the beginning of 1994, the share of non-state employment was officially 42 percent (see table 7-6). By the end of 1994, approximately 60 percent of the labor force appear to be occupied chiefly in the private sector. However, multiple occupations were the rule, and a person's public occupation was almost always his or her registered employment, whereas private activities tended to generate more income.

Retail trade and catering appear to be almost completely in private hands. In services, private enterprise also predominates, not least in financial services (notably commercial banks and insurance companies). The surprising feature is that most of industry was privatized, while construction, transportation, and agriculture stayed overwhelmingly in the public sector.

The standard Russian complaint about privatization was initially its excessive tardiness. Yet given that Russia has pursued the fastest priva-tization the world has seen, that argument has lost all validity. Speed was the top priority, and it was adhered to. It is even stranger to hear Russians argue that sales would have led to a faster privatization. Poland and Hungary stuck to sales, and their privatizations were evidently slower than Czechoslovakia's and Russia's.[125]

Presumably it is easier to privatize quickly during the early stages of transformation. Poland stands out as the country that discussed large-scale privatization rather than undertaking it. The longer the discussion proceeded, the more potential problems were raised.[126] Various groups could better assess their interests as well as their prospects, which meant that important vested interests were mobilized against an early resolution. As a result, many enterprises were left without effective owners and consequently were mismanaged. The Russian government, however, kept up such a strong political momentum that the people accepted privatization.

Another reason why fast early privatization is easier is that most enterprises appear profitable before stabilization has begun to be felt. Then people are still happy to accept shares from them. For society, private ownership of even bad enterprises is also valuable. The government can more easily refuse private rather than state-owned enterprise subsidies. The scaling down of unprofitable enterprises and reallocation of their resources is surely better done by concerned private owners than by disinterested civil servants. Hungary and Poland, on the contrary, have been left with a large number of unprofitable and parasitical state enterprises that demand massive subsidies and thus pose a threat to both stabilization and welfare. The surprise is that the Russian government did not make more serious mistakes in such a quick process.

A common argument against voucher privatization was that people would not value their vouchers but would sell them too cheaply. Prices at voucher auctions were quite low, implying that large Russian enterprises were worth only a few million dollars.[127] The low prices can be interpreted in many ways. One interpretation is that people did not believe that outside owners would be remunerated, presuming that the inside owners would appropriate all surplus as wages or fringe benefits. Another interpretation is that people did not believe in the viability of large Russian enterprises in which they could invest. A third explanation could be that access to voucher auctions was restricted because of both a lack of information and high transportation costs. Yet another possibility is that uncertainty was too great for many people to handle. Finally, they might simply have been uninterested in savings and investment and may just have preferred to sell their vouchers.

It is too early to say anything about the distribution of wealth, but under these conditions of poorly defined property rights, poorly functioning markets, few skilled investors, and a need for massive structural change, the emergence of quite an uneven distribution of wealth appears inevitable. Even so, free distribution leads naturally to a more equal distribution than does sales, in which the few investors with money to spare can purchase state assets at low prices. Notwithstanding that more assets have been distributed to employees of enterprises than to the public at large, the number of employees benefitting from some privatization is assessed at 40 million.

Privatization is also being blamed for corruption. It is true that privatization and corruption have risen seemingly in tandem, but the causality is not evident. Arguably, in 1992 and 1993 the main sources of corrupt income were export restrictions and cheap credits, not privatization. The privatization process undoubtedly has been accompanied with corrupt practices, but it is surprising that they have not been more apparent. Even if the government has failed in its demands for transparency in much of the local privatization, the privatization itself has gone surprisingly quickly. Moreover, the establishment of private property rights by corrupt means implies a single crime, which is better than the regular payment of bribes for the use of public property. The highly publicized and transparent voucher auctions have undoubtedly restricted corruption. Considering the weakness of the Russian state and especially its legal system, it is amazing that such an orderly privatization could be carried out.

Another criticism has been that the Russian privatization is not "real," because it has not led to restructuring. However, the massive structural changes in 1994 have presumably overruled this objection. In 1992 and most of 1993, Russian enterprises showed good profitability because of the lax monetary policy. They therefore felt no compulsion to restructure regardless of ownership. Liberalization gives enterprises the freedom to act; macroeconomic stabilization, which makes money scarce, forces them to act. When enterprises are put under duress, restructuring will vary with ownership, but until late 1993, Russian enterprises did not face hard budget constraints. Similarly, it has been argued that privatization has not led to any improvement in Russia's economic performance, but how could there be much amelioration with such high inflation?

A serious drawback with Russian privatization, however, is the predominance of insider ownership. Joseph Blasi's study of 200 enterprises in 1994 gives some idea of the ownership configuration that has emerged. Senior managers held 8 percent of the stock, other employees 58 percent, outsiders 21 percent, and property funds 13 percent.[128] Thus, if insiders, workers, and managers collude, it is difficult for outsider owners to exercise their rights as shareholders. Given that profits are taxed far more than wages in Russia, workers and managers have strong incentives to minimize profits, keep wages high, and maximize fringe benefits. Because the market price of a share should reflect the expected future value of the proceeds, Russian shares should have low market values as long as insiders dominate and try to keep profits low.

However, a great many enterprises need more capital than the hidden profits they can accumulate. It will be a long time before commercial banks function well enough to provide a substantial share of the capital needed. Meanwhile, real interests are likely to stay too high for bank credits to be worthwhile as a source of enterprise financing. If enterprises are to attract equity financing, they will have to show profits and offer decent yields to outside investors.

Another problem common to many privatized enterprises is that their managers are not up to the new problems they face in a market economy. A representative VTsIOM poll in August 1993 found that only 31 percent of employees thought their current management was capable of considerably improving their enterprise's economic situation, whereas 45 percent thought the opposite.[129] The trend was toward increasing skepticism, although this was long before any monetary squeeze. During the last years of *perestroika,* state enterprises were left alone by the state. In the first two years of economic transformation, extremely few managers were sacked. However, in the winter of 1993–94, the situation seemed to change because many managers proved that they were completely unable to do anything at all when demand fell. From December 1993 on, thousands of enterprises stopped production for various periods because of a lack of demand. The standstills started taking their toll on managers. In the first round of 215 shareholder meetings in the Nizhny Novgorod region, no less than 29 managers were fired.[130]

Despite extensive insider shareholding, there was a mechanism to eject managers. Typically, most of an enterprise's outside shares were owned by one voucher fund with a stake of 10 to 20 percent of the shares. The voucher fund could gang up with some of the insiders (usually a director who aspired to the post of director general and his allies). Any outsider could usually see the unsuitability of the incumbent manager, leaving the local property committee with little choice but to sack him.[131] In general, it was unfortunate that no ouster of old enterprise managers occurred during the early stages of the transformation. That was politically impossible, because the managers had almost come to rule Russia by then.

Outside share ownership was usually concentrated in the hands of one or two blockholders. Most were voucher funds, which as a rule were only interested in the value of the shares and their yields, because their business was to buy and sell shares. A smaller group of big voucher funds (such as Alpha Capital) actively challenged managers and tried to bring about industrial restructuring. A second type of blockholder was a rich individual or a private firm taking on the posture of an aggressive corporate raider. Such a blockholder would be prepared to challenge sitting managers or, if possible, to buy cheaply and strip an enterprise of its assets. So far, inside owners have blocked such an approach. A third group of blockholders were foreigners who often acted in consort with a Russian enterprise. They tended to be cautious because they were afraid of arousing hostile reactions.[132]

Although the current privatization strategy has discriminated against outside owners, muscular corporate raiders are emerging as the stars of the Russian economic show. Considering the state of the economy, with its low property values, lack of legal security, and high risks, it is evident that huge fortunes will be made by some individuals. The standard assumption, however, is that most voucher funds are either too small or too timid and will be wiped out. Fears that voucher distribution could result in ownership that is too widely disbursed already appear misplaced. The opposite problem—excessive concentration of ownership—could easily emerge, although the government has done so much to disperse ownership.

During the last quarter of 1993, the government tried to redress the balance between insiders and outside shareowners. In October 1993, a presidential decree "On Measures to Assure the Rights of Shareholders" was issued. It provided many protective measures for minority owners, though many (notably independent share registries) were hard to implement, because the interests of the insiders were stronger than the law.[133] A reflection of the weakness of outside owners was the dominant tendency among privatized enterprises not to pay any dividends. Out of a sample of 290 enterprises at the end of 1993, 70 percent stated that they could not pay dividends, leaving the voucher funds in an awkward situation.[134] To strengthen the position of the voucher funds, the privatization program for 1994 raised the limit for shareholding in one company by a voucher fund from 10 percent of shares to 25 percent.[135]

The conventional wisdom states that Russia has failed to attract direct foreign investment. However, even according to the balance of payments statistics, which tend to be understated, Russia received $1.7 billion in such investment in 1993.[136] (Goskomstat's statistics on foreign investment put the figure at $2.9 billion.) Moreover, foreign investments are not focused on trade, which comes in third place; machine-building comes in first, followed by energy. Similarly, the dominance of Moscow and of St. Petersburg has been broken. Admittedly, Moscow and its surrounding region obtained 26 percent of foreign investment in 1993, followed by distant places such as Krasnoyarsk, Omsk, Arkhangel'sk, Birobidzhan, Belgorod, Mari, and Komi.[137] Foreign enterprises have penetrated beyond the two big cities and moved into production in a serious fashion, even if the actual foreign investment remains limited.

An important accomplishment of voucher privatization is that it has contributed to the development of capital markets. In 1993, vouchers accounted for most trade in securities, and extensive trade in shares would be a natural development. In 1994, a boom on the stock market followed, though the share values peaked in September 1994 and fell by half in November. Still, the presence of a stock market led to a considerable inflow of foreign portfolio investment that exceeded $2 billion in 1994.[138]

For a long time, it has been argued that private ownership is alien to Russians. The Russian language did not even have a word for "private," much less one for "privatization." However, when Russians wanted to privatize, they just borrowed the word—as is certainly the case with new concepts all over the world. For some time, the awkward and unclear *razgosudarstvlenie* ("destatization") was used; but since 1990, the standard word for privatization has been *privatizatsiya*. Similarly, all kinds of capitalist concepts, from futures to brokers, have entered the Russian language. This cultural barrier had evidently been exaggerated.

CHAPTER EIGHT

Conclusions

MY PURPOSE in this book has been to provide a broad analytical picture of the Russian economic transformation and assess to what extent it has succeeded. In this concluding chapter, I offer a summary of achievements and failures of the reforms and draw more general lessons from the Russian experience.

Initially, I scrutinize all kinds of empirical evidence and quantify it as far as possible. The rest of the chapter is devoted to three kinds of broader perspectives. A preeminent issue is to what extent the fundamental tasks of the transition were carried out in the initial stage of the reform. This book pinpoints the old rent-seeking elite as the prime obstacle to successful reform. Within the old establishment, the military-industrial complex (VPK) was widely seen as the main impediment, but that turned out to be wrong. Therefore, I examine the relative weights of various industrial lobbies. Finally, I draw some general conclusions from the Russian transformation.

Economic Results

This section provides an overview of what has been accomplished in the Russian reforms and what was still lacking as of late 1994 with regard to institutional change, macroeconomic stabilization, production, foreign trade performance, social developments, and structural change.

272

Institutional Change

Today, it is easy to forget how fundamental the institutional changes have been in Russia. The transformation has been so far-reaching that it is hard to remember how absurd the old communist system actually was, and the current debate therefore focuses on the shortcomings of the new system. It would be useful to return to the initial criteria used in this book to define a market economy and sum up what has happened to the political system, ownership, allocation, monetization, and budget constraints on enterprises.

The political changes have been extraordinary. The ruling Communist party was outlawed in August 1991 and its offices were closed. No new ruling party has emerged. Although the KGB has survived as an organization, its repression has ceased. On December 12, 1993, a new Russian constitution—most reminiscent of that of France—was approved by the electorate in a referendum. It provides for an ordinary division of legislative, executive, and judicial powers, although the executive power of the president is uncommonly great. The new Russian Federal Assembly that was also elected on December 12, 1993, has proved quite a responsible and disciplined legislature, unlike the old predemocratic Supreme Soviet. In the lower house, the State Duma, eleven party factions provide political structure and a certain party discipline. Even before the real democratic breakthrough in August 1991, Russia had a diversified press, representing all kinds of views. Television has also become fairly independent. What has changed least is probably the government administration, still dominated by old communist state and party officials, and with an organizational structure that is both hierarchical and unwieldy. Regardless of important flaws (notably little effective rule of law and state powers that are too strong), Russia has basically become a democratic society.

Thanks to the achievements of privatization, about 60 percent of the labor force officially worked in the private sector by the end of 1994. In November, only 35 percent of all officially registered enterprises in Russia remained under state and municipal ownership (though they had 54 percent of the fixed capital), illustrating that the most capital-intensive activities are the last to be privatized.[1] With tens of millions of property owners of apartments, private plots, summerhouses, shares, and enterprises, a sufficiently broad base for the future democratic and market economic development of Russia has probably been created.

The centralized allocation of production has virtually ceased. Since 1993, hardly any state orders have applied to goods not meant for use by the state budget sector. In late 1994, the Russian Ministry of the Economy assessed that 22 percent of the volume of commodities in the economy was subject to some price regulation, which appears small by an international comparison.[2] Imports are only regulated through customs tariffs. Oil exports, however, have remained subject to export quotas. Moreover, since all production, transportation, and sales of natural gas are controlled by the state monopoly Gazprom, gas exports may be considered regulated. Oil and natural gas make up half of Russia's exports and are subject to nontariff export barriers. The liberalization of oil exports remains the focal point of Russian attempts at deregulation. However tardy it has been, Russian liberalization of trade and prices has gone far, and market allocation prevails.

Despite high inflation, monetization of the Russian economy has proceeded. The exchange rate of the ruble was essentially unified on July 1, 1992, though subsidized imports provided a limited exception until the end of 1993. Domestic barter shrunk swiftly. Barter has lingered in trade with the former Soviet republics (FSRs). However, outside of the former Soviet Union (FSU), barter accounted for only 11 percent of Russian exports and 14 percent of imports in 1993, most of it in trade with China.[3] Russia's foreign trade has become not only marketized but also monetized. However imperfect Russian commercial banks are, their structure is competitive, and there are more than 2,000 of them.

Finally, Russian enterprises were forced to face hard budget constraints after 1993, with the exception of the largest enterprises, notably Gazprom. Elephantine enterprises continue to exact discretionary decrees on tax exemption issued by President Yeltsin and Prime Minister Chernomyrdin. Yet this is a phenomenon limited to perhaps 100 large enterprises. The others can get neither state subsidies nor state credits on an individual basis.

Regardless of what perspective one chooses, the institutional changes in Russia have been quite impressive. The total effect of market imperfections is not so significant that it would disqualify Russia as a market economy. The outstanding problem, however, is the limited degree of the rule of law, which boosts transaction costs. Historically, it has taken a long time for legality to evolve. Russia certainly possesses an impressive degree of economic and political pluralism, which spurs development of the rule of law.

Table 8-1. *Macroeconomic Stabilization, 1991–94*

	1991	1992	1993	1994 (Preliminary)
Inflation (consumer price index, year end, percent)	144	2,520	840	224
Inflation (industrial wholesale prices, year end, percent)	236	3,275	890	233
Wage (year end, percent change)	—	1,245	775	271
Budget deficit (percent of GDP)	~30	19.7	9.4	10
M0 (year end, percent change)	120	886	675	—
M2 (year end, percent change)	126	643	416	—
Exchange rate (year end, rubles per dollar)	170	415	1,247	3,550
Employment (millions)	73.8	72.0	71.0	69.6
Unemployed (year end, millions)	—	3.6	4.1	5.3
Unemployed (year end, percent of labor force)	—	4.9	5.5	7.1

Note: Unemployment is assessed by Goskomstat according to the ILO/OECD methodology.
Sources: Goskomstat Rossii, *Rossiiskaya Federatsiya v tsifrakh v 1993 godu* (Moscow, 1994), pp. 129, 268; International Monetary Fund, *Economic Review: Russian Federation* (Washington, D.C., 1993), pp. 85, 88; Institute for Economic Analysis, *Rossiiskie ekonomicheskie reformy: poteryanny god* (Moscow, 1994), pp. 72, 79; Government of the Russian Federation, *Russian Economic Trends*, vol. 2, no. 4 (1993), pp. 119–22; *OMRI Daily Digest*, January 5, 1995; Goskomstat Rossii, *Sotsial'no-ekonomicheskoe polozhenie Rossii 1994 g.* (Russia's socioeconomic situation, 1994) (Moscow, 1995), pp. 4, 84, 119, 135.

Macroeconomic Stabilization

Contrary to Yegor Gaidar's original intention, Russia did not go through any real economic shock therapy. Its macroeconomic stabilization has been extremely gradual, with consumer prices rising by 2,520 percent in 1992, 840 percent in 1993, and 224 percent in 1994 (see table 8-1). The outstanding problem has been a large budget deficit.

The budget deficit, properly calculated, has gradually declined, from an estimated 30 percent of GDP in 1991 to almost 20 percent in 1992 (including both import subsidies and subsidization of credits) and to just over 9 percent in 1993. In 1994, however, the budget deficit rose to an estimated 10 percent of GDP (see table 8-1). Considering the dearth of financing, this budget deficit remained impermissibly large. It is true that the money supply has not risen nearly as fast as prices, but that is only a reflection of rising velocity and a flight from the ruble.

The real exchange rate has appreciated considerably despite the halfway stabilization, as signified by the rise in the average Russian wage from $7 a month in January 1992 to $114 a month in December 1993 (see table 6-2). The nominal exchange rate has moved along different trajectories. After hitting a low of 230 rubles per dollar in January 1992, it appreciated and remained fairly high during the first half of 1992 with a rate of 113 rubles per dollar in early June. A steady nominal devaluation still amounting to a gradual real revaluation followed until June 15, 1993, when the exchange rate reached a low point of 1,116 rubles per dollar. To everyone's great surprise, the nominal exchange rate began appreciating to about 985 rubles per dollar during August. The steady but limited nominal devaluation resumed in September and continued until January 1994. By the end of 1993, the rate was 1,247 rubles per dollar. A substantial real revaluation had occurred. After Gaidar's resignation on January 16, 1994, the exchange rate fell by an unprecedented 19 percent between January 14 and January 19, when it was 1,607 rubles per dollar. After a slight recovery, a steady but mitigated devaluation resumed. However, the real revaluation had almost ceased, reflecting the lack of credibility of the government's intentions to stabilize the currency further. In September 1994, the ruble started falling faster, by 20 percent in one month. The depreciation accelerated in October. In one week (October 3–10), the ruble fell by 17 percent; and during a single day, October 11, the exchange rate plummeted by 27 percent from 3,081 rubles per dollar to 3,926 rubles per dollar. Two days later it had recovered to 2,994 rubles per dollar. But the steady devaluation resumed, and the ruble exchange rate had fallen to 3,550 rubles per dollar at the end of 1994 (see figure 8-1).[4]

The positive side of the attempted Russian stabilization has been the slow growth of unemployment. When properly accounted for, only 7.1 percent of the labor force was out of work at the end of 1994, which is less than the European average. This includes people on leave without pay, about 2 percent of the labor force on average; but even so, Russian unemployment only approaches the western European average. The widespread worries of an explosion of unemployment have turned out to be highly exaggerated. There are several explanations for the surprisingly low unemployment, which have been investigated by Richard Layard. One reason is the slow stabilization. A more surprising one is that the Russian labor market has showed an impressive flexibility. In 1993, no less than 25 percent of workers in large and medium-size enterprises left their jobs, while 21 percent of their labor force was hired for new jobs by such enterprises. Real wages are almost perfectly flexible, and wages swing sharply between localities, branches, and enterprises. Apart from the coal industry, trade unions are quite weak. There is hardly any wage pressure, although no real income policy has been pursued. The emergence of large wage arrears is a telling reflection of the extraordinary weakness of labor. Hence, unemployment benefits are extremely low—

Figure 8-1. *Decline of the Ruble: Ruble/Dollar Exchange Rates, 1991–94*

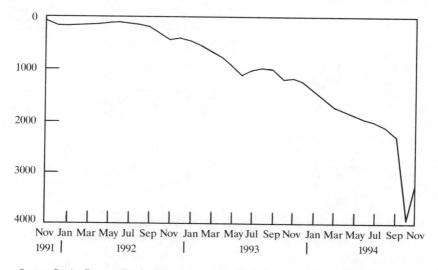

Sources: *Russian Economic Trends, 1993*, vol. 2, no. 4, pp. 120–21; *Russian Economic Trends, 1994*, vol. 3, no. 3, pp. 124–27.

about one-tenth of the average wage—leaving people little choice but to work if they can. Moreover, the strike rate is also low, at about one-tenth of the average of the Organization for Economic Cooperation and Development (OECD) countries. Yet layoffs have remained rare. Only 1.5 percent of workers in the large and medium-size enterprises were actually laid off in 1993. On the one hand, wages were so low and flexible that they were not a crucial cost to enterprises. On the other hand, enterprises had plenty of money for a long time because of the loose monetary policy, and the labor market was perceived as tight. Moreover, for rent-seeking enterprises, a large number of workers increased their political clout when trying to exact subsidies from the state.[5] The key problem has not been unemployment but inflation. Over time, however, unemployment is becoming a more serious concern.

Development of Production

It is surprisingly difficult to establish what has actually happened to production during the transition. Structural changes have evidently been massive, and there has been a substantial decline in total production; but

Table 8-2. *Production, 1991–94*

	1991	1992	1993	1994 (Preliminary)
Gross domestic product (trillions of rubles)	1.3	18.1	162.3	630
Growth in percent: GDP	−12.9	−18.5	−12.0	−15
Industrial production	−8.0	−18.0	−16.2	−21
Agricultural production	−4.5	−9.4	−4.0	−7
Transportation	−7.4	−23.6	−25.1	−26
Investment	−15.5	−39.7	−16.0	−26
Retail trade sales	−3.2	−3.5	1.9	4
GDP: Alternative estimate	−7	−12	−9	−10
Electricity production	−1.3	−5.6	−5.1	−8

Sources: Goskomstat Rossii, *Rossiiskaya Federatsiya v tsifrakh v 1993 godu*, pp. 8, 13–14, 157; Evgeny Gavrilenkov and Vincent Koen, "How Large Was the Output Collapse in Russia? Alternative Estimates and Welfare Implications," IMF Working Paper, November 17, 1994, p. 24; Goskomstat Rossii, *Sotsial'no-ekonomicheskoe polozhenie Rossii 1994 g.*, pp. 3, 16.

the degree of decline is a matter of great dispute. According to official statistics, the total decline in GDP during the systemic change from 1991 to 1994 amounts to a cumulative 38 percent (see table 8-2).

There are two important statistical illusions that must be addressed. The old Soviet statistics reported more production than actually occurred, with enterprises exaggerating their achievements to reach plan targets. Anecdotal evidence suggests an average overreporting of 5 percent of GDP. The reason for overreporting disappeared from 1991 to 1992, which presumably caused a onetime plunge in recorded production. In addition, the private sector and (following reform) public enterprises were motivated to underreport their full production to evade taxes. During the first half of 1992, many enterprises took to selling 5 to 10 percent of their production from trucks for cash to escape the problems of acute cash shortages.[6] This omission has presumably risen over time, with the easing of various old communist controls over enterprises.

A striking feature of the Soviet economy was not that it had a second economy, but rather how small it was in comparison with those in the West.[7] In December 1994, the chairman of Russia's State Committee on Statistics (Goskomstat) estimated the growing undeclared economy at 20 percent of Russian GDP.[8] An alternative measurement is electricity consumption, which is usually closely correlated to production: It fell by only 12 percent from 1991 to 1994.[9] However, because of fixed costs, this is probably an underestimate.

Until September 1993, Goskomstat was subordinate to the Supreme Soviet. It was therefore reluctant to take account of any of the statistical

Table 8-3. *Consumption and Accumulation, 1990–94:*
Structure of Utilization of GDP

Percent of utilized GDP

	1990	1991	1992	1993	1994 (Preliminary)
Private consumption	47.7	42.1	33.5	42.1	47
Public consumption	21.8	19.6	16.1	18.0	22
Gross accumulation	30.3	38.0	34.6	26.8	27
Investment	28.9	24.4	19.2	21.3	24
Change of stocks	1.4	13.6	15.5	5.4	3
Net exports	0.2	0.3	15.7	13.1	4
Total utilized GDP	100.0	100.0	100.0	100.0	100

Sources: Goskomstat Rossii, *Rossiiskaya Federatsiya v tsifrakh v 1993 godu*, pp. 101–02; Institute for Economic Analysis, *Rossiiskie ekonomicheskie reformy: poteryanny god*, p. 73 (original source: Goskomstat Rossii); Goskomstat Rossii, *Sotsial'no-ekonomicheskoe polozhenie Rossii 1994 g.*, p. 7.

biases that made the economic picture look worse. Since September 1993, Goskomstat has operated under the government's aegis and has started revising the most obvious biases, such as the neglect of the swiftly growing retail trade. In a further attempt to compensate for the most evident statistical flaws, Evgeny Gavrilenkov and Vincent Koen have cautiously estimated that the real decline in GDP was 28 percent between 1991 and 1994 (see table 8-2). However, their caution appears excessive. A total real decline in GDP on the order of 20 percent during the three years of transition appears more plausible.

There have also been real adjustments. Some of these are positive. Hoarding by enterprises should stop with the transition to a market economy, increasing use of available resources. This is a onetime adjustment, but it might be stretched out over a few years. In fact, enterprise stocks increased sharply by 15.5 percent of GDP in 1992, because monetary policy was so soft that enterprises were not forced to economize. In 1993, however, the increase in stocks was limited to 5.4 percent of GDP (see table 8-3). The transition from a seller's to a buyer's market will lead to a contraction of real demand, with consumers demanding less and imposing higher quality standards. Enterprises will cut input stocks and will find it more difficult to dispose of their stocks of final output.

Moreover, the transition to a market economy implies a substantial change in demand structure. When demand begins to matter, much unnecessary production just disappears. Demand decreases for arms and goods that were previously highly subsidized, such as agricultural machinery and meat; meanwhile, domestic producers are not prepared to

Table 8-4. *Conversion of Enterprises in the Military-Industrial Complex,*
1991–94

Percent change compared with one year earlier

	1991	1992	1993	1994 (First half)
Volume of production	−14	−18	−16	−27
Military goods	−26	−38	−30	−39
Civilian goods	−4	−7	−11	−36
Production personnel	−4	−9	−12	−15

Source: Gavrilenkov and Koen, "How Large Was the Output Collapse in Russia?" p. 27 (original source: Center for Economic Analysis).

satisfy many new demands. Table 8-4 shows a staggering decline of 68 percent in the production of military goods from 1991 to 1993, a decline that accelerated in 1994. As a consequence, at the end of 1994, the State Committee for Defense Industry was considering giving up 60 percent of the 680 military-industrial enterprises to the civilian sector, because these enterprises no longer produced significant amounts of arms.[10] Most arms manufacturers simply stopped making them, implying a great actual conversion of the military industry. A long overdue need for economic restructuring usually restricts economic growth. Many enterprises find that their market has shrunk, and it takes time for them to reorient themselves. Massive structural change is bound to cause supply bottlenecks and disruptions, and this is compounded by external shocks, restricting critical imports.[11]

All parts of the economy have not contracted equally, and huge structural shifts have occurred. Not surprisingly, investment has fallen the most, by a cumulative 63 percent from 1991 to 1994. Investment should be low if inflation is both high and unpredictable and relative prices are vacillating wildly. A positive surprise is that transportation has fallen far more than production, by a cumulative 58 percent from 1991 to 1994. Transportation is a cost item, and its shrinkage suggests that enterprises have started economizing on costs, which they should as their budget constraints harden. This is a plausible interpretation as the decline in transportation has accelerated.[12] Russia was overindustrialized in the sense that industry accounted for a larger share of GDP than would be rational in a market economy. Therefore, it is a positive adjustment that industrial production has fallen significantly more than GDP, by a cumulative 46 percent from 1991 to 1994 (see table 8-2). On the positive side, agricultural production has fallen relatively little—19 percent from

Table 8-5. *Foreign Trade, 1991–94*

Billions of U.S. dollars

	1990	1991	1992	1993	1994
Exports outside the FSU	71.1	50.9	42.4	43.0	48.0
Imports outside the FSU	81.8	44.5	37.0	27.0	35.7
Trade balance	−10.7	6.4	5.4	16.0	12.3

Sources: Goskomstat Rossii, *Rossiiskaya Federatsiya v tsifrakh v 1993 godu*, p. 106; Institute for Economic Analysis, *Rossiiskie ekonomicheskie reformy: poteryanny god*, p. 72; Goskomstat Rossii, *Sotsial'no-ekonomicheskoe polozhenie Rossii 1994 g.*, p. 3.

1991 to 1994. In this case, both underreporting and efficiency in usage have likely increased, suggesting that the effective decline may have been minor. Incredibly, after revising the retail trade statistics and taking unregistered trade into consideration on the basis of surveyed family budgets, retail trade sales actually rose by 2 percent from 1991 to 1994. These figures are partially estimated; but with their traditional conservatism, statisticians are more likely to underestimate than to overestimate. The structure of the national income has thus become more socially oriented after socialism.

Foreign Trade

Russian foreign trade was almost in free fall at the collapse of the USSR. Exports outside the FSU fell by 40 percent and imports by as much as 55 percent between 1990 and 1992 (see table 8-5). The decline in exports stopped in the middle of 1992, as the Russian economy became much more open. In central Europe, exports to the West had skyrocketed by 20 to 40 percent the first year after liberalization and stabilization. For Russia, however, exports outside the FSU only recovered slowly in 1993 and 1994. There are two obvious explanations. Much of the Russian exports (notably of oil and natural gas) remained under state control. What was more important, however, was probably that no real macroeconomic stabilization occurred in Russia. Russian enterprises were not forced to export to survive.

The development of Russian imports has been mystifying. They continued to decline in 1993 to only one-third of their 1990 level. Yet the Russian import regime has been quite liberal, without any quantitative restrictions. Even if import tariffs have been rising, they can hardly explain this dramatic development. As a result, Russia gained an impressive trade surplus of $16 billion in 1993 and $12 billion in 1994. Presumably, this is an exaggeration, and a considerable part of this surplus probably pertains to capital flight. Still, Russia had a surprisingly large trade surplus, which allowed it to build up its international reserves in 1993.

In 1991, trade between the former members of the Council for Mutual Economic Assistance (CMEA) collapsed. In 1992 and 1993, the same thing happened to trade between the FSRs. The volume of Russia's trade with the FSRs declined by half from 1991 to 1993.[13] Russia was compelled to reduce its exports to the other FSRs, because they lacked international financing, while Russia gained greatly in terms of trade. Moreover, the FSRs preferred to export outside the FSU rather than to Russia. Russia's recorded trade surplus toward the FSRs was 5.3 percent of GDP in 1992. This was reduced to 3.2 percent of GDP in 1993, when Russia's exports to the FSRs amounted to less than $14 billion (see tables 4-3 and 4-4). Russia's total exports were about $57 billion in 1993. Then its three main export markets were (in order) Ukraine, Germany, and China. This illustrates how Russia's foreign trade was reaching out in three directions, though the West accounted for about half of Russia's foreign trade.[14]

Because Russia had taken over the whole Soviet debt, the country suffered from a considerable debt burden. In November 1994, the Russian Ministry of Finance revealed that total Soviet debt at the end of 1991 had in fact been $103.9 billion, after debt to Eastern Europe had been included. By the end of 1994, total Russian and Soviet foreign debt had risen to $119.3 billion, 43 percent of Russia's GDP or 2.6 times Russia's exports in 1994.[15] However, much of the $29 billion in Soviet debt to Eastern Europe at the end of 1993 was balanced by Soviet counterclaims. Russian claims on the third world were larger but far more spurious.

Table 8-6 lists Soviet and Russian debt at the end of 1993. Out of a total of $112.8 billion, only $8.8 billion was new Russian debt. The main creditor was Germany. The outstanding balance of the loans it had supplied to the USSR amounted to $22.2 billion, while its claims on Russia were only $1.9 billion. Evidently, Western governments and commercial banks had provided credits to boost Mikhail Gorbachev and the USSR to a far greater extent than to support democracy and a market economy in Russia. The only positive exceptions were the international financial organizations, which had outstanding claims in Russia of $3.5 billion. However, they had never given anything to the USSR, which was not even

Table 8-6. *Russian Foreign Debt as of January 1, 1994*

Billions of U.S. dollars

TOTAL	112.78
Soviet debt	103.94
To Paris Club states	34.82
Germany	15.90
Italy	5.22
United States	2.72
France	2.58
Austria	1.82
To other state creditors	33.02
Former socialist countries	29.00
South Korea	1.42
Kuwait	1.00
To commercial banks	28.34
German	6.25
Italian	4.02
French	2.11
Austrian	1.22
American	1.22
Trade credits	7.77
Russian debt	8.84
To Paris Club states	5.19
United States	2.00
Germany	1.89
France	0.76
To international financial organizations	3.54

Source: Institute for Economic Analysis, *Rossiiskie ekonomicheskie reformy: poteryanny god*, p. 86 (original source: Russian Ministry of Finance).

a member of the IMF or the World Bank. These data underscore how meager Western financial support for Russia had been.

On the whole, Russia's foreign trade performance turned out better than many had feared. However, the trade surplus was accomplished by a decline in imports rather than by any major recovery of exports. The debt burden became more worrisome over time, as exports just about kept pace with interest.

Social Developments

A concern raised by anyone critical of the change of economic system in Russia is the excessive social costs caused by the transition to capitalism. However, this theme is more often touched on in inflammatory antireform propaganda than seriously analyzed. The real picture is not all that bleak, although social costs of the transition have been extensive.[16]

The losses of bank savings that were inflated away in 1992 were substantial for many, but by issuing too much money the communist state had promised more than it could deliver. It would have been worse to safeguard savings rather than current incomes. Currency reform would probably have hit savings equally hard. This was a cost induced by the communist regime, not by the reformers.

The second big social cost was an instant adjustment of real wages. However, wages had intentionally been raised sharply in December 1991 to provide advance compensation for the price shock and to conform with the Soviet practice of paying annual bonuses in December. Therefore, December wages are not useful benchmarks for comparison with other months; the relevant point of reference is the wage before the massive overhang arose. A reasonable starting point would be 1987, after which little real economic growth occurred. The fall in real wages would then be 35 percent in January 1992, and by 1993 it averaged around 20 percent (see table 6-2).[17]

Real monetary incomes increased by 10 percent in 1993 and 16 percent in 1994. Of these incomes, wages accounted for about 70 percent and social transfers 16 percent in 1993.[18] A characteristic of the new era is that Russians obtain an ever smaller share of their income from their wages, because a multitude of other earning opportunities open up with the transition to a market economy. Therefore, real wages have fallen much more than real incomes, and people live off their total income. By early 1994, real incomes were only down by about 10 percent from the 1987 standard.[19]

Moreover, even in 1987, shortages were palpable and the quality of goods and services dismal. Only the elimination of queuing should increase consumer welfare by 5 percent of total income and at least 6 percent of consumers' expenditures in 1995, according to calculations undertaken by Andrei Illarionov, Richard Layard, and Peter Orszag.[20]

As enterprises have been exposed to harder budget constraints, quality has obviously improved at an accelerated pace. Moreover, less of both actual production and consumption is being recorded than previously under the socialist system. Goskomstat's survey data on consumer expenditures of 49,000 households showed that by the end of 1992, these households spent about 50 percent more on consumption than what was indicated by Goskomstat's measured consumer expenditures. Goskomstat has tried to make adjustments, but ordinary statistical conservatism will likely incline it to a downward bias.[21]

In addition, a large informal sector of the market economy had developed that was not (and should not have been) included in GDP by standard definitions. By the end of 1993, Russia had about 50 million private plots of land, and their area had increased by 250 percent from 1990 until 1993.[22] These plots produce much that is never delivered to the market. All over Russia, new private homes are being constructed, and old ones are being repaired. Little of this is recorded, but it does contribute to the general economic welfare.

In early 1992, retail sales were allegedly collapsing, but this turned out to be a statistical illusion. In reality, much retail trade had been transformed into informal trade. After plausible adjustments had been made, retail sales fell by 3 percent from 1991 to 1992, while formal retail trade declined by 35 percent (which was first presented as the actual development). Retail sales rose by 2 percent in 1993 and by 4 percent in 1994, and underreporting is all too likely.[23]

Another test of economic welfare is how people use their incomes. With the introduction of a market economy and reasonable availability of goods, the notorious forced substitution of goods came to an end. At last, people could buy what they really wanted. Naturally, wastage not registered in statistics also diminished. As foreign trade was liberalized and decentralized, the structure of imports became more rational and contributed to improved economic welfare through better allocation.

Of their expenditures on purchases of goods and services in 1993, Russians spent 46 percent on food, 44 percent on nonfood consumer goods, and 8 percent on services. One important reason why the share of food expenditures rose was that food (especially meat) had been heavily subsidized before. Even so, the average consumption of meat per person dropped by only 6 percent from 1991 to 1993, according to Goskomstat.[24] The Center for Economic Reform of the Russian Government argues that the actual fall was only 3.5 percent from 1991 to 1993, and that the 1991 level was restored in early 1994.[25] If we turn our attention to consumer durables, sales have increased massively. For these commodities, turnover taxes used to be very high, and shortages were pervasive.

One of the most surprising observations is that Russians increased their savings—currency, bank deposits, and purchases of hard currency—from 4.8 percent of their income in 1992 to 14.3 percent in 1993, and then to 27 percent by the third quarter of 1994. Such a high savings ratio rules out the idea of abject poverty, even if a sense of insecurity was a major cause. Moreover, almost two-thirds of the savings went to the purchase of foreign exchange, also indicating a feeling of insecurity.[26]

But how can consumption increase if production falls? As has been discussed, the fall of production in Russia has been highly exaggerated. Moreover, as shown in table 8-2, the changed structure of production benefits consumers. Naturally, the same happened on the consumption side. An oddity of the Soviet economy was that extremely little GDP went to private consumption (traditionally slightly more than 40 percent of GDP). Previously, producer and consumer markets had been strictly divided through the separate circulation of cash and noncash rubles. Money was "soft" in the enterprise sphere—that is, enterprises could often exact additional money from the state if needed, whereas the great difficulty was in getting an allocation of the rationed inputs. Consumers, on the contrary, always faced hard budget constraints. When they had run out of money, the state did not care to give them any more.

In 1992, the ongoing battle between consumers and enterprises ceased, and the consumers suddenly found themselves in the same market as enterprises. However, consumers faced hard budget constraints, while enterprises still enjoyed soft budget constraints because of the then-loose monetary policy. Hence, enterprises crowded out consumers, and the share of GDP that went to private consumption diminished drastically, from 47.7 percent in 1990 to a paltry 33.5 percent in 1992. This effect alone amounted to a decline in private consumption of 30 percent (if GDP had been constant) and was the dominant cause of the declining standard of living. In 1993, as monetary policy became somewhat firmer, the share of private consumption in GDP rose to 42.1 percent and to 47 percent in 1994 (see table 8-3). Russia still has a long way to go before it reaches a private consumption of two-thirds of GDP, as is usual in Western countries. The precondition for such a development is that enterprises are squeezed through a tough monetary policy. Stiff macroeconomic stabilization thus brings important benefits to consumers, contrary to the conventional wisdom. The point is that enterprises should be exposed to hard budget constraints as tough as those on consumers.

Many accounts from Russia sound as if no social services existed. However, Russia continues to have ample, well-defined social benefits: free health care, free education at all levels, pensions, family benefits, and subsidized housing. Much of the financing of these benefits is covered by extrabudgetary funds, the safest form of financing. With the transition to a market economy, unemployment benefits have been introduced. In 1993, pensions fluctuated at around 34 percent of the average wage. Unlike wages, pensions are indexed quarterly, and the effective minimum during the last quarter of 1993 was 24 percent of the average wage. Contrary to popular belief, Russian pensioners have not borne a disproportionate share of the economic burden of the adjustment process.[27] (Under communism it was far worse: Millions of women who had not worked in the public sector were not entitled to any pensions until 1985.) Social services provided by enterprises suffered a decline. When they were forced to cut costs, enterprises tended to relinquish pioneer camps and houses of culture—typical communist artifacts—first. Next, however, came child care, kindergartens, and day-care centers.[28]

From 1990 to 1994, state budget allocations to both medical care and education fell sharply, even as a share of official GDP. The government gave priority to the privileges of the great industrial lobbies (that is, the gas and oil industry and the agrarian sector) over the needs of the general population.[29] Still, in 1994, total social expenditures from federal and local budgets, pension and social insurance funds, and enterprises amounted to about 21 percent of GDP, which is not low for a country at Russia's level of economic development. Direct public expenditures from federal and local budgets amounted to about 4.3 percent of GDP for health and about 4.3 percent for education.[30]

Even if the actual average standard of living has not fallen much, income distribution during the transition has widened. Richard Layard has investigated this phenomenon and has found that income distribution is roughly like that of the United Kingdom. There is still less inequality of income in Russia than in the United States. However, the statistical picture changes considerably over time, as minimum wages are adjusted irregularly, notably only once in 1994. A more striking feature is that a major redistribution of earned income has taken place—from the old to the young; from the unskilled to the skilled; from the city to the country; and from industry to finance, trade, and the legal profession. Many people have lost a great deal, but others have gained, and the income distribution appears to have altered surprisingly little.[31]

The ultimate concern is that the Russian mortality rate has gone up sharply (see table 8-7). Judith Shapiro has undertaken an excellent study of the Russian mortality crisis.[32] Mortality has increased in most former communist countries. However, it has risen especially sharply in the FSU,

Table 8-7. *Demographic Indicators, 1991–94*

	1991	1992	1993	1994
Population, year end (millions)	148.7	148.7	148.4	148.2
Births (per 1,000 inhabitants)	12.1	10.7	9.4	9.4
Mortality (per 1,000 inhabitants)	11.4	12.2	14.5	15.6
Infant mortality (per 1,000 births)	17.8	18.0	19.9	18.7

Sources: Institute for Economic Analysis, *Rossiiskie ekonomicheskie*, p. 72 (original sources: Goskomstat Rossii); Goskomstat Rossii, *Sotsial'no-ekonomicheskoe polozhenie Rossii 1994 g.*, pp. 160–61; *Open Media Research Institute Daily Digest*, February 15, 1995.

and not at all in the Czech Republic and Slovakia. About three-quarters of the additional deaths in Russia in 1993 were caused by cardiovascular disease and violent death (the foremost cause of the latter being accidents). It is primarily men who die early, and the life expectancy of Russian men has fallen to 59 years. Infectious diseases have increased quickly, but they caused only 1.8 percent of all Russian deaths in 1993. Cancer is not a major killer in Russia, accounting for only 1.7 percent of all deaths in 1993 and barely rising. (This clarifies that statements about mass poisoning of Russians by pollution have little foundation.) Moreover, if the prime problem were the collapse in Russian health care (though it is certainly a contributing cause), the increases in the various causes of death would be more evenly distributed.

Judith Shapiro's explanation is that the increased mortality in Russia is caused primarily by stress. Both cardiovascular diseases and accidents are stress-related. Russian men drank and smoked too much, ate food high in fat content, and exercised little before, but they did not suffer from as much stress. Many Russians, especially men, do not know how to handle the new problems they are experiencing in the transition. In addition, there are many reasons to assume that stress increases with inflation. The higher the inflation, the greater the variations from month to month in real wages and relative prices. Life becomes highly unpredictable, and many face greater strains than they can handle. As soon as inflation falls to a low level, life becomes more predictable and less stressful.[33] Even if the transition to a market economy almost inevitably increases stress and thus mortality, a prolonged transition and inflation are likely to cause many more deaths.

Despite Russia's hardships, the country saw the greatest immigration in its history in 1992 and 1993, with almost 1 million people a year immigrating from other FSRs (926,000 in 1992 and 923,000 in 1993) and with only 369,000 emigrating from Russia to other FSRs. Half of the émigrés came from Ukraine, Kazakhstan, and Uzbekistan, the three next-biggest FSRs. Half of the emigrants went to Ukraine. These migration figures are partly a reflection of ethnic discrimination in Central Asia and partly a sign that Russia is doing better economically than most other FSRs. Moreover, the migration flows are likely to have been bigger than recorded.[34]

Another inescapable cost of Russia's transition from an inert command economy to a flexible market economy is that risk increases. The cost of risk is highly subjective, but no doubt it is perceived as substantial. Russians appear to regard the fall in their standard of living as greater than this critical review of Russian economic statistics would suggest. There are many reasons for this. Russians are used to believing that official statistics exaggerate how well they are doing, and they find it hard to believe that the opposite has become the case. The share of Russian income from wages has fallen, but people do not value windfall gains they make from occasional trade and other sources as much as they do wages.

The collapse of communism was certainly costly, and real incomes did fall with it, primarily in 1991. However, given the statistical evidence, it is unlikely that there was any significant decline in the average standard of living after 1991. Such a great readjustment, though, is stressful as long as it lasts. The sooner it is over, the better off the Russians are likely to be.

Restructuring

After three years of systemic change, Russia displays a full panoply of markets. Contrary to what would ordinarily be the case in the West, the labor market in Russia appears the most flexible market. The markets for goods and services function less smoothly but are still decentralized. The capital markets are (not surprisingly) the least developed but appear to be advancing swiftly.

The proof of a market economy is that market-oriented structural changes actually take place. What is worth noting is restructuring prompted by demand and costs rather than by government policy or supply bottlenecks. There is plenty of evidence of such changes in Russia.

One observation is that the proportions of Russia's production are becoming less distorted. While GDP has shrunk sharply, virtually all structural changes correspond to market demands. In particular, Russia's overindustrialization in comparison with the West already belongs to the past. The service sector has risen to near-normal Western proportions, accounting for 55 percent of GDP in 1994.[35] Moreover, sheer costs (such as transportation) have fallen sharply. This shows that enterprises have at long last started bothering about costs. In 1993, consumer-oriented branches did not contract much, if at all: agricultural production fell officially by 4 percent, housing construction increased by 1 percent, and retail trade rose by 2 percent.[36] In reality, these indicators are all probably underreported, because many private activities are simply not recorded. In addition, a whole financial sector has developed.

For industry, demand took precedence over supply problems and determined the decline in production after the second half of 1993. The manufacturing of arms and agricultural equipment, which had been highly subsidized, declined significantly. A large number of products that no one wanted to buy were no longer produced.

Utilization of GDP has also assumed more normal proportions, as private consumption has increased from a minimal 33.5 percent of GDP in 1992 to a still small 47 percent of GDP in 1994 (see table 8-3). Considering that about two-thirds of GDP goes toward private consumption in Western countries, the consumption share in Russia should increase substantially if stabilization squeezes excess resources out of enterprises and the public sector.

The distribution of enterprises of different sizes is also becoming more normal. Small enterprises currently account for 10 percent of employment, and there are 75,000 small private manufacturing enterprises. Their number doubled in 1993.[37]

The country structure of Russia's foreign trade is becoming more normal, in accordance with the gravity model, which states that a country trades primarily with rich nations in its region. In 1993, about 60 percent of Russia's foreign trade outside of the FSU was with the West and only 15 percent with the former CMEA. Similarly, trade with other FSRs fell by 50 percent from 1991 to 1993.[38] This is a positive structural normalization after the end of the earlier bloc protectionism.

Although Russia's exports were already determined by demand, the commodity structure of Russia's imports has adjusted to the domestic market. Imports of previously heavily subsidized goods (notably grain and investment goods) have plummeted, while a multitude of import items have emerged on the Russian market, eliminating shortages. Currently, consumer goods constitute about half of Russian imports, which are obviously the most scarce in domestic supply, because the Soviet economy all but ignored them. Trade with the USSR was traditionally dominated by vast enterprises because of the centralization of Soviet foreign trade. Now a multitude of small foreign enterprises (especially from countries in the region) have broken in on the Russian market.

Most of the initial structural changes have led to eliminating production of goods and services no longer in demand. Other measures involve cost-cutting. The first positive supply effects are apparent in trade. Supply effects in production take longer to evolve.

The early emphasis on trade and cost-cutting has prompted public outrage over speculation and destruction of production, but these are natural stages in the development of a market. If the market is stopped on its way toward balance, its development may cease, as has happened in many overregulated countries in the third world. The vital preconditions of desirable structural changes are that enterprises remain independent and bother about their profits, while bargaining remains free and prices adjust to the market.

How Was the Window of Opportunity Used?

As Russia experienced in August 1991, immediately after a democratic breakthrough, a window of opportunity opens as never before or after. A strong sense of crisis then prevails, which gives a boost to popular idealism; and for a brief time, idealism or the common interest may take precedence over vested interests. For Russia, this window of opportunity was opened by the abortive coup and essentially closed by the Sixth Congress of People's Deputies in April 1992. As was discussed in chapter 1, it was vital to undertake a few central tasks in this period. The question is how well the Russian reformers used this opportunity.

A breakthrough period is one of institutional and political vacuum. If the state has more or less collapsed (as was the case in Russia in 1991), it is so weak that it needs to be rebuilt. These fundamental tasks are actually easier to handle in such a vacuum than later on when various interest groups have become organized. The tasks can be characterized as technically simple but politically difficult. The first premise is that real reformers hold power, and they must display political will and the ability to implement fundamental reforms. Reformist technocrats can carry out radical changes and build the pillars of a new better society from above.

Yet the political vacuum also offers great opportunities for small interest groups to use the weak state to acquire enormous riches for themselves, at the expense of society at large. These dangerous vested interests were primarily state enterprise managers, much of the old bureaucracy, rent-seeking traders, and banks. State enterprise managers gained extraordinary political strength in the interregnum between communism and the rise of the new political system. In short, the government needs to swiftly construct a framework for a normal functioning society. The three prime tasks that should ideally be accomplished in this period are the building of democratic institutions, macroeconomic stabilization-cum-liberalization, and launching of large-scale privatization.

First of all, the foundation of a democratic society needs to be established. Parliamentary elections should be held and a constitution adopted. There are only a few principles in an ordinary constitution that are truly essential, and little time is needed to write a good one. The problem is having it adopted. The longer discussions last, the more vested interests make themselves felt, and the initial sense of crisis abates. Political parties are then less prone to make necessary compromises. Therefore, the quality of a constitution is likely to deteriorate during prolonged discussions. Similarly, democracy and common interests tend to dominate early parliamentary elections after a democratic breakthrough, and democrats can more easily be united when the prime issue is democracy than when their differing ideologies tear them apart. A new parliament can defend the common concerns of society against the vested interests of the old establishment. A parliament can stand up more effectively against interest groups if the deputies answer to and are disciplined by political parties.

Second, liberalization and macroeconomic stabilization need to be undertaken. Both can be carried out within a few months. The aim should be to free up the economy as much as possible so that all markets can start functioning. However, when prices are liberalized in the presence of a substantial monetary overhang, they will rise. To avoid inflation, a strict macroeconomic stabilization is required. The budget deficit should be minimized, and monetary policy should be strict and characterized by a positive real interest rate.

Third, the principles of large-scale privatization are like those of a constitution. They are easily comprehended, but the longer they are discussed, the greater the political tension becomes. Contradictory claims are inevitable. Some interest groups will benefit more from corrupt revenues from state enterprises than from privatization, and they will therefore resist it. The single possible method of swift large-scale privatization appears to be based more or less on free distribution of ownership to a large share of the populace.

Russia has a mixed record. Curiously, it succeeded in large-scale privatization, although its stabilization was somewhat unsuccessful and its political changes occurred too late. When Russia is compared with the two front-runners—Poland and Czechoslovakia—that attempted swift changes in their economic systems, the experiences are found to have been strangely different. Only Czechoslovakia held early parliamentary elections. Both Poland and Russia held their first postcommunist parliamentary elections more than two years after the democratic breakthrough and almost two years after radical reform had been launched. It is difficult to imagine worse timing, with the first euphoria of a market economy having passed and with no clear upturn in sight. The election went accordingly. In their attempts at macroeconomic stabilization, Czechoslovakia did perfectly well and Poland relatively so, while Russia initially failed, although it avoided hyperinflation. Czechoslovakia and Russia are the countries that have done best in large-scale privatization, if success is measured in terms of speed and share of large state enterprises transferred to private hands. In Poland, an intellectually rigorous discussion on privatization led to little large-scale privatization.

It is not strange that Czechoslovakia undertook all three fundamental changes in proper fashion, because it benefitted from much better initial conditions. It seems by no means inevitable, however, that Poland succeeded in macroeconomic stabilization but failed in large-scale privatization, while Russia did the opposite. A simple explanation is that Russia learned from Poland's mistakes, though its preconditions were less favorable, complicating stabilization. However, that answer is hardly convincing. It is amazing that Russia could do better than Poland in one important regard despite its own greater disorder and complexity.

These three political developments in Russia need to be analyzed more closely to assess what was right and wrong. They can be judged by the following criteria:

—Strong and stable leadership in the field;
—Support from the supreme political leader (President Yeltsin);
—Development of a new administration;
—Use of international advice and experiences;
—Clear and sophisticated strategy;

—Elaboration of an operative program;
—Recognition of relevant interests without losing strategy;
—Parliamentary mandate;
—Public outreach; and
—Swift implementation.

Yeltsin was certainly a strong, democratically elected, and legitimate Russian leader. He had primary responsibility for the building of democracy, although he delegated a great deal of power to Gennady Burbulis, his chief political strategist as state secretary and first deputy prime minister for five months, and to Sergei Shakhrai, his chief constitution writer who served in various positions. Still, the main responsibility rests with President Yeltsin himself. The new political administrations that evolved—the presidential apparatus and the regional administrations— were not related to democratization and were increasingly taken over by the old *nomenklatura*. A large contingent of domestic and foreign advisors advocated early parliamentary elections and swift adoption of a new constitution. However, Yeltsin heeded advice urging him to work with the old parliament and not waste time on elections or constitutions, as the primary issue was economic reform.

In effect, Yeltsin had no political strategy at all, and no program. Hence, relevant interests were not consulted, and no parliamentary mandate was sought when it was possible to do so. Yeltsin did reach out to the public on these issues occasionally, but without taking a consistent line. He hesitated between compromise and all-out confrontation until he eventually was forced to fire the not very representative yet sovereign parliament. The cost was great on many accounts. Democratization was delayed and might fail as a consequence. The antireform-oriented parliament caused considerable damage to the economic transformation in many ways. At the end of 1993, however, Russia enacted a constitution calling for strong presidential powers and a distribution of legislative, judicial, and executive powers, which was adopted through a referendum. Democratic parliamentary elections with political parties were held, and the evolution of the parties intensified in their aftermath. In short, little was done for democratization in the period of extraordinary politics, though some amends were made a year and a half too late at great cost.

In November 1991, Yegor Gaidar assumed the initiative on liberalization and macroeconomic stabilization as deputy prime minister and initially minister of finance as well as minister of the economy. His first problem was that the Supreme Soviet overruled his attempt at assuming control over the Central Bank of Russia (CBR) on November 22. Moreover, at the beginning of April 1992, Gaidar gave up his key position as minister of finance to an old *apparatchik,* Vasily Barchuk, who had no ambitions for macroeconomic stabilization. Boris Fedorov subsequently held the job and did a great deal, but only for 13 months and long after the program was launched. Russia had five ministers of finance in two and a half years, and this lack of continuity harmed stabilization.

President Yeltsin appears to have been seriously involved in liberalization and stabilization for two or three months at the end of 1991. But by March and April 1992, he was letting Gaidar down, joining forces with the industrial lobby against his own government. Little was done to establish a new reformist administration, and the reformers drowned in a sea of old *apparatchiki.* Yet advice from the international community and foreign advisors was used extensively and rather skillfully. The economic strategy adopted was reasonably clear and sophisticated, though it could have been better. The difficult Russian preconditions made it all the more important to have a robust plan.

Unfortunately, no proper reform program was presented early on. The government tried to accommodate the interests of its worst enemy, the state managers lobby, rather than trying to reach out to the people. As a result, it compromised its strategy. No attempt was made to reinforce the parliamentary mandate President Yeltsin first received on November 1, 1991, after his big reform speech. Given that the reform program could have been ready as early as November or December 1991, it could have been possible to have a reasonable program adopted by the old Supreme Soviet, but this was never attempted. Gaidar did make some efforts at reaching out to the people through extensive publicity, but it was far too small an attempt. The initial implementation of both liberalization and stabilization was brave in the face of extraordinary confusion and political resistance, but it was not forceful enough.

Gaidar did not manage to hold sway. Too many mistakes had been made, and the environment was extremely hostile, hardly allowing for any mistakes at all. Apart from the ten factors on this chapter's list, two other shortcomings were relevant to macroeconomic stabilization. Russia was effectively in state bankruptcy, but the West was slow to offer financial assistance, although Russia could comply with normal requirements for such aid in terms of economic policy. In addition, the retained ruble zone presented a great temptation toward monetary irresponsibility for all involved, as any issuer of credit acted as a free rider.

Of the ten factors listed, only three were fulfilled. The main shortcoming was probably the opposition Gaidar encountered from both the CBR and the parliament, while the West just looked on passively. Gaidar's political contribution was insufficient as well. He failed to attract the president's serious and lasting interest in financial stabilization. The government was not cleansed of outright opposition or hostile bodies. Gaidar did not even publicize an economic program and did little to appeal to the people at large. His relations with the parliament were terrible, though this was primarily the parliament's fault. Gaidar's worst mistake was on the issue of subsidized credits to both industry and agriculture in early April 1992, when he made a strategic compromise with the greatest enemies of stabilization. His attempts at macroeconomic stabilization never recovered. The death knell to Gaidar's policy was his nomination of Viktor Gerashchenko for chairman of the CBR. Presumably both financial stabilization and Gaidar's fate as a politician would have benefitted from his taking a firmer stand. He simply gave in too easily on major principles. It must be emphasized how difficult the situation was, however; without Gaidar, the Russian economic transformation might not have been started.

For large-scale privatization, the period of extraordinary politics was fully utilized. The honor must go to Anatoly Chubais, who was Minister of Privatization from November 1991 to November 1994. He managed to capture Yeltsin's imagination with ideas such as "the voucher—a ticket to a free economy." The president provided firm support for the privatization policy until June 1994. Chubais created a new administration for the execution of privatization and avoided relying on old communist officials when at all possible. He made good use of the best international advice available, which was paid for through international technical assistance; but he made sure that advice was provided within a policy framework set by the Russians. Early on, a clear set of priorities was outlined. It took longer for stabilization to elaborate on a full strategy, but the issues were more numerous and complex.

Chubais formulated a privatization program designed to encourage public consumption at the earliest convenience. It balanced the interests of all legitimate stakeholders. Chubais worked closely with the Supreme Soviet and succeeded in persuading it to accept his privatization program by making tactical rather than strategic concessions. On June 11, 1992, the Supreme Soviet adopted the privatization program for 1992—the last major piece of reformist legislation it ever promulgated. During the sharpest frontal attack against the privatization program in April 1993, Chubais made no compromises and stood firm, prepared to resign if he lost. The privatizers used television propaganda and advertising extensively to explain their program to the public. Privatization was carried out in a decentralized way. This implied a big capacity for privatization and the satisfaction of local interests, which could be mobilized against conservative branch ministries in Moscow. Local corruption remained a major drawback.

This brief overview of three central elements of Russian politics leads to several conclusions. The top politicians had a great deal of leeway at this time, and the significance of that leadership is evident. Yeltsin hesitated and did not know what he really wanted. Gaidar failed and compromised rather than take a firm stand on principles, while Chubais displayed great political will but compromised when it was necessary and permissible. The impact of theoretical conceptualization and understanding was also great. A general contempt for political philosophy prevailed, and this prevented many from gaining useful insight. Liberalization and stabilization were understood by Gaidar but few others; understanding among the elite, much less among the people, was completely absent. The ideas of privatization were well understood by the leading privatizers, and they preached these ideas through the most massive propaganda campaign in the new Russia. Foreign advisors with useful insights were on hand to confer with all concerned, but the problem was the lack of ability and will to use their expertise. The communist establishment resisted every change, and it is doubtful whether any variations in its opposition really mattered. Few concepts were as viciously attacked as Chubais's privatization program.

However, in three regards, Gaidar's task was more formidable than that of Chubais. First, foreign financial assistance was needed for stabilization, and it was missing. Second, the lack of clarity surrounding the dissolution of the Soviet Union undermined stabilization more than anything else. And third, the stabilization program was more vulnerable than the privatization program to the initial thunder from state enterprise managers. Chubais had more time and political leeway to amend the privatization program. Yet in the end, political skills remained of fundamental importance; therefore Chubais was quite successful, and Gaidar much less so. Yeltsin seems not to have thought much about political strategy, though his political intuition and acumen compensated for his lack of strategic thinking.

Why Did the Military-Industrial Complex Fail as a Lobby?

My focus in this book has been on the actual political economy of the Russian transformation. The radical economic reformers have been presented as the positive force. From the outset, neither the major dangers nor the principal adversaries were by any means clear.

The threats to public finance during the transition turned out to be different from what many who had anticipated a continuation of the problems during the last years of Soviet power had expected. In 1988, wages had started rising excessively, and the coal miners' strike in the summer of 1989 had made its mark regarding the rising power of the new independent trade unions. Much of the public discussion therefore focused on the danger of a societal explosion after the price liberalization. The government was not very afraid of social unrest, but it did fear excessive wage claims, prompting a discussion about incomes policy. In reality, no wage pressure was felt, and the strike rate was very low. In fact, most strikes from 1992 were caused by unscrupulous employers who refused to pay legitimately earned wages. The difference was that before 1992, the managers and the workers had been on the same side against the state. Beginning in 1992, enterprises were independent, pitting managers against workers, with the former being much stronger than the latter.

Another fear was of a populist increase in social expenditures, because such endeavors had characterized the Congress of People's Deputies of the USSR since its inception in 1989. This was indeed populism, but it was spearheaded by the democrats led by Yeltsin. From 1992 on, the opposition against the democrats was on the contrary mobilized by the industrialist lobby for its own interests, and social expenditures were not among them.

State Enterprise Managers—The Key Resistance

The main adversaries of the radical reformers were not ideologically minded communists but state enterprise managers. The managers were not necessarily against reform as such; but they saw the transition process as an opportunity to enrich themselves, and they did so by causing all kinds of distortions in the regulatory framework. My general conclusion is that enterprise managers were prone to be asocial in the transition period. For that reason, their arguments should be ignored, and a reformist government should seek no political support from them. In the interests of society, the government should instead swiftly impose proper market regulation from above to introduce new incentives that promote profit-seeking rather than rent-seeking.

The name of the game was rent-seeking. The military-industrial complex (VPK) and the agrarians benefitted from state budget subsidies. With the transition to a market economy, subsidized credits became a major source of revenue to agriculture, commercial banks with access to cheap state loans, and some industries. Traders reaped rents from price controls, export restrictions, and multiple exchange rates. Rent-seeking enterprise managers had an interest in seeing price and trade controls as well as inflation maintained, because these both generated and concealed their incomes. These managers were not ideological, merely economically rational and ruthless.

It is important to make a distinction between managers and their enterprises as well as between the managers' lobby and industry. The collapse of the command economy broke down the state's control over enterprise managers. Curiously, it also destroyed the limited control of work collectives over their managers that existed in the late Soviet period. After the branch ministries had lost their supervision, the state was no longer an effective owner, and no new principal emerged. The managers were completely in charge of their enterprises and virtually unassailable. In effect, they enjoyed extensive quasi-property rights over the enterprises they ran. There was a widespread realization that this was a brief window of opportunity when great fortunes could be made through embezzlement and rent-seeking. The managers had much to gain from any asocial behavior. The risk of punishment was minute, because most of these asocial gains were not even illegal.

The costs of these economic distortions were of several kinds. The drop in national income became larger than necessary. It is equally disturbing that many culprits grew quite wealthy. The greatest cost, however, might be that the pillars of the new society were seriously deformed from the outset of reform. To understand the resistance to reform on various fronts, it is necessary to analyze the strength of the various lobbies for state enterprise managers. They divided naturally along divergent branches.

The Strength of Various Lobbies

From the Soviet experience, it was not evident which branch lobby would prove to be the strongest and most harmful. The VPK was generally perceived to be the strongest lobby, and in broad terms the defense sector appears to have consumed about one-quarter of GDP in the final years of the USSR. The agrarian lobby—25,000 directors of *sovkhozy* and chairmen of *kolkhozy*—had laid claim to large resources ever since the Brezhnev era. The energy lobby (or more accurately, the gas, oil, and coal lobbies) accounted for half of Soviet (later Russian) exports. The strong foreign trade establishment benefitted greatly from its monopoly. In the late Soviet era, many foreign traders made vast fortunes by buying commodities domestically at low controlled prices and selling them on the world market at prices many times higher.

The government was acutely aware of the threat from the VPK. However, the government took it on with impressive decisiveness, and the VPK fared badly. Despite its size (about one-tenth of the Russian labor force at the beginning of 1992), it received a minimum of state orders and subsidies. Production of military goods fell by 68 percent from 1991 to 1993 (see table 8-4).

The winners were the oil, gas, and agrarian lobbies. The agrarian lobby received about half the subsidized credits and the most budget subsidies in 1993. The gas industry was exempt from virtually all taxes, and the oil lobby did not pay much in taxes either. How then can it be explained that the VPK, which was assumed to be supreme, failed completely in rent-seeking, in a period of extraordinary rent-seeking by other industries?

Mancur Olson's *Logic of Collective Action* explains well why the threat to stabilization did not come from the workers or the Russian people:

> Unless the number of individuals in a group is quite small, or unless there is coercion or some other special device to make individuals act in their common interest, *rational, self-interested individuals will not act to achieve their common or group interests.*[39]

If civil society and participation are minimal, a small and powerful group such as the Russian state enterprise managers would be expected to be particularly well organized, as indeed was the case. It follows from the logic of collective action that under these conditions, the greatest threat would come from the state managers. The foremost student of these theories in the Soviet Union happened to be Yegor Gaidar, who had written a book about their significance for Soviet economic reform. He feared that managers would have the support both of their workers and of the people at large, and concluded:

> The relations that have arisen between the state and society have become a serious impediment to a financial cure of our country. As previously, economic paternalism reigns. In discussions between enterprises, industries, and the state, public opinion is almost never on the side of the state: the state must collect less taxes, but at the same time give out more budgetary resources . . . if [this position] is not overcome, no success in the struggle with inflation is to be expected. Only on the basis of popular support can the resistance of partial branch and regional interests be broken, with long overdue measures to financially cure the economy and deeply restructure the archaic structure of the economy, originating from the period of industrialization.[40]

Any group of state enterprises is small, and this criterion does not allow for an assessment of the relative strength of various industries as lobbies. The other part of Mancur Olson's thesis, the presence of "coercion or some other special device to make individuals act in their common interest," makes it possible to make more distinctions between different industries. The question can be stated more broadly: What bonds of cohesion are at hand?

The first option is direct coercion. It is apparent in two Russian industries. One—coal mining—offers ample opportunities for coercion. This may explain why the most militant trade unions in the former Soviet bloc have emerged among coal miners (in Poland, Romania, Russia, and Ukraine). The other is agriculture. Peasants are highly dependent on their bosses. In the Russian countryside, the scale is large and distances enormous. For geographical reasons, there are few possible suppliers and purchasers of many goods. Coercion is possible not least because there is hardly any recourse to law in the villages, rendering rule by threat of terror possible.

A milder form of coercion is to threaten workers with dismissal. This threat is most deterring in small localities where few other jobs may be available (that is, in agriculture, company towns, and the northern territories). It is most intimidating to the old and unskilled, who work primarily in agriculture; the highly skilled work force of the VPK is not easily threatened.

The effectiveness of a lobby is also dependent on the degree of its commonality of interest. A basic question is to what extent various members within a potential lobby are allies and competitors. Then the output of the lobby members needs to be considered. Enterprises producing the same kind of homogenous commodity do not compete over anything but price. If the price is set by the state, they do not even compete over that; but they do have a common interest to pressure the state to grant them larger resources through subsidies. Within agriculture and the energy industry, enterprises collude easily, because they produce homogenous commodities. But in machine-building and light industry, each enterprise is on its own, competing in design, technology, and quality with several other enterprises within the same industry. The half-dozen Russian airplane manufacturers must realize that a few of them will disappear and a few survive. Why then should they collaborate? Even under the old regime, they were fierce competitors—the Ministry of Defense had insisted on having several producers to develop new armaments in competition with one another. The prime issue for a particular military-industrial enterprise, therefore, is not its total production of arms, but whether the arms it produces will be bought. Orders are not likely to increase equally at each enterprise in times of increasing arms procurement. Moreover, the dependence of VPK enterprises on the Ministry of Defense is limited, because they produce more civilian than military goods. As soon as the market is introduced, the VPK is therefore likely to be a weaker lobby than either the agrarian or energy lobby, because it is less cohesive. The same is true of light industry. The number of enterprises in an industry appears far less important than the nature of its product. There are fewer military-industrial enterprises and on average they are larger than state farms, but the latter have more cohesive interests.

The consumer value of an industry's output is also of some significance. Food is of course vital. Energy provided half of Russia's exports, while armaments were abundant both in Russia and abroad. Therefore, it might have been easier to mobilize public support for agriculture and energy extraction, but many people argued that military research and development was a national resource that Russia simply could not do without.

Another important quality of a product is its ability to generate cash, which in turn can be used as bribes. Exports provide not only hard currency earnings but also the possibility of concealing money and transactions abroad. The Russian gas and oil lobbies have earned a reputation for great corruption, and they have undoubtedly used their large foreign currency accounts to purchase illicit favors.

It could also be argued that public goods in general suffer in the economic transition and that armaments belong in this category, along with law and order, public health, and education. The change in economic system also involved a fundamental change of values. The military might of the country became less important, while food became more so. Social status also changed, as top state officials (including generals) lost status, while business executives gained social clout.

The Weakness of the State

So far, this discussion has focused on the "demand side" of rent-seeking—that is, the strength groups of enterprises exert in pressuring the state. However, there is also the supply side, or the degree to which the state is likely to be trapped by various lobbies. In general, the more state intervention (and the less transparency), the easier it will be for enterprise lobbies to claim so-called compensation from the state. The worst kind of state intervention is to legislate a monopoly. The agricultural sector was characterized by multiple monopolies. Domestic trade in certain products (notably grain) was monopolized by the Federal Joint Stock Company Roskhleboprodukt, the former Ministry of [Grain] Procurement. Foreign trade in grain was controlled by the foreign trade monopoly enterprise Exportkhleb. Credits to agriculture was allocated through Rosselkhozbank. These monopolies all joined hands to put pressure on the state, because their interests were closely related. Similarly, at the end of 1993 the gas industry was the most regulated (after agriculture had been liberalized), and Gazprom was a state gas monopoly company, the Russian successor to the former Ministry of Gas Industry of the USSR.

A lower degree of state intervention is price regulation. This was characteristic of energy, agriculture, and transportation (that is, two of the high-rent industries), but hardly any others. It would be natural to assume that the energy lobby would fight for higher prices. However, energy enterprise managers did not demand price liberalization. The government received no support from them when it tried to liberalize energy prices, although in the spring of 1993 coal and gas prices in Russia were as low as 4 percent of world market prices. If their incentives are scrutinized, it is not so strange that the energy managers failed to request higher output prices. Naturally, they optimized their personal security and incomes.

The vital question to energy managers was whether the economic system would actually change. Essentially, there were three options. First, the old command system could stay in place or might be revived. Under the old system, profits were essentially irrelevant, because they were confiscated by the state at the end of the year, while the energy industry got huge state transfers for investment. Personal connections, on the contrary, had been of the utmost importance to the managers' well-being, and these relationships would presumably be damaged by an advocacy of higher output prices. It would probably have been irrational under the old system for a manager in the energy industry to push for higher output prices.

The second option was an intermediate system—neither a planned nor a market economy. An enterprise manager under such a system could make a fortune through arbitrage, selling cheap energy at high prices abroad. Therefore, managers of energy enterprises would have a strong vested interest in keeping official prices low and maximizing formal regulations, rendering the economic system so nontransparent that it would conceal their illicit rents and help them to maximize graft. Presumably, this was the situation in 1992. To add insult to injury, the managers of energy enterprises could claim state subsidies, on the grounds that they avoided raising prices for the benefit of society. Nor did the managers antagonize other industries or risk hitting any demand barriers, as they did in the first half of 1994, when prices had risen and monetary policy had become more restrained.

A third possibility was the introduction of a formal market economy. Actual profit taxation in Russia was prohibitive in 1993 and 1994. The official profit tax rate was not very high at 35 percent of profits, but local taxes were added. Moreover, allowed depreciation was about 1 percent of real capital. Enterprises also paid a large share—up to 80 percent—of their after-tax net profits to various social commitments imposed by the state or merely by tradition. In effect, this was an additional profit tax. Finally, the tax inspectors and tax police worked on commission and independently under what were effectively lawless conditions, taking whatever profit they happened to find. The increasingly militant behavior of the tax authorities boosted incentives for rent-seeking rather than profit-seeking. Thus, even under actual market conditions, managers of energy enterprises could not rationally opt for profit-seeking, because official profits were actually confiscated. They could either conceal profits or choose rent-seeking.

More generally, rent-seeking is facilitated if rules of conduct between the state and enterprises are unclear. In the interregnum between socialism and the market economy, there were no rules at all. High inflation also has the effect of dissolving economic norms. Cheap or subsidized credits were an important vehicle of rent-seeking, illustrating how inflation obscures economic reality. In 1992, enterprise managers soon bravely stated that they did not demand subsidies, only credits, but at a reasonable interest rate. Naturally, they did not discuss real interest rates but only nominal ones. In this way, subsidized credits were accepted as the norm from the early summer of 1992 until September 25, 1993, when Boris Fedorov finally succeeded in abolishing subsidized credits through a presidential decree after the parliament had been dissolved.

Whatever regulation that was left provided an incentive for enterprise managers to opt for rent-seeking instead of profit-seeking, regardless of whether it was price control, trade barrier, multiple exchange rate, or subsidized financial support. It was therefore all the more important that both liberalization and macroeconomic stabilization were particularly far-reaching and consistent in Russia and the FSRs. Their economic systems were more sensitive to rent-seeking than those in Eastern Europe, not to mention the West.

The Politics of Lobbyism

The politics of lobbyism are such that a clever lobbyist should be against any firm rule. The best would of course be to buy the whole top layer of the state. To a considerable extent, this was the situation in Russia. A deputy of the Supreme Soviet was hardly prohibited from selling his services to lobbyists. Whatever his motives might have been, Ruslan Khasbulatov himself stood up in defense of the VPK and the agrarians.

Gradually, the various lobbies managed to place their representatives in the government. At the end of May 1992, two former general directors of military-industrial enterprises, Georgy Khizha and Vladimir Shumeiko, became deputy prime ministers, with Khizha supervising the VPK. Simultaneously, the general director of Gazprom, Viktor Chernomyrdin, became deputy prime minister for energy. The minister of agriculture, Viktor Khlystun, however, was a reformer, albeit a rather ineffective one. Only in the spring of 1993 did Aleksandr Zaveryukha, a true agrarian lobbyist, join the government as deputy prime minister for agriculture. Khizha, Chernomyrdin, and Zaveryukha all fought for the interests of their lobbies. Khizha was sacked for that reason in December 1992, although Chernomyrdin was promoted and Zaveryukha survived. Under Chernomyrdin's rule in 1994, the gas and oil lobbies had a free ride. In terms of government representation, the VPK was certainly not at a disadvantage either. Moreover, Yury Skokov, an adamant champion of the VPK, was one of Yeltsin's closest friends and secretary of the Security Council until the spring of 1993.

Although most branch ministries had been formally abolished, many survived in one way or another, and every industry had substantial representation in and around the government. The Ministry of Agriculture was presumably the largest branch ministry. In the Ministry of Finance and the CBR as well, the branch ministries had representatives that defended their industries. This presence increased the pressure on the government, although it was in itself not decisive.

State enterprise managers coalesced in enterprise associations, and most appear to have been members of several such groups. The most visible organization of enterprise managers was the Russian Union of Industrialists and Entrepreneurs, headed by Arkady Volsky. It covered a broad range of industry, though its core was in civil engineering. The organizations of the VPK shifted, but in early 1994, the Russian Association of Commodity Producers, led by Yury Skokov, became a powerful organization. Most enterprises fought on their own, often as branch lobbies, and sometimes as one united lobby. In the latter instance, it could be very dangerous. The whole industrial lobby campaigned for low energy prices and cheap credits, notably in the campaign against stabilization in the spring of 1992, which to a considerable extent was led by Volsky. He called the appointment of Viktor Chernomyrdin as prime minister his victory in December 1992. But Volsky did not manage to deliver more rents to his favorites, the big automotive factories, than the agrarian and energy lobbies expropriated.

The agrarian lobby was tightly organized all along as the Agrarian Union, which also sponsored the Agrarian Party in the parliamentary elections in December 1992. The lobby had several leaders: Vasily Starodubtsev, Mikhail Lapshin, Aleksandr Zaveryukha, and Vladimir Isakov. At least Starodubtsev and Isakov were outright communistic and antidemocratic, whereas Volsky was a suave leader and a centrist in Russian politics. Both Volsky and Skokov were strong leaders and sophisticated politicians with excellent personal connections. None of the agrarian leaders could compete with them; but even so, the agrarian lobby won.

None of these factors appear to explain the difference between the fortunes of the successful energy and agrarian lobbies and that of the VPK. Two political factors, however, do appear to have been important.

The first was the government's frontal attack against the VPK, initially stating that arms procurement would be cut by 85 percent. In the end, the cut stopped at 68 percent; but even so, it amounted to a tremendous and decisive blow. The VPK never recovered. This was one of Yegor Gaidar's greatest achievements.

The second important political measure took place in December 1993, with the parliamentary elections and the adoption of the new constitution. As a consequence, the Russian parliament became structured along political party lines, and the patent acceptance of all demands from lobbies ceased. The agrarians, however, were abundantly represented in the new parliament, making the agrarian lobby even more privileged than before.

In light of all this, it seems appropriate to add to Mancur Olson's requirements for a truly strong lobby that it be small and coercive, produce homogenous commodities, and have cash for bribes. The points made about how the state should defend itself are hardly novel. Any kind of state regulation is bound to stimulate rent-seeking. The literature on democratization teaches that a weak state can defend itself, partly through swift and principled action, and partly through the building of democratic institutions. The state needs to reach out to its citizens through democratic mechanisms, and it must avoid discreet deals with the old rent-seeking elite.

How to Discipline State Enterprise Managers

From this line of reasoning, numerous conclusions can be drawn about how policy should have been pursued in the early transition period. The community of state managers turned out to be extraordinarily powerful immediately after the launching of the systemic change. They used their power for extravagant rent-seeking, primarily through subsidized credits and arbitrage in foreign trade facilitated by export restrictions.

Russian trade unions were feeble. However, in the one industry in which independent trade unions were strong—the coal industry—they contributed significantly to rent-seeking. This is what would be expected.

If trade unions exist in only one industry, that industry is likely to benefit at the expense of the state. For the purpose of minimizing rent-seeking, it would be better to have either no trade unions at all or strong, widespread ones. In any case, the needs of the people at large were neglected. Their interests are best represented by political parties, which need democratic parliamentary elections both to be formed and to be represented in the government.

The transition to a market economy instantly changed the distribution of power within the state enterprise managers lobbies. Lobbies that had relied on hierarchical state power (notably the VPK) lost out, while those to which the market forces brought cohesion benefitted. It was logical that the agrarian, gas, oil, and coal lobbies turned out to be the strongest. The steel lobby would have been another plausible candidate, but its strength was less apparent.

New private enterprises are likely to form weak lobbies, if any at all, because their focus is on profit-seeking rather than rent-seeking, and there are many small, disparate enterprises in this group. However, two private (or at least commercial) lobbies were evident from the beginning of the economic transition. The first new lobby consisted of commodity exchanges, which had thrived on arbitrage between low regulated prices and free market prices. It was badly beaten by the price liberalization. The other commercial lobby represented the 2,000 commercial banks. One-third of these banks (and all the major ones) were organized into the Association of Russian Bankers, which was called the fifth state power in the spring of 1994. The banks fell into two categories: old, big, mainly state-owned, rent-seeking banks surviving on centralized credits from the CBR; and market-oriented banks. Naturally, the bankers' association focused on rent-seeking interests, calling for more cheap credits from the CBR, and money is also a homogenous product.

Initially, the Russian government was only successful in its battles with the lobbies of state enterprise managers when it attacked their illicit interests swiftly and hard, for the good of society. An outstanding example is the sudden reduction in arms procurement in January 1992, which was a brilliant piece of politics by Yeltsin and Gaidar. A second example is the complete liberalization of agriculture undertaken by Boris Fedorov in the fall of 1993 after the parliament had been dissolved. It proved how much the government actually could do in this period of weak institutions, if someone at the top was decisive enough. Part of this liberalization was rescinded in 1994 because of the agrarian lobby's new strength in the parliament. However, much of the liberalization remained in force.

A third example is the attempt at monetary stabilization beginning in October 1993. Despite all the political events, the parliamentary elections in December 1993, and the changes in government, it was possible to sustain this most severe blow to the lobby of big enterprise managers until the summer of 1994, long after the politicians behind the policy (Fedorov and Gaidar) had left the government.

One important reason for this relative success was that the monetary squeeze divided the enterprises. Chernomyrdin saw them falling into three parts. One group of big enterprises had come close to a standstill and eventually had to be closed. Another group was doing well and would survive, while the third experienced serious trouble but could be restructured with considerable effort.[41] The losers were down and out, marked by their failure. They still demanded cheap credits, but they could no longer convincingly argue that they were viable enterprises for the future. The winners, on the other hand, suffered from a shortage of working capital, which had been run down by inflation. They needed to replenish it with ordinary bank credits, but in the spring of 1994, positive real interest rates hovered at around 150 to 180 percent a year. The winners began to realize that real interest rates would stay high until the budget deficit was reduced. As a result, they no longer supported general demands for cheap credits, and they wanted to cut the state budget deficit. The directors lobby had been severely split because of decisive state measures.[42]

All government compromises and concessions to the state managers lobby, on the contrary, turned out to be economic and political failures. The government did not become stronger but in fact was stalemated when it invited chief lobbyists to become deputy prime ministers in late May 1992. At the same time, the government gave in to pressure from the managers, offering subsidized credits and failing to liberalize energy prices. As a result, the macroeconomic stabilization policy was completely undermined. Nor did the managers thank the government; their criticism of it only increased. The lesson to be learned is that the managers behave better when they are under pressure from hard budget constraints than if the government tries to compromise with them.

In the spring of 1992, the government established a tripartite commission composed of government entities, employers associations, and trade unions. In effect, the employers were representatives of managers of the big state enterprises, the most rent-seeking ones. The trade unionists were third-rank old communist officials, representing no one but the lower tiers of the *nomenklatura*. They neither could nor would deliver on anything, whereas promises from the government were real. Fortunately, little came of the tripartite commission. Volsky typically wanted to go further in this direction, calling for a roundtable discussion of all economic issues: "It is necessary to set all basic influential forces around one table. They are known." He further warned against "underestimating the danger of a coming social explosion," but argued against new elections, stating that "people are deadly tired of politics," which low participation in by-elections had shown.[43] It is difficult to comprehend why people would revolt when they did not engage in any social actions (neither strikes nor elections) while freedom prevailed. The problem, on the contrary, was that people reacted too little and that civil society was too weak. Both the behavior and the demands of the directors lobby were highly unsocial. For instance, the directors did not pay honestly earned wages, while they continued to hold enterprise funds as flight capital abroad. This clarified that the directors themselves were not afraid of social unrest. Volsky understood the interests of the state enterprise managers very well, and his views could be taken as starting points for what the government should not do.

Conversely, there was little need for an incomes policy in Russia (and much less so than in Central Europe) because the workers were far too weak in relation to their managers. Any incomes policy would have aggravated this imbalance of power even further.[44] Even if there were work councils that existed by law, they meant little in real life.

The prime counterweights to the power of the state enterprise managers lobby were the reformers in the government and the will of the people. The best way the popular will could be expressed was through democratic parliamentary elections. They finally took place in December 1993—far too late, and long after stabilization had been undermined—leading to poor results from the reformers and great divisiveness among them. Even so, real political parties were created, reducing the influence of vested interests. The Agrarian Party received 8 percent of the vote, because it had a real social base. Volsky's Civic Union obtained 2 percent, making it clear how small the social and political base of the state managers lobby actually was.

Although the reformers were not particularly strong in the new Federal Assembly, this entity held up much better against the enterprise lobbies than had the Supreme Soviet. The agrarian lobby *was* strong (as it tends to be in democratic parliaments), and the coal industry got its subsidies, because of intermittent strikes among coal miners. In the spring of 1994, both the government and the Duma turned down demands from the military and the VPK for more resources despite a concerted and highly public campaign by both the Ministry of Defense and the VPK. Gazprom, however, remained the last Russian enterprise with soft budget constraints. It trusted that Prime Minister Chernomyrdin would guarantee it tax breaks, and he did. The oil lobby successfully continued to insist on corrupt export controls through the end of 1994. The other industrial lobbies were left without rents to collect.

The lessons to learn from all this are surprisingly simple. First, the stabilization and liberalization program must be as comprehensive as possible. In particular, this means liberalizing trade, energy prices, and agricultural prices, and introducing positive real interest rates early on. Second, the government should not negotiate with enterprise lobbies but should pressure them instead through a strict monetary policy. Third, there is less need for incomes policy in Russia than in most other places, and there is little need to worry about trade unions, strikes, and social unrest. Fourth, it is necessary to call early democratic parliamentary elections, fielding candidates from political parties. The elections are likely to beat all the enterprise lobbies apart from the agrarians.

Lessons From the Russian Transformation

Many conclusions can be drawn from the Russian transformation. One advantage of a large and complex country is that it provides a serious test for all kinds of hypotheses. In many other countries, opponents of an idea may claim that special conditions facilitated success. If a program succeeds under as complex a set of conditions as existed in Russia, it is fairly robust.

My first conclusion is that the economic transformation has succeeded in Russia to the extent that it has become a market economy. It was indeed possible to undertake such a conscious and deliberate economic transition. However imperfect the Russian reform program, the Gaidar team did formulate a reasonably viable economic strategy that was carried out to a considerable extent, despite massive resistance from the corrupt, the criminal, and the rent-seeking. The development of both political and economic pluralism and decentralization has gone far. Moreover, much of the old repressive apparatus has fallen apart and no longer has any ideological force. Thanks to this great dispersion of political and economic power, Russia appears compelled to stay a pluralist society with a market economy. No one could plausibly concentrate all the power in Russia in Moscow again.

The transformation of the Russian economy is well illustrated by three front-page photos from *Izvestiya* in July 1994. They picture Russians in 1985, queuing for vodka, and in summer 1992, queuing for bread—but in 1994, they are shown queuing to buy shares.[45] In the winter of 1991 and 1992, people feared famine in Russia. By the summer of 1994, the major concern was financial scandals with the potential of hurting millions of private speculators who had large savings and a high acceptance of risk. It is difficult to imagine a faster transition in popular concerns, and this in turn reflects the successful transformation of the Russian economy. Before 1988, most Russians seemed convinced that the Russian nation was fundamentally unsuitable for entrepreneurship. In 1994, a standard Russian saying ran: "Those who do not take risks will not drink champagne." An entire culture had been transformed.

Russia has also proved that it is not essentially different from other countries. It is true that Russia is extremely complex and has many peculiarities, but that does not mean that the ordinary laws of social science do not apply in Russia. Of the key issues the Russians faced, building democracy and the nation received the least skillful treatment, because it was handled as a uniquely Russian matter to which universal social theory did not really apply. Nowhere has this study revealed anything that suggests that Russia is an exception when it comes to social science. Russian conditions have instead provided social theorists with a tougher test. Good theory has stood the test, whereas poor theory has proven faulty.

The Russian transformation has been a manifestation of idealism by those who believed in building a better society—one characterized by individual freedom, democracy, a market economy, widespread private ownership, and the rule of law. The ruling spirit during the first two years of Russian transformation was indeed ideological and idealistic. Later on, the idealists lost out; but they had already laid the foundation for a free economy and a free society.

The social stratum posing the greatest danger to successful reform was indeed the old establishment—primarily state enterprise managers, but the state bureaucracy as well. The state managers needed to be disciplined through liberalization, macroeconomic stabilization, privatization, and corporate governance, while the old state bureaucracy needed to be cut back and rejuvenated. Because of their strength in contrast with the weakness of the rest of society, the FSRs required more radical liberal reform programs than had east central Europe, where the quality of both the state administration and civil society was higher. The people and the workers, on the contrary, have caused no serious problems at all in Russia. The fear of populism in its strict sense has essentially been misplaced.

Because of the combination of a weak state and a old, vicious elite, a radical and consistent liberal strategy was vitally needed in Russia. To be successful, it had to combine democratization, marketization, and privatization. Macroeconomic stabilization, with its many serious problems, provides a good illustration. However radical the Gaidar reform was, it simply was not radical and consistent enough. A fundamental mistake was to disregard the need for liberalization of domestic trade because of a lack of belief in the market as a mechanism of allocation. The conception of monetary policy was rudimentary at best, lacking a clear commitment to an early positive real interest rate, and no clear policy on the ruble zone was adopted. The government deviated severely from the basic liberalism of its program, such as maintaining price controls on energy, import subsidies, and export controls, which turned out to be impermissible concessions under the conditions that existed in Russia. Finally, the reformers faced formidable political resistance from a coalition of state enterprise managers, an antireform parliament, and a central bank that insisted on subsidized credits to the rent-seeking elite.

Any aberration from a simple, consistent, liberal model appears to have been more costly in Russia than in eastern Europe. For instance, both Poland and Czechoslovakia maintained price controls on energy after their initial deregulations, but the effects were not nearly as devastating as they were in Russia. Russia was thus more sensitive to deviations from the radical liberal reform model. At the same time, it was more difficult to be consistent in Russia, with its complicated preconditions. Therefore, the Russian transformation has in fact established the broader viability of the radical liberal reform model, which has proved successful in Poland, the Czech Republic, Estonia, and Latvia.

The social costs of the economic transformation have also been wildly exaggerated. The total decline in the actual material standard of living has not exceeded 10 percent. Who could have believed that communism's demise would be so cheap? Social costs have risen because of the slow transition. This has caused more corruption and higher inflation than was necessary, and both function as regressive taxes. Moreover, stabilizing an economy through a monetary squeeze is socially more costly than stabilizing through strict fiscal policy. The problem is political. Russians feel alienated because few understand this extraordinary transformation. Characteristically, an opinion poll in 11 regions of Russia in the spring of 1994 found that 89 percent of respondents found the situation in the country alarming, a crisis, or catastrophic, while about three-quarters simultaneously assessed their personal situations as satisfactory or good.[46]

The main remaining problem in Russia appears to be criminality. A nationwide legal system is a complex structure requiring tens of thousands of lawyers and establishment of a legal ethic among the people. To write and adopt laws and clamp down on the most obvious criminals are two important but comparatively easy tasks. To educate all the lawyers needed, however, will take decades. Considering that the legal capacity of functioning courts will be quite small for years to come, Russia needs to adopt a very liberal legal system. Otherwise, corruption will remain a dominant vice. The extent to which public commodities and services may be sold illicitly by Russian officials for their own benefit should be minimized.

Although the international community has interacted with Russia throughout the transformation, foreign nations have not been particularly forthcoming in offering assistance to Russia. The openness and great variety of contacts and exchanges and some of the advice have been beneficial. However, the leading Western powers neglected to help Russia financially when the best reform program was launched and Russia was actually stabilizing. The IMF emphatically supported maintaining the ruble zone, which was seriously harmful; and it argued long and hard against pegging the exchange rate as a nominal anchor, which had been useful in a number of other stabilizations. The IMF and its efforts in Russia reflect the wishes of the leading Western countries to look concerned but to actually provide a minimum of financing.

Political leadership in Russia has been vitally important to the success of reforms in various spheres. The records of the political leaders are as varied as could be expected. President Yeltsin has been a strong leader. He picked the reform team and the reform strategy. To begin with, he pushed reform with great force and persuasiveness and promoted his policies among the public. Yeltsin's support for the privatization program was persistent until June 1994. Yet his weaknesses were also evident. He had no apparent political strategy on essential issues such as the building of democracy, and he failed to organize a political party. Yeltsin jeopardized his liberalization and stabilization program to side with the state enterprise managers in the spring of 1992. His close associates have included many contradictory figures. Aleksandr Rutskoi and Khasbulatov were foisted on him by events, but Oleg Lobov and Skokov were, ominously, his preferred confidants. In the end, his commitment to liberal and democratic values appears tenuous at best.

Yegor Gaidar stands out as the most competent economist who has served in the Russian government. During his first half-year in government, he proved his ability to conceptualize a program and implement it with considerable decisiveness. However, after April 1992 he lost most of his vigor and seemed to be a lame duck politically. When he returned to government in September 1993, he tilted the balance of power to the advantage of the reformers and facilitated substantial reforms.

Anatoly Chubais is an amazing politician who has smoothly done everything right, to an extent that rarely happens. He has combined ideological principles with effective execution of his ideas. It is not surprising that he has lasted the longest in the Russian government of the radical reformers.

Boris Fedorov made all the difference as minister of finance in 1993. His extraordinary accomplishments toward Russian stabilization underscore how much one individual can mean in such a volatile situation.

Viktor Chernomyrdin has reflected the changes in the economic situation in Russia and his own status rather than any particular views. In 1992, he was a loyal representative of the rent-seeking natural gas monopoly. In 1993, as prime minister, he pitted conservatives against reformers without any apparent ambition other than maintaining some balance in the government and accruing more power. In 1994, Chernomyrdin became the dominant politician with regard to economic issues. He toyed with the idea of financial stabilization, but he was not fully absorbed by his responsibilities as prime minister in a market economy. He provided himself and his rent-seeking associates in the energy lobby with large illegitimate tax exemptions, making them the richest men in Russia.

The final conclusion I can draw is that radical economic reform was the right choice for Russia in the fall of 1991, and much has been accomplished since then. However, the economic transformation in Russia should have been more consistent from the beginning. A more far-reaching liberalization and a firmer financial stabilization would have restricted both rent-seeking and corruption. The economic changes should have been supported by early democratic reforms. Yet the case has nevertheless been made: Russia could (and did) reform, and it has become a market economy.

Abbreviations

AKKOR	Association of Peasant Farms and Agricultural Cooperatives of Russia
CBR	Central Bank of Russia
CC	Central Committee
CIS	Commonwealth of Independent States
CMEA	Council for Mutual Economic Assistance (also COMECON)
CPSU	Communist Party of the Soviet Union
EBRD	European Bank for Reconstruction and Development
EC	European Community
ECE	UN Economic Commission for Europe
ECU	European Currency Unit
EPU	European Payments Union
FBIS	Foreign Broadcast Information Service
FSR	Former Soviet Republic
FSU	Former Soviet Union
GDP	Gross domestic product
GKI	State Committee for the Management of State Property (also called Goskomimushchestvo)
Goskomstat	State Committee for Statistics
Goskomtsen	State Price Committee
Gosplan	State Committee for Planning
Gossnab	State Committee for Material and Technical Supplies
IBRD	International Bank for Reconstruction and Development (the World Bank)
IMF	International Monetary Fund
MFU	Macroeconomic and Finance Unit at the Russian Ministry of Finance
MICEX	Moscow Interbank Foreign Currency Exchange
MVES	Ministry of Foreign Economic Relations
OECD	Organization for Economic Cooperation and Development
RSFSR	Russian Soviet Federated Socialist Republic

SDR	Special drawing rights
USSR	Union of Soviet Socialist Republics
VAT	Value-added tax
VPK	Military-industrial complex
VTsIOM	All-Russian Center for the Study of Public Opinion

Chronology

Date	Event
1991	
June 12	Boris Yeltsin elected president of Russia
August 19–21	Abortive Communist coup
October 28	Yeltsin's big reform speech
November 6–8	Reform government appointed
December 8	Belovezhsky agreement between Belarus, Russia, and Ukraine on the abolition of the USSR and the foundation of the CIS
December 21	The CIS broadened to 11 countries at meeting in Alma-Ata
December 25	Mikhail S. Gorbachev resigns as president of the USSR
1992	
January 2	The big price liberalization
February 27	Shadow program with the IMF signed
April 3	Gennady Burbulis ousted as first deputy prime minister
April 6	Sixth Congress of People's Deputies convened
May–June	Vladimir Lopukhin sacked as minister of fuel and energy; three industrialists appointed deputy prime ministers: Viktor Chernomyrdin, Vladimir Shumeiko, and Georgy Khizha
June 11	Supreme Soviet adopts Privatization Program for 1992
July 1	Formal separation of the Russian ruble from other noncash rubles
July	Russia and the IMF sign a standby agreement
July 17	Viktor Gerashchenko appointed acting chairman of the Central Bank of Russia
August 19	Yeltsin announces voucher privatization
December 12	Yegor Gaidar ousted as acting prime minister by the Seventh Congress of People's Deputies
December 14	Chernomyrdin appointed prime minister
1993	
March 28	Congress of People's Deputies fails to impeach Yeltsin

319

Date	Event
April 16	Oleg Lobov appointed first deputy prime minister and minister of the economy
April 20	Technical credits to other former Soviet republics abolished
April 25	Referendum
May	Agreement with the IMF on a Systemic Transformation Facility
July 24	Demonetization of Soviet ruble banknotes
September 7	Agreement on the formation of a ruble zone of a new type
September 18	Gaidar replaces Lobov as first deputy prime minister and minister of the economy
September 21	Yeltsin dissolves Congress of People's Deputies and Supreme Soviet
September 25	Subsidized credits abolished
October 3–4	Armed uprising in Moscow; storming of the White House
December 12	Parliamentary elections and referendum on the new constitution

1994

January 5	Agreement on monetary union with Belarus signed
January 16	Gaidar resigns as first deputy prime minister and minister of the economy
January 20	Boris Fedorov resigns as deputy prime minister and minister of finance
April	Renewed agreement with the IMF on Systemic Transformation Facility
October 11	"Black Tuesday"—a one-day collapse of the exchange rate of the ruble

Cast of Characters

Leonid Abalkin. Born in 1930. Economist and reform communist. One of Mikhail Gorbachev's chief economic advisors. Deputy prime minister and chairman of the USSR government's Reform Commission, July 1989–January 1991. Director of the Institute of Economics of the Academy of Sciences since 1986.

Sergei Aleksashenko. Young economist and reformer. Russian deputy minister of finance from 1993 to March 1995. Appointed by Boris Fedorov. Member of the Shatalin group.

Stanislav Anisimov. Born in 1940. Soviet state official and advocate of branch interests who stayed on in the reform government. USSR minister of material resources in 1991. Russian minister of trade, 1991–92.

Georgy Arbatov. Born in 1923. Soviet foreign policy specialist. Advisor to all Soviet leaders from Brezhnev to Gorbachev on U.S. foreign policy. Director of the U.S. and Canada Institute of the Academy of Sciences.

Petr Aven. Born in 1955. Economist and reformer. Russian minister of foreign economic relations, November 1991–December 1992. Member of the Gaidar team. Currently president of Alpha Bank.

Vasily Barchuk. Born in 1941. Soviet financial official. Russian first deputy minister of finance, 1991–92. Russian minister of finance, 1992.

Oleg Bogomolov. Born in 1927. Economist and reform communist. Director of the Institute of the Economy of the World Socialist System of the Academy of Sciences since 1969 (institute was renamed the Institute of International Economic and Political Research in 1990).

Maxim Boycko. Young economist and radical reformer. Chief executive officer of the Russian Privatization Center since 1993. Advisor to Anatoly Chubais.

Gennady Burbulis. Born in 1945. Democratic politician. Emerged as reformist deputy from Sverdlovsk (Yekaterinburg) in 1989. Political advisor to Boris Yeltsin. Russian first deputy prime minister, November 1991–April 1992. State secretary in the President's Administration, April–December 1992.

Viktor Chernomyrdin. Born in 1938. Industrialist and state official. Centrist. Prime minister since December 1992. USSR minister of the gas industry, 1985–89. Chairman of the state concern Gazprom, 1989–92. Russian deputy prime minister for the fuel and energy complex, May–December 1992.

Anatoly Chubais. Born in 1955. Economist and radical reformer from St. Petersburg. Minister of privatization, November 1991–November 1994. First deputy prime minister for economic affairs since November 1994. Deputy prime minister since June 1992. Member of the Gaidar team.

Sergei Dubinin. Economist and reformer. Russian first deputy minister of finance appointed in early 1993 by Boris Fedorov. Acting minister of finance, January–October 1994.

Boris Fedorov. Born in 1958. Economist and radical reformer. Leader of the newly founded political party Forward, Russia. Russian minister of finance, second half of 1990. Russian minister of finance and deputy prime minister in 1993.

Yegor Gaidar. Born in 1956. Outstanding economist and radical reformer. Leader of the political party Russia's Democratic Choice. Economic editor of the journal *Kommunist,* 1987–90. Economic editor of *Pravda* in 1990. Director of the Institute of Economic Policy, 1990–91. Deputy prime minister and minister of economy and finance, November 1991–spring 1992. First deputy prime minister from March 1992 and acting prime minister, June–December 1992. First deputy prime minister and minister of the economy, September 1993–January 1994. Director of the Institute of Economic Problems of the Transition Period since December 1992.

Viktor Gerashchenko. Born in 1937. Soviet bank official. Chairman of the USSR State Bank, 1989–91. Chairman of the Central Bank of Russia, July 1991–October 1994.

Sergei Glaz'ev. Born in 1961. Economist and socialist. Russian first deputy minister of foreign economic relations, November 1991–December 1992. Minister of foreign economic relations, December 1992–September 1993.

Leonid Grigor'ev. Economist and reformer. Member of the Gaidar team and the Shatalin group. Russian deputy minister of finance and chairman of the Committee on Foreign Investment, November 1991–92.

Sergei Ignat'ev. Economist and reformer from St. Petersburg. Member of the Gaidar/Chubais team. Russian deputy minister of finance, November 1991–92. Deputy chairman of the Central Bank of Russia, 1992–93. Deputy minister of the economy since 1993.

Ruslan Khasbulatov. Born in 1942. Chechen. Economist who emerged as a democratic deputy in 1990, but turned against the democrats in 1992 and became a leading antireformer. First deputy chairman of the RSFSR Supreme Soviet, 1990–91. Chairman of the Russian Supreme Soviet, 1991–93.

Georgy Khizha. Born in 1938. Manager from the military industry in St. Petersburg. Forceful antireformer. Deputy prime minister for industry, May–December 1992.

Viktor Khlystun. Born in 1946. Agrarian academic and official. Minister of agriculture, November 1991–94. Reformist who avoided controversy.

Vladimir Kosmarsky. Economist and radical reformer. First deputy minister of labor, 1992; acting minister of labor, first half of 1992.

Oleg Lobov. Born in 1937. Construction engineer, Communist party and state official. Old friend of Boris Yeltsin from Sverdlovsk. Important antireformer. Russian first deputy prime minister, April–November 1991. First deputy prime minister and minister of the economy, April–September 1993. Secretary of the Security Council since September 1993.

Vladimir Lopukhin. Born in 1952. Economist and reformer. Russian minister of fuel and energy, November 1991–May 1992. Russian deputy minister of the economy, August–November 1991.

Yury Luzhkov. Born in 1936. State official. Mayor of Moscow since June 1992. Focused on property relations in Moscow.

Vladimir Mashchits. Born in 1953. Economist and reformer. Chairman of the Russian State Committee for Economic Cooperation With States–Members of the Commonwealth of Independent States, December 1991–94. Member of the Shatalin group.

Georgy Matyukhin. Old reform economist. Chairman of the Central Bank of Russia, 1990–June 1992.

Andrei Nechaev. Born in 1953. Economist and reformer. Russian minister of the economy, February 1992–93. Member of the Gaidar team.

Ella Pamfilova. Born in 1953. Radical reformer. Russian minister of social protection, November 1991–January 1994. Member of the Gaidar team.

Nikolai Petrakov. Born in 1937. Economist and reform communist. One of Mikhail Gorbachev's chief economic advisors and his personal economic assistant, 1990–91. Director of the Institute of the Problems of the Market since 1991. Member of the Shatalin group.

Yury Petrov. Born in 1939. Communist party official and friend of Boris Yeltsin from Sverdlovsk. Antireformer. Chief of the President's Administration, August 1991–93.

Aleksandr Rutskoi. Born in 1947. Major general. Russian vice president, June 1991–93. Leading antireformer.

Yevgeny Saburov. Born in 1946. Economist and reformer. Russian deputy prime minister and minister of the economy, August–November 1991.

Boris Saltykov. Born in 1940. Economist and reformer. Russian minister of science and higher education since November 1991. Member of the Gaidar team.

Sergei Shakhrai. Born in 1956. Lawyer and democratic deputy. One of President Yeltsin's chief advisors on legal and national issues. Intermittently deputy prime minister since December 1991. Leader of the centrist Party of Unity and Accord in the elections of December 1993.

Stanislav Shatalin. Born in 1934. Economist and reform communist. One of Mikhail Gorbachev's chief economic advisors. Member of the USSR Presidential Council, March–December 1990. Leader of the Shatalin group that elaborated on the 500-day program of Grigory Yavlinsky in August 1990.

Aleksandr Shokhin. Born in 1951. Economist, state official, and reformer. Originally number-two man on the Gaidar team, but moved toward the political center. Russian deputy prime minister, November 1991–October 1994, originally for social affairs, but from June 1992 for foreign economic relations. Russian minister of labor, August–November 1991. Deputy leader of the centrist Party of Unity and Accord in the elections of December 1993.

Vladimir Shumeiko. Born in 1945. Enterprise manager and state official. Moderate reformer. Chairman of the Russian Federation Council since February 1994. Russian first deputy prime minister, June 1992–January 1994.

Ivan Silaev. Born in 1930. Soviet state official. RSFSR prime minister, June 1990–September 1991, as a compromise candidate between Yeltsin and the communists. USSR deputy prime minister, 1985–90. Chairman of the Interrepublican Economic Committee (replacing the USSR government), September–November 1991.

Yury Skokov. Born in 1938. Enterprise manager and state official. Close friend of Yeltsin from Moscow. Strong antireformer. RSFSR first deputy prime minister, 1990–91. Economic and security advisor to the Russian president, 1991. Secretary of the Security Council, April 1992–March 1993. Currently chairman of the Association of Commodity Producers.

Oleg Soskovets. Born in 1949. Manager in the metallurgical industry and state official. USSR minister of metallurgy, 1991. Minister of industry of Kazakhstan, 1992. First deputy prime minister of Russia since 1993. Represents the interests of state industry.

Vasily Starodubtsev. Born in 1931. Agrarian activist and hard-line communist. One of the instigators of the August 1991 attempted coup. Both before and after August 1991, chairman of the Agrarian Union. Author of the book *Are Kolkhozy Necessary?*

Aleksandr Titkin. Born in 1948. Enterprise manager. Russian minister of industry, November 1991–October 1992. Presumably the staunchest antireformer and advocate of branch interests in the Gaidar government.

Dmitry Vasil'ev. Young economist and radical reformer from St. Petersburg. Deputy chairman of the GKI since November 1991, Chubais's right-hand man, and one of the main designers of the privatization program.

Sergei Vasil'ev. Young economist and radical reformer from St. Petersburg. Economic counselor of Gaidar, November 1991–December 1992. Director of the Working Center for Economic Reform of the Russian Government, 1992–93. Deputy minister of the economy since 1994.

Andrei Vavilov. Young economist and reformer. Brought in as Russian first deputy minister of finance by Gaidar in early 1992, but has stayed at his post.

Arkady Volsky. Born in 1932. Quintessential Soviet *apparatchik* and political survivor. Since 1990, chairman of the Russian Union of Industrialists and Entrepreneurs and its predecessor, the main lobbying organization of large state industrial enterprises. Occupied various posts in the CPSU CC apparatus, 1966–88, including personal economic advisor to Yury Andropov and Konstantin Chernenko, 1983–1985. Leading centrist opponent of radical economic reform in 1992. Leader of the Civic Union in the elections of December 1993.

Yury Yarov. Born in 1942. Communist party and state official. Russian deputy prime minister since December 1992.

Yevgeny Yasin. Born in 1934. Economist and reformer. Since November 1994, Russian minister of the economy. Has participated in the writing of all major economic reform programs since 1989 and has gradually been radicalized. Member of the Shatalin group.

Grigory Yavlinsky. Born in 1952. Economist, reformer, and politician. Chairman of the liberal Yabloko faction in the Russian State Duma. Chief author of the original 500-day program in 1990 and leading member of the Shatalin group. Russian deputy prime minister for economic reform in the fall of 1990. Deputy chairman of the Interrepublican Economic Committee (replacing the USSR government), September–November 1991. Rival of Gaidar.

Vitaly Yefimov. Born in 1940. State official. Russian minister of transportation since 1990. Conservative Soviet technocrat who stayed on in the Russian government and worked for branch interests against reforms.

Boris Yeltsin. Born in 1931. Communist party and state official who turned democrat after falling out with the Communist Party of the Soviet Union in the fall of 1987. First party secretary of Sverdlovsk *oblast*, 1976–85. First party secretary of Moscow City, 1985–87. USSR minister of construction, 1987–89. Chairman of the RSFSR Supreme Soviet, May 1990–June 1991. Since June 1991, Russia's first democratically elected president.

Notes

1. Boris Fedorov, "Rossiiskiye finansy v 1993 godu (The Russian finances in 1993)," *Voprosy ekonomiki*, no. 1 (January 1994), pp. 4–5.
2. "V. S. Chernomyrdin's Speech at the Expanded Meeting of the Government of the Russian Federation on March 4, 1994," *Rossiiskaya gazeta*, March 5, 1994.

Chapter One

3. Anders Åslund, *Gorbachev's Struggle for Economic Reform*, 2d ed. (Cornell University Press, 1991).
4. Wlodzimierz Brus and Kazimierz Laski, *From Marx to the Market: Socialism in Search of an Economic System* (Oxford University Press, 1989).
5. János Kornai, *The Socialist System. The Political Economy of Communism* (Princeton University Press, 1992), pp. 360–65; I have provided a similar presentation in Anders Åslund, "Prospects of the New Russian Market Economy," *Problems of Post-Communism*, vol. 41 (Fall 1994), pp. 16–20.
6. Kornai, *The Socialist System*, pp. 360–61.
7. Anders Åslund, *Post-Communist Economic Revolutions: How Big a Bang?* (Center for Strategic and International Studies, 1992); Anders Åslund, "A Critique of Soviet Reform Plans," in Anders Åslund, ed., *The Post-Soviet Economy: Soviet and Western Perspectives* (St. Martin's Press, 1992), pp. 167–80.
8. Åslund, *Gorbachev's Struggle for Economic Reform*, p. 225.
9. See, for instance: Adam Przeworski, *Democracy and the Market: Political and Economic Reforms in Eastern Europe and Latin America* (Cambridge University Press, 1991); Juan J. Linz, *The Breakdown of Democratic Regimes: Crisis, Breakdown, and Reequilibration* (Johns Hopkins University Press, 1978); Guillermo O'Donnell and Phillippe C. Schmitter, *Transitions From Authoritarian Rule: Tentative Conclusions About Uncertain Democracies* (Johns Hopkins University Press, 1986).

10. Mancur Olson, *The Logic of Collective Action: Public Goods and the Theory of Groups* (Harvard University Press, 1971).

11. Douglass C. North, *Structure and Change in Economic History* (W. W. Norton and Co., 1981).

12. Michael Bruno and others, eds., *Inflation Stabilization: The Experiences of Israel, Argentina, Brazil, Bolivia, and Mexico* (MIT Press, 1988).

13. Oliver E. Williamson, *Markets and Hierarchies: Analysis and Antitrust Implications: A Study in the Economics of Internal Organization* (Free Press, 1975).

14. Yegor T. Gaidar, *Ekonomicheskiye reformy i ierarkhicheskiye struktury* (Economic reforms and hierarchical structures) (Moscow: Nauka, 1990), p. 4.

15. Leo Pasvolsky, *Economic Nationalism of the Danubian States* (London: Macmillan, 1928); Thomas J. Sargent, "The Ends of Four Big Inflations," in Thomas J. Sargent, *Rational Expectations and Inflation* (Harper & Row, 1986), pp. 40–109.

16. David Lipton and Jeffrey Sachs, "Creating a Market Economy in Eastern Europe: The Case of Poland," *Brookings Papers on Economic Activity*, 1:1990, pp. 75–133; Leszek Balcerowicz, *800 dni szok kontrolowany* (800 days of controlled shock) (Polska Oficyna Wydawnicza "BGW", 1991); Olivier Blanchard and others, *Reform in Eastern Europe* (MIT Press, 1991); János Kornai, *The Road to a Free Economy. Shifting From a Socialist System: The Example of Hungary* (W. W. Norton, 1990); Ralf Dahrendorf, *Reflections on the Revolution in Europe* (London: Chatto & Windus, 1990).

17. I remember a meeting with Ruslan Khasbulatov's chief economist, Anatoly Milyukov, in February 1992. I argued that the necessary industrial decline would be 35 to 40 percent—that is, a bit more than in Poland. Milyukov simply responded that such a decline was unacceptable. In fact, it became larger.

18. Åslund, *Post-Communist Economic Revolutions*.

19. Anders Åslund, "Lessons of the First Four Years of Systemic Change in Eastern Europe," *Journal of Comparative Economics*, vol. 19, no. 1 (1994), pp. 22–38.

20. "Russia Requires Radical Reform and Strong Power" (Interview with Arkady Volsky), *Izvestiya*, August 3, 1992; "Thirteen Points of Volsky's Program," *Izvestiya*, September 30, 1992.

21. Leszek Balcerowicz, "Understanding Postcommunist Transitions," *Journal of Democracy*, vol. 5 (October 1994), pp. 75–89.

22. One of the better examples is Ronald I. McKinnon, "Gradual Versus Rapid Liberalization in Socialist Economies: The Problem of Macroeconomic Control," in Michael Bruno and Boris Pleskovic, eds., *Proceedings of the World Bank Annual Conference on Development Economics 1993* (The World Bank, 1994), pp. 63–94.

23. Anders Åslund, "Soviet and Chinese Reforms—Why They Must Be Different," *The World Today*, vol. 45 (November 1989), pp. 188–191.

24. Wlodzimierz Brus, "Marketization and Democratization: The Sino-Soviet Divergence," Working Paper 63 (Stockholm: Stockholm Institute of Soviet and East European Economics, 1992), pp. 4–5.

25. Goskomstat SSSR, *Narodnoe khozyaistvo SSSR v 1989 g.* (The national economy of the USSR in 1989) (Moscow: Finansy i statistika, 1990), p. 9.

26. Jeffrey Sachs and Wing Thye Woo, "Reform in China and Russia," *Economic Policy*, no. 18 (April 1994), p. 106.

27. Ibid., pp. 105–13.

28. Peter Murrell and Mancur Olson, "The Devolution of Centrally Planned Economies," *Journal of Comparative Economics*, vol. 15, no. 2 (1991), pp. 239–65.

29. Minxin Pei, "The Puzzle of East Asian Exceptionalism," *Journal of Democracy*, vol. 5 (October 1994), pp. 90–103.

30. Anders Åslund, "Gorbachev's Economic Advisors," *Soviet Economy*, vol. 3 (July/September 1987), pp. 246–69; Anders Åslund, "Changes in Soviet Economic Policy-Making in 1989 and 1990," in Anders Åslund, ed., *Market Socialism or the Restoration of Capitalism?* (Cambridge University Press, 1992), pp. 92–120.

31. Our collaboration with the Russian reformers has been amply documented in four books. Since 1991, the Stockholm Institute of Soviet and East European Economics has held a conference each year in June in Stockholm on the advancement of Russian economic reform (Anders Åslund, ed., *The Post-Soviet Economy*); Anders Åslund and Richard Layard, eds., *Changing the Economic System in Russia* (St. Martin's Press, 1993); Anders Åslund, ed., *Economic Transformation in Russia* (St. Martin's Press, 1994); Anders Åslund, ed., *Russian Economic Reform at Risk* (London: Pinter, forthcoming).

32. Vincent Koen, "Measuring the Transition: A User's View on National Accounts in Russia," IMF Working Paper WP/94/6 (International Monetary Fund, January 1994), p. 8; Goskomstat Rossii, *Sotsial'no-ekonomicheskoe polozhenie Rossii 1993 g.* (Russia's social-economic situation in 1993) (Moscow, 1994), p. 6.

33. Richard Layard and Andrea Richter, "Labour Market Adjustment—The Russian Way," in Åslund, ed., *Russian Economic Reform at Risk*.

34. Robert Di Calogero, K. Wilhelm Nahr, and Richard T. Stillson, "Money and Banking Statistics in Former Soviet Union (FSU) Economies," IMF Working Paper WP/92/103 (International Monetary Fund, December 1992).

35. Yevgeny Vasil'chuk, "The Customs Statistics Complement the Picture of Foreign Trade," *Finansovye izvestiya*, June 23, 1994.

Chapter Two

1. Anders Åslund, *Gorbachev's Struggle for Economic Reform*, 2d ed. (Cornell University Press, 1991).

2. Ibid., p. 28; Mikhail S. Gorbachev, *Izbrannyye rechi i stat'i* (Selected speeches and articles), vol. 2 (Moscow: Politizdat, 1987), pp. 75–108.

3. Gorbachev, *Izbrannyye rechi i stat'i*, p. 86.

4. Anders Åslund, "Heritage of the Gorbachev Era," in U.S. Congress, Joint Economic Committee, *The Former Soviet Union in Transition*, vol. 1 (Government Printing Office, May 1993), pp. 184–95.

5. "'We Are Taking Over'" (Interview with B. N. Yeltsin), *Newsweek*, January 6, 1992, pp. 11–12.

6. A devastating illustration of Gorbachev's emptiness is his book: Mikhail S. Gorbachev, *The August Coup: The Truth and the Lessons* (London: Harper-Collins, 1991).

7. Andrei Amalrik, *Will the Soviet Union Survive Until 1984?*, 2d ed. (Penguin, 1980), p. 34.

8. This section is based on Åslund, *Gorbachev's Struggle for Economic Reform*, pp. 61–68.

9. *Konstitutsiya (Osnovnoi Zakon) Soyuza Sovetskikh Sotsialisticheskikh Respublik* (Constitution [Fundamental Law] of the Union of Soviet Socialist Republics) (Moscow: Yuridicheskaya literatura, 1985), p. 9.

10. "M. S. Gorbachev's Speech," *Pravda*, December 1, 1990.

11. M. S. Gorbachev, "To Be the Party of the People, the Party of *Perestroika*," *Pravda*, December 2, 1990.

12. Åslund, "Heritage of the Gorbachev Era," pp. 184–95.

13. For an excellent account of how *glasnost* proceeded, see Alec Nove, *Glasnost in Action: Cultural Renaissance in Russia* (Boston: Unwin Hyman, 1989).

14. The two seminal articles were: Vasily I. Selyunin and Grigory I. Khanin, "Cunning Numbers," *Novy mir*, vol. 63 (February 1987), pp. 181–201, and Nikolai P. Shmelev, "Advances and Debts," *Novy mir*, vol. 63 (June 1987), pp. 142–58.

15. The main recipients were Vietnam, Cuba, and Mongolia, which were members of the CMEA. Other prominent recipients were Angola, Mozambique, Ethiopia, and South Yemen.

16. Peter Reddaway, "Empire on the Brink," *New York Review of Books*, January 31, 1991, pp. 7–9.

17. Åslund, *Gorbachev's Struggle for Economic Reform*, pp. 204–06.

18. Goskomstat SSSR, *Narodnoe khozyaistvo SSSR v 1989 g.* (The national economy of the USSR in 1989) (Moscow: Finansy i statistika, 1990), p. 50.

19. Åslund, "Heritage of the Gorbachev Era," pp. 191–92.

20. Mikhail S. Gorbachev, *Perestroika: New Thinking for Our Country and the World* (Harper & Row, 1987), p. 118.

21. "'I Want to Stay the Course'" (Interview with M. S. Gorbachev), *Time*, December 23, 1994, p. 14; Anders Åslund, "Russia's Road from Communism," *Daedalus*, vol. 121 (Spring 1992), pp. 78–79.

22. The term sovereignty assumed a meaning closer to that of autonomy than to that of independence in Russian language usage during these years.

23. Juan J. Linz and Alfred Stepan, "Political Identities and Electoral Sequences: Spain, the Soviet Union, and Yugoslavia," *Daedalus*, vol. 121 (Spring 1992), pp. 123–39.

24. Åslund, *Gorbachev's Struggle for Economic Reform*, pp. 212–14.

25. This section is primarily based on Åslund, *Gorbachev's Struggle for Economic Reform*, pp. 204–14.

26. Goskomstat SSSR, *Narodnoe khozyaistvo SSSR v 1990 g.* (The national economy of the USSR in 1990) (Moscow: Finansy i statistika, 1991), p. 7.

27. Grigory Yavlinsky, Aleksei Mikhailov, and Mikhail Zadornov, "A Concept

of the Transition of the Economy of the USSR to the Market," *Delovoi mir*, July 31, 1990.

28. *Perekhod k Rynku: Kontseptsiya i Programma* (Transition to the market: conception and program) (Moscow: Arkhangelskoe, August 1990), p. 235. Except for Yasin, all these economists were young; almost all were in their 30s.

29. Roman Frydman, Andrzej Rapaczynski, John S. Earle and others, *The Privatization Process in Russia, Ukraine and the Baltic States* (Central European University, 1993), pp. 26–30.

30. " 'I Want to Stay the Course' " (Interview with M. S. Gorbachev), *Time*, December 23, 1991, p. 14.

31. Ibid.

32. Joint Working Group on Western Cooperation in the Soviet Transformation to Democracy and the Market Economy, *Window of Opportunity: The Grand Bargain for Democracy in the Soviet Union* (Pantheon Books, 1991).

33. Personal observations in Moscow in early 1990.

34. Anders Åslund, "How Small Is Soviet National Income?," in Henry S. Rowen and Charles Wolf, Jr., eds., *The Impoverished Superpower: Perestroika and the Soviet Military Burden* (Institute for Contemporary Studies, 1990), pp. 43–45.

35. UN Economic Commission for Europe, *Economic Survey of Europe in 1991–1992* (United Nations, 1992), p. 105. Soviet statistics for 1991 are extremely shaky; and because the country ceased to exist before the year ended, little can be done to improve the statistics.

36. Compare David Lipton and Jeffrey D. Sachs, "Prospects for Russia's Economic Reforms," *Brookings Papers on Economic Activity*, 2:1992, pp. 216–19.

37. Goskomstat SSSR, *Narodnoe khozyaistvo SSSR v 1989 g.*, p. 11.

38. A number of alternative assessments have been made by the CIA and the World Bank, among others. However, significant discrepancies remain, especially with regard to the military.

39. Goskomstat SSSR, *Narodnoe khozyaistvo SSSR v 1989 g.*, pp. 688–91.

40. Ibid., p. 695.

41. The ten CMEA countries were Bulgaria, Cuba, Czechoslovakia, the German Democratic Republic, Hungary, Mongolia, Poland, Romania, the Soviet Union, and Vietnam.

42. Richard E. Baldwin, *The Potential for Trade Between the Countries of EFTA and Central and Eastern Europe*, Occasional Paper 44 (Geneva: European Free Trade Association, June 1993), pp. 10–27.

43. It is possible that this decline is exaggerated, because the prices in CMEA trade were artificial and inflated. However, the decline was substantial in any case.

44. Åslund, *Gorbachev's Struggle for Economic Reform*, pp. 187–98.

45. M. S. Gorbachev, "To Strengthen the Key Link in the Economy," *Pravda*, December 10, 1990.

46. UN Economic Commission for Europe, *Economic Survey of Europe in 1992–1993* (United Nations, 1993), p. 289.

Chapter Three

1. Boris N. Yeltsin, trans. Catherine A. Fitzpatrick, *The Struggle for Russia* (Times Books, 1994), pp. 105–06.

2. "Communique of the Central Commission of the All-Russian Referendum on the Results of the Referendum, Taking Place on April 25, 1993," *Rossiiskaya gazeta*, May 6, 1993.

3. Yeltsin, *The Struggle for Russia*, p. 115.

4. Ibid., pp. 35–36.

5. Ibid., p. 113.

6. "B. N. Yeltsin's Speech," *Sovetskaya Rossiya*, October 29, 1991.

7. Adam Przeworski, *Democracy and the Market: Political and Economic Reforms in Eastern Europe and Latin America* (Cambridge University Press, 1991), p. 87.

8. Keith Bush, "El'tsin's Economic Reform Program," *Report on the USSR*, November 15, 1991, p. 1.

9. "B. N. Yeltsin's Speech."

10. Ibid.

11. Expert Institute, Russian Union of Industrialists and Entrepreneurs. "Russian Reform: The First Step," mimeo, Moscow, January 1992, p. 6.

12. Ibid., pp. 88–89.

13. Yeltsin, *The Struggle for Russia*, pp. 126–27.

14. "Decree on Reorganization of the Government of the RSFSR," November 6, 1991, *Izvestiya*, November 7, 1991.

15. "Decree on the Organization of the Work of the Government of the RSFSR Under the Conditions of Economic Reform," November 6, 1991, *Ekonomika i zhizn'*, no. 48, November 1991, Enclosure, p. 3.

16. "B. N. Yeltsin's Speech."

17. Ibid.

18. Yeltsin, *The Struggle for Russia*, p. 127.

19. Richard Pipes, *The Russian Revolution* (Vintage Books, 1991), pp. 298–300, 320–23.

20. Yeltsin, *The Struggle for Russia*, p. 129.

21. Ibid., p. 127.

22. "I dislike the style of the IMF bureaucracy and its Moscow buddies. They do not look like promoters of free market democracy and civilized principles of international relations. They resemble neo-Bolsheviks who love expropriating other people's money, imposing undemocratic, alien rules and stifling economic freedom [sic]." Georgi A. Arbatov, "A Neo-Bolshevik Brand of Capitalism," *International Herald Tribune*, May 12, 1992; Arkady Volsky in *International Herald Tribune*, January 31, 1994.

23. "B. N. Yeltsin's Speech."

24. Yeltsin, *The Struggle for Russia*, p. 145.

25. Ibid., p. 147.

26. "B. N. Yeltsin's Speech."

27. Yeltsin, *The Struggle for Russia,* p. 146.

28. Ibid., p. 200.

29. Ibid., p. 150.

30. Ibid., p. 149.

31. Keith Bush, "Russia: Gaidar's Guidelines," *RFE/RL [Radio Free Europe/ Radio Library] Research Report,* vol. 1, April 10, 1992, p. 22.

32. Pravitel'stvo RSFSR, Postanovlenie ot 19 noyabrya 1991 g. "Ob organizatsii raboty po podgotovke proektov pervoocherednykh normativynykh aktov, neobkhodimyckh dlya osushchestvleniya radikalnoi ekonomicheskoi reformy" ("RSFSR Government, Decree of November 19, 1991, on the Organization of the Work on the Preparation of Drafts of Priority Legislative Acts, Necessary for the Implementation of Radical Economic Reform"), mimeo.

33. "Memorandum of Russia's Government," *Nezavisimaya gazeta,* March 3, 1992; Bush, "Russia: Gaidar's Guidelines," p. 22.

34. "B. N. Yeltsin's Speech."

35. Ibid.

36. Marek Dabrowski, "Debate on the Guidelines of Russian Economic Reform at the End of 1991 and in 1992," in Marek Dabrowski, ed., *Program Gajdara: Wnioski dla Polski i Europy Wschodniej.* (The Gaidar programme: lessons for Poland and Eastern Europe) (Warsawa: Fundacja Friedricha Eberta and Centrum Analiz Spoleczno-Ekonomicznych, 1993), pp. 36–46.

37. Egor T. Gaidar, "Inflationary Pressures and Economic Reform in the Soviet Union," in P. H. Admiraal, ed., *Economic Transition in Eastern Europe* (Oxford: Blackwell, 1993), pp. 82–90.

38. Marek Dabrowski, "The First Half-Year of Russian Transformation," in Anders Åslund and Richard Layard, eds., *Changing the Economic System in Russia* (St. Martin's Press, 1993), pp. 7–9; Jeffrey Sachs, "Goodwill Is Not Enough," *The Economist,* December 21, 1991, pp. 101–04. At a meeting between Yeltsin, Burbulis, Gaidar, and seven foreign economic advisors on December 11, 1991, Jeffrey Sachs spoke on behalf of the foreign advisors. He focused on four points: 1. It was necessary to reinforce the Central Bank and monetary policies. 2. There was a need for a substantial domestic oil tax. 3. Russia could become a world leader on privatization and should give 25 percent of the shares to the workers immediately. 4. It would be possible to mobilize $15–20 billion per year in international financial support. (Personal notes)

39. "B. N. Yeltsin's Speech."

40. Ibid.

41. Ibid.

42. Gaidar, "Inflationary Pressures and Economic Reform in the Soviet Union," p. 84.

43. "B. N. Yeltsin's Speech."

44. Yegor Gaidar, "The Race With the Crisis," *Novoye vremya,* no. 48 (November 1991).

45. Ibid.

46. Personal conversations with Gaidar in December 1991.

47. "B. N. Yeltsin's Speech."

48. Georgy G. Matyukhin, *Ya byl glavnym bankirom Rossii* (I was Russia's main banker) (Moscow: Vysshaya shkola, 1993), p. 69.

49. Yegor Gaidar, "The Race with the Crisis," *Novoye vremya*, no. 48 (November 1991), p. 12.

50. "B. N. Yeltsin's Speech."

51. "Gaydar Reports on Meeting," Moscow Television, 2120 GMT, December 28, 1991, in Foreign Broadcast Information, *Daily Report: Soviet Union*, December 30, 1991, p. 40. (Hereafter FBIS, *Soviet Union*).

52. Yegor Gaidar, "The Race with the Crisis," *Novoye vremya*, no. 48 (November 1991).

53. Personal conversation in December 1991.

54. "Memorandum of the Government of Russia," *Nezavisimaya gazeta*, March 3, 1992.

55. "B. N. Yeltsin's Speech."

56. Ibid.

57. Ibid.

58. Ibid.

59. "Gaydar Reports on Meeting," Moscow Television, 2120 GMT, December 28, 1991, in FBIS, *Soviet Union*, December 30, 1991, p. 41.

60. Personal conversation with Gaidar in December 1991.

61. "B. N. Yeltsin's Speech."

62. Yeltsin, *The Struggle for Russia*, p. 148.

63. Ibid., p. 124.

64. "I realized that a person of his type could no longer remain prime minister." Ibid., p. 124.

65. Sergei Chugaev, "Who Enters the Russian Reform Government," *Izvestiya*, November 5, 1991; personal investigation in Moscow.

66. Yeltsin, *The Struggle for Russia*, pp. 172–73.

67. "Stsenarii ekonomicheskoi reformy. Avgust-dekabr' 1991 goda. Privatizatsiya i razgosudarstvlenie ekonomiki" (Scenario of economic reform, August–December 1991: privatization and destatization of the economy), mimeo, Moscow, August 1991, 54 pp.

68. Yeltsin, *The Struggle for Russia*, p. 126.

69. Yegor T. Gaidar, *Ekonomicheskie reformy i ierarkhicheskie struktury* (Economic reforms and hierarchical structures) (Moscow: Nauka, 1990); Gaidar, "Inflationary Pressures and Economic Reform in the Soviet Union," pp. 63–90; Yegor Gaidar, "At the Beginning of a New Phase," *Kommunist*, no. 2 (January 1991), pp. 8–19.

70. Yeltsin, *The Struggle for Russia*, pp. 125–26.

71. Ibid., pp. 125, 155–56.

72. Ibid., pp. 156–57.

73. The outstanding exception was Professor Yevgeny Yasin.

74. I have reviewed this debate more briefly in Anders Åslund, "The Gradual Nature of Economic Change in Russia," in Åslund and Layard, eds., *Changing*

the Economic System in Russia, pp. 19–38. The discussion on privatization has been put into chapter 7.

75. Nikolai Petrakov, "The Crisis of Economic Reform in Russia," *Voprosy ekonomiki,* no. 2 (February 1993), pp. 64–65.

76. Ibid.

77. Leonid Abalkin, "Economic Reform: Results and Perspectives," *Ekonomicheskaya gazeta,* no. 21, May 1992. When I hosted a seminar with Ruslan Khasbulatov at the Stockholm School of Economics in May 1990, he was asked about the monetary overhang in the Soviet Union. Khasbulatov could not understand that more money could be a problem, because that would mean that everyone was richer and more could be produced.

78. "Prices, Money, Credits" (Interview with Viktor Gerashchenko), *Ekonomika i zhizn',* no. 46, November 1992.

79. British Broadcasting Corporation (BBC), *Survey of World Broadcasts,* SU/ 1477 C4/2.

80. Yury Yaremenko and others, "Is It Necessary to Let the Prices of Fuel Free?", *Nezavisimaya gazeta,* April 1, 1992.

81. Ibid.

82. Ibid.

83. Irina Demchenko, "As Long As There Is No Oil Price, Any Economic Forecast Is Uncertain," *Izvestiya,* March 16, 1992.

84. "Nobody Stands Behind Me; My Profession is Banker" (Interview with Viktor Gerashchenko), *Literaturnaya gazeta,* September 2, 1992.

85. Viktor Gerashchenko, "The Reform Is Not a Horse; It Cannot Drag Itself Out," *Rossiiskaya gazeta,* April 24, 1993.

86. Viktor Gerashchenko, "A Realistic Approach Is Missing," *Rossiiskaya gazeta,* April 2, 1993.

87. Aleksandr Rutskoi, "Is There a Way Out of the Crisis?", *Pravda,* February 8, 1992.

88. Nikolai Petrakov and others, "The Government Has Lost Control Over the Economic Processes," *Nezavisimaya gazeta,* March 6, 1992.

89. Leonid Abalkin, "Reflections on the Strategy and Tactics of Economic Reform," *Voprosy ekonomiki,* no. 2 (February 1993), p. 6.

90. Oleg Bogomolov, "There Is Neither Time, Nor Effective Power," *Nezavisimaya gazeta,* February 7, 1992.

91. Nikolai Fedorenko and others, "The Storm of Market Redoubts Does Not Succeed So Far," *Izvestiya,* March 18, 1992.

92. Petrakov and others, "The Government Has Lost Control Over the Economic Processes."

93. Rutskoi, "Is There a Way Out of the Crisis?"

94. Ibid.

95. Ibid.

96. Ibid.

97. Ibid.

98. Fedorenko and others, "The Storm of Market Redoubts Does Not Succeed So Far."

99. Abalkin, "Economic Reform: Results and Perspectives."

100. Georgy Arbatov, "'Gaidarism' Is a Reaction to Own Marxism," *Nezavisimaya gazeta,* March 13, 1992.

101. Petrakov and others, "The Government Has Lost Control Over the Economic Processes."

102. Fedorenko and others, "The Storm of Market Redoubts Does Not Succeed So Far."

103. Petrakov and others, "The Government Has Lost Control Over the Economic Processes"; Bogomolov, "There Is Neither Time, Nor Effective Power"; Oleg Bogomolov, "Is Russia Threatened with Hyperinflation?", *Cato Journal,* vol. 12 (Winter 1993), p. 596. In this they received ample support from Steve H. Hanke and Kurt Schuler, who in a multitude of publications argued that only a currency board was important, also dreaming the financial issues away. Steve H. Hanke and Kurt Schuler, "Currency Boards and Currency Convertibility," *Cato Journal,* vol. 12 (Winter 1993), pp. 687–705.

104. "Program for Khasbulatov," *Nezavisimaya gazeta,* April 3, 1992.

105. "Ruslan Khasbulatov Does Not Believe in IMF Assistance," *Izvestiya,* April 4, 1992.

106. Abalkin, "Reflections on the Strategy and Tactics of Economic Reform," p. 5.

107. Ibid., p. 7.

108. Sergei Parkhomenko, "Volsky Creates A Party of Pragmatists," *Nezavisimaya gazeta,* May 13, 1992.

109. "Thirteen Points of Volsky's Program," *Izvestiya,* September 30, 1992.

110. Arkady Volsky, "To Defend State Industry," *Ekonomicheskaya gazeta,* November 1992.

111. "Program for Khasbulatov," *Nezavisimaya gazeta,* April 3, 1992.

112. Vladimir Ispravnikov, "Is Any Way Out of the Dead End to Be Seen?", *Voprosy ekonomiki,* no. 2 (February 1993), p. 36; Vladimir Ispravnikov and others, "Does the Government Take the View of the Computer Into Account?", *Izvestiya,* March 26, 1992.

113. Nikolai Petrakov, "Monetary Stabilization in Russia: What Is to Be Done?", *Cato Journal,* vol. 12 (Winter 1993), p. 608.

114. See the section on social costs in chapter 6.

115. Larisa Piyasheva, "Confessions of the Economic Commissar to the President of the Republic," *Moskovskie novosti,* no. 5, February 2, 1992.

116. "MN Founders Divided Over Yavlinsky's Reform Assessments," *Moscow News,* no. 22, 1992.

117. Georgy Arbatov, "Where Did the Money Go?", *Nezavisimaya gazeta,* April 3, 1992.

118. "Gaydar Reports on Meeting," Moscow Television, 2120 GMT, December 28, 1991, in FBIS, *Soviet Union,* pp. 39–40.

119. Ibid.

120. Quite a few Western conservatives were persuaded by the reform communists on these points. See Paul Craig Roberts, "Russia's Informal Revolution," *Cato Journal,* vol. 12 (Winter 1993), p. 603: "Oleg Bogomolov . . . reports, again

correctly, that prior to price liberalization, property should have been privatized, monopolistic structures demolished." Judy Shelton, "What Went Wrong?", *Cato Journal*, vol. 12 (Winter 1993), p. 617: "Lest anyone be tempted to categorize Petrakov among those political hardliners in Russia today who are opposed to free markets and democratic reform in general, it is important to point out that Petrakov chose to resign his post as Gorbachev's chief economic adviser in January 1991. . . . Petrakov's most stinging criticism of the Gaidar program is that prices were 'freed' in the absence of meaningful competition."

121. Abalkin, "Reflections on the Strategy and Tactics of Economic Reform," p. 5; Ispravnikov, "Is Any Way Out of the Dead End to Be Seen?", p. 36.

122. Petrakov and others, "The Government Has Lost Control Over the Economic Processes."

123. "Program for Khasbulatov."

124. Arbatov, " 'Gaidarism' Is a Reaction to Own Marxism"; Petrakov, "The Crisis of Economic Reform in Russia," pp. 67–68; Petrakov, "Monetary Stabilization in Russia: What Is To Be Done?", pp. 608–09.

125. Vladimir Kotov, "Russia's Road to the Market: Victory or Defeat?", *Nezavisimaya gazeta*, March 13, 1992; Yefrem Maiminas, "Alternative—Beyond the Borders of the Market," *Nezavisimaya gazeta*, March 19, 1992; Aleksei Ulyukaev, "About 'the Advice From Outsiders'," *Nezavisimaya gazeta*, March 27, 1992; Konstantin Gofman, "To Reestablish State Control Is Possible Only With Terror," *Nezavisimaya gazeta*, March 27, 1992; Mikhail Lantsman, "Khasbulatov's Program Is Oriented to Hyperinflation," *Nezavisimaya gazeta*, April 4, 1992; Aleksei Ulyukaev, "The Steps of Reform: A Spring Account," *Moskovskie novosti*, April 12, 1992; Sergei Vasil'ev, "Structural Crisis—A Preparation to Growth," *Nezavisimaya gazeta*, May 27, 1992; Mikhail Leont'ev, "The Stabilization of Production on the Corps of the Financial System," *Izvestiya*, July 23, 1992.

126. Boris L'vin, "How to Make Revolution," *Nezavisimaya gazeta*, March 10, 1992; Vitaly Naishul', "Perspectives of Liberal Reforms," *Nezavisimaya gazeta*, October 21, 1992; Vitaly Naishul', "Economic Reforms: A Liberal Perspective," in Anders Åslund, ed., *Economic Transformation in Russia* (St. Martin's Press, 1994), pp. 174–81.

127. "Spring '92 Reforms in Russia," *Moscow News*, no. 21, 1992, and no. 22, 1992.

128. Expert Institute, Russian Union of Industrialists and Entrepreneurs, "Russian Reform: The First Step," pp. 1–49.

129. Rudiger Dornbusch and Sebastian Edwards, "The Macroeconomics of Populism," in Rudiger Dornbusch and Sebastian Edwards, eds., *The Macroeconomics of Populism in Latin America* (University of Chicago Press, 1991), pp. 9–10.

130. Russian Academy of Sciences, Economic Department and the International Fund "Reform," "Sotsial'no-ekonomicheskie preobrazovaniya v Rossii: Sovremennaya situatsiya i novye podkhody" (Social-economic transformation in Russia: The contemporary situation and new approaches), mimeo (Moscow, January 1994), pp. 1–32.

131. Yeltsin, *The Struggle for Russia*, p. 156.

132. Ibid., p. 152.

133. Ibid., pp. 157, 159–60.

134. John Lloyd and Leyla Boulton, "Yeltsin's Deputy Quits as Shake-up Continues," *Financial Times*, April 4–5, 1992, p. 2.

135. Yeltsin, *The Struggle for Russia*, p. 159.

136. Expert Institute, Russian Union of Industrialists and Entrepreneurs, "Russian Reform: The First Step," p. 7.

137. Yeltsin, *The Struggle for Russia*, p. 158.

138. "Gaydar Reports on Meeting," Moscow Television, 2120 GMT, December 28, 1991, in FBIS, *Soviet Union*, December 30, 1991, p. 39. Possibly Gaidar wanted to distance himself from his competitor Yavlinsky, who was an outstanding publicizer; the 500-day program had certainly been a publicity success.

139. Expert Institute, Russian Union of Industrialists and Entrepreneurs, "Russian Reform: The First Step," pp. 8–9.

140. Ibid., p. 7.

141. "Viktor Chernomyrdin's Cabinet," *Izvestiya*, December 24, 1992.

142. Yeltsin, *The Struggle for Russia*, p. 157.

143. Personal experience in February 1994.

144. Yeltsin, *The Struggle for Russia*, p. 129.

145. Mancur Olson, *The Logic of Collective Action: Public Goods and the Theory of Groups* (Harvard University Press, 1965), p. 143.

146. Although political advice was not the task of foreign economic advisors, we did provide ample suggestions, which received little attention because the economic politicians we talked to were moderately interested in politics. Jeffrey Sachs and I emphasized the need for a democratic base of reform and early parliamentary elections. As Sachs said in June 1991: "The successful transformation of the socialist economies, whether in Eastern Europe or in the Soviet Union, has to be based on three fundamental factors. The first is political democratization." (Jeffrey Sachs, "The Grand Bargain," in Anders Åslund, ed., *The Post-Soviet Economy: Soviet and Western Perspectives* [St. Martin's Press, 1992], p. 209). Marek Dabrowski emphasized: "First, it is important to make optimum use of the 'political credit' and time given to the reform government to go as far as possible in reform policy. This amount of political credit is only available to the first really postcommunist government, and it lasts for a limited time only. This necessitates shock therapy rather than a gradualist approach. Second, the Polish experience shows that most of the painful decisions should be built into the initial decisive stabilization and liberalization package." Dabrowski, "The First Half-Year of Russian Transformation," p. 14. A favorite topic of mine was the need for public education. Gaidar accepted this and tried to do quite a bit, but it was far from enough.

147. Yeltsin, *The Struggle for Russia*, p. 154.

148. John Lloyd, "Power Battle 'May Destroy' Russian Reform Plans," *Financial Times*, January 16, 1992, p. 1.

149. John Lloyd, "Yeltsin Deputy Attacks Government," *Financial Times*, December 19, 1991, p. 1.

150. Yeltsin, *The Struggle for Russia,* p. 127.

151. Ibid., p. 165.

152. Yeltsin explains his sacking of Lopukhin thus: "So if some middle-aged industrialist comes to me and says in a worried voice, 'Boris Nikolayevich, I have worked for forty years in the petroleum industry. What is your Lopukhin doing? . . . everything's going to hell in a handbasket,' of course I lose my patience. I feel I have to make some changes." Yeltsin, *The Struggle for Russia,* p. 168.

153. Ibid., p. 168.

154. Ibid., pp. 165–69; Mikhail Leont'ev, "Russian Reform: the Beginning of Agony? Yeltsin Has Started Taking Apart the Gaidar Team," *Nezavisimaya gazeta,* June 2, 1992.

155. Yeltsin, *The Struggle for Russia,* pp. 172–73.

156. Ibid., p. 198.

157. Ibid., pp. 31, 168, 173, 199.

158. Ibid., p. 174.

159. The main protagonist of this argument was Vladimir Mau who was a political advisor to Gaidar. See his comments on David Lipton and Jeffrey D. Sachs, "Prospects for Russia's Economic Reforms," *Brookings Papers on Economic Activity,* 2:1992, pp. 268–69.

160. "Decree on Measures to Stabilize the Economy of the Agroindustrial Complex," *Rossiiskaya gazeta,* April 7, 1992.

161. Pyotr Varov, "Parliament Outmaneuvers Russia's Government," *Kommersant,* November 25, 1991.

162. Matyukhin, *Ya byl glavnym bankirom Rossii,* pp. 52–70.

163. Ibid.

164. In hindsight, Gaidar thought that it would have been better to try to support Matyukhin, while he still saw no possibility to get Fedorov approved by the Supreme Soviet. (Personal conversation in March 1993)

165. Aleksei Zuichenko, "Russia's Parliament Is About to 'Correct' Reform," *Nezavisimaya gazeta,* April 3, 1992; "Appointment," *Moskovskie novosti,* no. 15, April 12, 1992.

166. Admittedly, Gaidar had also appointed a young reform economist, Andrei Vavilov, first deputy minister of finance as his own man at the ministry of finance.

167. Aleksei Kiva, "It Would Be Good Not to Forget About the Experiences of Others: Realism Is the Only Policy That Stands," *Nezavisimaya gazeta,* February 1, 1992.

Chapter Four

1. Armenia, Azerbaijan, Belarus, Kazakhstan, Kyrgyzstan, Moldova, Russia, Tajikistan, Turkmenistan, Ukraine, and Uzbekistan.

2. The CIS treaty was subject to ratification by the parliaments of the countries concerned. Azerbaijan's parliament initially failed to ratify the CIS treaty, and the country in effect fell out of the CIS for a while. However, after a change of

rule in Azerbaijan in 1993 and substantial losses in the war with Armenia, Azerbaijan ratified the CIS treaty in the fall of 1993.

3. Georgia joined after a serious war with secessionists over the autonomous republic of Abkhazia from Georgia, which was won by the secessionists in September 1993 because of support from at least parts of the Russian military.

4. "Declaration of the Governments of the Republic of Belarus, the Russian Federation and Ukraine on Coordination of Economic Policy," *Rossiiskaya gazeta*, December 10, 1991.

5. Aleksei Portansky, "Russia Starts Selling Debts of Third Countries," *Izvestiya*, July 2, 1994.

6. Statement by Grigory Yavlinsky as head of the Soviet delegation to the IMF and World Bank annual meeting in Bangkok in September 1991 (Stephen Fidler and others, "G7 Agrees to Relieve Moscow's Debt Crisis," *Financial Times*, October 15, 1991, p. 1; Kenneth Gooding, "Soviet Revelations Boost Gold Price," *Financial Times*, October 1, 1991, p. 36).

7. "Decree of the Council of Ministers—Government of the Russian Federation on the Signing with States—Republics of the Former USSR of Agreements on the Regulation of Questions of Legal Succession With Regard to the Foreign State Debt and Assets of the Former USSR," *Rossiiskaya gazeta*, May 28, 1993.

8. This section draws heavily on the following: Jeffrey Sachs and David Lipton. "Remaining Steps to a Market-Based Monetary System in Russia," in Anders Åslund and Richard Layard, eds., *Changing the Economic System in Russia* (St. Martin's Press, 1993), pp. 127–62; Brigitte Granville, "So Farewell Then Rouble Zone," in Anders Åslund, ed., *Russian Economic Reform at Risk* (London: Pinter, forthcoming); International Monetary Fund, *Economic Review: Financial Relations Among Countries of the Former Soviet Union* (International Monetary Fund, February 1994); International Monetary Fund, *Economic Review: Trade Policy Reform in Countries of the Former Soviet Union* (International Monetary Fund, 1994); Anders Åslund, "The Nature of the Transformation Crisis in the Former Soviet Countries," in Horst Siebert, ed., *Overcoming the Transformation Crisis: Lessons for the Successor States of the Soviet Union* (Tübingen: J.C.B. Mohr, 1993), pp. 39–56.

9. Milton Friedman, *Money Mischief: Episodes in Monetary History* (Harcourt Brace Jovanovich, 1992), p. 242, quoted in Jeffrey Sachs and David Lipton, "Remaining Steps to a Market-Based Monetary System in Russia," p. 128.

10. International Monetary Fund, *Economic Review: Financial Relations Among Countries of the Former Soviet Union*, p. 9; Benedicte Vibe Christensen, *The Russian Federation in Transition: External Developments*, Occasional Paper 111 (International Monetary Fund, February 1994), p. 33.

11. Sachs and Lipton, "Remaining Steps to a Market-Based Monetary System in Russia," p. 128.

12. Anders Bornefalk, "The Ruble Zone: A Case of Irrationality?" Working Paper 90, Stockholm Institute of East European Economics, August 1994.

13. Sachs and Lipton, "Remaining Steps to a Market-Based Monetary System in Russia," p. 127.

14. David Lipton and Jeffrey D. Sachs, "Prospects for Russia's Economic

Reforms," *Brookings Papers on Economic Activity,* no. 2, 1992, p. 237 (emphasis in original).

15. Ivan Zhagel', "Russia Tightens Monetary Policy," *Izvestiya,* May 25, 1992.

16. [International Monetary Fund], "The Coordination of Monetary Policy in the Ruble Area," mimeo, April 29, 1992, p. 4.

17. [International Monetary Fund], "Guidelines for the Conduct of Monetary Policy in the Ruble Area," mimeo, April 29, 1992, p. 3.

18. [International Monetary Fund], "The Coordination of Monetary Policy in the Ruble Area," mimeo, April 29, 1992, p. 5.

19. It was presented by John Odling-Smee, head of the Second European Department of the IMF at the meeting in Tashkent. Strangely, Ernesto Hernández-Catá states: "The Fund has never opposed the introduction of national currencies in the FSU." But somewhat contradictorily he admits in the same paragraph: "The views of the IMF have evolved gradually toward a recognition that the introduction of independent currencies in most, if not all, the countries of the Former Soviet Union (FSU) is probably inevitable and may well be in the interest of all the countries involved." He tries to justify the Tashkent proposal with political expediency: "The IMF staff did propose guidelines for the conduct of monetary policy in the ruble area, at the May 1992 meeting of central bank governors in Tashkent, Uzbekistan. But it did so because, with the exception of the Baltic countries and Ukraine, most FSU states appeared to favor the ruble area option." (Ernesto Hernández-Catá, "The Introduction of National Currencies in the Former Soviet Union: Options, Policy Requirements and Early Experiences," mimeo, International Monetary Fund, June 24, 1993, p. 2.) As late as May 22, 1993, John Lloyd, the well-informed Moscow bureau chief of the *Financial Times,* reported that the IMF had "changed its position of encouraging the former Soviet states to remain in the rouble zone" in connection with the currency reform in Kyrgyzstan on May 15, 1993. (John Lloyd, "Most CIS States to Get Own Currencies," *Financial Times,* May 22–23, 1993, p. 2.)

20. Lipton and Sachs, "Prospects for Russia's Economic Reforms," pp. 236–39; Ivan Zhagel', "Russia Tightens Monetary Policy," *Izvestiya,* May 25, 1992.

21. "The CIS on the Maastricht Road?" *Ekonomicheskaya gazeta,* no. 51, December 1992.

22. Jozef M. van Brabant, "Convertibility in Eastern Europe Through a Payments Union," in John Williamson, ed., *Currency Convertibility in Eastern Europe* (Institute for International Economics, September 1991), pp. 63–95; Oleh Havrylyshyn and John Williamson, *From Soviet disUnion to Eastern Economic Community* (Institute for International Economics, October, 1991), pp. 53–60; John Williamson, *Trade and Payments After Soviet Disintegration* (Institute for International Economics, June 1992), pp. 29–31; Daniel Gros, "A Multilateral Payments Mechanism for the Former Republics of the Soviet Union and Eastern Europe," in Daniel Gros, Jean Pisani-Ferry, and André Sapir, eds., *Inter-State Economic Relations in the Former Soviet Union* (Centre for European Policy Studies, 1992) Working Document no. 63, pp. 41–47; Rudiger Dornbusch, "A Payments Mechanism for the Soviet Union and Eastern Europe," in Gros, Pisani-Ferry and Sapir, eds., *Inter-State Economic Relations in the Former Soviet Union,*

pp. 31–40; Rudiger Dornbusch, "Payments Arrangements Among the Republics," in Olivier Blanchard and others, *Post-Communist Reform: Pain and Progress* (MIT Press, 1993), pp. 81–108.

23. Williamson, *Trade and Payments After Soviet Disintegration*, p. 29.

24. Some of the arguments against payments union were provided early on with regard to Eastern Europe by Peter B. Kenen, "Transitional Arrangements for Trade and Payments among the CMEA Countries," *IMF Staff Papers*, vol. 38, no. 2 (June 1991), pp. 235–67. See also Zdenek Drabek, "Convertibility or a Payments Union? Convertibility!", in John Flemming and J.M.C. Rollo, eds., *Trade, Payments and Adjustment in Central and Eastern Europe* (Royal Institute of International Affairs, 1992), pp. 57–74. A full-fledged refutal of a payments union for the FSU was presented by Holger Schmieding, *No Need for a Monetary Halfway House: Lessons From the European Payments Union for Post-Soviet Currency Arrangements*. Kiel Discussion Paper, no. 189 (August 1992). A broader criticism is offered by Barry Eichengreen, "A Payments Mechanism for the Former Soviet Union: Is the EPU a Relevant Precedent?," *Economic Policy*, no. 17, (October 1993), pp. 309–53. The general argument for fast convertibility early on in the transition from communism has been outlined by Andrew Berg and Jeffrey D. Sachs, "Structural Adjustment and International Trade in Eastern Europe: The Case of Poland," *Economic Policy*, no. 14 (April 1992), pp. 117–73.

25. C. Michalopoulos and D. Tarr, "Transitional Trade and Payments Arrangements for States of the Former USSR," mimeo (World Bank, June 1992), p. 10, cited in Granville, "So Farewell Then Rouble Zone," p. 4.

26. Jeffrey D. Sachs, *Poland's Jump to the Market Economy* (MIT Press, 1993), p. 52.

27. International Monetary Fund, *Economic Review: Financial Relations Among Countries of the Former Soviet Union*, p. 43.

28. Egor T. Gaidar, "Inflationary Pressures and Economic Reform in the Soviet Union," in P. H. Admiraal, *Economic Transition in Eastern Europe* (Oxford: Blackwell, 1993), p. 84.

29. Lipton and Sachs, "Prospects for Russia's Economic Reforms," p. 237.

30. Ardo H. Hansson, "The Trouble with the Ruble: Monetary Reform in the Former Soviet Union," in Åslund and Layard, *Changing the Economic System of Russia*, pp. 163–82.

31. I heard Rudiger Dornbusch making this point at an important seminar at the Central Economic-Mathematical Institute in Moscow in September 1991 (Rudiger Dornbusch, "Monetary Problems of Post-Communism: Lessons From the End of the Austro-Hungarian Empire," *Weltwirtschaftliches Archiv*, vol. 128, no. 3 (1992), pp. 391–424). Jeffrey Sachs made these points repeatedly with the Russian reform leaders, with reference to the following: Thomas J. Sargent, "The Ends of Four Big Inflations," in Thomas J. Sargent, *Rational Expectations and Inflation* (Harper & Row, 1986), pp. 95–97; Leo Pasvolsky, *Economic Nationalism of the Danubian States* (London: George Allen & Unwin, 1928), pp. 204–31.

32. Joakim Karlsson, "Former Soviet Republics: Widely Differing Performance," *Östekonomisk Rapport*, vol. 6, no. 6 (May 17, 1994), p. 3. The only FSRs that did not have hyperinflation in 1993 were the three Baltic countries,

Russia, and Kyrgyzstan. Tajikistan, Ukraine, Georgia, Turkmenistan, and Armenia had annual inflation rates ranging from 7,000 to 11,000 percent.

33. Hansson, "The Trouble with the Ruble: Monetary Reform in the Former Soviet Union," pp. 163–82.

34. Ardo H. Hansson and Jeffrey D. Sachs, "Monetary Institutions and Credible Stabilizations: A Comparison of Experiences in the Baltics." Mimeo. Paper presented at the conference on Central Banks in Eastern Europe and the Newly Independent States, University of Chicago Law School, April 22–23, 1994.

35. Hernández-Catá, "The Introduction of National Currencies in the Former Soviet Union: Options, Policy Requirements and Early Experiences," p. 8.

36. They were, notably, Jeffrey D. Sachs, Ardo Hansson, and Boris Pleskovic.

37. International Monetary Fund, *Economic Review: Financial Relations Among Countries of the Former Soviet Union*, p. 3.

38. BBC, *Summary of World Broadcasts: The Soviet Union*, February 17, 1992, pp. SU/1306 C2/6–7.

39. John Anderson, "Notes on Interrepublic Trade Agreements," Moscow, mimeo, February 24, 1992; International Monetary Fund, *Economic Review: Trade Policy Reform in the Countries of the Former Soviet Union* (International Monetary Fund, 1994), pp. 16–17; International Monetary Fund, *Economic Review: Financial Relations Among the Countries of the Former Soviet Union*, p. 11; Pavel Teplukhin and Tatyana Normak, "Trade Between States of the Former Soviet Union (FSU)," *Russian Economic Trends*, vol. 2, no. 4 (1993), pp. 88–91.

40. Goskomstat Rossii, *Sotsial'no-ekonomicheskoe polozhenie Rossii 1993 g.* (The socio-economic situation in Russia, 1993) (Moscow, 1994), p. 90.

41. International Monetary Fund, *Economic Review: Financial Relations Among Countries of the Former Soviet Union*, pp. 4, 33–34; Granville, "So Farewell Then Rouble Zone."

42. Georgy G. Matyukhin, *Ya byl glavnym bankirom Rossii* (I was the main banker in Russia) (Moscow: Vysshaya shkola, 1993), p. 58.

43. Most coupons circulated at par with the Russian ruble and only complemented them as cash. In Ukraine and Belarus, however, the national coupons were also meant to bar outsiders from local price-controlled produce. Until early 1993, the Belarusian coupon was worth more than the Russian ruble, although the Belarusian account ruble fell below the rate of the Russian account ruble in the fall of 1992. The Ukrainian coupon, which was introduced in January 1992, was initially worth more than Russian cash rubles, but because of excessive emission, its value soon fell below that of the Russian ruble.

44. Granville, "So Farewell Then Rouble Zone," p. 9.

45. "Decree of the President of the Russian Federation on Measures to Defend the Monetary System of the Russian Federation," *Rossiiskaya gazeta,* June 24, 1992.

46. Lipton and Sachs, "Prospects for Russia's Economic Reforms," pp. 240–41.

47. P. Filippov, V. Golubev, and G. Tal', "Gerashchenko Neglects Russia's Interests," *Izvestiya,* September 17, 1992.

48. Granville, "So Farewell Then Rouble Zone," p. 10; Brigitte Granville and Andrei Lushin, "The New Style Rouble Zone or the Old Soviet Union 'Revis-

ited'," Macroeconomic and Finance Unit, Russian Ministry of Finance, mimeo, October 15, 1993, pp. 1–2.

49. Personal observation during visit to Riga in August 1992 and conversation with the chairman of the Bank of Latvia, Einars Repse.

50. International Monetary Fund, *Economic Review: Financial Relations among Countries of the Former Soviet Union*, pp. 6, 34.

51. Daniel Gros, "Intra CIS Payments: The Interstate Bank Project: Its Genesis and Demise." Advisory Group on Interstate Economic Relations, mimeo, Brussels, June 1994; International Monetary Fund, *Economic Review: Financial Relations Among Countries of the Former Soviet Union*, pp. 5, 18–20, 35–37; Oleg Vyugin, Gerard Duchène, and Daniel Gros, "The Ruble Space Should Be Serviced by an Interstate Clearing Bank," *Izvestiya*, January 13, 1993; Macroeconomic and Finance Unit, Russian Ministry of Finance, "On the Establishment of an Interstate Bank for Trade between CIS States," mimeo, Moscow, July 19, 1993.

52. Boris Fedorov, "Russian Finances in 1993," *Voprosy ekonomiki*, no. 1, 1994, p. 56; International Monetary Fund, *Economic Review: Financial Relations Among Countries of the Former Soviet Union*, p. 12.

53. International Monetary Fund, *Economic Review: Financial Relations Among Countries of the Former Soviet Union*, p. 43.

54. Exceptions were made for Belarus, Turkmenistan, and Uzbekistan, which were relieved of interest. International Monetary Fund, *Economic Review: Financial Relations Among Countries of the Former Soviet Union*, p. 13.

55. Boris Fedorov, "An Illegal, Senseless and Harmful Action for Russia," *Izvestiya*, August 6, 1993; Andrei Illarionov, "How Much Does Friendship Cost? How the Central Bank Finances the Former Union Republics," *Izvestiya*, September 16, 1994; Sergei Dodzin and others, "Cash Transfers to Other Republics," Macroeconomic and Finance Unit, Russian Ministry of Finance, mimeo, August 4, 1993.

56. International Monetary Fund, *Economic Review: Financial Relations Among Countries of the Former Soviet Union*, pp. 37–39.

57. "Communication by the Central Bank of the Russian Federation," *Rossiiskaya gazeta*, July 27, 1993.

58. However, there were serious inconsistencies in the statistics presented by the CBR. Andrei Veselov, "The Central Bank Found about Three Trillion, but So Far Keeps Quiet about That," *Izvestiya*, September 14, 1993.

59. "Declaration by the Government of the Russian Federation," *Rossiiskaya gazeta*, July 27, 1993.

60. Georgia made its coupon the sole legal tender in August 1993. In September 1993, its monthly inflation was 53 percent and in October 102 percent. Turkmenistan introduced its manat on November 1, 1993, and its monthly inflation in November 1993 was 429 percent. The monetary reforms in Moldova and Azerbaijan were more gradual. Moldova had monthly inflation of 64 percent in September and 59 percent in December 1993. Azerbaijan had 59 percent inflation in December 1993. (Karlsson, "Former Soviet Republics: Widely Differing Performance," p. 3.)

61. Boris Yeltsin, *The Struggle for Russia* (Times Books, 1994), p. 219. Boris Fedorov denies having participated in a meeting mentioned by Yeltsin with Chernomyrdin and Gerashchenko, and he was evidently taken by surprise. (Boris

Fedorov, "An Illegal, Senseless and Harmful Action for Russia," *Izvestiya*, August 6, 1993.)

62. "The Problem With Cash Eliminated," *Nezavisimaya gazeta*, July 7, 1993.

63. Veselov, "The Central Bank Found about Three Trillion, But So Far Keeps Quiet about That," *Izvestiya*, September 14, 1993.

64. Boris Fedorov, "An Illegal, Senseless and Harmful Action for Russia," *Izvestiya*, August 6, 1993; "About the Decision of the Central Bank of Russia on the Exchange of Bank-Notes," *Segodnya*, August 6, 1993; Anders Åslund and others, "Destructive Results of the Central Bank Currency Action," Macroeconomic and Finance Unit, Russian Ministry of Finance, mimeo, July 26, 1993.

65. "Soglashenie o prakticheskikh merakh po sozdaniyu rublevoi zony novogo tipa" (Agreement on practical measures for the creation of a ruble zone of a new type), mimeo, Moscow, September 7, 1993.

66. "Central Asian Republics Join Russian Ruble Zone," *Kommersant*, August 4, 1993, pp. 6–7.

67. "Soglashenie ob ob"edinenii denezhnoi sistemy Respubliki Belarus' s denezhnoi sistemoi Rossiiskoi Federatsii" (Agreement on the Unification of the Monetary System of the Republic of Belarus with the Monetary System of the Russian Federation), mimeo, Moscow, September 8, 1993; "Soglashenie ob ob"edinenii denezhnoi sistemy Respubliki Uzbekistan s denezhnoi sistemoi Rossiiskoi Federatsii" (Agreement on the Unification of the Monetary System of the Republic of Uzbekistan with the Monetary System of the Russian Federation), mimeo, Moscow, September 17, 1993.

68. International Monetary Fund, *Economic Review: Financial Relations Among Countries of the Former Soviet Union*, pp. 45–47; Granville and Lushin, "The New Style Rouble Zone," pp. 5–7; Fedorov, "The Russian Finances in 1993," pp. 56–58; Steve Liesman, "Kazakhstan Threatens to Issue Own Money," *Moscow Times*, October 30, 1993, p. 12; Ivan Zhagel', "In the Zones of Ruble, Karbovanets and Manat: The Unification of the Monetary Systems of Russia and Kazakhstan Did not Take Place," *Izvestiya*, November 5, 1993; Aleksandr Shokhin, "We Have Adequate Answers to Threats to Make Russians Hostages in Near Abroad," *Izvestiya*, November 16, 1993.

69. Kazakhstan introduced its tenge on November 15, 1993, and recorded 56 percent inflation for that month. Uzbekistan started circulating its sum-coupon on November 16, 1993, and its inflation rate was 60 percent for that month. Armenia launched its dram on November 22, and the Armenian inflation rate that month was 438 percent. Tajikistan's monthly inflation reached 177 percent in December 1993. (Karlsson, "Former Soviet Republics: Widely Differing Performance," p. 3; International Monetary Fund, *Economic Review: Financial Relations Among Countries of the Former Soviet Union*, p. 7.)

70. Fedorov, "Russian Finances in 1993," p. 58.

71. The original signatories were Armenia, Belarus, Kazakhstan, Kyrgyzstan, Moldova, Russia, Tajikistan, and Uzbekistan. Azerbaijan joined later, and Turkmenistan became an associate member.

72. International Monetary Fund, *Economic Review: Financial Relations Among Countries of the Former Soviet Union*, p. 8.

73. "Agreement on the Order of the Unification of the Monetary System of the Republic of Belarus With the Monetary System of the Russian Federation and the Mechanism of the Functioning of the Common Monetary System," *Nezavisimaya gazeta*, January 25, 1994; "Zayavlenie glav pravitel'stv Rossiiskoi Federatsii i Respubliki Belarus' o predstoyashchem ob"edinenii denezhnoi sistemy Respubliki Belarus' s denezhnoi sistemoi Rossiiskoi Federatsii" (Declaration by the Heads of the Governments of the Russian Federation and the Republic of Belarus on the Impending Unification of the Monetary System of the Republic of Belarus With the Monetary System of the Russian Federation), mimeo, Moscow, January 5, 1994.

74. "The Constitution of the Russian Federation," *Izvestiya*, December 28, 1993.

75. "Der Rücktrittsbrief Gajdars an Jelzin," *Frankfurter Allgemeine Zeitung*, January 18, 1994; Ustina Markus, "The Russian-Belarusian Monetary Union," *Radio Free Europe/Radio Liberty Research Report*, vol. 3, no. 20 (May 20, 1994), p. 30.

76. Fedorov, "Russian Finances in 1993," pp. 58–59.

77. Markus, "The Russian-Belarusian Monetary Union," p. 31; Aleksandr Starikevich and Nikodim Dubalevich, "The Unification of the Monetary Systems Is Also Dangerous for Belarus," *Izvestiya*, March 11, 1994.

Chapter Five

1. This chapter is primarily based on legal texts, newspaper articles, and memoranda from our Macroeconomic and Finance Unit at the Russian Ministry of Finance.

2. "The State and Its Apparatus" (Interview with Vladimir Kvasov), *Rossiiskie vesti*, March 26, 1994.

3. Vincent Koen and Steven Phillips, *Price Liberalization in Russia: Behavior of Prices, Household Incomes, and Consumption During the First Year*, Occasional Paper no. 104, International Monetary Fund, Washington, D.C. (June 1993), pp. 2–3.

4. Maxim Boycko, "Price Decontrol: The Microeconomic Case for the 'Big Bang' Approach," *Oxford Review of Economic Policy*, vol. 7, no. 4 (Winter 1991), p. 36.

5. "Decree of the President of the RSFSR on Measures to Liberalize Prices," *Ekonomika i zhizn'*, special issue (December 1991), p. 2.

6. Koen and Phillips, pp. 2, 4.

7. "Decree on Measures to Liberalize Prices," *Ekonomika i zhizn'* (December 1991), p. 3.

8. Ibid.

9. Leyla Boulton, "Moscow Prepares for Backlash As Price Controls End," *Financial Times*, January 2, 1992, p. 1; John Lloyd, "Russians Shocked by Fourfold Price Rises," *Financial Times*, January 3, 1992, p. 1.

10. "Yegor Gaidar," *Rossiiskaya gazeta*, July 3, 1992.

11. The attitude toward the liberalization of primarily domestic but also for-

eign trade was probably the point of greatest divergence between the reform government and its foreign advisors, while there was general agreement on maximal price liberalization. All the foreign advisors advocated an instant and thorough liberalization of domestic trade, but few Russian reformers did so. The strongest proponent of free domestic trade was Gaidar's advisor Sergei Vasil'ev, now deputy minister of the economy, with responsibility for deregulation. Gaidar himself understood the need for the liberalization of both domestic and foreign trade, but he made substantial compromises. Although Boris Fedorov's ideals might have been slightly less liberal than Gaidar's, he was more resolute in pushing through liberalization in 1993. (Marek Dabrowski, "The First Half-Year of Russian Transformation," pp. 9–11; Anders Åslund, "The Gradual Nature of Economic Change in Russia," pp. 20–22, in Anders Åslund and Richard Layard, eds., *Changing the Economic System in Russia* [St. Martin's Press, 1993]).

12. (Russian government), *Programma uglubleniya ekonomicheskikh reform: Proekt* (Program for the Deepening of Economic Reforms: Draft), (Moscow, June 1992), pp. 52–54.

13. Ibid.

14. "Decree of the President of the Russian Federation on the Freedom of Trade," *Rossiiskaya gazeta*, February 1, 1992.

15. "Street Capitalism," *Economist*, April 25, 1992, p. 57; Vitaly Kolbasyuk, "In Moscow Starts a Trade Renaissance," *Nezavisimaya gazeta*, May 29, 1992.

16. "Decree of the President of the Russian Federation on Some Measures to Implement the Decree of the President of the Russian Federation 'On the Freedom of Trade'," *Rossiiskaya gazeta*, June 26, 1992.

17. Personal observations in Moscow during frequent visits. On the illegal organization of flower sales in Moscow, see Fedor Korov'ev and Bogdan Skabichevsky, "Kings and Carnations," *Nezavisimaya gazeta*, March 27, 1992.

18. Rustam Arifdzhanov, "The Moscow Trader Leaves the Street," *Izvestiya*, May 4, 1994.

19. L. Rozenova, "The Difficult Road of Free Prices," *Ekonomicheskaya gazeta*, no. 18 (May 1992).

20. Irina Demchenko, "The Government Tries to Regulate Prices, But Prices Are Capable of 'Deregulating' the Government," *Izvestiya*, January 10, 1993; Michael Dobbs, "Russia Rescinds Jan. 1 Price Controls," *International Herald Tribune*, January 19, 1993, p. 14.

21. Koen and Phillips, p. 10; meeting with L. Rozenova, Chairwoman of the State Price Committee, July 19, 1993.

22. "Decree of the Council of Ministers—Government of the Russian Federation on Powers of the Executive Organs of Krais, Oblasts and Federal Cities on Licensing Certain Kinds of Activities," *Rossiiskaya gazeta*, June 19, 1993; Viktor Belikov, "Licensing Is Being Introduced on Entrepreneurship," *Izvestiya*, November 13, 1992; Mikhail Berger, "Decree on the Expansion . . . of Corruption in the Localities," *Izvestiya*, June 3, 1993.

23. The main source of this section is Petr Aven, "Problems in Foreign Trade Regulation in the Russian Economic Reform," in Anders Åslund, ed., *Economic Transformation in Russia* (St. Martin's Press, 1994), pp. 80–93. Additional details

have been drawn from: International Monetary Fund, *Economic Review: Russian Federation* (Washington, D.C.: International Monetary Fund, June 1993), pp. 35–40; and International Monetary Fund, *Economic Review: Trade Policy Reform in the Countries of the Former Soviet Union* (Washington, D.C.: International Monetary Fund, February 1994), pp. 35–40. In accordance with Russian practice, in the following "foreign trade" means foreign trade outside of the CIS. Statistics and foreign trade regulation treat trade with the CIS as a separate category of "interstate trade" (see chapter 3).

24. Goskomstat Rossii, *Rossiiskaya Federatsiya v tsifrakh v 1992 godu* (The Russian Federation in numbers in 1992) (Moscow, 1993), pp. 31–32.

25. Sergei Glaz'ev, "There Are Forces Which Resist the Creation of Currency and Export Control," *Rossiiskaya gazeta,* June 25, 1993; "A Closed Economy Means a Backward Economy," *Finansovye izvestiya,* June 18, 1993; Sergei Glaz'ev, "Success Depends on the Utilization of the Competitive Advantages of Russian Enterprises," *Nezavisimaya gazeta,* September 9, 1993; "Foreign Economic Freedom Did Not Suit Everybody," *Finansovye izvestiya,* November 19, 1993; David A. Dyker, "Recentralization or Liberalization in Foreign Trade?", *Radio Free Europe/Radio Liberty (RFE/RL) Research Report,* vol. 2, no. 30, July 23, 1993, pp. 6–9.

26. Aven, "Problems in Foreign Trade Regulation in the Russian Economic Reform," pp. 88–89.

27. Tat'yana Koshkareva, "In Front of the Noses of the Russian Consumers an Iron Curtain Has Been Let Down," *Segodnya,* March 22, 1994.

28. International Monetary Fund, *Economic Review: Russian Federation,* pp. 132–33, 140; Macroeconomic and Finance Unit, Russian Ministry of Finance, "Centralized Imports: The Current System and Policy Alternatives," mimeo, Moscow, June 4, 1993, pp. 1–4.

29. Andrei Lushin, "Trade Policy Developments," mimeo, Macroeconomic and Finance Unit, Russian Ministry of Finance, Moscow, November 27, 1993, pp. 1–2.

30. Lushin, "Trade Policy Developments," Appendix 1.

31. "Decree of the Council of Ministers—Government of the Russian Federation on Measures to Liberalize Foreign Economic Activities," *Rossiiskaya gazeta,* November 11, 1993.

32. Dyker, pp. 6–9; Dmitry Kuznets, "The Government Intends to Liberalize Foreign Trade," *Segodnya,* April 20, 1994.

33. Aven, "Problems in Foreign Trade Regulation in the Russian Economy," p. 91.

34. Goskomstat Rossii, *Rossiiskaya Federatsiya v tsifrakh v 1992 godu* (The Russian Federation in numbers in 1992), pp. 38, 43, 46, 47. This is a compilation from different tables. The number of enterprises cited varies. They are increasingly divided, definitions vary, and ever more enterprises fall outside of statistics, but the point is how few they were at the outset of the reforms.

35. Anette N. Brown, Barry Ickes, and Randi Ryterman, "The Myth of Monopoly: A New View of Industrial Structure in Russia," mimeo, The World Bank,

Washington, D.C., August 6, 1993, p. 6; Vladimir Capelik and Andrei Yakovlev, "Monopoly in the Soviet Economy," *Kommunist*, October 1990, p. 69; Vladimir Capelik, "The Development of Antimonopoly Policy in Russia," *RFE/RL Research Report*, vol. 1, no. 34 (August 28, 1992), p. 66; Heidi Kroll, "Monopoly and Transition to the Market," *Soviet Economy*, vol. 7, no. 2 (April–June 1991), p. 147.

36. Brown, Ickes, and Ryterman, "The Myth of Monopoly."

37. Ibid., pp. 13–20, 27, 34.

38. Capelik, "The Development of Antimonopoly Policy in Russia," pp. 66–70.

39. "Statute on the RSFSR State Register for Associations and Monopolistic Enterprises Active on Product Markets," *Ekonomicheskaya gazeta*, no. 1 (January 1992).

40. Vladimir E. Capelik, "Should Monopoly Be Regulated in Russia?", *Communist Economies and Economic Transformation*, vol. 6, no. 1 (1994), pp. 22–24.

41. Ibid., pp. 19–30.

42. Paul L. Joskow, Richard Schmalensee, and Natalia Tsukanova, "Competition Policy in Russia During and After Privatization," *Brookings Papers on Economic Activity: Microeconomics*, 1994, p. 336.

43. Ibid., pp. 344–48.

44. Conversations with Western business executives and the Russian State Price Committee in October and November 1993.

45. "State Program for Demonopolization of the Economy and the Development of Competition," *Rossiiskaya gazeta*, April 14, 1994; Joskow, Schmalensee, and Tsukanova, "Competition Policy in Russia During and After Privatization," pp. 345, 357.

46. Jacques Delpla, "Price Policy in Russia: The Case of Energy," mimeo, Macroeconomic and Finance Unit, Russian Ministry of Finance, Moscow, April 26, 1993, p. 4.

47. Goskomstat Rossii, *Rossiiskaya Federatsiya v tsifrakh v 1992 godu* (The Russian Federation in numbers in 1992), p. 164.

48. Personal conversation with Yegor Gaidar in March 1993.

49. Boris N. Yeltsin, *The Struggle for Russia* (Times Books, 1994), p. 168.

50. "Memorandum on Economic Policy of the Russian Federation," *Ekonomicheskaya gazeta*, no. 10, March 1992; John Lloyd, "Russian Oil Price to Rise by 550 Percent in June," *Financial Times*, March 26, 1992, p. 30.

51. Yeltsin, *The Struggle for Russia*, pp. 165–67.

52. Andrew Berg and others, "Energy Prices and Inflation in Russia," mimeo, Monetary and Finance Unit, Russian Ministry of Finance, Moscow, July 26, 1993, p. 2; "Decree of the Government of the Russian Federation on State Regulation of Prices of Energy Resources, Other Kinds of Production and Services," *Ekonomicheskaya gazeta*, no. 21, May 1992, Supplement.

53. Berg and others, "Energy Prices and Inflation in Russia," p. 2; "Decree of the President of the Russian Federation on State Regulation of Prices of

Certain Kinds of Energy Resources," *Rossiiskaya gazeta*, September 19, 1992; "Russia Plans to Double Energy Prices," *International Herald Tribune*, September 11, 1992, p. 11.

54. "Decree of the President of the Russian Federation on the Transformation of the State Gas Concern 'Gazprom' into the Russian Joint Stock Company 'Gazprom'," *Rossiiskaya gazeta*, November 11, 1992; " 'Gazprom'—the Biggest Monopolist in the World," *Izvestiya*, July 22, 1992; "Russia's Gas Industry," *Finansovye izvestiya*, November 29, 1992; "Decree of the Government of the Russian Federation on the Order of Utilization of Hard Currency, Received From Export of Natural Gas in 1993," *Rossiiskaya gazeta*, December 25, 1992; "Decree of the President of Russia on the Assurance of Reliable Gas Supplies to the Consumers of the Russian Joint Stock Company 'Gazprom' in 1994–1996," *Rossiiskaya gazeta*, December 22, 1993; Jacques Delpla, "Gradually Raising 1% of GDP Through a New Gas Excise Tax," mimeo, Macroeconomic and Finance Unit, Russian Ministry of Finance, Moscow, January 2, 1994, p. 5.

55. Mikhail Berger, "One More Difficult Step on the Road to the Market: The Prices of Petroleum Products Have Been Let Free," *Izvestiya*, May 26, 1993.

56. "Decree of the President of the Russian Federation on Measures to Stabilize the Situation in the Coal Industry," *Rossiiskaya gazeta*, June 26, 1993; Sergei Leskov, "Free Prices on Coal Can Strengthen or Break Russia's Economy," *Izvestiya*, June 23, 1993; Sergei Leskov, "The Miners Are Not Satisfied with the Liberalization of Prices and Demand Meetings with the President and Prime Minister of Russia," *Izvestiya*, June 24, 1993; Lev Fainshtein, "Metallurgists and Miners Did Not Agree on the Price," *Kommersant'-Daily*, July 13, 1993; Radmir Kil'matov, "The Cabinet Is Suggested to Find Means Again," *Kommersant'-Daily*, September 10, 1993; "Prices: A New Blow to the Citizens' Pockets—Electricity and Gas Are Becoming More Expensive," *Rossiiskie vesti*, March 30, 1994.

57. "Decree of the Government of the Russian Federation on State Regulation of the Price of Natural Gas and Other Energy Resources," *Rossiiskaya gazeta*, July 24, 1993; Delpla, "Gradually Raising 1% of GDP Through a New Gas Excise Tax," p. 5; Rustam Narzikulov, "The End of the Energy Paradise," *Segodnya*, November 16, 1993.

58. "Decree of the Council of Ministers—Government of the Russian Federation on the Correction of the System of Electricity Tariffs," *Rossiiskaya gazeta*, August 13, 1993.

59. "The Dynamics of Prices of Energy," *TEK*, no. 3–4, 1994, p. 9; Elena Yakovleva and Irina Savvateeva, "Russia on the Eve of 'Freeing of Gas Prices': What Will it Bring to Us All?", *Izvestiya*, November 26, 1994.

60. Irina Savvateeva, "The Energy Prices Rise Faster Than All Others," *Izvestiya*, March 25, 1994; "Russia's Government Will As Previously Regulate the Prices of Gas and Heating," *Segodnya*, June 21, 1994.

61. "Decree of the President of the Russian Federation on the Formation of State Food Funds for 1992," *Ekonomichskaya gazeta*, no. 5, February 1992.

62. Conversations with various officials at the Russian Ministry of Agriculture in Moscow in July 1993.

63. Anders Åslund, "State Credits to Agriculture Are Gifts to Monopolies," *Izvestiya*, September 21, 1993.

64. Petr Aven, "Problems in Foreign Trade Regulation in the Russian Economic Reform," pp. 89–90; Douglas Galbi and Andrei Uspenskii, "Grain Subsidies: Progress Report for 1993," mimeo, Macroeconomic and Finance Unit, Russian Ministry of Finance, Moscow, August 30, 1993.

65. "Decree of the President of the Russian Federation on Measures to Stabilize the Economy of the Agro-Industrial Complex," *Rossiiskaya gazeta*, April 7, 1992; "Decree of the Government of the Russian Federation on Additional Measures to Assure a Timely Harvest and Procurement of Agricultural Products in 1992," *Rossiiskaya gazeta*, July 14, 1992; "No More Grain Than Usual, But Less Sensationalism," *Rossiiskaya gazeta*, July 18, 1992; Valery Konovalov, "The Price of Grain Will Be Given by the President," *Izvestiya*, July 24, 1992; Natal'ya Gorodetskaya, "There Will Not Be Russian Currency," *Nezavisimaya gazeta*, October 2, 1992; "Decree of the Government of the Russian Federation on Urgent Measures for Support of Cattle and Animal Husbandry (1992)," *Rossiiskaya gazeta*, November 7, 1992.

66. Galbi and Uspenskii, "Grain Subsidies: Progress Report for 1993"; Marina Amelina, Douglas Galbi, and Andrei Uspenskii, "The Distribution of Central Bank Credits for Grain Procurement," mimeo, Macroeconomic and Finance Unit, Russian Ministry of Finance, September 3, 1993.

67. "Law of the Russian Federation on Grain," *Rossiiskaya gazeta*, May 29, 1993.

68. Anders Åslund, "State Credits to Agriculture Are Gifts to Monopolies," *Izvestiya*, September 21, 1993; "Decree of the Supreme Soviet of the Russian Federation on Urgent Measures to Assure the Harvest of 1993," *Rossiiskaya gazeta*, July 23, 1993.

69. Boris Fedorov, "The Russian Finances in 1993," *Voprosy ekonomiki*, no. 1, January 1994, p. 36; Yelena Yakovleva, "The State Withdraws From Russia's Grain Market," *Izvestiya*, December 28, 1993; Yelena Yakovleva, "The Prices of Bread Will Rise, But Differently in Different Cities," *Izvestiya*, October 15, 1993; "Decree of the President of the Russian Federation on the Annulment of Certain Articles of the Law of the Russian Federation 'On Grain'," *Rossiiskaya gazeta*, December 29, 1993; Nikolai Chernykh, "The Prices of Food Continue to Be Liberalized," *Kommersant'-Daily*, October 12, 1993; "Omsk Suffers From Overproduction of Grain," *Izvestiya*, November 11, 1993.

70. Nanette van der Laan, "Parties Meet to Agree on New Speaker," *Moscow Times*, December 28, 1993, p. 3; Aleksandr Frolov, "The Algebra of Compromise," *Sovetskaya Rossiya*, February 26, 1994.

71. "Decree of the Government of the Russian Federation on Economic Conditions for the Functioning of the Agro-Industrial Complex of the Russian Federation in 1994," no. 120, mimeo, Moscow, February 23, 1994; Andrei Illarionov, "The Agrarian Bosses Want to Be Fed by the Whole People," *Izvestiya*, February 8, 1994.

72. Dmitry Volkov, "Zaveryukha Declared the End of Imports of Food,"

Segodnya, January 29, 1994; Dmitry Kuznets, "They Will Sell the Harvest With Force," *Segodnya*, March 23, 1994; Center for Economic Analysis, Government of the Russian Federation, "Dynamics of Purchases and Deliveries of Agricultural Products in Russia in 1993 and January–March 1994," *Segodnya*, June 30, 1994.

73. Boris Fedorov, "Agriculture," *Izvestiya*, June 21, 1994.

74. Goskomstat Rossii, *Sotsial'no-ekonomicheskoe polozhenie Rossii 1994 g.*, p. 168.

75. "The Ministry of Thieves in Law," *Izvestiya*, July 20, 1994.

76. Ibid.

77. Arkady Vaksberg, *The Soviet Mafia* (St. Martin's Press, 1991); Konstantin M. Simis, *USSR: Secrets of a Corrupt Society* (London: J. M. Dent & Sons, 1982); Ilja Zemtsov, *La corruption en Union sovietique* (Paris: Hachette, 1976).

78. "The Ministry of Thieves in Law."

79. Sergei Leskov, "A Series of Resignations in the Government," *Izvestiya*, August 25, 1993; Semen Vasil'ev, "Arrests in the Central Bank," *Kommersant'-Daily*, July 13, 1993; Leonid Berres, "Scandal Due to the Privatization of Houses by the Military," *Kommersant'-Daily*, July 13, 1993.

80. Based on many conversations with business executives in Russia.

81. Vadim Belykh, "The Time of Thieves in Law," *Izvestiya*, April 8, 1994.

82. Vasily Kononenko, "The Russian Authorities Prepare an Attack on Organized Criminality," *Izvestiya*, May 26, 1994; "Federal Program of the Russian Federation for Stepping up the Fight Against Crime During 1994–1995," *Rossiiskaya gazeta*, June 1, 1994; "The President Goes for Extraordinary Measures in the Struggle Against the Raging of Criminality," *Izvestiya*, June 15, 1994; John Lloyd, "Anti-Crime Measures Split Russians," *Financial Times*, June 27, 1994, p. 3.

83. Goskomstat Rossii, *Sotsial'no-ekonomicheskoe polozhenie Rossii 1993 g.*, p. 166; Goskomstat Rossii, *Sotsial'no-ekonomicheskoe polozhenie Rossii 1994 g.*, p. 170.

84. Arkady Vaksberg, "Crime No Punishment," *Moscow Times*, December 30, 1992; Victor Yasmann, "Corruption in Russia: A Threat to Democracy?", *RFE/RL Research Report*, vol. 2, no. 10 (March 5, 1993), pp. 15–18; "The Ministry of Thieves in Law."

85. Center for Economic Reforms, Government of the Russian Federation, "The Economic Situation in the Russian Federation, April 19–26, 1994," *Segodnya*, May 5, 1994; Goskomstat Rossii, *Sotsial'no-ekonomicheskoe polozhenie Rossii 1994 g.*, p. 131.

Chapter Six

1. I have learned much about macroeconomic stabilization under Russian conditions, primarily from Jeffrey Sachs but also from David Lipton and Stanley Fischer. This chapter draws greatly from Jeffrey D. Sachs, "Prospects for Monetary Stabilization in Russia," in Anders Åslund, ed., *Economic Transformation*

in Russia (London: Pinter, 1994), pp. 34–58, and Jeffrey D. Sachs, "Russia's Struggle with Stabilization: Conceptual Issues and Evidence." Paper presented at the Annual [World] Bank Conference on Development Economics, April 28–29, 1994, Washington, D.C. Other important general sources are: Stanley Fischer, "Russia and the Soviet Union Then and Now," in Olivier Jean Blanchard, Kenneth A. Froot, and Jeffrey D. Sachs, eds., *The Transition in Eastern Europe*, vol. 1 (University of Chicago Press, 1994), pp. 221–52; Jeffrey D. Sachs and David Lipton, "Remaining Steps to a Market-Based Monetary System," in Anders Åslund and Richard Layard, eds., *Changing the Economic System in Russia* (St. Martin's Press, 1993), pp. 127–62; David Lipton, "Reform Endangered," *Foreign Policy*, no. 90 (Spring 1993), pp. 57–78; Stanley Fischer, "Prospects for Russian Stabilization in the Summer of 1993," in Åslund, ed., *Economic Transformation in Russia*, pp. 8–25; Boris G. Fedorov and Andrei I. Kazmin, "1993: The First Experiences of the Russian Financial and Monetary Stabilization Policy," in Åslund, ed., *Economic Transformation in Russia*, pp. 26–33; Boris G. Fedorov, "The Russian Finances in 1993," *Voprosy ekonomiki*, no. 1 (January 1994), pp. 4–85. For data, I draw extensively on International Monetary Fund, *Economic Review: Russian Federation* (International Monetary Fund, 1993); Macroeconomics and Finance Unit (MFU), *Weekly Monetary Reports*; and the government of the Russian Federation, *Russian Economic Trends*.

2. Anders Åslund, "Lessons of the First Four Years of Systemic Change in Eastern Europe," *Journal of Comparative Economics*, vol. 19 (1994), pp. 22–38.

3. Statement made at a seminar at the Central Economic-Mathematical Institute in Moscow in September 1991.

4. Sachs and Lipton, "Remaining Steps to a Market-Based Monetary System," p. 127.

5. International Monetary Fund, *Economic Review: Russian Federation*, pp. 89–91; Government of the Russian Federation, *Russian Economic Trends*, vol. 2, no. 4 (1993), pp. 11–12.

6. These official Russian interest rates are not properly compounded. The official interest of 20 percent per annum was insignificantly higher (that is, 22 percent per annum) but the real rate of 50 percent per annum was already 63 percent per annum, and an official rate of 80 percent per annum was actually 117 percent per annum. The higher the interest rate, the greater the discrepancy. I owe this observation to Brigitte Granville.

7. Georgy G. Matyukhin, *Ya byl glavnym bankirom Rossii* (I was Russia's main banker) (Moscow: Vysshaya shkola, 1993), pp. 58–69.

8. Government of the Russian Federation, *Russian Economic Trends*, p. 117.

9. International Monetary Fund, *Economic Review: Russian Federation*, p. 93.

10. Government of the Russian Federation, *Russian Economic Trends*, p. 116.

11. Ibid., p. 106.

12. International Monetary Fund, *Economic Review: Russian Federation*, p. 93.

13. Ibid.

14. Mikhail Delyagin and Lev Freinkman, "Extrabudgetary Funds in Russian

Public Finance," *Radio Free Europe/Radio Liberty (RFE/RL) Research Report,* vol. 2, December 3, 1993, pp. 49–54; International Monetary Fund, *Economic Review: Russian Federation,* p. 93.

15. Government of the Russian Federation, *Russian Economic Trends,* p. 106.

16. Ibid., p. 22.

17. Much of the following is based on Boris Fedorov, "The Russian finances in 1993," *Voprosy ekonomiki,* pp. 4–85.

18. "Declaration on the Economic Policy of the Government and the Central Bank of Russia," in Ministry of Finance of the Russian Federation, *Rossiiskie finansy v 1993 godu* (Russian finances in 1993) (Moscow, January 1994), pp. 130–33.

19. International Monetary Fund, *Economic Review: Russian Federation,* p. 133.

20. Viktor V. Gerashchenko, "The Monetary-Credit System in Russia in the Transition Period," *Biznes i banki: Bankovskaya gazeta,* no. 38, September 1994, in Foreign Broadcast Information Service, *Daily Report: Central Eurasia,* October 13, 1994, p. 23. (Hereafter FBIS, *Central Eurasia.*)

21. Aleksei Mikhailov, "The Currency Summer '93," *Moskovskie novosti,* no. 30, July, 25, 1993.

22. "Decree of the Council of Ministers—Government of the Russian Federation on Proportions of Compensation of the Difference in the Interest Rate of Advantageous Credits," no. 3633, *Sobranie Aktov Prezidenta i Pravitel'stva Rossiiskoi Federatsii,* no. 39, September 27, 1993.

23. Mark Nagel, "The 1994 Budget," mimeo, Moscow, May 16, 1994.

24. Yeltsin, *The Struggle for Russia,* pp. 259–60.

25. Fedorov, "Russian Finances in 1993," pp. 39–41; Oksana Dmitrieva, "Political Games Around the Budget," *Moskovskie novosti,* no. 28, July 11, 1993; Aleksandr Bekker, "'The Siberian Accord' Demands a Revision of Taxes," *Segodnya,* April 6, 1994.

26. Stanley Fischer, "Prospects for Russian Stabilization in the Summer of 1993," pp. 8–25; Jeffrey D. Sachs, "Prospects for Monetary Stabilization in Russia," pp. 34–58; Valery Vyzhutovich, "The Art of Demanding Sacrifices," *Izvestiya,* December 6, 1994.

27. Petr Zhuravlev, "The New Russian Deputies Have Been Suggested to Leave Work," *Segodnya,* December 28, 1993.

28. "Der Rücktrittsbrief Gajdars an Jelzin," *Frankfurter Allgemeiner Zeitung,* January 18, 1994.

29. FNS Kremlin Package, "Press Conference by Russian Prime Minister Viktor Chernomyrdin," mimeo, January 20, 1994.

30. Yelena Kolokol'tseva and Dmitry Volkov, "A Temporary Coalition Government Has Been Formed," *Segodnya,* January 21, 1994; Mikhail Leont'ev, "Apparently, the Prime Minister Tried Again," *Segodnya,* January 25, 1994; Andrei Zhdanov and Faina Osmanova, "In Throes a New Government Is Born," *Nezavisimaya gazeta,* January 21, 1994.

31. Jacques Delpla and Charles Wyplosz, "Russia's Unconventional Transi-

tion," in Anders Åslund, ed., *Russian Economic Reform at Risk* (London: Pinter, forthcoming).

32. Geraschenko, "The Monetary-Credit System in Russia in the Transition Period," FBIS, *Central Eurasia*, October 13, 1994, p. 22.

33. Otto Latsis, "In an Unreliable Balance," *Izvestiya*, July 14, 1994.

34. Estimate by Brunswick Brokerage Research from December 1994.

35. Institute for Economic Analysis, *Rossiiskie ekonomicheskie reformy: poteryanny god* (Russian economic reforms: a lost year) (Moscow, December 1994), p. 7.

36. Nagel, "The 1994 Budget," p. 2.

37. A. Deshabo, "Business Is Good Only for Cash," *Izvestiya*, June 25, 1994; Boris Fedorov, "A New Tax Policy Immediately!", *Izvestiya*, June 7, 1994; Sergei Pepelyanev, "Most Changes in the Tax Legislation Remain Insignificant," *Finansovye izvestiya*, May 26, 1994; Andrei Koptyaev, "A Tax Reform is Almost Inevitable," *Finansovye izvestiya*, February 3, 1994.

38. Andrei Grigor'ev, "The Budget Is Becoming a Stumbling-Block for the Government's Economic Policy," *Segodnya*, September 27, 1994.

39. Andrei Illarionov, "The Budget as a Mirror of the True Intentions of the Government," *Izvestiya*, May 18, 1994.

40. Institute for Economic Analysis, *Rossiiskie ekonomicheskie reformy: poteryanny god*, pp. 13, 27, 74.

41. Otto Latsis, "What Skid in the Engine of Power?", *Izvestiya*, November 1, 1994.

42. Mikhail Leont'ev, "Chubais Has Been Appointed Gaidar," *Segodnya*, November 9, 1994.

43. Information from Brunswick Brokerage Research in Moscow, December 1994.

44. Institute for Economic Analysis, *Rossiiskie ekonomicheskie reformy: poteryanny god*, p. 8.

45. Mikhail Sarafanov, "The Export of Energy Remains Under Control," *Finansovye izvestiya*, October 11, 1994; Yelena Yakovleva and Irina Savvateeva, "Russia on the Eve of 'Oil Liberty'," *Izvestiya*, November 26, 1994.

46. Mikhail Berger, "The Question of Freedom of Our Exports Can Cost a Minimum of 7 Billion Dollars," *Izvestiya*, November 24, 1994; Irina Savvateeva, "Oil Lobbyists Put Russia on the Verge of Financial Catastrophe," *Izvestiya*, December 8, 1994.

47. John Thornhill, "Moscow's Reformers Score Oil Victory," *Financial Times*, January 6, 1995, p. 2.

48. In this section, I shall primarily draw on the work by Jacek Rostowski: Jacek Rostowski, "The Inter-Enterprise Debt Explosion in the Former Soviet Union: Causes, Consequences, Cures," *Communist Economics & Economic Transformation*, vol. 5, no. 2 (1993), pp. 131–59; Jacek Rostowski, "Interenterprise Arrears in Post-Communist Economies," IMF Working Paper WP/94/43 (International Monetary Fund, April 1994); I also consult: Sachs and Lipton, "Remaining Steps to a Market-Based Monetary System," pp. 127–62; David

Bigman and Sergio Pereira Leite, "Enterprise Arrears in Russia: Causes and Policy Options," IMF Working Paper WP/93/61 (International Monetary Fund, August 1993); Barry W. Ickes and Randi Ryterman, "Roadblock to Economic Reform: Inter-Enterprise Debt and the Transition to Markets," *Post-Soviet Affairs,* vol. 9 (July–September 1993), pp. 231–52.

49. Government of the Russian Federation, *Russian Economic Trends,* p. 116.

50. Bigman and Pereira Leite, "Enterprise Arrears in Russia: Causes and Policy Options," pp. 1, 10.

51. Goskomstat Rossii, "The Socio-Economic Situation on November 15," *Delovoi mir,* November 24, 1994.

52. Rostowski, "Interenterprise Arrears in Post-Communist Economies," pp. 1–2.

53. Goskomstat Rossii, "The Socio-Economic Situation on November 15."

54. For a particularly absurd article on these lines, see V. Sokolov and Ye. Gil'bo, "An Alternative Budget Is Proposed," *Ekonomika i zhizn',* no. 48 (November 1994).

55. Bigman and Pereira Leite, "Enterprise Arrears in Russia: Causes and Policy Options," p. 1.

56. Goskomstat Rossii, "The Socio-Economic Situation on November 15."

57. Rustam Arifdzhanov, "In Russia There Is a Red Debt of Arrears," *Izvestiya,* October 7, 1994.

58. Mikhail Delyagin, "The Unification of Promissory Notes Can Soften the Crisis of Arrears," *Finansovye izvestiya,* October 6, 1994.

59. Igor' Karpenko, "The President Signed a Package of Economic Decrees," *Izvestiya,* December 22, 1994; Dmitry Volkov, "Messrs Panskov and Zadornov Agree on the Assessment of the Budget Deficit," *Segodnya,* December 21, 1994.

60. Andrei Illarionov and Mikhail Dmitriev, "Small Secrets of the Federal Budget," *Izvestiya,* November 19, 1994.

61. I was in Volgograd in February 1994, when the Volgograd Dzerzhinsky Tractor Factory organized such a demonstration in obvious collusion with the *oblast* administration.

62. Rustam Arifdzhanov, "Whom Do the Trade Unions Save?", *Izvestiya,* October 27, 1994; Institute for Economic Analysis, "Survey of Russian Economy," mimeo, Moscow, November 15, 1994, figure 4.

63. Lev Makarevich, "The Threat of Mass Bankruptcies Has Reached the Banks," *Finansovye izvestiya,* December 8, 1994.

64. Goskomstat Rossii, *Rossiiskaya Federatsiya v tsifrakh v 1993 godu* (The Russian Federation in numbers in 1993) (Moscow, 1994), p. 12.

65. Rostowski, "Interenterprise Arrears in Post-Communist Economies," pp. 1–2.

66. The best understanding of the weakness of Soviet power in the early 1980s has been expounded by Zbigniew Brzezinski, "Tragic Dilemmas of Soviet World Power: The Limits of a New-Type Empire," *Encounter,* vol. 61 (December 1983), pp. 10–17. An extraordinary insight into what President Reagan's policy would imply for Russia was provided by Richard Pipes, "Can the Soviet Union Reform?", *Foreign Affairs,* vol. 63 (Fall 1984), pp. 47–61.

67. "B. N. Yeltsin's Speech," *Sovetskaya Rossiya*, October 29, 1991.

68. The following criticism of the West closely follows Jeffrey D. Sachs, particularly "Russia's Struggle with Stabilization: Conceptual Issues and Evidence," paper presented at the Annual [World] Bank Conference on Development Economics, April 28–29, 1994, Washington, D.C.; Peter Norman and John Lloyd, "G7 Stays Hand Over Soviet Debt Safety Net," *Financial Times*, November 12, 1991, p. 4; "G7 Agrees Debt Deal With Soviet Republics," *Financial Times*, November 22, 1991, pp. 1, 16; "Memorandum on Mutual Understanding Concerning the Debt of Foreign Creditors of the Soviet Socialist Republics and Its Successors," *Izvestiya*, October 29, 1991; and conversations with Russian and Western officials present and involved at that meeting.

69. Ian Davidson and others, "West Ponders Value of Shoring Up Soviet Centre," *Financial Times*, November 5, 1991, p. 4.

70. "Gates on Soviet Breakup, Weapons Proliferation," *News Backgrounder*, United States Information Service, December 11, 1991.

71. Jim Hoagland, "Seeing Yeltsin's Days as Numbered, Bush Holds Back," *International Herald Tribune*, February 12, 1992. An important dissenting voice in the U.S. administration at the time was Secretary of Defense Dick Cheney, who in December 1991 argued that this might be the only chance the West would get to help the former Soviet Union to achieve democracy and stability, but he lost (David White, "Last Chance to Help Soviet Union Says Cheney," *Financial Times*, December 14, 1991, p. 2).

72. "Discover Russian Reform," *International Herald Tribune*, November 13, 1991, p. 8.

73. "Helping Post-Soviet Reform," *Financial Times*, December 17, 1991, p. 16.

74. Lionel Barber, "US to Hold Aid Conference to Bolster Soviets," *Financial Times*, December 13, 1991, p. 1; Anthony Robinson and Patrick Blum, "Western Donors Cement Links With CIS States," *Financial Times*, May 26, 1992, p. 2; Aleksandr Zhitnikov, "Humanitarian Aid: 170 Thousand Tons for 10 Billion Rubles," *Izvestiya*, March 12, 1992.

75. The White House, Office of the Press Secretary, "Multilateral Financial Assistance Package for Russia," Press Release, April 1, 1992; Quentin Peel, "Western Aid to Fill Trade Gap for Russia," *Financial Times*, April 2, 1992, p. 2.

76. "Memorandum on Economic Policy of the Russian Federation," *Ekonomicheskaya gazeta*, no. 10, March 1992; Otto Latsis, "With a Delay of 47 Years," *Izvestiya*, April 28, 1992.

77. Steven Greenhouse, "Russians Say I.M.F. Demands May Nullify Benefits of Loans," *New York Times*, June 16, 1992, p. A12.

78. Leyla Boulton, John Lloyd, and Quentin Peel, "Russia to Cut Deficit and Inflation," *Financial Times*, July 7, 1992, p. 1; Peter Norman, "G7 Passes the Future of Russia to the IMF," *Financial Times*, July 13, 1992, p. 11; Aleksandr Shal'nev, "The IMF Opens Access to the West's Finances to Russia," *Izvestiya*, August 6, 1992; Mikhail Berger, "Russia Will Probably Become the Biggest Client of the World Bank," *Izvestiya*, August 7, 1992.

79. Aleksandr Shal'nev, "The IMF and the World Bank Intend to Cut the Promised Aid to the CIS Substantially," *Izvestiya*, September 17, 1992.

80. Sachs, "Russia's Struggle With Stabilization: Conceptual Issues and Evidence," pp. 25–26, 53; International Monetary Fund, *Economic Review: Russian Federation*, pp. 93, 132–33.

81. Full-fledged criticism of the IMF was published at the time, but it had no impact: Jeffrey Sachs and David Lipton, "Russia on the Ropes: How the IMF Is Missing Its Chance to Spur Recovery," *Washington Post*, September 29, 1992, p. C1.

82. Sachs, "Russia's Struggle With Stabilization: Conceptual Issues and Evidence," p. 59.

Chapter Seven

1. Roman Frydman and others, *The Privatization Process in Russia, Ukraine and the Baltic States* (Budapest: Central European University Press, 1993), pp. 34–36.

2. Ibid.

3. Ibid., pp. 18–19.

4. Observations from many conversations with Russian enterprise managers.

5. Frydman and others, *The Privatization Process in Russia, Ukraine and the Baltic States*, pp. 20–22.

6. Goskomstat Rossii, "The Social-Economic Situation and Development of Economic Reforms in the Russian Federation in 1992," *Ekonomicheskaya gazeta*, no. 4, January 1993.

7. Frydman and others, *The Privatization Process in Russia, Ukraine and the Baltic States*, pp. 22–26.

8. *Perekhod k Rynku: Kontseptsiya i Programma* (Transition to the market: concept and program) (Moscow: Arkhangelskoe, August 1990), pp. 68, 222.

9. "RSFSR Law on the Privatization of State and Municipal Enterprises in the RSFSR," *Ekonomika i zhizn'*, no. 31, July 1991.

10. Ibid., p. 15.

11. "Draft USSR Law on the Basic Foundations of Destatization and Privatization of Enterprises," *Izvestiya*, June 26, 1991.

12. "B. N. Yeltsin's Speech," *Sovetskaya Rossiya*, October 29, 1991.

13. Leonid Grigor'ev, "Ulterior Property Rights and Privatization: Even God Cannot Change the Past," in Anders Åslund, ed., *The Post-Soviet Economy: Soviet and Western Perspectives* (St. Martin's Press, 1992), pp. 196–208.

14. Anders Åslund, "Has Poland Been Useful as a Model for Russia?" in Anders Åslund, ed., *Economic Transformation in Russia* (St. Martin's Press, 1994), pp. 157–73.

15. "The Stakes Are Set" (Interview with Dmitry Vasil'ev), *Rossiiskaya gazeta*, February 10, 1992.

16. "B. N. Yeltsin's Speech."

17. Irena Grosfeld, "Prospects for Privatization in Poland," *European Economy*, no. 43 (March 1990), pp. 147–49, discusses the nature of *nomenklatura* privatization. The implication was that state managers transferred enterprise assets to themselves, mostly together with powerful accomplices. Many methods

were used. A state manager could set up a small enterprise of which he was a major owner and to which he sold produce of the state enterprise cheaply. This was done so that the profit pertained to his private enterprise and not to the state enterprise he managed. A popular technique in Russia was management courses. They could be provided by the manager and his friends to the state enterprise, and they could be bought very dearly.

18. "Basic Provisions of the Program of Privatization of State and Municipal Enterprises in the Russian Federation for 1992," *Ekonomicheskaya gazeta*, no. 2, January 1992.

19. "B. N. Yeltsin's Speech."

20. "Basic Provisions of a Program of Privatization of State and Municipal Enterprises in the Russian Federation in 1992."

21. "Privatizing State Property" (Interview with Anatoly Chubais), *Moscow News*, no. 3, March 1992, p. 10.

22. "Basic Provisions of a Program of Privatization of State and Municipal Enterprises in the Russian Federation in 1992."

23. Ibid.

24. "Privatization Gives the Treasury 92 Billion" (Interview with Anatoly Chubais), *Komsomolskaya pravda*, February 20, 1992.

25. "State Program for the Privatization of State and Municipal Enterprises of the Russian Federation for 1992," *Rossiiskaya gazeta*, July 9, 1992.

26. An exceptional, not very authoritative, early statement by a privatization official asserted that 70 percent of state property was to be sold off over the next decade. Leyla Boulton, "Russia to Sell 70% of State Assets," *Financial Times*, November 27, 1991, p. 2.

27. Much of the following is based on an excellent article: Andrei Shleifer and Maxim Boycko, "The Politics of Russian Privatization," in Olivier Blanchard and others, *Post-Communist Reform: Pain and Progress* (MIT Press, 1993), pp. 37–80.

28. "Privatization Gives the Treasury 92 Billion."

29. Ibid.; "Property Free of Charge Does Not Make a Man an Owner" (Interview with Anatoly Chubais), *Izvestiya*, February 26, 1992; "The Stakes Are Set" (Interview with Dmitry Vasil'ev), *Rossiiskaya gazeta*, February 10, 1992; Petr S. Fillipov, "And So We Create a Class of Owners-Serfs?", *Rossiiskaya gazeta*, March 10, 1992.

30. Larisa I. Piyasheva and others, "To Give Away for Free," *Izvestiya*, February 14, 1992; Vasily I. Selyunin, "In Spite of Everything, It Will Be Done Our Way," *Izvestiya*, March 23, 1992; A. Isaev and others, "Nevertheless, It Will Be Necessary to Give [State Property] Free of Charge," *Rossiiskaya gazeta*, April 7, 1992.

31. Personal observations and conversations during many months in Moscow; Yury Andreev, "Double Standards," *Nezavisimaya gazeta*, March 17, 1992.

32. "Privatization Gives the Treasury 92 Billion."

33. Vladimir Todres, "The Bitterness of the Parliament's Struggle With the Government Grows," *Nezavisimaya gazeta*, May 30, 1992.

34. "An Efficient Form of Privatization," *Ekonomicheskaya gazeta*, no. 19, May 1992.

35. Philip Hanson and Elizabeth Teague, "The Industrialists and Russian Economic Reform," *Radio Free Europe/Radio Liberty (RFE/RL) Research Report*, vol. 1 (May 8, 1992), pp. 5–6.

36. "The President's Address to Citizens," *Rossiiskaya gazeta*, August 20, 1992.

37. "B. N. Yeltsin's Speech," *Rossiiskie vesti*, August 25, 1992.

38. For descriptions of the voucher scheme see: Frydman and others, *The Privatization Process in Russia, Ukraine and the Baltic States*, pp. 66–71; Bozidar Djelic, "Mass Privatization in Russia: The Role of Vouchers," *RFE/RL Research Report*, vol. 1 (October 16, 1992), pp. 40–44; Bozidar Djelic and Natalia Tsukanova, "Voucher Auctions: A Crucial Step Toward Privatization," *RFE/RL Research Report*, vol. 2 (July 23, 1993), pp. 10–18.

39. "The President's Address to Citizens."

40. Igor' Karpenko, "We Have No Disagreements With V. Chernomyrdin About the Program of Privatization" (Interview with Anatoly Chubais), *Izvestiya*, January 19, 1993.

41. Shleifer and Boycko, "The Politics of Russian Privatization," in Blanchard and others, *Post-Communist Reform: Pain and Progress*, pp. 48–49, 59–63.

42. Aleksandr Bekker, "The Servile Boris Nikolaevich," *Segodnya*, June 15, 1994.

43. Shleifer and Boycko, "The Politics of Russian Privatization," in Blanchard and others, *Post-Communist Reform: Pain and Progress*, pp. 43–48; Sergei Sninsky, "State Holdings Instead of Auctions," *Nezavisimaya gazeta*, March 11, 1992; "From Netting Out to Corporatization" (Interview with Vladimir Shumeiko), *Rossiiskaya gazeta*, June 4, 1992.

44. Larisa I. Piyasheva, "The New Head of the Socialist Dragon," *Nezavisimaya gazeta*, April 25, 1992.

45. Shleifer and Boycko, "The Politics of Privatization," in Blanchard and others, *Post-Communist Reform: Pain and Progress*, pp. 43–48.

46. Irina Demchenko, "The President Thought and Decided that Chubais Is More Right Than Lobov," *Izvestiya*, September 14, 1993.

47. "The Fourth Option of Corporatization of State Enterprises," *Ekonomicheskaya gazeta*, no. 1, January 1993; "Once Again About the Fourth Option of Privatization," *Ekonomicheskaya gazeta*, no. 16, April 1993.

48. Yelena Kotelynikova, "The Supreme Soviet Scrutinizes Presidential Guarantees," *Kommersant'-Daily*, July 15, 1993.

49. Richard Rose, "The Russian Response to Privatization," *RFE/RL Research Report*, vol. 2 (November 26, 1993), p. 55.

50. Mary Cline, "Attitudes Toward Economic Reform in Russia," *RFE/RL Research Report*, vol. 2 (May 28, 1993), pp. 43–49.

51. Relevant contributions include: David Lipton and Jeffrey D. Sachs, "Privatization in Eastern Europe: The Case of Poland," *Brookings Papers on Economic Activity*, 2:1990, pp. 293–341; Jeffrey D. Sachs, "Privatization in Russia: Some Lessons From Eastern Europe," *American Economic Review*, vol. 82 (May 1992); Andrei Shleifer and Robert Vishny, "Privatization in Russia: First Steps," in Olivier Jean Blanchard, Kenneth A. Froot, and Jeffrey D. Sachs, eds., *The*

Transition in Eastern Europe, vol. 2 (University of Chicago Press, 1994). Maxim Boycko and Andrei Shleifer, "The Voucher Program for Russia," in Anders Aslund and Richard Layard, eds., *Changing the Economic System in Russia* (St. Martin's Press, 1993), pp. 100–111. Jeffrey Sachs played an important role in the internal privatization debate early on—for instance, pushing for 25 percent of shares to be given to employees initially (in meetings with President Yeltsin on December 11 and 13, 1991). Later on, major Western advice came from Andrei Shleifer and Jonathan Hay, who worked permanently at the GKI from December 1991 under Dmitry Vasil'ev. But a large number of Western professionals played significant yet little noticed roles.

52. Mikhail Berger, "Goskomimushchestvo Is Preparing Itself to Transfer Property," *Izvestiya,* March 27, 1992.

53. Much of the following is based on: Andrei Shleifer and Maxim Boycko, "The Politics of Russian Privatization," in Blanchard and others, *Post-Communist Reform: Pain and Progress,* pp. 37–80.

54. Vasily Kononenko, "The Government Approved the Program of Privatization for 1993," *Izvestiya,* November 30, 1992; "The State Program of Privatization," *Izvestiya,* June 27, 1992.

55. "State Program for the Privatization of State and Municipal Enterprises of the Russian Federation for 1992," *Rossiiskaya gazeta,* July 9, 1992; "The State Program of Privatization."

56. "Resolution of the Supreme Soviet of the Russian Federation on the Delimitation of State Property in the Russian Federation into Federal Property, State Property of Republics Belonging to the Russian Federation, *Krai, Oblasti,* Autonomous Regions, Autonomous Districts, the Cities of Moscow and St. Petersburg and Municipal Property," *Ekonomicheskaya gazeta,* no. 3, January 1992.

57. Igor' Karpenko, "The Program of Privatization for 1993," *Izvestiya,* May 20, 1993.

58. "Basic Provisions of the Program of Privatization of State and Municipal Enterprises in the Russian Federation for 1992," *Ekonomicheskaya gazeta,* no. 2, January 1992.

59. Karpenko, "We Have No Disagreement With V. Chernomyrdin About the Program of Privatization"; Karpenko, "The Program of Privatization for 1993"; Igor' Karpenko, "The Draft Program of Privatization for 1993 Was Approved by the Government of Russia," *Izvestiya,* June 1, 1993.

60. "We Have No Disagreement With V. Chernomyrdin About the Program of Privatization" (Interview with A. Chubais), *Izvestiya,* January 19, 1993.

61. "The State Program of Privatization of State and Municipal Enterprises in the Russian Federation," *Rossiiskaya gazeta,* January 4, 1994.

62. "'Text' of Privatization Program Edict," ITAR-TASS, July 22, 1994, in Foreign Broadcast Information Service, *Daily Report: Central Eurasia,* July 25, 1994, pp. 18–19. (Hereafter FBIS, *Central Eurasia.*)

63. "Privatizing State Property" (Interview with Anatoly Chubais), *Moscow News,* no. 3, March 1994, p. 10.

64. Formally, there are 89 regions, but Chechnya was for all purposes outside of Moscow's reach.

65. Bozidar Djelic and Natalia Tsukanova, "Voucher Auctions: A Crucial Step Toward Privatization," *RFE/RL Research Report*, vol. 2 (July 23, 1993), p. 12.

66. "Privatization Gives the Treasury 92 Billion."

67. Roman Frydman and others, *The Privatization Process in Central Europe*, vol. 1 (Budapest: Central European University Press, 1993).

68. In November 1991, a small team of advisors affiliated with the Harvard Institute for International Development (HIID) joined the GKI full-time. In March 1992, a joint World Bank/European Bank for Reconstruction and Development (EBRD) team was added, and in May 1992, the GKI selected a consortium of Western advisors through an international tender. In addition, Western investment bankers have been involved in preparing privatization of particular enterprises, especially the International Finance Corporation and CS First Boston, but a large number of Western advisers representing a broad range of expertise have been involved in the Russian privatization program. In particular, the U.S. Agency for International Development provided a great deal of financing. (Bozidar Djelic and Jeffrey Sachs, "Russia: Breakthrough Year in 1993," in Rodney Lord, ed., *Privatisation Yearbook 1993* [London: Privatisation International, 1993], pp. 84–85.)

69. Anatoly Chubais and Maria Vishnevskaya, "Main Issues of Privatization in Russia," in Åslund and Layard, eds., *Changing the Economic System in Russia*, p. 92.

70. The State Committee of the Russian Federation for the Management of State Property, *Annual Report 1992* (Moscow, 1993), p. 6.

71. Chubais and Vishnevskaya, "Main Issues of Privatization in Russia," in Åslund and Layard, eds., *Changing the Economic System in Russia*, p. 89.

72. "Decree on the Acceleration of Privatization of State and Municipal Enterprises," *Zakon*, no. 2 (February 1992), pp. 1–10.

73. John Lloyd, "Russia's Third City Leads the Way in State Property Sales," *Financial Times*, February 6, 1992, p. 2.

74. The State Committee of the Russian Federation for the Management of State Property, *Annual Report 1992*, pp. 7, 28–29. The statistics are bad for many reasons. New statistical routines were being set up, and in the enormous rush to privatize quickly, statistics were more important for exhortation than actual control. Goskomstat data tend to treat the original number of enterprises as the relevant figure, whereas some GKI data take into account how many enterprises there were at the time of privatization. (Aleksandr Margolin, "Why Was the Small-Scale Privatization Slowed Down?", *Rossiiskie vesti*, July 14, 1993.) In addition, the categorization of enterprises does not seem to have been worked out. For instance, small enterprises were not supposed to be transformed into shareholding companies, but that was a common form of privatization of small enterprises (see Margolin, 1993, p. 4). The privatization process frequently took a long time, and clearly the perception of when an enterprise had become private varied by months.

75. Margolin, "Why Was the Small-Scale Privatization Slowed Down?"

76. Aleksandr Radygin, "The Peak of Privatization Through 'Voluntary Initiatives' Is Over," *Finansovye izvestiya*, February 17, 1994.

77. "Economic Production and Price Dynamics as of October 25," *Delovoi mir,* November 2, 1994, pp. 4–5.

78. The State Committee of the Russian Federation for the Management of State Property, *Annual Report 1992,* p. 6.

79. Margolin, "Why Was the Small-Scale Privatization Slowed Down?" Statistics vary considerably by source.

80. Ibid.

81. The State Committee of the Russian Federation for the Management of State Property, *Annual Report 1992,* p. 6.

82. Igor' Karpenko, "The Principles for Privatization in Moscow Have Been Determined," *Izvestiya,* December 12, 1992.

83. Based on personal conversations in and around Moscow shops in 1992.

84. Personal observations and conversations with salespeople in Moscow during the reform period; Yakov Orlov, "Trade Is Primarily Privatized in a 'Collective' Fashion," *Segodnya,* December 28, 1993.

85. Repeated personal conversations with Chubais in late 1991 and the first half of 1992.

86. Anatoly Yershov and Igor' Karpenko, "At the Fair in Nizhny Novgorod Trucks Were Sold for Vouchers," *Izvestiya,* November 2, 1992.

87. Goskomstat Rossii, *Rossiiskaya Federatsiya v tsifrakh v 1993 godu* (The Russian Federation in numbers in 1993) (Moscow, 1994), p. 46.

88. Shleifer and Boycko, "The Politics of Russian Privatization," in Blanchard and others, *Post-Communist Reform: Pain and Progress,* pp. 53–56; Frydman and others, *The Privatization Process in Russia, Ukraine and the Baltic States,* pp. 76–82; Igor' Karpenko, "The Decree on the Corporatization of Enterprises is Coming Into Force," *Izvestiya,* July 7, 1992.

89. "Report on Privatization," *RFE/RL Daily Report,* April 8, 1994.

90. Goskomstat Rossii, *Sotsial'no-ekonomicheskoe polozhenie Rossii 1993 g.* (The socio-economic situation in Russia in 1993) (Moscow, 1994), p. 94.

91. S. Mikhailov, "Once Again About the Results and Problems of Privatization in 1993," *Ekonomicheskaya gazeta,* no. 19, May 1993.

92. "Decree on State Guarantees About the Rights of Citizens of Russia to Participate in the Privatization," *Rossiiskaya gazeta,* May 19, 1993.

93. Yelena Dzhaginova, "A Quarter of the Population of Russia Do Not Know What to Do With Their Vouchers," *Segodnya,* January 26, 1994.

94. "Privatization in Public Opinion," *Izvestiya,* July 2, 1994.

95. Information from the GKI.

96. All-Russian Center for the Study of Public Opinion (VTsIOM), *Ekonomicheskie i sotsial'nye peremeny* (Economic and social changes), no. 6, October 1993, p. 52.

97. Yury Levada, "A Critical Balance of an 'Extraordinary' Year," *Moskovskie novosti,* no. 1, January 3, 1993.

98. Aaron Trehub, "Housing Policy in the USSR/CIS: Perestroika and Beyond," *RFE/RL Research Report,* vol. 1 (February 7, 1992), pp. 38–39.

99. Frydman and others, *The Privatization Process in Russia, Ukraine and the Baltic States,* pp. 74–75; "Housing: Free and Forever," *Rossiiskaya gazeta,* Jan-

uary 4, 1993; "Model Statute on the Privatization of the Housing Fund in the RSFSR," *Ekonomicheskaya gazeta*, no. 1, January 1992.

100. Goskomstat Rossii, *Rossiiskaya Federatsiya v tsifrakh v 1993 godu*, p. 52; "The Socio-Economic Situation and the Development of Economic Reforms in the Russian Federation in the First Half of 1993," *Ekonomicheskaya gazeta*, no. 31, July 1993; "Privatization of Housing Turned Millions of People Into Proprietors," *Finansovye izvestiya*, July 2, 1993; "Economic Production and Price Dynamics as of October 25," *Delovoi mir*, November 2, 1994, pp. 4–5.

101. Richard Rose, "The Russian Response to Privatization," *RFE/RL Research Report*, vol. 2 (November 26, 1993), p. 55; Maria Matskevich and Leonid Kesel'man, "In Moscow, the Leading Employees Favor the Privatization of Industry," *Nezavisimaya gazeta*, March 12, 1992.

102. Yury Levada, "Lessons of a Difficult Year," *Moskovskie novosti*, no. 1, January 2–9, 1994.

103. When I visited a family farm outside Moscow in the spring of 1992, I learned that either the farmer or one of his children stayed up all night with a rifle to check that no one stole anything, tried to burn their houses, or moved the fences at adjacent private plots.

104. Timothy N. Ash, Robert Lewis, and Tanya Skaldina, "Russia Sets the Pace of Agricultural Reform," *RFE/RL Research Report*, vol. 1 (June 19, 1992), p. 60.

105. Don Van Atta, "Yeltsin Decree Finally Ends 'Second Serfdom' in Russia," *RFE/RL Research Report*, vol. 2 (November 19, 1993), p. 34.

106. Olga Melyukhina, "Russia's Peasant Farms Are at a Financial Impasse," *Finansovye izvestiya*, April 14, 1994.

107. Sheila Marnie, "The Unresolved Question of Land Reform in Russia," *RFE/RL Research Report*, vol. 2 (February 12, 1993), pp. 35–36; Van Atta, "Yeltsin Decree Finally Ends 'Second Serfdom' in Russia," pp. 34–35.

108. Don Van Atta, "Rutskoi Loses Responsibility for Agriculture," *RFE/RL Research Report*, vol. 2 (April 30, 1993), pp. 11–16.

109. "Decree of the Government of the Russian Federation on the Order of Reorganization of *Kolkhozy* and *Sovkhozy*," *Ekonomicheskaya gazeta*, no. 3, January 1992.

110. Goskomstat Rossii, *Sotsial'no-ekonomicheskoe polozhenie Rossii 1993 g.*, p. 42.

111. "Decree of the President of the Russian Federation on the Regulation of Land Relations and the Development of Agrarian Reform in Russia," *Izvestiya*, October 29, 1993.

112. Yelena Yakovleva and Anatoly Yershov, "How Peasants in Nizhny Novgorod Learned How to Purchase Land," *Izvestiya*, November 13, 1993.

113. Goskomstat Rossii, *Sotsial'no-ekonomicheskoe polozhenie Rossii 1993 g.*, pp. 42–43; Stephen K. Wegren, "Rural Reform in Russia," *RFE/RL Research Report*, vol. 2 (October 29, 1993), pp. 43–53.

114. Goskomstat Rossii, *Sotsial'no-ekonomicheskoe polozhenie Rossii 1993 g.*, pp. 44–45.

115. Ibid., p. 95.

116. Ibid., p. 184.

117. Ibid., p. 96.

118. Ibid., pp. 96–97; Anastasiya Naryshkina, "There Are About 150 Exchanges Left in Russia," *Segodnya*, June 23, 1994.

119. Goskomstat Rossii, *Sotsial'no-ekonomicheskoe polozhenie Rossii 1993 g.*, pp. 98–99.

120. Frydman and others, *The Privatization Process in Russia, Ukraine and the Baltic States*, pp. 32–33.

121. "Law of the Russian Federation on Insolvency (Bankruptcy) of Enterprises," *Ekonomicheskaya gazeta*, no. 1, January 1993.

122. Gleb Cherkasov, "Bankrupts Do Not Go to the Debt Pit," *Segodnya*, June 18, 1994.

123. "Decree of the Government of the Russian Federation on Some Measures to Implement Legislation on Insolvency (Bankruptcy) of Enterprises," *Rossiiskaya gazeta*, May 27, 1994; "Decree of the President of the Russian Federation on the Sale of State Debtor Enterprises," ITAR-TASS, June 3, 1994, in FBIS, *Central Eurasia*, June 6, 1994, pp. 23–24; Interview with Maxim Boycko, Chief Executive Officer of the Russian Privatization Center, and his colleagues in Moscow, December 15, 1994.

124. Petr Zhuravlev, "Anatoly Chubais Affirms that He Opened the Door to the Market," *Segodnya*, March 24, 1994.

125. Irena Grosfeld and Paul Hare, "Privatization in Hungary, Poland and Czechoslovakia," *European Economy*, special ed. no. 2 (1991), pp. 129–56.

126. Ivan Major, *Privatization in Eastern Europe: A Critical Approach* (Aldershot, Hants; Brookfield, Vermont: Edward Elgar, 1993).

127. Maxim Boycko, Andrei Shleifer, and Robert W. Vishny, "Privatizing Russia," *Brookings Papers on Economic Activity*, 2:1993, p. 160.

128. Joseph Blasi, "Privatizing Russia—A Success Story," *New York Times*, June 30, 1994, p. A23.

129. VTsIOM, *Ekonomicheskie i sotsial'nye peremeny*, p. 54.

130. Fred Hiatt, "Privatizing a Noodle Factory Has Russians in a Stew," *Washington Post*, March 29, 1994, p. A14.

131. Conversations with managers, officials, investors, and economists in Volgograd and Moscow in January and February 1994.

132. Boycko, Shleifer, and Vishny, "Privatizing Russia: First Steps," in Blanchard, Froot, and Sachs, eds., *The Transition in Eastern Europe*, pp. 169–71.

133. "Decree on Measures to Assure the Rights of Shareowners," *Rossiiskaya gazeta*, November 6, 1993.

134. Yelena Kotelynikova, "Shareholders Do Not Receive the Promised Dividends," *Kommersant'-Daily*, January 20, 1994.

135. "State Program of the Privatization of State and Municipal Enterprises in the Russian Federation," *Rossiiskaya gazeta*, January 4, 1994.

136. Goskomstat Rossii, *Sotsial'no-ekonomicheskoe polozhenie Rossii 1993 g.*, p. 88.

137. Sergei Rybak, "2.9 Billion Dollars of Foreign Capital in the Russian Economy," *Segodnya*, March 24, 1994.

138. Information from the Brunnswick brokerage in Moscow, December 1994.

Chapter Eight

1. "All Not Yet Lost for Budget" (Interview with Deputy S. Burkov), *Rossiiskaya gazeta*, November 30, 1994.

2. Yelena Yakovleva and Irina Savvateeva, "Russia on the Eve of 'Freeing of Gas Prices': What Will it Bring to Us All?", *Izvestiya*, November 26, 1994; Aleksandr Bekker, "Russian Prices Are 75 Percent Free," *Segodnya*, December 2, 1994.

3. "In 1993 Russia Exported $4.94 Billion and Imported $3.74 Billion Through Barter," *Segodnya*, April 1, 1994.

4. "Russian Economic Trends: Monthly Update," mimeo, Moscow, October 17, 1994; John Thornhill, "Russian Output Halved in 3 Years," *Financial Times*, December 31, 1994, p. 2.

5. Richard Layard and Andrea Richter, "Labour Market Adjustment: The Russian Way," in Anders Åslund, ed., *Russian Economic Reform at Risk* (London: Pinter, forthcoming).

6. Personal assessments from Tatyana Dolgopyatova and Elvira Naibullina, who both conducted ongoing interviews with enterprise managers, communicated in July 1993.

7. Gur Ofer and Aaron Vinokur assess the second economy GDP at only about 3 to 4 percent of Soviet GDP in 1973, far less than anywhere in the Western world. (Gur Ofer and Aaron Vinokur, *The Soviet Household Under the Old Regime: Economic Conditions and Behavior in the 1970s* [Cambridge University Press, 1992], p. 84).

8. *Radio Free Europe/Radio Liberty (RFE/RL) Daily Report*, December 6, 1994.

9. Evgeny Gavrilenkov and Vincent Koen, "How Large Was the Output Collapse in Russia? Alternative Estimates and Welfare Implications," IMF Working Paper, November 17, 1994, p. 29.

10. "The State Committee for Defense Industry Considers the Possibility of Transferring 60% of the MIC Enterprises to the Civilian Sector," *Segodnya*, December 14, 1994.

11. Jan Winiecki, "The Inevitability of a Fall in Output in the Early Stages of Transition to the Market: Theoretical Underpinnings," *Soviet Studies*, vol. 43, no. 4 (1991), pp. 669–76; János Kornai, *Transformational Recession*, Discussion Paper no. 1, Collegium Budapest, Institute for Advanced Study, June 1993.

12. Road transportation has undoubtedly increased as a share of total transportation and is heavily underreported, unlike other forms of transportation. Still, pipeline and railway transportation (which are well documented) are the dominant forms of transportation in Russia. Officially, road transportation accounted for as little as 0.6 percent of all transportation measured as ton-

kilometers (Goskomstat Rossii, *Rossiiskaya Federatsiya v tsifrakh v 1993 godu* [Moscow, 1994], p. 222).

13. Goskomstat Rossii, *Sotsial'no-ekonomicheskoe polozhenie Rossii 1993 g.* (Moscow, 1994), pp. 89–90.

14. Goskomstat Rossii, *Sotsial'no-ekonomicheskoe polozhenie Rossii 1993 g.*, pp. 84, 91; John Lloyd, "Russian Trade Turns Westward," *Financial Times*, November 24, 1994, p. 4.

15. Institute for Economic Analysis, *Rossiiskie ekonomicheskie reformy: Poteryanny god* (Moscow, 1994), p. 86 (original source: the Russian Ministry of Finance).

16. My main sources are various studies by Richard Layard and Andrei Illarionov with coauthors: Andrei Illarionov, "The Fall of the Standard of Living: Myth or Reality?", *Izvestiya*, February 17, 1994; Michael Ellam and Richard Layard, "Prices, Incomes, and Hardship," in Anders Åslund and Richard Layard, eds., *Changing the Economic System in Russia* (St. Martin's Press, 1993), pp. 39–61; Andrei Illarionov, Richard Layard, and Peter Orszag, "The Conditions of Life," in Anders Åslund, ed., *Economic Transformation in Russia* (London, Pinter, 1994), pp. 127–56; Government of the Russian Federation, *Russian Economic Trends*, vol. 2, no. 4 (1993), pp. 32–41.

17. As table 6-2 illustrates, it is difficult to generalize on the basis of Russian wage statistics. The monthly shifts in real wages are huge; no regular wage indexation existed, minimum wages were raised irregularly, and in December large bonuses were added. Therefore, it is difficult to choose the appropriate time of measurement for a short-term comparison.

18. Goskomstat Rossii, *Rossiiskaya Federatsiya v tsifrakh v 1993 godu*, p. 269; Goskomstat Rossii, *Sotsial'no-ekonomicheskoe polozhenie Rossii 1994 g.*, p. 143.

19. Government of the Russian Federation, *Russian Economic Trends*, vol. 2, no. 4 (1993), pp. 110–11; *Russian Economic Trends: Monthly Update*, May 31, 1994.

20. Illarionov, Layard, and Orszag, "The Conditions of Life," p. 129.

21. Ibid., pp. 129–30.

22. Goskomstat Rossii, *Sotsial'no-ekonomicheskoe polozhenie Rossii 1993 g.*, p. 45.

23. Ibid., p. 4; Gavrilenkov and Koen, "How Large Was the Output Collapse in Russia?," p. 23.

24. Goskomstat Rossii, *Sotsial'no-ekonomicheskoe polozhenie Rossii 1993 g.*, pp. 149–51.

25. Government of the Russian Federation, *Russian Economic Trends*, vol. 3, no. 1 (1994), p. 50.

26. Goskomstat Rossii, *Sotsial'no-ekonomicheskoe polozhenie Rossii 1993 g.*, pp. 149–51; Goskomstat Rossii, "Russia's Socioeconomic Condition as of October 31," *Delovoi mir*, November 10, 1994.

27. Government of the Russian Federation, *Russian Economic Trends*, vol. 2, no. 4 (1993), p. 38.

28. Maxim Boycko and Andrei Shleifer, "The Russian Restructuring and So-

cial Assets," in Anders Aslund, ed., *Russian Economic Reform at Risk* (London: Pinter, forthcoming).

29. Andrei Illarionov, "The Budget as a Mirror of the Government's True Intentions," *Izvestiya*, May 18, 1994.

30. The picture is obscured, because no data have yet been presented on the extrabudgetary funds for 1994. Judith Shapiro, "How Small Is Russian Social Expenditure?," *Socio-Economic Survey,* vol. 2, no. 1 (Moscow, November 1994), pp. 1, 3–6.

31. Illarionov, Layard, and Orszag, "The Conditions of Life," pp. 133–35; Government of the Russian Federation, *Russian Economic Trends,* vol. 2, no. 4 (1993), pp. 35–37.

32. Judith Shapiro, "The Russian Mortality Crisis and Its Causes," in Anders Åslund, ed., *Russian Economic Reform at Risk* (London: Pinter, forthcoming).

33. Shapiro, "The Russian Mortality Crisis and Its Causes."

34. A. Koretsky, "Instead of Money—Public Advice," *Kommersant'-Daily,* October 12, 1994.

35. *RFE/RL Daily Report,* December 6, 1994.

36. Table 8-2; Goskomstat Rossii, *Sotsial'no-ekonomicheskoe polozhenie Rossii 1993 g.,* p. 3.

37. Ibid., p. 96.

38. Ibid., pp. 84–86, 89–90.

39. Mancur Olson, *The Logic of Collective Action: Public Goods and the Theory of Groups,* 2d ed. (Harvard University Press, 1971), p. 2 (emphasis in original).

40. Yegor T. Gaidar, *Ekonomicheskie reformy i ierarkhicheskie struktury* (Economic reforms and hierarchical structures) (Moscow: Nauka, 1990), p. 208.

41. Viktor Chernomyrdin, "No Exits on the Road to Market," *Financial Times,* May 16, 1994, p. 15.

42. Observations from interviews with enterprise managers in Volgograd, February 7–11, 1994.

43. "Russia Needs a Radical Reform and Strong Power" (Interview with Arkady Volsky), *Izvestiya,* August 3, 1992.

44. Shrewdly, Volsky argued for a tax-based income policy with a progressive tax on unjustified increases in the wage fund. "Thirteen Points of Volsky's Program," *Izvestiya,* September 30, 1992.

45. Rustam Arifdzhanov, "Queues as a Mirror of Our Evolution," *Izvestiya,* July 7, 1994.

46. Vladimir Petukhov and Andrei Ryabov, "Do Not Stop Us From Living, Help Us to Survive: About the Social Frame of Mind of Russians," *Rossiya,* no. 19, May 18–24, 1994.

Index

Abalkin, Leonid, 18, 36–37, 74, 75, 79, 80, 83, 85, 321
Afghanistan, 26
Agrarian party, 200, 201, 306, 310
Agricultural sector: antireform elements, 162, 164, 165–66; current status, 166–67; export policy, 166; Gorbachev's reforms, 27, 29; liberalization of, 56, 145, 161–67, 171–72; monopoly structures, 163–64; as political interest group, 92, 164, 165–66, 171–72, 200, 201, 300, 303, 306–07, 308–09, 311; price system, 162, 164–65; production levels, 280–81; in Soviet economy, 14, 44; subsidized credits, 163, 164–66, 199
Aleksashenko, Sergei, 38, 321
Allison, Graham, 40
Allocation: agricultural markets, 142, 162; confidence in market role in, 141–42, 162; in market economy, 3; in socialist economy, 3–4; in Soviet economy, 44–45; at time of price liberalization, 141
Amalrik, Andrei, 28
Andropov, Yuri, 48
Anisimov, Stanislav, 89, 321
Arbatov, Georgy, 78, 81–82, 321
Armenia, 116, 118, 123, 124, 131, 132
Arrears: types of, in Russian economy, 208. *See also* Interenterprise arrears
Aven, Petr, 18, 73, 89, 94, 146, 147, 148, 151, 217, 321
Azerbaijan, 35, 103, 116, 125

Baker, James A., 216
Balcerowicz, Leszek, 16
Banking lobby, 147, 308
Bankruptcy system: for control of interenterprise arrears, 209, 214; development of, 264–65; role of, 264

Barchuk, Vasily, 98, 191, 295, 321
Barter economy, 113, 274
Barsukov, Mikhail, 95
Belarus, 58, 103, 116, 117–18, 125, 131; trade agreement, 133–34, 201
Bogomolov, Oleg, 74, 77, 83, 321
Boycko, Maxim, 18, 240, 321
Brezhnev, Leonid, 14, 15, 237
Brezhnev Constitution, 30
Brown, Anette, 153–54
Budget deficit: after ruble collapse, 207; Chernomyrdin administration, 203–04, 205; early reform success, 187, 189; extrabudgetary funds and, 203–04; Marxist analysis, 75, 79; opportunities to cut, in Russian economy, 181–82; reform goals, 66, 70, 292; reform outcomes, 275; in Soviet Union before collapse, 47–49, 52, 177; stabilization strategies, 199–200, 207; tax revenue, 196
Burbulis, Gennady, 17–20, 54, 72, 86, 87, 99, 191, 322
Bush, George, 99, 216, 217

Camdessus, Michel, 218
Capital flight: in credit expansion, 192–93; exchange rate policy and, 177
Central Bank of Russia, 55, 56; Belarus trade agreement, 133–34; CIS credits policy, 125–29, 194–96; CIS currency policy, 110; criminal enterprise in, 169; data sources, 23; demonetization of ruble, 130; direct lending by, 182; expansion of money supply by, 179; foreign trade policy, 147, 148; in interenterprise arrears problem, 210, 211, 212, 214; as obstacle to macroeconomic stabilization, 182, 197, 206, 211, 221, 296;

political status, 97, 98; refinance policy, 188, 194; reform team relations, 97–98; trade balance management, 123–24

Chernomyrdin, Viktor, 95, 133, 194, 305; career, 322; composition of government, 201–02; economic reform policy, 56–57, 202–07; Gerashchenko and, 197, 199, 201; performance of, 315; political support for, 55, 193, 306, 311; price policy, 89, 144, 159, 161, 165–66; privatization policy, 243

Chile, 11

China, 82; reform experience, 13–16, 176

Chubais, Anatoly, 18, 20, 54, 57, 73, 99, 194, 202; career, 322; as first deputy prime minister, 201, 206; performance of, 315; privatization policy, 228, 230, 233, 234, 239, 240, 243, 244, 245, 246, 248, 249, 252, 296–97

Civic Union party, 56–57, 310

Coal industry, 96, 157, 158, 160, 301, 307–08

Commission on Credit Policy, 193, 194

Committee on Foreign Investment, 246

Commodity exchanges, 165, 264, 308

Commonwealth of Independent States: agreements, 104–05; authority of, 103, 104; barter economy, 113; currency and payment arrangements, 107–19, 120–21; demonetization of ruble, 129–31; economic issues in breakup of Soviet Union, 106–09; exchange rate issues, 107; financing issues, 108; foreign debt issues, 105; formation of, 58, 103; inflation control, 108; Interstate Bank, 127; membership, 103–04; monetary authority, 109; nationalist trends and, 104; outcomes of currency and payment agreements, 134–36; policy goals, 108–09; as political entity, 102–03; Russia in, 105, 106–07; Russian credit expansion, 190, 194–96; Russian credit policy, 125–29; Russian reform process and, 65–66, 84; Russian trade balance, 121–23; trade among, 107, 108. See also Ruble zone

Communist party: after coup attempt, 57, 62; Gorbachev's reorganization of, 33–34, 51; in 1993 elections, 200; remnants of, in Russian government, 62, 90, 95, 143–44

Communist system. See Socialist system

Congress of People's Deputies: as democratic body, 61; dissolution of, 56, 198; First, 32, 33; in land reform, 39,

260, 261; opposition to radical reform by, 54, 55, 93–94, 97–98; in privatization effort, 242

Consumer spending and saving, 10, 284–86, 290; money demand, 179–80; price reforms, 139; in Soviet Union, 43–44

Corruption and crime, 69–70, 142; cause for rise in, 168–69; in decentralization of privatization program, 237; in demonetization of ruble, 130; efforts against, 170–71; in export market, 151; free trade and, 143, 144–45; future challenges, 314; implementation of reforms and, 9, 10; in import regulation, 149; institutional, 90, 169; organizations for, 168; political interest groups, 302–03; privatization efforts and, 229, 268; pyramid schemes, 203; socialist strategies for controlling, 78; Soviet legacy, 6, 7; trends, 167–68, 170

Council for Mutual Economic Assistance, 32, 46, 111, 113, 145, 177

Council of Ministers, 89–90, 91, 92

Coup of August 1991, 1, 34, 53, 54

Credits expansion, 56, 67, 97, 191–93; agricultural subsidies, 163–65; to CIS/FSR states, 125–29, 190; Fedorov intervention, 194–96; in netting out interenterprise arrears, 212; strategies for controlling, 4, 194–96, 199; in transition to market economy, 4

Crime. See Corruption and crime

Czechoslovakia, 9, 11, 12, 63, 70, 82, 115, 176, 293, 313; privatization experience, 227, 229, 236, 240, 247

Dabrowski, Marek, 19

Data sources, 21–24; production levels, 278–79

Defense spending, 26, 27, 181; in 1994 budget, 204–05; demand structure, 279–80; political influence of defense industry, 300–01, 302, 305–07; reform policy, 66; in Soviet economy, 43–44, 49–50, 214–15

Democratic Russia party, 60, 261

Democratization: challenges to, 7–8; functioning of lobbies in, 310–11; Gorbachev's proposals, 33; importance of, in transition to market economy, 7, 292; Russia's transition, 273; speed of implementation, 11–12, 60–61, 294

Deng Xiaoping, 13–14

Dolgikh, Vladimir, 48

Dornbusch, Rudiger, 84, 180
Dubinin, Sergei, 203, 206, 322

Economic theory: concepts of
privatization, 228–32; effectiveness of
lobbies, 305, 307; populist paradigm,
84–85; power of political lobbies, 92,
300–03; quantity theory of money, 179–
80, 221; of reform team members, 70–
73; socialist, 73–86; state susceptibility
to lobbying, 303–05
Edwards, Sebastian, 84
Electricity, 160, 196
Emerson, Michael, 111
Employment and unemployment statistics:
agricultural, 14; distribution in private
enterprise, 224, 273–74; by size of
enterprise, 154
Energy sector, 145, 147; current status,
161; macroeconomic stabilization, 196,
205, 207; as political interest group,
157, 158, 160, 171, 205, 300, 303–04;
price system, 157, 158–61; reform
goals, 157; resistance to reform,
156–57
Enterprise managers: associations of, 92–
93, 306; autonomy of, 225; insularity of,
92, 186; mechanisms for ouster of, 225,
269–70; money supply policy and, 210;
motivation and behavior in market
economy, 9, 137–38, 176; motivation and
behavior in socialist system, 42–43,
178; as obstacles to reform, 96–97,
99, 101, 186–87, 298–300; performance
in market economy, 269; in political
structure, 54, 95; in privatization
debate, 234–35; understanding of
interest market, 182; withholding
employee funds, 183, 213–14; Yeltsin
and, 95, 99, 101
ESOPs (employee share-owning
programs), 234
Estonia, 35, 116, 117, 118
European Commission, 110, 111
European Payments Union, 111
Exchange rate, 4; after stabilization, 203;
capital flight response, 177, 192–93; CIS,
107; 1994 collapse, 205, 222; current, 4;
data sources, 23–24; early reform policy,
188; Fedorov wager, 197; floating, 67; in
macroeconomic stabilization, 183;
reform goals, 70; reform outcomes, 275–
76; reform policy, 147–48; 1993 rise in,
197; in Soviet system, 146

Export policy, 150–52; agricultural
interests and, 166; current, 4; oil, 200,
207, 274
Extrabudgetary funds, 192, 203–04

Federal Assembly, 273, 310–11
Federal Joint Stock Company
(Roskhleboprodukt), 89, 142, 162–63,
166
Federation Council, 202
Fedorov, Boris, 18, 20, 38, 55, 56, 98, 128,
132, 133, 135, 144, 218, 295;
accomplishments, 194, 196, 197–98, 220–
21, 315; agriculture policy, 164, 165;
background, 194, 322; foreign trade
policy, 149; Gerashchenko and, 197;
price policy, 159–60; resignation from
government, 200
Fillipov, Petr, 233, 245
Fischer, Stanley, 40
Five-hundred-day program, 27, 37–38, 71–
72, 223, 226, 229
Foreign assistance, 80; beneficial
interventions, 219; as commodity credits,
218; in developing privatization
program, 247–48; failure of, 99, 101,
220, 314; as humanitarian aid, 216–17;
international financing, 41, 70, 183; lack
of response from Western nations, 215–
16, 219–20; negative outcome of, 190;
Russian expectations, 67–68, 80;
subsidized grain sales, 163. See also
International Monetary Fund
Foreign investment in Russia: after ruble
collapse, 206; after stabilization, 202–
03; liberalization of, 224–25;
privatization program and, 231–32, 240,
270–71
Foreign policy, Gorbachev's, 32
Foreign trade: among CIS states, 105, 107,
108; crisis at time of USSR collapse,
145–46; crisis before USSR collapse, 49–
50, 145–46; current profile, 290–91; data
sources, 24; debt concerns of Western
nations, 215; energy sector in, 157;
liberalization of, 145–52; reform goals,
70, 146; reform outcomes, 281–83. See
also Export policy; Import policy; Trade
policy
Foreign Trade Organization
(Exportkhleb), 142
Former socialist republics/Former Soviet
Union: attempt by Russia to limit credit,
125–27; attempt to reestablish ruble
zone, 131–34; demise of ruble zone,

119–31, 135–36; distribution of Soviet assets and debt, 105–06; economic issues, 102; ethnicity/nationalist issues, 104; exchange rate issues, 107; foreign trade issues, 107–08; Interstate Bank, 127; macroeconomic characteristics, 178–79; monetary authority issues, 106–07; reform vs. conservative approach in Russian policymaking, 108–09; resistance to trade liberalization in, 147; subsidies from Russia, 108; support for ruble zone, 110, 111; Western support for, 215, 217. *See also* Payments mechanisms for FSRs/FSU

Four-hundred-day program, 37

Free enterprise: as characteristic of market economy, 137; energy sector reform, 156–61; liberalization of, 139–45; monetary policy in growth of, 156; opportunities in Soviet Union, 30–31; presidential decrees, 142, 143, 144; record-keeping for, 145; regional authority, 144–45; in Russia as market economy, 4

Friedman, Milton, 106, 179

FSR. *See* Former socialist republics/ Former Soviet Union

FSU. *See* Former socialist republics/ Former Soviet Union

Gaidar, Yegor, 9, 17, 18–19, 54, 56, 83, 132, 133, 135, 193, 246; agriculture policy, 162, 165; background, 322; CBR and, 97–98; conflict with parliament, 94–95, 98–99; credits policy, 193; currency reform, 186; early reform successes, 187–89; energy policy, 158; foreign trade policy, 146; hopes for foreign aid, 68; on market efficiency, 8; monetary policy, 114; performance of, 220–21, 315; political functioning, 87–88, 93, 96; political mistakes, 101, 294–96, 297; price policy, 140, 141; reform program, 64, 65, 66; reform team, 72–73; resignation from government, 200–01; return to government, 198; on sequence of reforms, 82; on state managers, 301; Yeltsin and, 54

Gates, Robert, 216

Gavrilenkov, Evgeny, 279

Gazprom, 141, 159, 200, 211, 274, 303, 305, 311

General Agreement on Tariffs and Trade (GATT), 152

Georgia, 103, 116, 117, 123

Gerashchenko, Viktor, 133, 135, 191, 194, 296; background, 322; Chernomyrdin and, 197, 199, 201; in demonetization of ruble, 130; on interenterprise arrears, 210; in macroeconomic stabilization program, 55, 197, 198, 199, 206, 221–22; monetary policy, 75, 125, 127, 198; new ruble zone policy, 56; resignation of, 206

Germany, 8, 83, 217, 282

Glasnost, 27, 31–32

Glaz'ev, Sergei, 18, 147, 149, 322

Goals of economic reform: Abalkin program, 37; accomplishments, 3; antimonopoly policy, 154, 156; CIS, 108–09; comprehensiveness, 100; economic recovery, 69; energy sector, 156–58, 159–60; exchange rate, 68, 69; foreign trade, 146; Gorbachev's, 27–28, 31; inflation control, 222; land reform, 161, 164; in Marxist analysis, 75–86; at outset, 7; price liberalization, 68, 139; privatization, 69, 223, 241, 249; shortcomings, 70; socialist theorists, 85; Yeltsin's, 64–65, 66

Goldman Sachs, 246

Golovkov, Aleksei, 91

Gorbachev, Mikhail, 13–14, 16, 58, 90–91, 215; economic legacy, 29–31, 47–48, 51; 500-day program, 37–38; as instigator of reform, 26; on nationalist trends, 34–35; political authority, 15; political legacy, 31–36, 51, 52; political skills, 27, 28; reform goals, 27–28, 31–32, 51; Yeltsin on, 28

Gorbachev's Struggle for Economic Reform, 2

Gosbank, 18

Goskomstat, 22, 23

Gosplan, 89, 95, 141

Gossnab, 89, 141, 153

Grand Bargain, 40, 71, 72

Grigor'ev, Leonid, 19, 38, 246, 322

Group of Seven, 215, 217, 218

Growth rate, Soviet economy, 42–43

Hapsburg Empire, 9, 115, 136

Hay, Jonathan, 247

Hayek, Friedrich, 83

Hoagland, Jim, 216

Homicide, 167–68

Housing: new construction, 285, 290; privatization of, 257–59

Human resources: market economy expertise, 15–16; of Russia, 50, 181

Hungary, 11, 82, 209, 226, 227, 265, 266, 267

Hyperinflation: definition, 5; in introduction of Russian reforms, 40; in non–ruble zone currencies, 117–18; risk in credit expansion, 193; ruble zone outcome, 132, 135, 219–20

Ickes, Barry, 153–54
Igrat'ev, Sergei, 323
Ilyushin, Viktor, 95
Immigration trends, 288–89
Import policy: current, 4, 149, 152, 274; grain, 163, 164; liberalization, 148–49; performance of, 281–82, 290–91; subsidies, 149, 196
Income distribution, 84–85, 176, 287
Incomes policy, 68, 70, 183, 310
Industrial sector: associations, 306; Chinese reforms vs. Soviet reforms, 14; monopolies in, 153–54; obstacles to privatization, 96–97; as political lobby, 201–02, 234, 300–03; privatization of, 252–57; production levels, 176, 189–90, 278–80; response to loose monetary policy, 192; size of enterprises, 152; in Soviet economy, 44–45; support for ruble zone, 109–10
Inflation: cause of, 176; Chernomyrdin strategies, 201, 206–07; CIS interactions and, 108; in credit expansion, 191, 192, 193; current status, 4, 5; effects of stabilization program, 188, 202, 203, 221; Marxist economic analysis, 75–77; as monetary phenomenon, 190; monetary reform in post-Soviet economies, 178–81; money demand and, 179–80; official estimates, 23; options for Russia, 181–87; price policy and, 175; redistribution of wealth in, 176; in reform efforts, 56, 188, 222; response to interenterprise arrears policy, 212; 1993 rise in, 197–98; in ruble zone, 115; in Soviet Union before collapse, 47, 52
Interenterprise arrears, 67; accumulated debt, 211–13; as characteristic of market economy, 209; conversion to securities, 212, 213; course of, in reform period, 208–09; free market resolution of, 212–13; government arrears vs., 213; identification of, 208; inflation and, 76; issues of state credibility in, 211–12; legal mechanisms, 211; in monetary model of inflation, 179; money supply and, 209, 210; moral hazard in, 210, 213; netting out, 191, 212, 213; as poor payments problem, 210, 211; in postcommunist economies, 180;

recommendations for, 214; sources of, 180, 207–08, 209–10
Interest rates: to control credits, 194; in macroeconomic stabilization, 182; to restrain demand, 182; in Soviet Union before breakup, 178
International Monetary Fund, 23, 24, 190, 221, 314; exchange rate goals for Russia, 183, 218; import policy, 149; incomes policy, 68; on maintenance of ruble zone, 110–11, 118, 136, 218–20; standby agreement, 54–55, 192, 217–18; Systemic Transformation Facility, 56, 194
Interstate Bank, 127
Isakov, Vasily, 306
Ispravnikov, Vladimir, 74, 81
Izvestiya, 21

Japan, 8, 82, 217

Kagalovsky, Konstantin, 18
Kazakhstan, 116, 118, 128, 129, 131, 132, 289
KGB, 62, 95, 273
Khanin, Grigory, 43
Khasbulatov, Ruslan, 18, 74, 80, 83, 93, 97, 305, 315, 323
Khizha, Georgy, 95, 305, 306, 323
Khlystun, Viktor, 89, 161–62, 305, 323
Khrushchev, Nikita, 15
Koen, Vincent, 279
Kohl, Helmut, 99, 217
Kommersant, 21
Kornai, János, 3, 4
Korzhakov, Aleksandr, 95
Kosmarsky, Vladimir, 18, 91, 323
Kyrgyzstan, 116, 117, 118

Labor market, 5, 289
Land reform, 39, 56, 69, 161–62, 164; agrarian lobbies, 260, 261; obstacles to, 260; popularity of, 259–60; reform program, 261–63
Lapshin, Mikhail, 200, 306
Latin America, 8
Latvia, 116, 117, 118, 125
Law on Competition and the Restriction of Monopolistic Activities in Commodity Markets, 154
Law on Cooperatives, 30, 224
Law on Enterprise in USSR, 37
Law on Enterprises and Entrepreneurial Activity, 38, 139, 144, 224
Law on Foreign Investment, 224, 225
Law on Individual Labor Activity, 30, 224
Law on Land Reform, 39, 260

Law on Leasehold, 30
Law on Personal Privatization Accounts, 227
Law on Privatization of State and Municipal Enterprises, 227
Law on Property, 38
Law on State Enterprises, 29, 37, 48, 225, 226
Law on the Peasant Farm, 39, 260
Layard, Richard, 19, 276, 287
Leasing, of state enterprises, 225
Legal system: current status, 5, 274; early reform goals, 7; framework for privatization, 227–28, 247; future challenges, 314; Gorbachev's goals, 34; in interenterprise arrears problem, 211; liberalization of Russian economy and, 138
Lenin, V. I., 79
Liberal Democratic party, 200
Lipton, David, 17, 19, 109, 181
Lithuania, 35, 116, 117, 118, 125
Lobov, Oleg, 55, 71, 89, 94–95, 144, 238–39, 243, 323
Lopukhin, Vladimir, 73, 89, 94, 98, 323
Luxury goods, 8
Luzhkov, Yury, 237, 243, 323

Macroeconomic crisis: debate over depth of, 74–75; in Soviet Union before collapse, 47–49, 52
Macroeconomic stabilization: Chernomyrdin administration, 200–07; credits expansion and, 191–96, 199; early reform accomplishments, 187–91; Fedorov's accomplishments, 55, 194, 196, 197–98, 199; future challenges, 222; historical models, 8, 82–83; importance of, 174–77, 292; interenterprise arrears and, 209; monetary policy, 199–200; political context, 191, 193–94, 200–02, 221–22, 294–96, 309; preconditions for, 177; reform strategies, 181–87, 198–200; Russian performance in, 202–03, 220–22, 275–77, 293; setbacks in 1992 coalition government, 191–93; social costs, 176; unique challenges in Russia, 177–81; Yeltsin's goals, 64–65, 66
Market economy: characteristics of, 3–4, 137, 209; early demands for, 30; émigré expertise, 15–16; energy sector transition to, 156–61; evolution of, 8–9; functioning of lobbies in, 308; intellectual preparation for, 40; Marxist economic interpretation, 77–78; money

supply in functioning of, 137–38; outcomes of transition to, 289–91; as political factor, 205–06; proposals for transition to, in Soviet Union, 37–38; regulatory functioning in Russia and, 138; Russia as, 3–5, 311–12; state enterprises in, 138
Marxist economic thought, 74–86, 172–73
Mashchits, Vladimir, 18, 38, 73, 323
Mass media, 21, 273
Matyukhin, Georgy, 67, 97–98, 188, 323
Mikhailov, Aleksei, 37, 38
Ministry of Agriculture, 169
Ministry of Defense, 169
Ministry of Foreign Economic Relations, 147, 150, 169
Ministry of Fuel and Energy, 169
Ministry of the Economy, 89, 169
Mitterrand, François, 216
Models for reform: China as, 13–16, 82, 176; for control of crime in new economies, 7–8, 170–71; for currency policy in disintegration of empire, 9, 115; for economic transition, 8, 11–2, 82–83; for privatization, 226–27. See also Czechoslovakia; Hungary; Poland as economic model of reform
Moldova, 103, 116, 125
Monetary overhang: in collapse of socialist economy, 6; Marxist economic analysis, 75; reform strategies, 183–86
Monetary policy: accomplishments, 274; budget constraints for market economy, 4, 137–38, 176; challenges for post-Soviet economies, 39–40, 178–79; challenges to macroeconomic stabilization, 182–83; CIS currency and payments arrangements, 66, 106, 109–19; credit expansion, 191–93; currency reform, 183–86; demonetization of ruble, 129–31; in free enterprise expansion, 156; in functioning of market economy, 137–38; historical models, 9; inflation threat, 179; interenterprise arrears in, 209–10; macroeconomic stabilization, 199–200; Marxist economic analysis, 75–77, 79–80; money demand, 179–80; quantity theory of money, 179–80, 221; reform policy, 7, 65, 67, 70, 100; in Russia as market economy, 4–5; Soviet Union, 31; statistical data, 23; Yeltsin reform government, 56
Monopolies: agricultural, 162–63, 164; in constant money supply, 180; criticism of reform policy, 155–56; current status, 4,

156; definition, 154–55; in energy sector, 159–61; foreign trade and, 68; in liberalization process, 171; Marxist economic analysis, 78, 79–80; in price liberalization, 141–42, 155–56; in reform sequence, 82; Russian misconceptions, 10, 153–54, 172
Mortality rate, 287–88
Moscow Interbank Foreign Currency Exchange, 24
Mozhaev, Boris, 81

Nationalist movements, 34–35, 104
Natural resources, 50, 181
Nechaev, Andrei, 19, 73, 323
Nezavisimaya gazeta, 21
Nizhny Novgorod, 249, 252
Nomenklatura, 6, 13, 15, 51; in Central Bank policymaking, 98; privatization, 82, 226, 228–29, 252, 257; strategies for containing, 7; survival of, 62–63
North, Douglass C., 8

Oil economy: export policy, 150–51, 200, 207; political forces, 201–02, 205, 300, 311; prices, 76, 157, 158, 161; Soviet price system, 42; subsidies, 205
Olson, Mancur, 7, 8, 92, 300, 301, 307
Opinion polls, 24

Pace of reform, 9–12, 59, 80–81, 151, 172–73, 175–76, 249–51, 266–67
Pamfilova, Ella, 73, 323
Panskov, Vladimir, 206
Paramonova, Tatyana, 206
Pavlov, Valentin, 31, 186
Payments mechanisms for FSRs/FSU, 107–08; barter system, 113; bilateral clearing, 113; Central Bank policy, 211; implementation and outcomes, 115–19; independent national currencies, 114–15, 116–17; in liberalization of Russian foreign trade, 147–48; as obstacle to Russian monetary policy, 182–83; options, 109; payments unions/ multilateral clearing, 111–13. *See also* Ruble zone
Pension system, 287
Perestroika, 6, 13, 27
Petrakov, Nikolai, 18, 36, 37, 74–75, 77, 79, 83, 85, 323–24
Petrov, Yury, 95, 324
Piyasheva, Larisa, 81, 233–34
Poland as economic model of reform, 293, 313; influence of, 9, 16, 19, 83;

liberalization of foreign trade, 147, 149; price deregulation, 70, 142; privatization experience, 227, 229, 235, 240, 244, 247, 248, 266, 267; shock therapy, 10, 63; significance of, 11, 12, 37, 96; socialist assessment of reforms in, 83
Political functioning: corruption in, 169; economic reforms in context of, 2, 53–57, 294–98, 314–15; Gorbachev's reforms, 31–34; Gorbachev's style, 28; institutional reforms, 90–92; market forces in, 205–06; obstacles to radical reform, 86–101, 186, 221–22; privatization debate, 232–33, 242–46; referendum on reform, 55; regional distribution of tax revenues, 199; Soviet holdover, 90–91; subordination of Soviet economy to, 41–43; Yeltsin's style, 86–87. *See also* Political lobbies; Political structure
Political lobbies: agricultural sector, 92, 162, 164–66, 171–72, 200, 201, 300, 303, 306–07, 308–09; budget share, 205; Chernomyrdin administration and, 201–02, 205, 207; effectiveness of, 305–11; energy sector, 57, 160, 300, 303–04; industrial sector, 92, 160; in land reform process, 260, 261; in market economies, 308; as obstacles to reform, 299–303; opportunities for control of, 307–11; in privatization debate, 234; state susceptibility to, 92, 303–05
Political structure: CBR in, 97, 98; Chernomyrdin government, 201–02; CIS, 58–59; Council of Ministers, 89–90; dissolution of parliament, 56, 198; distribution of Soviet authority, 15; Federation Council, 202; Gorbachev's reforms, 33–36, 51–52; institutional reform, 57–63; institutional reforms, 88–90, 273; liberalization of Russian economy and, 138; *1993* elections, 56–57, 200–01; remnants of Communist party in, 62–63, 90, 143–44; Russian constitution, 59–61, 63; socialist, 3; Soviet, dissolution of, 59; support for reform process in, 6–7, 92, 100, 291–92; unreformability of Soviet Union, 31; Yeltsin's first government, 72–73
Price system: agricultural markets, 162, 164–65; at beginning of reform effort, 7; CIS agreements, 66, 105; current, 4, 171, 274; energy sector, 157, 158–61, 196; export goods, 151; liberalization of domestic enterprise, 139–45, 171–73, 175;

monopolistic enterprises in, 155–56; natural gas, 159, 160, 161, 196; reform goals, 66, 68; in reform sequence, 65, 66; regional authority in, 140, 144; socialist system, 14, 31, 42, 77–78, 139, 175

Privatization, 99; accomplishments, 3, 265–68, 273, 293, 296–97; allowable forms of ownership, 224; associations in, 225–26; bureaucratic structure for, 245, 246; compulsory, 242; conceptual development, 38–39, 228–32, 233–41; corruption and, 229, 237, 268; current status, 5; definition, 254; development of new enterprises, 263–64; foreign assistance for, 247–48; foreign investment and, 231–32, 240, 270–71; holding companies, 238; housing, 257–59; implementation and administration, 7, 39, 54, 243–48; large-scale, 252–57; leasing of state enterprises, 225; legal infrastructure, 38–39, 224–25, 227–28, 247; managers' participation, 234–35, 240; market considerations, 232; mechanisms of, 226–28, 248–49, 251; ownership issues, 230–31, 232–35, 253–54; ownership outcomes, 251–52, 253–54, 255–56, 268–69, 270; performance of managers in, 269–70; political debate, 232–33, 242–46; rate of, 249–51, 254–55, 266–67; reform goals, 7, 69, 70, 100, 223, 229–30, 241–42, 243, 292–93; in reform sequence, 54, 55, 81–82; restrictions, 232; shortcomings of reform process, 268–70; small-scale, 248–52; socialist interpretation, 78; Soviet legacy, 30–31, 38–39, 40, 223–26; stakeholder interests in, 229, 232–33, 237–41; statistical data, 22–23; voucher system, 235–36, 254–57, 267, 271; worker participation, 230–31, 233–34, 239, 240, 253–54. See also Land reform

Production: consumption trends, 286, 290; currency stability and, 174; oil, 157; reform outcomes, 176, 189–90, 277–81, 290, 291; reform policy, 139; in socialist analyses, 74–75, 79; Soviet price system, 139

Protection rackets, 169

Public opinion/perceptions: concerns about crime, 167, 170; credibility of stabilization program, 221; currency reform, 186; current, 314; demonetization of ruble, 130–31; failings of reform effort in influencing, 87–88, 100; populist economic appeals, 85–86; on privatization, 230, 231–32, 239; referendum on reform government, 55; understanding of free market

functioning, 142–43, 297; on voucher privatization, 255–56, 257

Public welfare spending, 181–82; current, 286–87; extrabudgetary funds for, 192; Soviet, 178; vs. interest group spending, 205, 207

Quantity theory of money, 179–80, 221

Real interest rates, 67, 100

Reform outcomes, 291–98, 315–16; agricultural market, 166–67; criteria for evaluation, 174–77, 293–94; economic crime as threat to, 167–71; foreign trade, 281–83; inflation as measure of, 175, 176, 177; institutional change, 273–74; liberalization, 171–73

Reform process: after dissolution of parliament, 56; after referendum, 55–56; agriculture sector, 161–67; antiinflation strategies, 181–87; antimonopoly policy, 152–56; author's involvement, 17–21; bureaucratic obstacles to, 89–92, 312–13; in Chernomyrdin administration, 202–07; Chinese course vs. Soviet course, 13–16; CIS in, 65–66, 84, 104; in communist context, 28; conceptual basis, 5–13, 16, 312; conceptual disagreement, 73–86; conditions at beginning of, 6, 16, 53, 177; course of, 53–57; course of interenterprise arrears during, 208–09; decline of Soviet Union, 31–40; development of private enterprise, 223–26; economic liberalization, 171–73; election of 1993 and, 56–57; elections of 1993 and, 200–01; enterprise managers as obstacles to, 92–93, 186–87, 298–300; 312–13; formulated as official program, 88; importance of macroeconomic stabilization, 174–77; income restructuring in, 176–77; initial round of radical reforms, 187–91; intensity of opposition, 86, 93; liberalization of domestic enterprise, 139–45; liberalization of foreign trade, 145–52; lobbies as obstacles to, 300–03; market restructuring in, 289–91; money supply in, 189–90; obstacles to, 272; political base, 92, 100, 291–92; political context, 86–99, 101, 200–02, 314–15; production performance, 176, 189–90, 277–81; radical approach, 2, 9–11, 63–70, 186–87, 313; rate of privatization, 249–51, 258; resistance to radical program, 191–98; scale and pace of, 9–12, 59, 80–81,

151, 172–73, 175–76, 249–51, 266–67; second stabilization effort, 198–200; sequence of implementation, 10–11, 65, 66, 81–82, 227; significance of Russian experience, 311–16; social base for, 96; social costs of, 69, 81, 283–89, 313–14; tax system, 66–67, 182; theorists of, 63; timing, 6, 65; transition to democracy, 7, 60, 292; unique characteristics of Russia, 10–11, 83; Western intervention, 215–22. *See also* Goals of economic reform; Reform outcomes
Retail sales, 139, 285
Rosnefteprodukt, 141
Rostowski, Jacek, 19, 212
Rozenova, Lira, 143–44
Ruble zone: alternative strategies, 109–19; Belarus-Russia agreement, 133–34; collapse of, 119–31; with currency convertibility, 114–15; economic outcomes, 115, 118, 134–36; International Monetary Fund recommendations, 110–11, 118, 136, 218–20; membership, 116, 117–18; of new type, 131–32; objections to, 109, 115; options after Soviet breakup, 103, 109; proponents, 109–11
Russian Union of Industrialists and Engineers, 12, 84, 234
Russian Union of Industrialists and Entrepreneurs, 76, 92, 306
Russia's Choice party, 200
Rutskoi, Aleksandr, 74, 77, 78, 94, 261, 315, 324
Ryterman, Randi, 153–54
Ryzhkov, Nikolai, 31, 48

Saburov, Yevgeny, 16–17, 71, 227, 324
Sachs, Jeffrey, 16, 18, 19, 20, 40, 98, 109, 114, 181, 218
Safety nets, 69, 222
Saltykov, Boris, 73, 324
Segodnya, 21
Selyunin, Vasily, 43
Shakhrai, Sergei, 324
Shapiro, Judith, 287–88
Shatalin, Stanislav, 18, 36, 37, 85, 324
Shleifer, Andrei, 19, 240
Shmelev, Nikolai, 40
"Shock therapy," 10, 37, 186–87, 275
Shokhin, Aleksandr, 17, 18, 54, 72–73, 91, 194, 203, 206, 324
Shortages, 146, 284; current status, 5; incentive to export and, 145; liberalization of foreign trade and, 148–49, 150; in Soviet Union, 47, 49, 177–78

Shumeiko, Vladimir, 95, 238, 305, 324
Silaev, Ivan, 70, 324
Singapore, 11, 82
Skokov, Yury, 71, 94, 95, 306, 324–25
Small enterprises: new, development of, 263; number of, 22, 290; privatization, 242, 248–52; prospects for reform, 14; in Soviet system, 14, 152, 153–54, 290
Socialist system: arrears in, 208; bureaucratic functioning, 90–91; characteristics of, 2–3, 178; concept of ownership in, 223–24; demise of, 6, 26–27; duration of, and resistance to change, 14–15; goals of, 223; Gorbachev's commitment to, 28, 33–34; measures of economic performance, 41–42; politics over economics in, 41–43; vs. free market system, 137
Social unrest, 99, 181, 222; attempted coup, 1, 34, 53, 54; as concern of politicians, 39; in price liberalization, 140
Soros, George, 219
Soskovets, Oleg, 201, 206, 207, 213, 325
South Korea, 11, 82
Soviet Union, 6; annual economic growth, 42–43; causes of collapse, 50–52, 214–15; dissolution of political structures, 57–63; distortion of economic structure, 43–47; economic costs of collapse, 134–36; economic issues in collapse, 106–09; economic issues in collapse of, 26–27, 41, 52, 177; economic thinking in, 36–40; foreign debts and assets, 105–06; foreign policy, 32; foreign trade crisis, 49–50, 145–46; Gorbachev's reform goals, 27–28; Gorbachev's role in collapse of, 35, 36; gross domestic product, 43–44; historical parallels, 9; international response to collapse, 215–22; macroeconomic crisis, 47–49, 52; nationalist movements in, 34–35; political structure, 15; positive economic legacy of, 50, 180–81; price system, 42, 139; private enterprise in, 30–31, 37, 223–26, 227–28; reform experience, 13–16; Russian debt burden, 282; statistical data, 23; subsidies to CIS states, 108; trade policy and practice, 46–47; transformation of bureaucratic entities, 89–90; unreformability of, 31; wastage in, 45–46
Stalin, Josef, 15, 175
Standard of living, 176, 287, 289
Starodubtsev, Vasily, 92–93, 162, 306, 325
State bonds, 196

State Committee on Material and
    Technical Supplies, 89
State Committee on the Management of
    State Property (GKI), 22–23, 244–47
State enterprises: current status, 5; leasing
    of, 225; legal framework, 225; as
    lobbies, 92; opportunity to control, 97;
    political motivation of, 42–43. *See also*
    Enterprise managers
State Planning Committee, 89
State Price Committee, 143–44
Steel production, 45
Stock market, 224
Street markets, 142–43
Supreme Soviet: as democratically
    representative body, 61; dissolution of,
    56, 198; in land reform process, 261;
    in privatization effort, 239, 243, 245,
    297
Sweden, 83
Systemic Transformation Facility, 56, 194

Taiwan, 11
Tajikistan, 116, 118, 124, 131, 132
Tariff policy: current, 4, 149, 152; exports,
    150, 151; imports, 149
Tax system: collections during loose
    monetary policy, 193; current status,
    222; falling VAT revenues, 196; foreign
    trade, 151; incomes policy, 68, 70;
    macroeconomic stabilization, 187–88;
    problems of Russian system, 204; reform
    options, 182; reform policy, 66–67;
    regional distribution, 199; socialist, 78,
    79, 178; Soviet, 47, 48
Titkin, Aleksandr, 89, 238, 325
Trade policy: Belarus-Russia agreement,
    133–34; CIS currency convertibility, 114;
    CIS payment mechanisms, 111–13;
    credits management, 125–29; current,
    152, 274; demonetization of ruble, 129–
    31; exchange rate, 145–48; Marxist
    economic analysis, 77–78; political
    lobbies, 147; reform policy, 68; in Russia
    as market economy, 4; Soviet system, 14,
    45–47; tax evasion in, 151. *See also*
    Export policy; Foreign trade; Import
    policy; Payments mechanisms for FSR/
    FSU; Ruble zone
Trade unions, 96, 157, 307–08, 310; current
    status, 276; in privatization debate, 239–
    40
Transportation services, 252, 280
Turkmenistan, 103, 116, 117, 123, 124,
    129

Ukraine, 12–13, 58, 103, 105, 117, 125, 289
Unemployment: current status, 222, 276–
    77; macroeconomic stabilization and,
    176; statistical data, 23
United Nations, 24
United States, 215, 216, 217
Uzbekistan, 116, 118, 123, 124, 131, 132, 289

Value-added tax, 66–67, 182; decline in
    revenues, 196; implementation, 187–88
Vasil'ev, Dmitri, 233, 248, 249, 325
Vasil'ev, Sergei, 18, 325
Vavilov, Andrei, 38, 325
Voilukov, Arnold, 76
Volsky, Arkady, 12, 56–57, 80, 81, 82, 92,
    94, 306, 310, 325

Wages: in period of credit expansion, 193;
    reform outcomes, 4, 198, 276–77, 284;
    reform policy, 68; in reform sequence,
    65; in Soviet Union, 29–30, 48; withheld
    by state enterprises, 183, 213–14
Wholesale markets, 141–42, 214
Williamson, John, 111–12
Williamson, Oliver E., 8
World Bank, 24, 217, 218

Yabloko party, 200
Yaremenko, Yury, 74, 85
Yarov, Yury, 144, 201, 325
Yasin, Yevgeny, 38, 84, 87, 206, 325
Yavlinsky, Grigory, 37, 40, 71–72, 83–84,
    110, 200, 226, 326
Yefimov, Vitaly, 89, 326
Yeltsin, Boris, 17, 20, 29; access to, 86; ac-
    complishments of, 100, 294, 314–15; anti-
    crime efforts, 170; Burbulis and, 86–87;
    career, 326; Chubais and, 244; on collapse
    of Soviet Union, 53, 58; in conflict with
    parliament, 94–95; on crime and corrup-
    tion, 69–70; in development of constitu-
    tion, 59–60; economic reforms, 38–39, 54,
    63–70; energy policy, 158; on foreign as-
    sistance, 67, 215; on Gorbachev, 28; 1994
    reformation of government, 206; political
    compromises of, 94–95, 99, 101, 295, 315;
    political style, 95–96, 294; in postpone-
    ment of elections, 60; on privatization, 69,
    228, 230, 235, 240; reform of political
    structures, 57–63; reform team, 70–73,
    93; on social costs of reforms, 69

Zadornov, Mikhail, 37
Zaveryukha, Aleksandr, 201, 305–06
Zhirinovsky, Vladimir, 200
Zyuganov, Gennady, 200